FORTRESS FARMING

A volume in the series

Cornell Series on Land: New Perspectives on Territory, Development, and Environment
Edited by Wendy Wolford, Nancy Lee Peluso, and Michael Goldman

A list of titles in this series is available at cornellpress.cornell.edu.

Fortress Farming

Agrarian Transitions, Livelihoods, and Coffee Value Chains in Indonesia

Jeff Neilson

CORNELL UNIVERSITY PRESS   ITHACA AND LONDON

First published 2025 by Cornell University Press

Library of Congress Cataloging-in-Publication Data

Names: Neilson, Jeff, author.
Title: Fortress farming : agrarian transitions, livelihoods, and coffee value chains in Indonesia / Jeff Neilson.
Description: Ithaca : Cornell University Press, 2025. | Series: Cornell series on land: new perspectives on territory, development, and environment | Includes bibliographical references and index.
Identifiers: LCCN 2024034365 (print) | LCCN 2024034366 (ebook) | ISBN 9781501780912 (hardcover) | ISBN 9781501780929 (paperback) | ISBN 9781501780943 (ebook) | ISBN 9781501780936 (pdf)
Subjects: LCSH: Agriculture—Economic aspects—Indonesia. | Land tenure—Indonesia. | Globalization—Economic aspects—Indonesia. | Coffee industry—Indonesia.
Classification: LCC HD2082 .N55 2025 (print) | LCC HD2082 (ebook) | DDC 338.1/737309598—dc23/eng/20241125
LC record available at https://lccn.loc.gov/2024034365
LC ebook record available at https://lccn.loc.gov/2024034366

Contents

Preface

It is surprisingly cold in the hamlet of Tondok Buntu, in the mountainous north of Sulawesi's Toraja highlands, and several villagers, wrapped in long sarongs, were squatting in the morning sun to warm themselves as a thick mist still hung in the valley below. Tondok Buntu consists of four imposing *tongkonan* ancestral houses, with their ornately carved exterior and sweeping roofs lined up opposite five rice barns—small-scale imitations of the houses. Community members are variously aligned with at least one, and usually several, such *tongkonan* across the Torajan landscape and so feel compelled to participate in ceremonial activity associated with the structures. A small Pentecostal church has been built at the eastern edge of the hamlet, and it being Sunday, villagers from neighboring hamlets were drifting through Tondok Buntu in readiness for the service.

Mama Lina,[1] along with other women in the village, had risen early to cook a stew of rice husks, taro stems, and sweet potato leaves to feed the pigs held in pens behind every house. Most of these pigs will never be sold and are instead taken to ceremonies directly from their pens. Such ceremonial demand remains strong. Buffalo herdsmen—usually young men or teenage boys—were taking their lumbering beasts out from their stalls and into the fields to graze. The larger bulls will later be hand-fed elephant grass to fatten them up and increase their value: this reached an astonishing half a billion Indonesian rupiah (IDR, or around 35,000 USD) in 2018 for bulls with the desired markings. All are destined for ritual sacrifice.

It was July, and the coffee harvest had begun. However, the rhythm of village life was only moderately affected, with another poor harvest, this time due, it seems, to unusually heavy rains during the earlier flowering period. Nevertheless, scatterings of coffee beans, still encased in their white parchment, were being dried on mats in the compound for sale the following day, while the sweet smell of slightly fermenting mucilage (the sticky substance that coats the parchment) still lingered from the manual pulping of recent days. Five liters of parchment coffee were thinly spread on one mat. Perhaps twenty on another. These small batches would be sold to one of the regular collectors, known locally as *tengkulak*, who visit the hamlet, or the coffee would otherwise be carried to the nearby Sapan market to exchange for what Mama Lina called *seng dapo'* (shopping money for the kitchen). The *tengkulak* would sell to local aggregators, or perhaps themselves transport the parchment coffee down to one of the two large mills that dominate the local coffee trade. One mill, owned by a Japanese coffee company, has been operating in Toraja since the 1970s. The other, known locally as the KUD, has a tight supply relationship with Starbucks and has rolled out its corporate sustainability program, called CAFE Practices, in these villages. Unlike in some other parts of Indonesia, the supply chain here is short, and farmers sell a high-quality product virtually directly into the international specialty coffee market. As a result, farm-gate prices are much higher here than on the Intercontinental Exchange (ICE) in New York.

Tondok Buntu lies in the heart of the North Torajan coffee belt. A locally renowned market at Sapan, held every six days and said by many to supply the best quality coffee in Sulawesi, is a short walk away. Yet despite direct exposure to the world coffee market, and the upstream influence of international coffee companies, the villagers' lives were not dominated by these forces. All thirty-two households living in Tondok Buntu in 2018 had access to a coffee plot, ranging in size from a hundred trees through to a few thousand (no household managed more than two hectares, or almost five acres), and almost everyone initially reported that coffee was their most important source of income. In later conversations, however, villagers explained how relatives living outside the highlands regularly send remittances for both daily household needs and for ceremonial participation, and these were of far greater value than coffee sales. Not all the coffee plots, moreover, were being actively cultivated. New plantings of between twenty and fifty trees were found near the village, and weeds were either cut by hand or sprayed with herbicide, but otherwise there was little sign of intensive crop maintenance: pruning was rare, and shop-bought fertilizers hadn't been applied for years on many farms. Overall, inputs of labor and capital are kept to a minimum, and coffee cherries are harvested by whoever is available from within the extended household—often elderly women and children. Wages are seldom paid for coffee-related work in Tondok Buntu.

Coffee is not the only crop grown in the hamlet. Coffee plots are interspersed across a diverse landscape mosaic of wet-rice fields (*sawah*), bamboo-dominated agroforests, grazing lands, and fallows. The steep terraced hillsides around the village, where *sawah* had been recently harvested, were now a dry yellow stubble. While every household in Tondok Buntu has a coffee plot, not everyone owns *sawah*. These fields are maintained—along with the rice barns—largely as a status symbol and cultural identity marker by the local nobility, a hereditary elite. Household labor for the *sawah* was augmented with labor from the broader community mobilized through extended kinship and caste relations and through small work groups known as *saroan*, where the labor of both planting and harvesting was compensated with a share of the harvest. Again, cash wages are rarely paid. Nek Simon, a former administrative head of the hamlet and a member of the hereditary elite, laughed as he squatted while inhaling a cigarette and explained that it didn't make economic sense to grow rice. Returns were meager and production costs high. Not even the largest landowners in the hamlet were producing enough rice to feed their family throughout the year. All bought rice from the market, traded into Toraja from the lowland Bugis territories. Nevertheless, Nek Simon explained that he would continue to cultivate rice because he considered it a gift from the ancestors, who were descended from heavenly beings (*to'manurung*). Indeed, the richly decorated rice barns, carved with pictographs abstractly portraying aspects of daily life, philosophical concepts, and beliefs, suggest that rice is no ordinary commodity in Toraja.

Mama Lina brought out a meal for Nek Tomas, a recent centenarian, who sat quietly on the *tongkonan* porch surveying the goings-on on that cool morning. The meal, which I shared with him, consisted of cooked rice with smoked buffalo meat left over from a funeral feast, and some tinned sardines from the market that had been mixed with fresh chili, shallots, and choko from the garden. The night before, Nek Tomas was animated as he told stories of the deprivations and fear he experienced during the Japanese occupation and retold what he knew about the exploits of Pong Tiku, a national hero who resisted the Dutch colonial occupation of Toraja in the early twentieth century and whose power stemmed largely from his control of the lucrative coffee trade. He recounted how coffee once had a vibrant economic role in Tondok Buntu. Following the defeat of an ill-fated Islamist rebellion in the late 1960s, for example, regional security dramatically improved for Torajans, and the coffee industry boomed. Nek Tomas recalled how you could then buy a buffalo bull from the sales from a single plot. Even in the remote north of Toraja, more than ten hours' drive from the provincial capital of Makassar, producing for the global market is not a novel or recent development—the first coffee boom had taken place here in the 1880s, followed by another in the 1920s. Even still, villagers are not clambering over each other to shore up control over coffee land; indeed, a market for such land is virtually nonexistent. Formal land titles remain rare.

The conversation turned to the coffee price, regularly posted in the marketplace by the Japanese buyer. It was not high enough to generate much excitement. Leaning against the rice barn and listening in, Pong Arno complained that it was impossible to buy a buffalo, or even a pig, from coffee proceeds these days. Coffee, and coffee lands, generate cash for daily consumption, and so can be critical for household food security, and yet coffee rarely offers a pathway for wealth accumulation or a means to participate in the prestige games of the ceremonial economy. These farms were, in the words of a coffee smallholder I met in the Karo highlands of Sumatra, a "livelihood fortress": *kopi itu sebagai benteng hidup saja* (coffee is just a livelihood fortress), *tapi ngak mungkin maju dengan kopi* (but

there's no way you can "get ahead" by planting coffee). It was an important livelihood resource when other options were exhausted or unavailable, and so it was
considered a fortress (*benteng*) against falling into dire food insecurity. Farming
provided something of a safety net, a refuge, but little more.

Across rural Southeast Asia, there are places like Tondok Buntu where livelihoods are influenced by interactions with commodity markets and the strategies
of powerful downstream companies, but this has not resulted in the predicted
rise to dominance of productivist farming. The productive forces of capitalism
have been resisted, or at least modified, at the farm level, by particularistic local
social institutions and by the evolving dynamics of broader economic structures.
In this book, I present the resulting household livelihood strategies as "fortress
farming," evident in Tondok Buntu and widespread across Indonesia's coffee-
growing regions (I believe they can be found even more broadly) and which
are fundamentally reshaping relationships with land and informing Indonesia's
agrarian transition. I further develop how and why such strategies have emerged
among Indonesian smallholder households and consider the wider implications
of such tendencies for our theoretical understanding of how late-industrializing
countries are experiencing broader processes of agrarian transition in the early
twenty-first century.

Acknowledgments

The fieldwork that underpinned this book was undertaken over an extended period, reaching back to my first visit to coffee-growing villages in Toraja during 1998. Consequently I am indebted to an unusually large number of people who have assisted in various ways throughout the subsequent twenty-five years, and hopefully I will be forgiven when I fail to mention them all.

Field research in Indonesia during the period 2007 until 2020 was enabled by a series of research grants provided by the Australian Centre for International Agricultural Research (ACIAR). In particular, I appreciate the roles played by ACIAR program managers such as Peter Horne, Dave Shearer, and Rodd Dyer, all of whom provided me with both technical and practical guidance during this period. I only hope that the unique role performed by ACIAR in supporting long-term partnerships between Australian-based researchers and their international collaborators, to examine a broad range of agricultural and rural challenges facing farmers in the Asia-Pacific region, will continue long into the future. For me, this has meant a close relationship with researchers at the Indonesian Coffee and Cocoa Research Institute (ICCRI), especially with Faila Hartatri, who was responsible for expertly leading countless field trips and household surveys right across the islands. Other important collaborators at ICCRI include Yusianto, Lya Aklimawati, and Sukrisno Widyotomo (*almarhum*). A special acknowledgment is required for Surip Mawardi (now retired from ICCRI and managing his own coffee farm in North Sumatra), who not only possesses an unparalleled depth of knowledge regarding all aspects of the Indonesian coffee industry, but also has dedicated his life to working tirelessly with, and improving the lives of, Indonesian coffee farmers through various field-based interventions. While we don't agree on all aspects of coffee-based livelihoods, his career has been a profound inspiration to me (and many others), and I feel fortunate to have learned so much from his intellect and passion.

ACIAR funding also supported collaboration with the University of Lampung, the Bandung Institute of Technology, the University of Indonesia, Hasanuddin University, the Christian University of Indonesia Toraja, the Committee on Sustainability Assessment (COSA), and the regional Agricultural Technology Assessment Institutes (BPTP) under the Indonesian Ministry of Agriculture. I have benefited enormously through field support and critical intellectual engagement with researchers from these various institutes, including Bustanul Arifin,

Hanung Ismono (*almarhum*), Nurul Sri Rahatiningtyas, Fathia Hashilah, Angga Dwiartama, Ben Derosari, Sjafruddin Kadir, Judith Ratu Tandi Arrang, Daniele Giovannucci, and Sikstus Gusli. The detailed survey work in the Semende region was further supported by the UK-based ISEAL Alliance, and I appreciate the support from Kristin Komives and Vidya Rangan from ISEAL. I acknowledge the leadership of this Semende survey work performed by Russell Toth from the University of Sydney, in partnership with J-PAL Southeast Asia and SurveyMETER.

The research approach I pursued for this book has depended on the in-kind support of individuals working within the coffee industry, and this started with my initial "apprenticeship" into the complex world of coffee quality and processing provided by Keiji Sato and Jabir Amien. I have also benefited from support provided by Laurent Bossolasco, Wagianto, Will Young, Shaughan Dunne, Andrew Ford, Kornel Gartner, Derby Sumule, Rudy Halim, Sarjana, Wisman Djaya, Asnawi Saleh, and many others. From 2007 until 2014, I worked closely with Tony Marsh, an independent coffee consultant whose industry knowledge was always insightful and whose companionship and general good humor during long road trips were much appreciated.

I have, of course, relied on the hospitality of countless coffee-growing households across Indonesia, many of whom have invited me into their homes to eat and stay, and special thanks are required to Piter Lepong, Agustinus Gono, and Patolla and their families, for ongoing generous hospitality during longer village stays. I thank Waris (in Sumatra) and Tono (in Sulawesi), who are two of the most reliable and accommodating drivers and friends that a field researcher could ask for.

Several very generous colleagues were willing to spend their valuable time reading and providing critical feedback on draft chapters. In some cases, this extended to the full manuscript at various stages of its development. I am highly appreciative of the time spent at this task by John Connell, Mark Vicol, Bill Pritchard, Neil Coe, Phil Hirsch, Simon Butt, Eve Warburton, David Guest, and Meine van Noordwijk, and to various conversations and exchanges I have had on agrarian change in Indonesia with John McCarthy. Feedback on the manuscript by two anonymous reviewers for Cornell University Press was also pivotal in helping refine key elements of the book. The overall encouragement, and especially the critical and insightful reading of the manuscript provided by Nancy Lee Peluso (and her coeditors of the Cornell Series on Land, Wendy Wolford and Michael Goldman), were eminently beneficial.

The writing of this book has only been possible because of the supportive academic environment provided through my ongoing employment at the University of Sydney, and I acknowledge my many colleagues from both the School of Geosciences and the Sydney Southeast Asia Centre who have made this a collegial and intellectually stimulating place to work. I started conceptualizing and writing parts of this book during a period of study leave spent at Wageningen University and Research and the University of Copenhagen in 2019, and I am appreciative of the support (intellectual and other) provided at that time by Simon Bush, Jacqueline Vel, Mark Vicol, Katy-Ann Legun, Gerben Nooteboom, Darmanto, and Niels Fold. Many of the ideas presented in the book were initially field-tested at seminars and conferences in Copenhagen, Wageningen, Leiden, Sydney, Berlin, and Jakarta, during which important, often critical, feedback helped me develop my argument. Of particular importance was a seminar and paper presented to farmers and coffee industry participants in Bandung, organized by Angga Dwiartama during November 2019, on the theme of "Fortress Farming." The feedback I received from that public airing of my ideas provided encouragement that I was articulating a sentiment that appeared to have broad resonance within that critical community.

I am especially fortunate to have worked with a number of talented research students who have chosen to examine different aspects of the Indonesian coffee industry with me, and whose insights I have benefited from immensely. These include Felicity Shonk, Fathia Hashilah, Josie Wright, Joshua Bray, Kayla Lochner, Triska Damayanti, Faila Hartatri, Fikriyah, Maxine Williams, Samuel Oomens, Peter Cooper, and Manann Donoghue. I have benefited from the perspectives of and discussions with the more than 250 Australian and Indonesian students I have taken on field schools to Indonesia since 2011. I have found these field schools to be fertile opportunities to generate new ideas, some of which have percolated into this book.

Nurrokhmah Rizqihandari (Qiqi) provided excellent cartographic assistance for the book and patiently, but always promptly, accommodated my numerous requests to make alterations to the maps. Yunie Rahmat spent many hours ensuring that the manuscript (including the illustrations, tables, and references) was formatted correctly and prepared in accordance with the requirements of Cornell University Press. As my keyboard dexterity has slowly worsened, this support was invaluable.

In Toraja, I am indebted to the many people who have shared their culture and allowed me to enter their social world, including foremost my parents-in-law (Indo' and Ambe Nek Bandoro), both of whom have now left us and whose absence we all feel so keenly, along with Nek Malisan (*almarhum*), Nek Arby, Rimba, Sam, Aras, Dinny and Danny, Minggu, Acis, Ratte, and so many others. The relief and support provided by my social community in Sydney has been just as critical, with special mention of Run Fridays (especially during COVID-19 lockdowns when the first draft of the manuscript was written), the Parkrun Group, Monday Swimming, AFL 9's, Last Friday of the Month, the bushwalking crew, MRC, and RM Golf. I am thankful to have two wonderful sisters, Kim and Michelle, whose reliable support could always be called on, as together we have learned to get by without the two people whose wise guidance provided such solid foundations for our lives.

My twenty-five-year relationship with Indonesian coffee has been closely paralleled by my even more fulfilling relationship with Relyta, whose love, generosity, and culinary brilliance has sustained me throughout. It was Relyta who first encouraged me to explore her ancestral homeland, and because of her and our beautiful children Eden and Jemma, I have been afforded the luxury of a home environment that has allowed me to spend far too much time in the task of writing this book.

FORTRESS FARMING

FORTRESS FARMING AND INDONESIAN COFFEE

Be to me a rock of refuge to which I may always go. Give the command to save me, for you are my rock and my fortress.

—Psalm 71:3

At the outset of the Industrial Revolution (around 1800), approximately three-quarters of the world's population were engaged in farming. By 1970, this had still only fallen to 51 percent as urbanization and industrialization occurred in some world regions while rural populations generally swelled in the Global South (Grigg 1975). By 2020, however, the share of farmers then dropped rapidly to only 27 percent, and, perhaps more surprisingly, the absolute size of this global agricultural workforce also fell, from 1.05 billion to 884 million between 2000 and 2020 (FAO 2020). Such global estimates are strongly affected by developments in India and (especially) China, but similar shifts have occurred elsewhere, including across Southeast Asia. Improvements in agricultural productivity combined with industrial growth were critical for drawing workers away from farming in Western Europe, in European settler states in North America and Australasia, and in Northeast Asia. The processes and pathways through which these national-scale agrarian transitions have occurred in different countries, however, have varied enormously and continue to be shaped by both socioeconomic developments within countries and sets of relations with the global economy. The society-wide transition away from farming has generally been associated with expanding economic output, improved living standards, and rising life expectancy. It has also been associated with the depletion and degradation of natural resources, increasing social inequality, and anthropogenic changes to the earth's climate system.

Southeast Asia is currently experiencing rapid structural transformation as national economies have expanded and industrialized, largely by participating in export-oriented value chains. According to some mainstream narratives, small-holder farming is even perceived to be a residual activity pursued by households unable, or unwilling, to participate in the modern economy. At the same time, half the region's population still lived in rural areas in 2020, and many, but not all, were engaged in farming. Furthermore, uncertainties abound about the ability of the world economy, and the biophysical resources on which it depends, to continue creating sufficient off-farm work to offer improved livelihoods to the region's rural communities. The Southeast Asia region, along with its largest economy, Indonesia, thus offers critical insights into the nature of contemporary agrarian transitions.

Given this backdrop, this book engages directly with recent debates on the future of smallholder farming and access to land under contemporary capitalism. The book's findings—informed by field research from across Indonesia—contrast with the situation analyzed by Li (2014) for marginalized Lauje communities in Sulawesi, where a particularly insidious form of capitalist relations emerged with the introduction of cocoa, ultimately resulting in pervasive land-lessness at a forest frontier. Instead, I observe that capitalist relations are less likely to dominate *within* farming when it is not the primary object of household investment, where labor is predominately unpaid family labor, and where access to land is so deeply embedded in social relations that markets for it struggle to operate smoothly. While Indonesian agrarian households do, at times, operate under peasant-type Chayanovian ideals, as described by van der Ploeg (2013), they are far more interested and willing to enmesh themselves in broader social patronage networks, and indeed to engage with various off-farm commercial opportunities, than suggested by van der Ploeg's autonomous peasant ideal. Indeed, the importance of off-farm income when analyzing agrarian change in Southeast Asia has been long recognized (Hart et al. 1989), becoming a defining feature of contemporary rural livelihoods in the region, as emphasized by Rigg (2001, 2019).

My book broadly agrees with the contention of Rigg, Salamanca, and Thompson (2016) that explanations for the persistence of smallholding in the Southeast Asian countryside require an improved understanding of broader contextual and structural factors. I further take up those authors' appeal that "more detailed and empirical work remains to be done on emergent, late-capitalist precarity in East Asia" (130). This book responds by making significant empirical and theoretical contributions to understanding the interactions between broader structural constraints, shifting relationships with land, and the nature of contemporary livelihoods in rural Southeast Asia. It also explores the locally specific social institutions that continually frustrate attempts to construct broad meta-narratives of agrarian change.

Fortress farming refers to a rural livelihood strategy whereby the household maintains access to farmland as a defensive strategy to enhance livelihood resilience, while actively tapping into resource flows from beyond the rural landscape. By invoking the metaphor of a fortress, I am not suggesting that smallholder farms are self-contained, autarkic, or inwardly focused, but rather that they are an important refuge in times of trouble. Such a farm is defensive, and fortresslike, as it involves a relationship with land oriented toward enhancing *livelihood resilience*. Livelihood resilience refers to "the capacity of all people across generations to sustain and improve their livelihood opportunities and well-being despite environmental, economic, social, and political disturbances" (Tanner et al. 2015, 23). The use of "fortress" follows similar defensive metaphors (a "moat") used by Karl Polanyi ([1944] 2001) in *The Great Transformation*. Through a detailed analysis of the rise and spread of industrial capitalism during the late eighteenth and nineteenth century in Europe, Polanyi presented societal responses to self-regulating markets as "counter-movements." Polanyi (173) described the 1795 Speenhamland Law (designed to provide relief to the rural poor at the onset of the Industrial Revolution) as "a moat erected in defence of traditional rural organization, when the turmoil of change was sweeping the countryside, and, incidentally, making agriculture a precarious industry." Fortress farming is often associated with nonproductivist farming practices rather than necessarily farming for wealth accumulation, and this is commonly enabled by diverse resource flows into the rural household from nonfarm sources. It is thus a household livelihood strategy that responds to an evolving institutional environment that encompasses, but also stretches well beyond, local rural landscapes. The emphasis on actively tapping resource flows thereby positions fortress farming in contrast to the so-called "new peasantries," which van der Ploeg (2008) describes as eschewing dependency relations in an overarching pursuit of autonomy.

My reference to "nonproductivist" farming requires some explanation. Productivist farming refers to farm systems oriented toward maximizing physical outputs as a dominant land-use logic, often with the generation of negative social and environmental externalities such as loss of community and land degradation. Ilbery and Bowler (1998) associated agricultural productivism with commercialization (a market orientation for farm outputs), commoditization (an emphasis on shifting structural relations of production, particularly in respect to the factors of land and labor), and industrialization (the application of technology to the production process, often through mechanization, synthetic inputs, and biotechnology). From the perspective of the Global North in the 1990s (Ilbery and Bowler 1998; Marsden 1995; Ward 1993), it appeared that productivist agriculture was giving ground to environmentally friendly production, localized food systems, and increased recognition of the amenity-based services provided by rural landscapes beyond commodity production (that is, post-productivism). Some of the more extreme temporal claims that post-productivism was the hallmark of a new era, however, have since been treated with far greater caution (Roche and Argent 2015). We should equally not ignore the reality that individuals will invariably attempt to improve their economic situation (sometimes through productivist farming), such that we often observe spatially heterogeneous mosaics of productivist and nonproductivist farm practices within, and across, landscapes (Wilson and Burton 2015). Fortress farming, however, highlights a general tendency toward nonproductivist land practices in late-industrializing countries.

The concept of "livelihoods" shines a light on the breadth of activities in which rural households are engaged—wage labor, petty trade, subsistence farming, commodity production, reciprocal labor and gift exchange, patronage relations, remittances, and ceremonial participation. As I will develop further in chapter 2, however, my conceptual understanding of livelihoods needs to be large enough to encompass not only the range of activities pursued to achieve an acceptable material standard of living, but also the desire to attain a wider sense of life meaning. This takes the notion of livelihood resilience within my concept of fortress farming into the realm of cultural practices, which inevitably vary across geographies and communities. In Indonesia, these oftentimes respond to place-specific *adat* practices, which are customary (but still somewhat fluid) sets of beliefs, rules, and traditions that influence cultural orientations and behavior in a community (even if they have been constructed through constant interaction with other communities). *Adat* can also shape resource access regimes (McCarthy 2006). Desires and aspirations also vary within communities and are of course dynamic rather than fixed, but the key point is that both culture and economy are integral to livelihoods—and to the desire to address livelihood resilience through fortress farming.

The livelihoods approach has, however, been accused of failing to address how wider, global processes impinge on local concerns (Scoones 2015). In contrast, my presentation of fortress farming focuses on the relationship between the broader institutional environment and household livelihood strategies. I develop an understanding of the institutional environment as a multiscalar set of political and social rules and routinized practices that coalesce in a particular place to shape economic activity, the distribution of resources, and ultimately how livelihoods are pursued. The institutional environment is multiscalar in the sense that it is intersected by rules and patterns of behavior forged by actors with influence at local, regional, national, and global scales. Institutional environments thus coevolve through the interplay between place-based cultural proclivities and the way places are embedded within broader relations of power—especially those forged by the state over territories—but I extend this to the role of powerful lead firms operating within so-called global value chains (GVCs). The GVC approach provides an alternative axis through which power (often exerted by multinational companies) can be examined to better understand the political economy of agrarian livelihoods. More particularly, the GVC framework has been applied to demonstrate how the specific strategies of lead firms, in managing their increasingly globalized supply chains, cocreate (with a range of nonfirm actors) the institutional environments that are now key determinants of development processes operating at local, regional, and national scales (Neilson and Pritchard 2009). I thus apply an institutionally enriched livelihood framework that borrows from the global value chain analytical toolkit to incorporate aspects of international and agrarian political economy, building on my previous work (Neilson 2019) and work with colleagues (Vicol et al. 2019).

Institutional environments are deeply shaped by history and culture in a partially path-dependent way, yet they are also dynamic and continually modified by the strategies, motivations, and practices of different actors. They evolve in particular places through the actions of, and the interactions between, smallholder farmers, cultural leaders, migrant workers, traders, industrialists, the state (or its representatives), activists and nongovernmental organizations (NGOs), researchers, international development agencies, multinational corporations, and consumers. The institutions and access regimes around land (a Polanyian fictitious commodity), for example, remain deeply embedded within persistent social relations that extend well beyond the market. I follow Granovetter (1985, 482), whose notion of embeddedness argued that "the behavior and institutions to be analyzed are so constrained by ongoing social relations that to construe them as independent is a grievous misunderstanding." Some institutions have global effects, while others are national in scope, such that we discern some commonalities across multiple sites within countries. In this sense, there are aspects of fortress farming that can be generalized. A key observation in this book, however, is that these institutions then interact with place-based situated histories to shape the localized institutional environments that influence livelihood decisions at the household level.

Fortress farming can help explain various anomalies encountered by those attempting to promote rural development. Such anomalies include the apparent unwillingness of households to transform into production-oriented agricultural entrepreneurs (despite efforts of some downstream buyers and the state encouraging them to do so). It explains the limited impact of value chain sustainability programs that seek to improve the lives of producers through the promotion of good agricultural practices. It explains the persistence, and importance, of agrarian landscapes—and access to land—even when wealth accumulation is primarily associated with nonagricultural economies. It explains the inability of farmers to coalesce into an influential political force despite their apparent demographic dominance in democratic countries like Indonesia. Finally, it explains the limited consolidation of land as a productive resource (smallholder persistence), despite exposure to the competitive pressures of capitalism.

Fortress farming scenarios have important policy implications for countries experiencing agrarian transition under conditions of late capitalism, and the changing role of land assumes central importance. Rigg et al. (2018, 328) assert that, to understand contemporary agrarian transitions in Asia, "it is necessary to think about the place, meaning and significance of land in rural livelihoods in transforming countries of Asia differently." Furthermore, the capacity of the manufacturing sector to continue generating jobs for relatively low-skilled workers from the countryside appears limited (Rodrik 2016), such that late-industrializing countries like Indonesia are unlikely to experience a transition that simply follows the paths of earlier industrializers in Western Europe, North America, or even Northeast Asia. I argue that the persistence of diversified rural livelihoods with partial dependence on access to land may be a longer-term feature of rural landscapes than is commonly assumed.

Throughout the book, I will use the term "smallholder" as a designation for households with access to farmland that supports, at least partially, their livelihood, and which can be managed primarily with household labor. In this way, I am largely equating smallholdings with "family farms," which Lowder, Sánchez, and Bertini (2021, 6) define as "those farms held by an individual, group of individuals or household whose labor is mostly supplied by the family" (this also conforms with an earlier definition provided by FAO 2014). In the Indonesian coffee sector, on which this book focuses, smallholdings are overwhelmingly managed by households who consider themselves to be owner-cultivators rather than renters (appendix table A7). An obvious question is how small is a smallholder? In their global analyses, Lowder, Sánchez, and Bertini considered smallholdings as any farm smaller than two hectares. The appropriateness of this definition, of course, varies with context. Within a given range of technology adoption, Indonesian coffee smallholdings are generally limited in physical extent by household labor constraints, and currently this indeed seems to set an upward limit of around two hectares for family farms. Based on the 2013 Agricultural Census data, an estimated 90 percent of Indonesian coffee-growing households managed less than three hectares in total. Family-farm smallholders dominate Indonesia's coffee sector.

In Indonesia, there is furthermore a clear distinction between smallholders and large commercial plantations (hundreds or even thousands of hectares in size) issued with long-term leases (*hak guna usaha*), which I will discuss in later chapters. Labor can be, and is, enlisted by smallholders through informal paid labor and extended household and patronage relations. While the extent of wage labor can be significant among some commodity-producing smallholders, it remains limited on Indonesian coffee smallholdings (appendix table A9), and sharecropping arrangements are also uncommon (appendix table A8). Within the broad categorization of smallholder, however, some class differentiation and local accumulation of land have also occurred.

The term "smallholder" may imply a level of economic and political agency that remains illusory for many Indonesians "living from the soil." Nevertheless, I generally use it in preference to "peasant"—another notoriously slippery term—which is often used to denote a particular social class. The term "peasant" is sometimes applied to intentionally highlight the exploitative nature of social relations between marginalized agrarian households and the broader political and economic systems within which they are embedded. As such, it has been reclaimed by various agrarian resistance movements in some parts of the world (most notably the international peasant organization La Via Campesina—"The Peasant Way") as a rhetorical strategy to demand a moral and political response to unacceptable social conditions. Elson (1997) argued, however, that we have likely witnessed the historical end of the peasantry as a social class, as rural populations have become progressively fragmented, to such an extent that the term seems increasingly anachronistic.[1] Similarly, Bernstein (2010, 112) suggests that "it is difficult to adhere to any notion of farmers—whether described as 'peasants,' 'family farmers' or 'small farmers'—as a single class." The Indonesian term *petani* (often translated simply as "farmer"), sometimes qualified as *petani rakyat* ("commoner farmer") or *petani kecil* ("small farmer"), closely correlates to "peasant" in the sense that it remains suggestive of an exploited social category. *Petani*, however, also suggests a degree of stasis that is incongruent with the empirical realities of diversified household livelihoods and mobility. Peluso (2017) emphasizes how the "smallholder slot" (in Indonesia) is a contingent and flexible category. As such, it too is heavily politicized, and Peluso (840) demonstrates how it became reified by the Indonesian state (through *petani kecil*) to indicate "a desired positionality in rural society," where the smallholder was projected to be "proud of one's productive work—as both an independent producer and a citizen of Indonesia." My use of "smallholder" is initially free of any judgment about whether these households are fully integrated into capitalist markets, whether they also engage in off-farm work, and whether they necessarily exist in a subordinate position within a larger, more dominant social system, or even exist as a class in opposition to the interests of capital. I will instead allow such inferences to emerge inductively through an analysis of my empirical material.

Why Indonesia?

After India and China, Indonesia's agricultural labor force is the world's third largest and so is of global significance. While the Indonesian economy has not grown as strongly as China's in recent decades, Indonesia is often considered an economic development success story, where "per capita incomes have risen more than sixfold over fifty years, poverty has fallen rapidly, and social indicators have improved significantly" (Hill 2018, 495). Involvement in farming, however, is a key correlate of poverty, and this is linked to high disparities in per capita incomes between places like Jakarta (and some resource-rich regions like East Kalimantan) and those in the eastern islands such as East Nusa Tenggara, where 70 percent of households remain engaged in farming and where poverty rates rank among the country's highest.

Although the Indonesian population—the world's fourth largest in 2023—continues to grow, the country has undergone an important demographic transition over the last fifty years. The total fertility rate (the number of children, on average, expected to be born to each woman during her life) has come down from 5.6 in the 1960s to 2.3 in 2019 and is expected to reach the replacement level of 2.1 by 2030, such that Indonesia's population is predicted (United Nations 2019) to peak, and then stabilize, at around 330 million by 2060, from a population of 270 million at the 2020 census. Declining fertility rates, together with ongoing urbanization, have meant that Indonesia's rural population peaked at 126 million as far back as 1992: it was 119 million by 2020 (World Bank 2024). The overall situation in rural Indonesia is not one where demographic pressure is the key driver of land shortages. Far more important in this respect have been the large corporate and state-based land appropriations (especially for commercial plantations) that commenced in the colonial period, peaked during the Suharto regime (1966–1998), and indeed continue today.

Southeast Asia's largest economy is experiencing an agrarian transition, as social and economic life drifts away from a dependence on agriculture (at the national scale) toward higher rates of urbanization, primarily nonagricultural economic growth, and the partial de-agrarianization of livelihoods. In 2010, probably for the first time in the long history of the archipelago, more Indonesians were living in urban rather than rural areas,[2] and agriculture, forestry, and fisheries contributed only 12.4 percent to the country's GDP by 2022 (figure 0.1). The share of the working-age population primarily employed in agriculture has declined (from 56 percent in 1980 to 29 percent in 2021), and even the absolute number of these workers (around thirty-eight million individuals in 2022) has been declining slightly since 2000. The number of agricultural *households*, however, has not decreased in lockstep with this, as part-time farming and intra-household livelihood diversification become more common. Agricultural households—defined by the agricultural census as those where "at least one household member undertakes an agricultural activity partly or wholly aimed to be sold or bartered"—still constituted 40 percent of all households in 2023, the same share as in 2013 and only a moderate decline from 2003. At the time of the 2013 Agricultural Census, nonfarm income was estimated to constitute around half the total for these households, notwithstanding considerable regional variation (table 0.1).

Furthermore, and as I will show later in this book, standard surveying methods fail to capture the full extent of kinship-linked resource transfers into rural

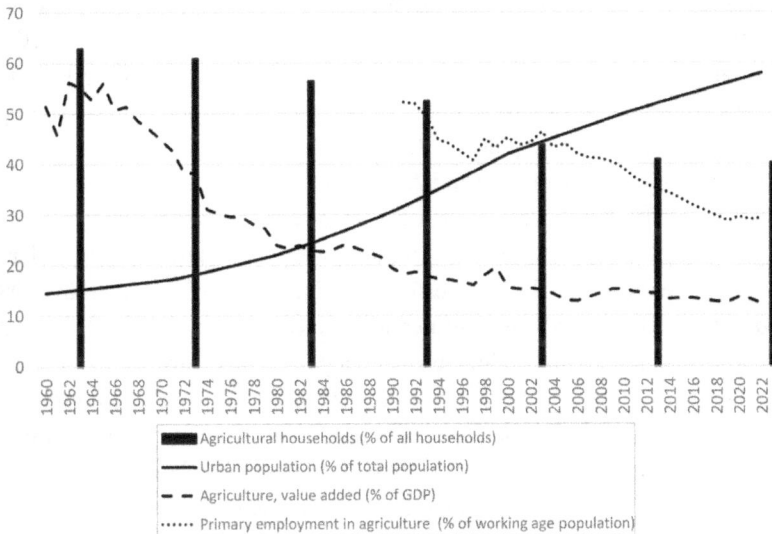

FIGURE 0.1. Deagrarianization of the Indonesian economy (1960–2023). *Sources:* World Bank 2024; BPS 2013; BPS 2023.

TABLE 0.1 Nonfarm income among agricultural households (2013)

PROVINCE	AVERAGE ANNUAL HOUSEHOLD INCOME (MILLION IDR)	AVERAGE ANNUAL NONFARM INCOME (MILLION IDR)	SHARE OF NONFARM INCOME IN TOTAL INCOME (%)
South Sumatra	31.9	6.6	21
Lampung	26.1	9.4	35
South Sulawesi	23.9	9.5	40
Aceh	23.7	10.8	45
North Sumatra	28.6	10.4	47
East Java	24.1	11.7	48
Bali	35.1	22.3	62
Indonesia	26.6	12.3	46

Source: BPS 2013.

communities. Despite a broad-brush portrait of a standard agrarian transition, suggesting some of the same modernizing tendencies witnessed elsewhere in the world, the specific characteristics of this transition, particularly as played out at the household scale, are far more complex.

The fact that 40 percent of Indonesian households are at least partly reliant on access to land (or other natural resources) for their livelihood is important. Production of rice and other food crops is widespread, with a third of Indonesia's fourteen million rice-growing households (in the 2013 agricultural census) using their entire rice harvest for own-consumption, and with many more selling only a small surplus on the market. Farming can also serve as an important safety net during times of personal and systemic crisis. This was well-documented during the 1998 Asian financial crisis, when the urban economy contracted sharply, leading to massive formal job losses, with many of these displaced workers subsequently working in farming (Manning 2000). A retreat to farming also occurred during the COVID-19 pandemic of 2020 and 2021.[3] Many others became dependent on family and social networks to survive, while many accessed government support payments. Admittedly, the return to farming was less pronounced in 2019 than in 1998. The reasons why this has been less so during COVID-19 than in 1998 are not yet entirely clear but seem related to the creation of a state-funded social protection system, notwithstanding its many imperfections, during the intervening twenty years. It may also be that increased mechanization in the rice-growing heartlands has meant that workers can no longer be reabsorbed by agriculture to the same extent, or that workers have indeed lost access to farmland through prior expropriations. In 1998, moreover, rapid exchange rate depreciation simultaneously facilitated a commodity boom, which benefited producers of export crops, and this was not the case during the pandemic. Of course, the ability of farming, and rural landscapes more broadly, to function as a safety net is only possible when access to land and rural social networks is sustained—and this is by no means guaranteed, and is highly dependent on prevailing institutional environments. Debates around this safety net role are addressed in chapter 1.

Many of those born in Indonesia's villages do establish higher-income lives away from farming, often through obtaining an education, engaging in off-farm work, and by migrating to urban areas, where they act as ambassadors attracting others away from a life of farming. During migratory experiences (*merantau*),[4] many individuals send remittances back to rural villages to support family members and their community, some retain intergenerational links with ancestral homelands, while others turn their back on the perceived backwardness (*sifat kampungan*) of their rural past and lead thoroughly urban lives. Others, however, have their dreams dashed by the harsh realities of city life, where jobs are not as plentiful as imagined, as they struggle to eke out a pitiable existence scavenging (sometimes literally) inside Indonesia's sprawling megacities. Some of these individuals eventually trickle back to natal villages to farm, if relationships with land and community have not been irredeemably severed.

Yet despite the generally urbanizing reality, many Indonesians seem reluctant to let go of a self-image as an agrarian nation (*negara agraris*). Farm practices are often deeply embedded within cultural institutions, exemplified by the privileged social position of rice farming in many communities. Ownership of rice fields and rice barns can be important social markers linked to ethnic and cultural identities that are imbued with meaning that extends well beyond any economic function. The ability of the nation (the *bangsa*) to feed itself is upheld by nationalist political manifestos and emotive appeals for food sovereignty (Neilson and Wright 2017). Revivalist movements for indigenous foods are celebrated at culinary festivals and across various social media platforms. Indonesians are proud of agricultural products linked to regional cultural identities and would like to see coffee continue to be marketed domestically and abroad under such ethnic markers as "Bali," "Preanger," or "Toraja." Agrarian transitions continue to be as much cultural as they are economic.

Later in this book, I present two regional case studies of fortress farming in greater detail: Toraja in southwest Sulawesi and Semende in southern Sumatra, both outer island upland regions. While both regions practice subsistence-oriented wet-rice cultivation, they have also had an extended engagement with commodity production through coffee. They are distinct from the heavily irrigated, and densely populated, rice-growing heartlands of Java's north coast and are located in provinces where agricultural households have a below-average reliance on off-farm work (table 0.1). These two regions have also not been subject to the palm oil boom of the Sumatran and Kalimantan lowlands, which has involved large-scale "corporate occupation" of rural space (Li and Semedi 2021, but see also McCarthy 2010, Cramb and McCarthy 2016, and Pye and Bhattacharya 2013). Neither Semende nor Toraja, however, has been unscathed by colonial encounters and the disciplining pressures of global capitalism. Both regions possess resilient customary *adat* institutions that have persisted—perhaps owing to their dynamism—into the current day. I have, however, observed the continued influence of *adat* cultural practices on institutional environments in other Indonesian coffee-growing regions where I have worked. The continued importance of *adat* in shaping resource access regimes was also highlighted by McCarthy (2006) in his study of Sama Dua in South Aceh. The influence of *adat* on fortress farming that I later describe in these two case studies, while clearly manifesting itself in unique ways in these places, also reflects a broader phenomenon of culturally embedded institutions and the continued relevance of customary rules and practices in shaping rural livelihood outcomes. This is important even if these same *adat* rules and practices are constantly in flux.

Why Coffee?

This book examines the unfolding agrarian transition shaping rural Indonesia in the early twenty-first century, full of its contradictions, frictions, and challenges, through the analytical frame of a single commodity, coffee. I explore how livelihoods are being dreamed, performed, and experienced by a subset of Indonesian rural society—the country's nearly two million households who were planting and harvesting coffee cherries for at least part of their livelihood during the 2000s and 2010s. Such smallholders were estimated to be responsible for around 99 percent of national coffee production in 2020, a share that has gradually increased since the colonial era. This smallholder domination contrasts with oil palm, which has emerged as the most commercially significant agricultural commodity in Indonesia in recent decades. Table 0.2, however, shows that in 2013, at the time of the most recently available full agricultural census, coffee was still being cultivated by a greater number of households than oil palm. While the 2018 intercensus was not a full enumeration, it suggests a declining number of coffee-growing households. Coffee is grown across a diverse geography, literally stretching from Aceh in the northwestern tip of Sumatra through to the highland border regions of Papua in the east, and on most islands in between.

Commercial coffee production is predominately based on the cultivation of one of two species—*Coffea arabica* and *Coffea canephora* (Robusta), with smaller amounts of *Coffea liberica* also grown in the Sumatran lowlands. Indonesian production consists of an estimated 85 percent Robusta, a hardier species that trades at lower prices and is grown at lower altitudes than Arabica. Semende is primarily a Robusta producing region, while Toraja is primarily Arabica. Coffee is widely

TABLE 0.2   Number of households cultivating Indonesia's major tree crops

TREE CROP	NUMBER OF HOUSEHOLDS (2013)	NUMBER OF HOUSEHOLDS (2018)	AREA CULTIVATED BY HOUSEHOLDS (HA, 2013)
Coconut	5,090,583	*Not available*	1,242,319
Rubber	2,888,542	2,630,765	4,542,093
Cocoa	2,186,755	1,370,428	1,097,187
Coffee	1,962,044	1,616,459	1,063,427
Cloves	1,623.089	*Not available*	493,668
Oil palm	1,458,319	1,872,016	3,133,710

Sources: BPS 2013; BPS 2019a.

grown within diverse agroforests, intercropped with fruit trees (durian, avocado, rambutan, banana), root crops (taro and sweet potato), vegetables, pepper vines, and shade trees used for fodder and mulch (*gamal, lamtoro, dadap*). It is some-times grown as a simple backyard garden crop, near the family home. Elsewhere, it is planted less intensively in remote forest frontiers and monocropped. As a result, coffee sometimes competes for land with conservation initiatives, includ-ing the UNESCO-listed Tropical Rainforest Heritage of Sumatra, much of which is situated adjacent to coffee-growing landscapes, and which UNESCO listed as "in danger" in 2011.

Coffee plantings are embedded within diverse regional landscapes. It has become somewhat conventional to present a false dichotomy between low-land wet rice (*sawah*) and upland swidden (*ladang*) communities,[5] forgetting the important—even primary—role performed by *sawah* in many Indonesian uplands, including many coffee-growing regions.[6] Although swidden landscapes with a primary focus on dryland rice (*padi ladang*) do exist in Indonesia, espe-cially on Kalimantan (van Noordwijk et al. 2008), swiddening also occurred on the outskirts of Indonesia's wet-rice cultivating valleys, and it is into these *ladang* systems that coffee was largely integrated.

With a few exceptions, coffee is cultivated using traditional, "unimproved" methods, and it has not been consistently supported through government-funded agricultural extension programs. Despite this, Indonesia was the fourth-largest coffee producer in the world in 2020 (ICO 2020) and in some years exceeds Colombia to be third. National production levels fluctuate annually, based largely on weather conditions, but in contrast to other producers like Brazil, Vietnam, Honduras, and Ethiopia, there has been little increase in output since the 1990s. In recent years, coffee cannot be considered a boom crop in Indonesia. Unlike Vietnamese smallholders, who generally irrigate their coffee farms intensively from both groundwater supplies and nearby rivers, systematic irrigation of cof-fee is not practiced in Indonesia. While coffee is a relatively easy crop to main-tain at low levels of labor input (especially with herbicides), the harvest of coffee cherries continues to be time-consuming and tedious. Unlike in Brazil, coffee harvesting in Indonesia has not been mechanized, such that the availability of harvest labor is a key production constraint. Indonesian coffee yields are low relative to other major coffee-producing countries (table 0.3). Roughly half of Indonesia's coffee-growing households apply no fertilizer at all (appendix table A2), and many of those that do apply it do so at low rates (Byrareddy et al. 2019). Low-input production is also reflected in the limited integration of smallholders with credit markets (appendix table A5). These low-input systems are significant for fortress farming, as they suggest the potential for increasing productivity if house-holds chose to reorient their allocations of either labor or capital toward coffee

TABLE 0.3   Coffee yields in major coffee-producing countries (2016–2020 average)

COFFEE PRODUCER	KG/HA
Vietnam	2,615
Brazil	1,502
Honduras	1,129
Colombia	988
India	707
Ethiopia	651
Indonesia	583

Source: FAO 2024

cultivation. Global coffee prices have been mostly low now for decades, despite growing global consumption (although prices increased significantly in 2023 and 2024 owing to global supply shortages). Generally low prices are due to improved supply responsiveness from Brazil and Vietnam (Sachs et al. 2019). In Indonesia, these low prices have instead resulted in gradually declining interest in the crop.

Only half of Indonesia's coffee-growing households identify coffee as their main agricultural activity, with 15 percent identifying nonfarm activities as their main source of income (BPS 2018). It seems rather straightforward to refer to "coffee farmers," but it is more accurate to refer to "coffee-growing households" in recognition of the pervasiveness of pluriactivity (or the tendency for a household to engage in a range of diversified livelihood activities). While this may seem obvious enough, it is remarkable how often discussions proceed in government offices, NGOs, coffee firms, and development agencies on the basis that the singular identity of "coffee farmer" possesses categorical meaning.

While few households cultivate *only* coffee, the single-commodity focus adopted in this book has several analytical advantages. Most importantly, it allows a concrete exploration of how the forces of contemporary capitalism, as manifest through specific value chain structures, are reshaping local institutional environments and intruding on the lives of rural producers. This is enabled, in a practical sense, by a frame of reference bounded by the contours of a particular industry with its own internal logic of value creation and accumulation (that is, a global value chain). The coffee sector has received relatively little recent attention by scholars of agrarian change in Indonesia, and limited policy attention from the Indonesian government. The lack of policy attention can be explained by the relative insignificance of coffee within a much larger and highly diverse national economy. In contrast, however, downstream coffee firms in the value chain have taken an active interest in the households that supply the basic commodity upon which their profitability depends, such that their influence can be strongly felt.

The Indonesian coffee industry also presents an opportunity to examine institutional evolution over a three-hundred-year history, as few other commodities have maintained their relative significance in Indonesia over the *longue durée*.

Methods

I first became familiar with Indonesian coffee-growing communities by way of the Toraja highlands, where I was engaged in an undergraduate research project. That project involved several stays in forest-margin communities throughout 1998 and 1999, all of which grew coffee, and indeed new forest plots were being cleared by ex-urban workers who had been laid off following the Asian financial crisis. The experience motivated me to undertake doctoral research on the global commodity chains (the preferred terminology at the time) that linked sites of rural production on Sulawesi with the burgeoning international specialty coffee sector. I spent a total of fifteen months during the 2002 and 2003 coffee harvests living in Sulawesi (and another twelve months in 2005 under a postdoctoral fellowship), undertaking ethnographic research with coffee-growing households across the southwestern peninsula of the island (Neilson 2004). I was a frequent visitor to the various highland markets, held on six-day cycles in Toraja, where I got to know many of the collectors. I attended farmer training sessions organized by buyers and learned from them about quality grades and the factors shaping (their perceptions of) bean quality and of their sourcing strategies and challenges.

Between 2005 and 2021, I was then involved in four subsequent research projects examining various aspects of the Indonesian coffee sector, funded by the Australian Research Council (ARC) and the Australian Centre for International Agricultural Research (ACIAR). This involved research visits to most of Indonesia's major coffee-producing regions (from west to east): Gayo, Sidikalang, Karo, Simalungun, Lintong, Rejang, Pasemah, Semende, Ogan Komering, Sumber Jaya, Liwa, Tanggamus, Preanger, Temanggung, Bondowoso, Ijien, Kintamani, Ruteng, Bajawa, and Wamena, along with regular return visits to Sulawesi. The key sites discussed in the book are shown in figure 0.2. I have visited some sites repeatedly over this period, allowing more in-depth semi-longitudinal analysis. These visits have involved structured and unstructured interviews (usually fueled by multiple cups of coffee) with farmers, collectors, commodity traders, village and district government heads, cooperative administrators, extension officers, NGOs, farmer associations, exporters, international development agencies, coffee roasters in major Indonesian cities and abroad, industry associations, factory owners, and senior bureaucrats and politicians in Jakarta. I have participated in dozens of industry events, workshops, exhibitions, and conferences that have discussed and promoted the development of the Indonesian coffee sector, and

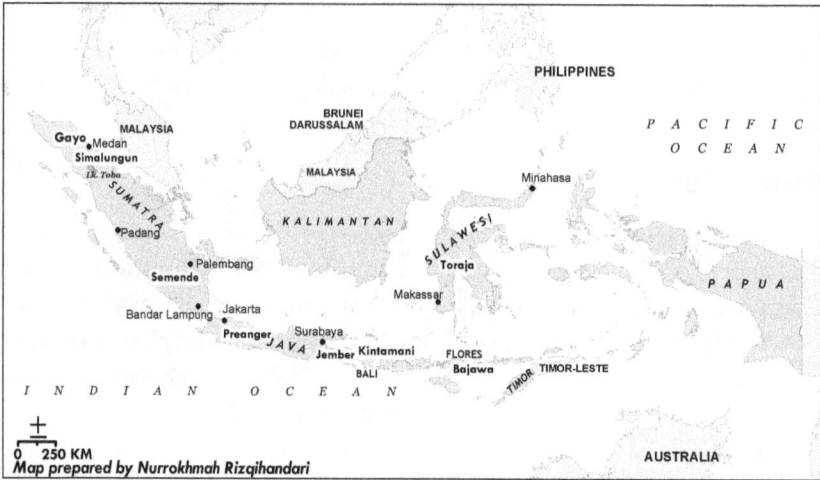

FIGURE 0.2. Map of Indonesia showing major sites mentioned in the book.

which have provided me with insights into the prevailing narratives that underpin industry and state attitudes toward coffee-related development.

During periods of fieldwork, and with considerable assistance from researchers at the Indonesian Coffee and Cocoa Research Institute (ICCRI), I have undertaken or supervised surveys of more than five thousand smallholder households across ten major coffee-producing regions (table 0.4). The specific aims of these surveys have varied. Some sought to understand farming practices at the forest margin, others assessed relationships with coffee roasters or studied the effects of sustainability programs, while others analyzed the introduction of Geographical Indication schemes. A central theme, however, has been to understand how coffee farming was integrated within broader rural livelihood strategies and land practices, and to understand household engagement with both downstream buyers and the state. While this book is not quantitatively focused, this survey work shaped my understanding of the livelihood strategies that vary across different regions and is drawn upon at different times to present key arguments.

Throughout the book (including the statistical appendix A), I also present the results of surveys undertaken by Indonesia's National Statistics Bureau (BPS, Badan Pusat Statistik). These surveys include the decennial Agricultural Census (Sensus Pertanian, ST), where every agricultural household in Indonesia is enumerated, and the 2018 Agricultural Intercensus (SUTAS); the associated Estate Crop Household Economic Survey (Survei Rumah Tangga Usaha Perkebunan, SKB), conducted on a representative sample of estate crop households in the year following the Agricultural Census; the decennial Population Census (Sensus Penduduk, SP), a complete enumeration of every individual within Indonesia; the annual (sometimes biannual) Labor Force Survey (Survei Angkatan Kerja Nasional,

TABLE 0.4   Case study sites involving household surveys

LOCATION	SAMPLE SIZE	YEAR	SURVEY PARTNER
Toraja, Sulawesi	66	2008	Jalesa
Gayo, Aceh	135	2008	UNSYIAH
Lampung, Sumatra	123	2008	UNILA
Toraja, Sulawesi	199	2009	ICCRI
Bajawa, Flores	207	2009	ICCRI/BPTP NTT/DELSOS
Manggarai, Flores	197	2009	ICCRI/BPTP NTT/DELSOS
Enrekang, South Sulawesi	197	2009	ICCRI
Kintamani, Bali	200	2013	ICCRI
Enrekang, South Sulawesi	98	2014	Universitas Indonesia
Semende, South Sumatra	1,588	2015, 2017, 2019	SurveyMETER
Simalungun, North Sumatra	200	2015, 2017	ICCRI
Sumedang, West Java	86	2015, 2017	ICCRI
Sidikalang, North Sumatra	72	2016	ICCRI
Bajawa, Flores	100	2016	ICCRI
Kintamani, Bali	56	2016	ICCRI
Lampung and Semende, Sumatra	550	2017	UNILA
Toraja, Sulawesi ("Tondok Buntu")	32	2018	Universitas Kristen Indonesia—Toraja (UKIT)
Toraja, Sulawesi	99	2018	Universitas Indonesia
North Sumatra and Aceh	1,306	2020	Enveritas (phone survey)
Total households	**5,511**		

SAKERNAS), and the annual National Socioeconomic Survey (Survei Sosial Ekonomi Nasional, SUSENAS), each covering a nationally representative sample of
around two hundred thousand households. This data is presented to provide supporting evidence for observations drawn from primary fieldwork, where, on the
balance of evidence, specific questions appear to have elicited accurate responses
and meaningful results. These datasets have also allowed me to ascertain the extent
(and limitations) to which my case specific findings can be generalized.

I present research findings primarily through ethnographic accounts from the
specific case studies of Toraja (Sulawesi) and Semende (Sumatra). Both sites represent regions with extended histories of engagement with global coffee markets and
involvement by international coffee buyers through value chain mechanisms, and
each has had a similar experience of the Indonesian state through development
programs and interactions with forest authorities. I identify concrete elements
from these cases that can be generalized as representative of institutional environments affecting Indonesian coffee-growing households more broadly by triangu-
lating observations with both my fieldwork elsewhere and with national datasets
(where available), while identifying those elements that are specific to each site.

My approach is essentially inductive, and I have abstracted the concepts of *institutional environment* and *fortress farming* as heuristic frameworks to help explain these field-based observations. My analytical method, however, has also involved what might be called "grounded theory" involving a recursive method of successive periods of data collection, analysis, and verification to reach my conclusions (Glaser and Strauss [1967] 1999; Knigge 2017). This has meant an iterative process of testing my observations against evolving theoretical frameworks. My presentation of fortress farming, and the analytical method used to develop it, have, however, been inevitably influenced by my positionality and subjectivities. I have worked collaboratively with coffee firms on action-research interventions at the farm level, previously sat on the Supervisory Board of the Sustainable Coffee Platform for Indonesia (SCOPI), and have collaborated with international development agencies. My funding from ACIAR has demanded ongoing engagement with such "research end-users," and this has exposed me, at times, to the pressures of what Li (2007) refers to as the "rendering technical" of development problems, but it has also provided insights into the perspectives of these influential actors that co-construct the institutional environments I have studied.

Through twenty-five years of marriage, I have become part of an extended Torajan family, which has allowed (on the one hand) insights into various cultural attitudes and life aspirations through casual observations and conversations, and through participation in family events and ceremonies. On the other hand, these, and other positional experiences, have also inevitably meant that I have brought to this research endeavor my own biases and subjectivities (as a white Australian male geographer interested in the multiscalar and networked nature of rural places), which have framed my understanding of industry dynamics and agrarian change, for better or for worse. As far as I can tell, there is little that can be done to effectively remove such positional biases entirely, but I have sought to be cognizant of my own subjectivity through constant reflexivity and by sharing research observations with research colleagues, various industry and state-based stakeholders, and with Indonesian rural households. Their feedback has helped to develop an intersubjective assessment of the processes at play and to iteratively construct my argument. Overall, my methodological approach has involved analyzing agrarian change processes through engaged fieldwork that seeks to understand the lived experiences and aspirations of those individuals and households growing coffee across Indonesia.

Book Structure

I have sought to develop an original and distinctive theorization of the ways multiscalar processes construct place-specific institutional environments, which in turn shape and reshape rural livelihood possibilities and land relations, often resulting in a dominant livelihood strategy of fortress farming. This in turn helps to explain the current unfolding of Indonesia's agrarian transition. The book is structured around this series of interlocking arguments, and this requires first setting out the broader institutional environments in Indonesia's coffee regions in some detail before returning to the core concern of household-scale livelihood change in my two case studies. This deliberately multiscalar analytical endeavor involves a constant jumping between scales from the global through to the local. An adequate (if necessarily still incomplete) analysis of the institutional environment requires an examination of the historical development of coffee growing and coffee-related institutions, and how these have intersected with key features of the Indonesian state, the governance of the value chain by lead firms, and land access regimes (this is pursued in chapters 2 to 5).

Chapter 1 first sets out the key theoretical considerations of the book, beginning with an understanding of agrarian change and the contemporary agrarian question, followed by a review of recent debates on livelihood theory and the contested role of farming as a social safety net. My interest in land is thus presented through a livelihoods lens where access to land can be a pivotal resource (or "capital") that households draw on to enhance livelihood resilience. I then make the case for introducing a global value chain approach to livelihoods theory and suggest that this can be most helpfully achieved through the conceptual development of the multiscalar institutional environment.

Chapter 2 reviews recent debates on processes of agrarian transition and what this means for changing rural livelihoods in contemporary Southeast Asia. Indonesia's unfolding agrarian transition frames my argument throughout the book, and, in this second chapter, I review the structural transformation of the Indonesian economy from its origins in Dutch colonialism, when coffee was introduced to the islands. This long-term perspective is critical to my broader conceptual framework, whereby contemporary institutional environments are shaped not only by specific actor strategies but are also deeply embedded within historical processes. Chapter 2 analyzes the structural transformation of the national economy since independence, including the role of export-oriented industrialization, and I raise the possibility that the country may now be experiencing "premature deindustrialization," contributing to a stalled or truncated agrarian transition.

This historical perspective is also essential as a prelude for understanding the evolution of the Indonesian state itself as an institution-shaping actor (or, more accurately, a collection of actors). Chapter 3, on patronage and the Indonesian state, analyzes how the state, through territorial control, is responsible for many of the transforming structures and processes that constitute the broader institutional environment for contemporary agrarian change. It examines the nature of the Indonesian state, its birth and evolving role in the lives of Indonesian rural communities. This involves analyzing recent state interventions, often enacted in partnership with NGOs and development agencies, to support the coffee sector through agricultural extension programs, village-level industrialization efforts, and support for farmer groups. It also includes the role of more generic state initiatives, like the recent spread of social protection programs. I emphasize how state programs, policies, and culture tend to reinforce vertically oriented patronage relationships rather than allowing class-based alliances, and I examine how this affects access to household livelihood resources (especially what is sometimes referred to as "social capital") while encouraging the prevalence of fortress farming.

Chapter 4, on global capital and coffee value chains, then complements the analysis of the state by introducing the role that lead firms (multinational coffee roasters) are performing in shaping contemporary institutional environments. This commences with a presentation of how rural households are inserted within a particular multiscalar structure—the global value chain for coffee. This then leads to an analysis of how lead firm strategies are having flow-on effects (providing both livelihood opportunities and constraints) within Indonesian rural communities. The focus is on understanding the specific mechanisms through which contemporary global capitalism affects smallholder livelihoods in rural Indonesia, but it does this in a nondeterministic way by highlighting how value chain influences are constantly rearticulated locally, most notably through a patronage-bound political economy.

Having developed a picture of how national economic development, the state and state policies, and value chain structures interact to shape institutional environments, in chapter 5 the book focuses in on the specific institutions that regulate access to land within coffee-growing communities. This chapter commences with a presentation of what I call the landlord state. I then explore how access to land is mediated through national land and forestry law, community-based forestry agreements, customary *adat* rights, formal land titling programs, and the evolving individualization of ownership. The institutional environment of land access that emerges in this chapter is one that appears forever partially formed and co-constructed with, and influenced by, place-specific customary practices in dialogue with formal laws, unwritten social norms, and uneven power relations.

Chapters 6 and 7 then provide fine-grained analyses of how place-specific institutional environments have encouraged dominant livelihood strategies and land relations that can be understood in terms of fortress farming. This is pursued in chapter 6 through a regional case study of livelihoods in Toraja, where land access regimes for coffee farming have remained relatively open (at least for certain genealogically bound social groups). The rural economy, however, is primarily sustained by remittances channeled through ceremonially driven patronage networks, and this encourages fortress farming strategies. Chapter 7 then draws on field research from Semende, where farming performs a far more central economic role in livelihoods than in Toraja. Customary land tenure arrangements also encourage a strong link between this cultural homeland and an émigré community, and fortress farming is also evident amid increasing pluriactivity and diverse resource in-flows. In both regional cases, we see fortress farming emerging in response to an institutional environment mutually constructed by developments in the national economy, state-based policies and programs, the upstream engagements of coffee lead firms, and place-specific land access regimes.

The final chapter concludes by examining the implications of fortress farming for the unfolding agrarian transition occurring across Indonesia that this book seeks to better understand. I argue for the usefulness of analyzing institutional environments, as co-constructed by the strategies of lead firms in value chains, in explaining the rise of particular livelihood strategies. At the same time, I call for greater sensitivity among value chain scholars toward the ways that localized institutional environments are mutually constituted by lead firm strategies and complex social landscapes, complicating opportunities for what I call livelihood upgrading. I then present my contribution to understanding contemporary agrarian change in Indonesia by considering the transformation of livelihood strategies through the lens of fortress farming and consider broader implications for other late-industrializing countries.

AGRARIAN CHANGE AND LIVELIHOODS IN A WORLD OF GLOBAL VALUE CHAINS

> The number of large farms may not be changing; the small farm may not be being swallowed up by the large; but thanks to the development of industry, both are passing through a complete revolution—a revolution bringing the small landowner into closer contact with the propertyless proletariat and shaping the interests of both to an increasingly convergent extent.
>
> —Karl Kautsky, *The Agrarian Question* (1899)

This chapter positions the key theoretical objectives of the book within a broader set of debates concerning the transformation of the world's agrarian communities. I pursue this by first reviewing key issues raised by "classical" agrarian scholars who observed earlier industrialization processes in Europe and who maintained an analytical focus on patterns of class differentiation with the rise of agrarian capitalism. I then seek to frame the contemporary agrarian question from a livelihoods perspective, which situates farming and access to land within a much broader range of economic activities and social networks. I propose the global value chain framework as a helpful analytical addition to the livelihoods perspective by addressing how broader global economic structures interact with livelihood opportunities at the household level.

Agrarian Questions

The future of agrarian communities in response to the forward march of market-based capitalism has been the core concern of agrarian studies for more than a century. It was classically framed as "the agrarian question," drawing on Karl Kautsky's seminal work *Die Agrarfrage*, published in 1899, which sought to understand the varied and distinctive ways that the (predominately German-speaking) peasantry was being transformed by the growth of industry and the development of capitalism in the second half of the nineteenth century.[1]

Kautsky ([1899] 1988) differed from Lenin's analysis in *The Development of Capitalism in Russia*, also first published in 1899. Lenin emphasized the inevitability of capitalist concentration *in* agriculture through processes of class differentiation creating classes of commodity-producing rural bourgeoisie (*kulaks*) and agricultural wage workers. Kautsky, however, considered it "obvious" that agriculture would pursue a unique path distinct from both industry and commerce, and presented the limits of capitalist agriculture through an analysis that retains contemporary resonance.

The "proletarianization of the peasantry," for Kautsky, involved peasant households clinging to smallholdings, even if land was principally considered a means of subsistence rather than a resource for generating profit and accumulating capital. At the same time, these "peasants" became engaged in supplementary employment in industry (as both agricultural laborers and outworkers), while (as petty commodity producers) having their farming surplus appropriated by town-based moneylenders, traders, and extractive states. This assessment approximates what, in contemporary settings, Bernstein (2010, 111) terms "classes of labor," to describe the working poor of the Global South who defy "inherited assumptions of fixed and uniform notions of 'worker,' 'farmer,' 'petty trader,' 'urban,' 'rural,' 'employed' and 'self-employed.'" Kautsky ([1899] 1988, 168) was not primarily concerned with how "the peasant becomes a proletariat" but with how "the peasant appears to remain as a peasant, but at the same time takes upon proletarian functions," and so sought to explain the unexpected persistence of household-based smallholdings within a broader capitalist system. Peasants, it seemed, were either becoming what would later be called semi-proletariats (Arrighi 1973) or becoming petty commodity producers (Bernstein 1986, 2010).

The persistence of smallholders in many rural landscapes thus presents something of a theoretical puzzle (Rigg, Salamanca, and Thompson 2016). Conventional Marxist analysis assumed that capitalism, as a progressive force, would inevitably transform agriculture toward capitalist production relations,[2] resulting in Leninist-inspired class differentiation. Peasant production, however, like that of many smallholders today, continued to rely on unpaid household labor, produced much of its own food and craft manufactures, and continued accessing land through customary arrangements. A key concern for Kautsky and, subsequently, the Russian agronomist Alexander Chayanov ([1925] 1966) was the dual function of the peasant household, in terms of being both a unit of production and consumption, such that it was not subject to the same laws of competition as the capitalist producer and so calculated its costs and benefits differently. Chayanovian observations that "labour, within the peasant farm, is not wage labour, and capital is not capital in the Marxist sense" (van der Ploeg 2013, 15) further prompted debates about whether there was a distinct mode of peasant production operating within a wider capitalist system. Chayanov thus downplayed processes of class differentiation *within* farming. Bernstein (2009, 66) contrasts this with the Leninist position where "the dynamic of the development of capitalist relations shapes the conditions, practices and fates of petty producers—and indeed is *internalized* within their enterprises and circuits of reproduction." According to Chayanov, however, capitalist relations were not fully internalized within the peasant household. Nevertheless, Chayanov (222) suggested that the farm household "becomes an inseparable part of the capitalist system, so far as the family farm exists within an economy dominated by capitalist relations; so far as it is drawn into commodity production and is a petty commodity producer, selling and buying at prices laid down by commodity capitalism." Chayanovian-inspired models of rural household economy have, however, generally been shunned by those working in both the Marxist tradition (for not following Lenin's position on class differentiation and for their alleged populism) and the liberal tradition (for challenging the notion of *Homo economicus* and rational economic decision-making). However, in Indonesia's fortress farming households, there are Chayanovian limits on the penetration of capitalist relations of production *within* farming itself, but this does not necessarily imply a "struggle for autonomy" (as suggested by van der Ploeg 2008), or that these same households are otherwise assuming an anticapitalist political stance. Moreover, rural households in Indonesia have become actively entwined (often enthusiastically so) in a myriad of market and nonmarket forces at, and beyond, the farm gate.

Hart, Turton, and White's (1989) edited publication *Agrarian Transformations* marked a shift in thinking about agrarian change in Southeast Asia, in that it placed the influence of these broader forces at the center of analysis. In that volume, White (1989) emphasized that there was no universal or all-purpose "agrarian question" awaiting investigation, nor was there any universal form of "agrarian differentiation." White and Wiradi (1989, 299) highlighted the potential implications of increasing nonfarm income for (the limits to) land-based agrarian differentiation:

> Wealthy households have many other avenues for profitable investment, and many demands for nonproductive expenditures, which compete with the alternative of land acquisition. On the other hand, the many small owners whose agricultural incomes do not provide reproduction at minimal levels are able, by participating in a variety of low-return nonfarm activities . . . to achieve subsistence incomes without the distress sale of their "sublivelihood" plots. These patterns . . . call for

interpretations of agrarian differentiation processes under conditions of commoditization and productivity growth which place the phenomenon of "part-time" farming and farm labor at all levels of the agrarian structure in more central focus.

Furthermore, Hart (1989) highlighted the influence of state patronage in shaping processes of agrarian differentiation, recognizing the varied forms in which power is manifest beyond relations of production, and so argued for conceptual frameworks in which "the institutional arrangements governing access to and control over resources and people are linked with larger economic and political forces" (2).

It can thus be said that rural class relations in contemporary Asia are no longer responding exclusively, if they ever were, to control over the productive assets of farmland itself (see, for example, White and Wiradi 1989; Rigg 2001; Bernstein 2010; Vicol 2019). Rigg's (2001) *More Than the Soil* made it clear that much of rural Southeast Asia has long been characterized by intense social and economic "inter-penetration" with the urban realm, and that it is fundamentally misleading to consider contemporary processes of rural development (or class differentiation) as being driven primarily by relations within farming. As presented by Rigg (2001, 200):

> One of the greatest surprises in the Thai countryside is the fact that accumulation seems to have occurred *without* dispossession. We have not seen . . . the emergence of a class of *kulaks* (wealthy peasants) nor a significant deepening in inequalities in ownership and access to land. Rural inequalities may indeed have become more entrenched over the last half century; this is not because peasants have been dispossessed but because wealth is being accumulated in other sectors, activities, and spatial arenas.

Meanwhile, some 45 percent of the world's population were still living in rural areas in 2020, many involved in smallholder farming or fishing, with global poverty still heavily concentrated outside of towns and cities, such that the "agrarian question of labour" (as Bernstein 2006 terms it) remains critically important.[3] An alternative framing of the agrarian question, then, is to ask why it is that, despite several decades of industrialization, many countries in the Global South still contain surprisingly large numbers of households retaining links to rural communities and the land, and to consider what the likely future is for these individuals and communities. As flagged in this volume's introduction, Elson (1997) argued that the twentieth century marked the end of the peasantry in Southeast Asia, following a "great age of the peasantry" from the mid-to-late nineteenth century until the early decades of the twentieth century. He put the situation by the close of the twentieth century as follows:

> Although the face of Southeast Asia even today remains superficially rural, the trajectory of peasant disappearance is fixed. The progeny of the late-nineteenth-century peasantry still live in the countryside, but not with the permanence, rural focus and sense of local identity their forebears had. They still grow rice, but they grow it more quickly, more often, and according to the template of modern agricultural science, and they grow a great variety of other cultigens as well. They sell the great bulk of what they produce, they produce it to sell, and they purchase the great bulk of what they use. They live in villages, but those villages are administrative creations which look upward and outward, not inwardly oriented local communities. They work outside the village, in a great range of specific and enduring occupations, in rhythms dissociated from those of rural production and at extremes of distance that would both frustrate and bewilder their predecessors. They move about with a facility and alacrity their forebears might both fear and envy. Their culture is not just that of the village but of the nation and the world, relayed to them through schools, newspapers, magazines, CDs, and the electronic media. (Elson 1997, xxii)

Certainly, any notion of an isolated and self-sufficient peasantry, let alone one with clearly delineated class interests, living within corporate villages, needs to be summarily dismissed. Rural smallholders engage with a broader hegemonic system of capitalist production as petty commodity producers, seasonal labor, remittance recipients, and small business owners. They also form relationships with their governments as citizens of modern nation-states. They are also community members with diverse social and cultural expectations. More than a quarter of a century after Elson sounded the death knell for the Southeast Asian peasantry, the apparent persistence of so many smallholder households may appear surprising. Many rural households continue to be primarily dependent on their own internal labor reserves for both production and reproduction, and partially depend upon access to natural resources for their livelihoods. Many remain engaged with production for own-consumption and have not embraced productivist farming. The critical question, then, has become how this considerable population has engaged with both rural production *and* with broader social and economic spheres well beyond the village, and what this means for land relations, sustainability, and the future of agrarian communities.

A Livelihoods Perspective

My approach to this analytical challenge is to apply, and further develop conceptually, a livelihoods perspective to agrarian change. Such a perspective has been used to describe a variety of research, policy, and project work that starts from an emphasis on people-centered development. The livelihoods perspective emerged in the late twentieth century as an integrating concept to address human well-being in a resource-constrained world (Chambers and Conway 1991), attempting to anchor development analysis in the day-to-day reality and aspirations of poor people (Carney 2002). Importantly, the perspective looks not only at employment and income. Rather, it examines the full breadth of activities in which people are engaged to survive, and sometimes prosper.

Chambers and Conway (1991) drew heavily on Amartya Sen's work on "capabilities," which Sen (1984) described as the ability to perform basic "functionings," where quality of life is improved by being able to perform those activities most valued by particular people in specific contexts. This was an explicit attempt to overcome the shortcomings of the narrower concept of "utility" used within mainstream economics, where the ability to consume within the monetary economy had come to be a proxy indicator of well-being. Strongly influenced by the work of Bourdieu (1977) and Long (2001), the actor-oriented livelihood paradigm has been developed further, in the Indonesian context, through the notion of livelihood styles (Nooteboom 2003; De Jong 2013). Drawing on field research in Sulawesi, De Jong (65) considers a livelihood style to reflect an "actor's conscious and unconscious objectives," which are established and maintained "within the framework of status systems, cultural ideals and geographic space and place." I borrow from such an understanding to highlight how a livelihood perspective considers not only attempts to address material deprivation, but also how culture shapes aspirations, nonmaterial aspects of well-being, and the ability to deliver meaning to people's lives. A focus on individual aspirations reminds us that livelihoods are embedded within deep-rooted cultural institutions in addition to economic structures.

Chambers and Conway (1991) further attempted to move beyond what they considered three conventional, but inherently limiting, modes of analysis: *production thinking*, where key social problems, such as hunger, are considered a consequence of underproduction rather than the capability to access what is produced; *employment thinking*, based on the assumption that jobs present a viable solution to address poverty, thus overlooking the lived realities of livelihood pluriactivity; and *poverty-line thinking*, where issues of deprivation and well-being can be distilled down into a measure of monetary income or expenditure (e.g., $1.90 per day) rather than a more holistic approach to well-being as understood by the capabilities approach. All three modes of analysis had been imported from urbanized industrial society contexts into the rural South, where their applicability as indicators of social development have proved more limited.

A livelihood perspective highlights household-level pluriactivity, which is a widespread reality across rural Southeast Asia (Andriesse and Phommalath 2012; Booth 2002; Kelly 2011; Rigg 2005; Rigg, Salamanca, and Thompson 2016; Rigg 2019), as indeed it is elsewhere in the rural world (Ellis 1998; Bernstein and Oya 2014). Put simply, it is wrong to equate rural lives with agriculture in any simple or totalizing sense, with poverty alleviation also becoming progressively de-linked from farming (Rigg 2006). More recently, Rigg (2019) has emphasized not only the rising importance of nonfarm income in Southeast Asia, but the extent to which rural and urban regions have become increasingly interwoven. This is evident with the establishment of industrial facilities in rural areas, commuting made possible by improved transport infrastructure, and the transfer of (usually urban-derived) remittances and social protection payments to rural households. Rigg's work has focused on Thailand, a geographically less fragmented country than Indonesia with better quality infrastructure, and he suggests that insular Southeast Asia might be undergoing a different kind of agrarian transition due to less spatial integration, less pluriactivity, and less urban-rural interpenetration (Rigg 2020). However, on average (and as presented earlier in table 0.1), off-farm income is estimated to contribute nearly half of total income for Indonesian agricultural households, and the prevalence of off-farm income (which includes nonfarm businesses, nonagricultural wages, and various transfers) is not restricted to Java. Many of the pluriactive livelihood patterns observed by Rigg in Thailand are indeed relevant to large parts of Indonesia.

Rural households construct and contrive a living by drawing on a combination of tangible assets (such as land, savings, and equipment) and intangible assets (such as their skills, health and education, and the capacity to make claims on relatives, patrons, friends, and the state). These assets were treated as livelihood *capital* by Johnson (1997), eventually resulting in the familiar five-fold categorization of household capital—natural, human, social, physical, and economic—where capital can be converted into a corresponding "resource" for a specific use.[4] In practice, these livelihood resources are often combined and can be mutually reinforcing, such as land being important not only for productive purposes (farming) but also essential for sustaining social relations (providing a home for family to return to, undertake rituals like funerals, or send remittances to). A key aim of this book is to understand the changing role of land as a livelihood resource. Moreover, the ability to access land is inextricably related to social capital, which is also pivotal in enabling individuals and households to tap into various resource flows from beyond the farm gate.

I have been using the term "household" in reference to livelihoods, recognizing that the household is of course internally differentiated—most obviously along gender and generational lines—and feminist theory has alerted us to the dangers of naively assuming the existence of a unitary household when many societies are becoming increasingly individualized (De Haan and Zoomers 2005). Razavi (2009, 198), meanwhile, highlighted the "severe limitations of methodological individualism for analyzing gender relations" within households, and suggests that we still need to be able to capture and reflect the "*common* interests that all household members have in the overall economic success of their households, however unequally the resources and the burdens are divided." The rural household is undoubtedly changing, but it remains a mostly coherent unit of both production and consumption within which the sharing and uneven control of resources through nonmarket mechanisms remain pervasive, such that it retains both broad functional and analytical utility. Diversified rural livelihood strategies, moreover, often only become evident at the household scale when farming by one household member complements off-farm income from another.

As with resource distribution within the household, economic institutions more broadly are inevitably "embedded" within social relations (Granovetter 1985). This has important implications for understanding how socially constructed institutional environments direct flows of wealth and resources in ways that ultimately affect livelihoods. The notion of "distributed livelihoods" (Ferguson 2015) is helpful here to capture the basic idea that social actors make choices about how financial resources are spent (and distributed). Ferguson highlights how much of the population (in both the Global North and Global South) survives through processes of redistribution. Drawing on work from southern Africa, Ferguson (2015) has called for a "new politics of distribution," highlighting the emergence of state-based welfare payments alongside the continued pervasiveness of traditional distribution networks prior to, and extending beyond, those being established by the state. Ferguson (97) presents the rural poor in southern Africa as embedded within a broader "distributive political economy" as wealth is divided into "smaller and smaller slivers as they work their way across social relations of kinship, clientage, allegiance, and solidarity." For Ferguson, distributive livelihoods assume central importance, and he describes distributive labor as that which "seeks to secure a transfer of resources from those who have them to those who don't" (101).[5]

The distribution of resources occurs through spending on goods and services in the economy, but this alone underestimates the extent of noneconomic and quasi-economic redistribution. An obvious way this occurs is through intra-household transfers to "dependents," but it also extends to broader kin relations, patronage networks, and state-funded social protection payments. Functionally this means that households (as a unit of essentially nonmarket resource sharing) can thus also be conceptualized well beyond the nuclear family. I argue that analyzing distributional flows into rural landscapes is critical for understanding contemporary agrarian transitions. Moreover, the importance of socially embedded redistribution means that, in some cases, rural smallholdings are maintained because they help ensure legitimate access to these flows.

Scoones (1998) provided an influential framework for the analysis of "sustainable rural livelihoods," which has been reflected in various schematic visualizations (figure 1.1) applied by organizations like the UK's Department for International Development and Oxfam (as presented by Carney 1999). Such frameworks generally included five key elements: (1) a contextual analysis of place-specific conditions and trends (sometimes presented as a "vulnerability context"); (2) livelihood assets, capitals, or resources (the "five capitals"); (3) transforming structures and processes, including influence and access; (4) livelihood strategies; and (5) livelihood outcomes. Despite the practical utility of these analytical frameworks, various concerns have been raised, with Natarajan et al. (2022) providing a useful recent summary of these critiques. Foremost among these concerns were that there was (1) an absence of politics and structural analysis; (2) a reification of the local over other spatial scales of analysis; (3) an inadequate focus on history and change; and (4) a failure to go far enough to decolonize Western-centric, development-related knowledge production. Natarajan et al.'s (2022) response to these concerns was an attempt to reformulate the sustainable livelihoods framework "fit for the 21st century" by "foregrounding a structural, spatially disaggregated, dynamic and ecologically coherent approach to framing rural livelihoods." Their proposed reformulation highlights the relationality of power and dispenses with the notion of livelihood capitals. While I am sympathetic to these critiques and to the aspirations of this reformulation, I tend to find greater practical utility in earlier articulations. Appendix B presents my own, less radical, reformulation of a livelihoods framework as applied to the arguments in this book.

Earlier people-centered livelihoods approaches implied a high degree of agency held by individuals and households, particularly when their "capitals" are enhanced. Possibilities for action, however, are also powerfully shaped by regimes of access and so are further filtered by political, historical, and institutional context (Scoones 2009 acknowledges this). In the words of De Haan and Zoomers (2005, 43, paraphrasing Marx), "people do make their own livelihoods, but not necessarily under conditions of their own choosing." Indeed, Scoones (2009, 187) argued that "one of the persistent failings of livelihoods approaches has been the failure to address wider, global processes and their impingement on livelihood concerns at the local level." This, too, was a key concern for Natarajan

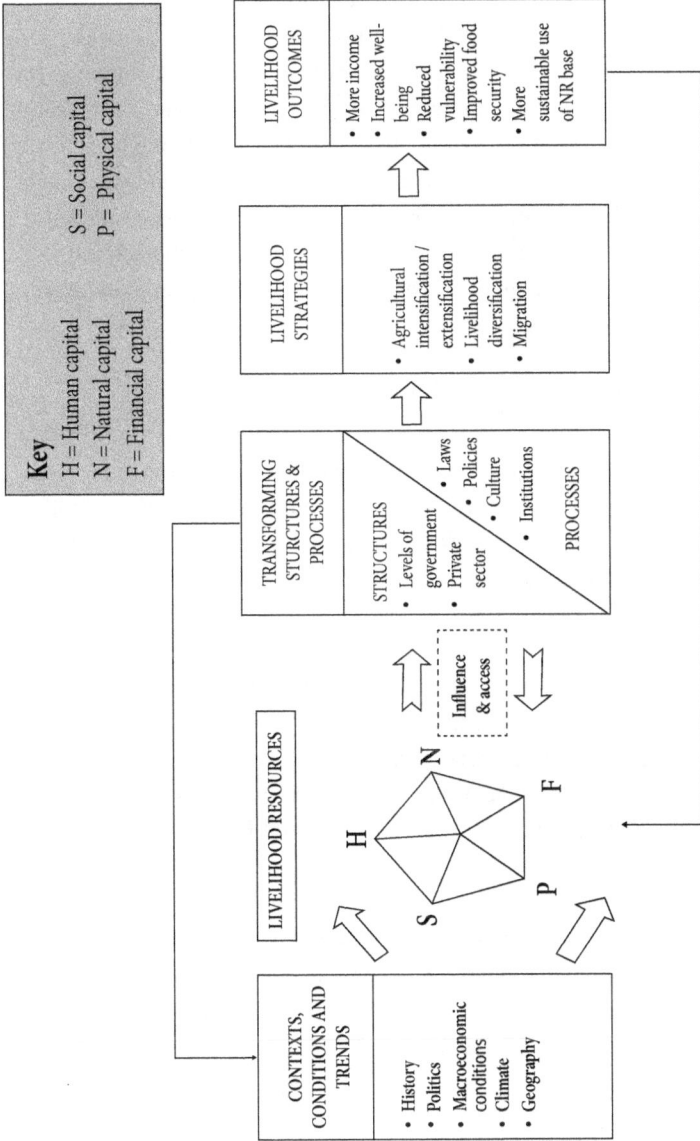

FIGURE 1.1. The influential Sustainable Livelihoods Framework used by the UK Department for International Development.

Source: Adapted from Scoones (1998) and Carney (1999).

et al. (2022). One of the key conceptual contributions I make to livelihoods theory in this book is to develop more fully the institutional environment as a set of multiscalar structures shaping livelihood opportunities, without, it should be emphasized, falling into the trap of structural determinism. Despite acknowledging that economic power increasingly rests with downstream actors involved in the processing and marketing of agricultural products, neither Scoones (2015) nor Natarajan et al. (2022) explicitly recognizes the merits of value chain analysis within a broader project to "bring multiscalar politics" back into livelihoods thinking. In contrast, my approach is to borrow insights from global value chain theory, which provide alternative axes through which broader economic structures can be examined as part of the institutional environment affecting livelihoods. I will return to this application of GVC theory after briefly addressing debates around livelihood safety nets.

Livelihood Safety Nets

Any contemporary rendering of the agrarian question needs to consider rural livelihoods that incorporate combinations of on-farm and off-farm activities. Such pluriactivity can assist with risk diversification and livelihood resilience, allowing households to reallocate their productive priorities depending on changing opportunities in the broader economy. Off-farm work, however, can also be interpreted as a sign of distress and uncertainty in a precarious world, precipitated by a crisis in farming. Those involved in precarious pluriactivity in rural Java use the term *serabutan* to describe the way they pick up different types of short-term farm and nonfarm work whenever they can get it (*serabutan* is also used to describe a somewhat chaotic or unorganized traffic situation). Meanwhile, Dorward (2009) presents a framework for rural livelihood strategies in terms of "hanging in," where current levels of welfare are maintained in the face of external stresses and shocks; "stepping up," where improvements in productivity or scale of production or productivity are viable; and "stepping out," where individuals switch to new activities (off-farm employment). In these terms, those Indonesian households engaged in *serabutan* work may be both hanging in and stepping out simultaneously. McCarthy (2020) similarly refers to the Indonesian situation where rural households "muddle through" by keeping one foot on the land while moving tentatively toward off-farm income generation as one of "advancing sideways." For McCarthy, Indonesia is experiencing neither a sustained agrarian transformation nor an agrarian crisis.

The prevalence of pluriactive part-time farmers, then, may reflect a risk-minimizing livelihood strategy, or it could be a temporary stage prior to agriculture being thoroughly reshaped by the productive forces of capitalism. It could also reflect a strategy (in the interests of capital) to suppress industrial wages. In China, it has been observed that capital accumulation proceeded without "expropriating farmland from peasant-workers and thereby putting the costs of labor reproduction on agrarian households, [which] allows urban employers to pay wages to the migrant workforce below family subsistence levels" (Jakobsen 2018, 177). This analysis is associated with the semi-proletarian thesis, which has been revisited (and given a more positive spin) in the cases of South Africa and China by Zhan and Scully (2018). These authors highlight the "double role" of semi-proletarianization in that farming *also* provides important livelihood security (a safety net) for multi-sited households when opportunities elsewhere falter.

Notions of an agricultural safety net have a long history. Polanyi ([1944] 2001, 96) described considerable urban-rural remigration during the Industrial Revolution, as "different groups were drawn for varying periods into the sphere of commercial and manufacturing employment, and then left to drift back to their original rural habitat." This seemed to function if the foundations of rural society weren't destroyed. Polanyi (96) continues:

> As long as domestic industry was supplemented by the facilities and amenities of a garden plot, a scrap of land, or grazing rights, the depen- dence of the labourer on money earnings was not absolute; the potato plot or "stubbing geese," a cow or even an ass in the common made all the difference; and family earnings acted as a kind of unemploy- ment insurance. [However,] the rationalization of agriculture inevitably uprooted the labourer and undermined his social security.

Similar observations were presented by the World Bank (2007) as the "safety net role of agriculture" or "farm-financed social welfare," whereby urban-rural remi- gration offers a safety valve when the urban economy, or an individual within it, experiences a crisis. With reference to Indonesia, Fane and Warr (2009) likewise refer to the "shock absorber" role of agriculture during a crisis. Rigg (2019, 139) explains the persistence of Thai smallholdings by suggesting that "while land and land-based farming activities may not be the most remunerative, they provide a degree of security that nonfarm work cannot." Drawing on work in north India, Pritchard, Vicol, and Jones (2017, 41) similarly describe how land featured in livelihood aspirations as "a bulwark of food (and by extension, livelihood) secu- rity through own-production capabilities."

The capacity of rural smallholdings to absorb labor is of critical impor- tance to the ability of farming to act as a safety net, and this will be a key theme I examine empirically in the case of coffee. The reported ability of wet-rice agri- culture (*sawah*) to absorb labor without impacting the physical stability of the system was central to Geertz's controversial arguments of "shared poverty" in

Java (Geertz 1963). Research in Jambi Province of Sumatra (Cramb et al. 2009, 337) demonstrated that this safety net function was not unique to *sawah* systems, suggesting that "swidden cultivation provides a safety net that smallholders can fall back on during crisis situations." McCarthy (2006) also reported a safety net role for farming in Sama Dua District of South Aceh during the 1998 financial crisis. Dove (1993) explained the prevalence of low-intensity rubber systems in Kalimantan based on the ability of rubber trees to respond to intermittent tapping (labor allocations) and so could be easily adjusted to the specific income needs of the household.

While this safety net function has been widely documented, it has also been critiqued as a "village myth" by Li (2009). Her critique (82) is summarized as follows: "A critical flaw in these observations . . . is that a large number of those who exit rural areas have no farms, and some of them have been landless for multiple generations. If 'farm-financed social welfare' works at all, it works for prosperous landowners. For the poor it is a mirage, with potentially lethal effects." The concern here appears to be not so much that villages and farms do not absorb workers during times of crisis (as they clearly do), but that many of the poor, because of past dispossession or pervasively uneven class structures, lack access to land on which they might farm. The ability of farming to function as a safety net is indeed precluded when there is no land available to farm. Li's concern is with those "expelled" from rural communities rather than those individuals who leave agriculture voluntarily and maintain support networks and resources in the village. In other contexts, including some of Indonesia's coffee-growing districts I describe in this book, migration away from rural areas frequently occurs as part of a deliberate strategy where links to a rural homeland are not severed, and are reflective of Indonesia's long-recognized pattern of circular migration (Hugo 1977). The perpetuation of faith in the safety net function of agriculture, however, is presumably said to be "lethal" if it is used discursively to justify the absence of other modes of social protection. Indeed, Hüsken and Koning (2006) describe the antipathy the Suharto government (1966–1998) held toward state-sponsored social security based on its belief that family and community bonds would take care of the poor, the elderly, and the needy.

Agricultural safety nets depend on access to both natural and social livelihood resources. The presence of informal social support structures, such as the celebrated Indonesian mutual aid system of *gotong royong*, however, need not imply any egalitarian ethos (Koentjaraningrat 1967). More broadly, the core contention of Scott's (1976) *Moral Economy of the Peasant* was that informal social institutions, such as the patron-client relations between smallholders and first-stage collectors, or that between sharecroppers and landlords, allowed subsistence claims to be made upon patrons during adverse circumstances (even if the normal feature of the relationship was essentially exploitative). Considerable investments in social relationships, however, are often required to ensure access to such livelihood security mechanisms, and the need for balanced reciprocity often imbues such relationships with a transactional character (Hüsken and Koning 2006). Hüsken and Koning further argued that while traditional social support structures and institutions were under pressure and couldn't be taken for granted (following the Asian financial crisis of 1998), they were surprisingly resilient. This suggests a need for institutional flexibility, and Popkin (1979, 245) highlighted how peasant movements (referring to Vietnam, but relevant to Indonesia) sought "not to restore traditional practices and institutions, but to *remake* them; they seek not to destroy the market economy, but to *tame* capitalism." Indeed, there has been a popular belief that the spirit of *gotong royong* was pivotal during the COVID-19 crisis to make up for government deficiencies in providing social support to the poor (Yulisman 2020). A livelihood perspective thus highlights the important role that both tangible resources (land) and intangible social resources can potentially perform in sustaining lives by providing safety nets.

State-based social protection is also changing rapidly and becoming incrementally more "densely woven" than before (McCarthy, McWilliam, and Nooteboom 2023a). An observer of rural Southeast Asia twenty years ago could have decried the absence of state-financed social security programs, but this too is changing (as I will discuss in chapter 3). In many Indonesian communities, most households are now receiving some form of direct social protection or cash payment from the state, as are many across Latin America and sub-Saharan Africa (Ferguson 2015). The contemporary agrarian question, then, needs to consider how evolving distributive practices are central to understanding the way capitalism is reshaping rural livelihoods and farm practices. More work is needed to understand how these varied modes of social support (farm-financed social welfare, informal and traditional support structures, and state-based social protection) intersect and combine to affect processes of agrarian change and the role of land as a livelihood fortress.

Institutions and Global Value Chains

Smallholder livelihoods are exposed to capitalist pressures not just (and arguably not even) by attempts to impose capitalist farming directly, but these pressures have long worked their influence at a distance. Bernstein (2006, 454) explains:

> Agriculture in capitalism today is not synonymous with, nor reducible to, farming, nor is it constituted simply as a set of relations between agrarian classes (landed property, agrarian capital, labor), as in the "classic"

agrarian question. Rather, agriculture is increasingly, if unevenly, integrated, organized, and regulated by the relations between agrarian classes and types of farms, on one hand, and (often highly concentrated) capital upstream and downstream of farming, on the other hand. Moreover, such integration and regulation operate through global as well as national (and more local) social divisions of labour, circuits of capital, commodity chains, sources and types of technical change (including in transport and industrial processing as well as farming), and markets.

McMichael (2013), through a "food regimes" theoretical lens, has made a similarly convincing case for the analytical centrality of broader global economic structures, and especially the pervasive role of agribusiness transnational corporations (TNCs), in shaping agrarian social relations and livelihoods. A key insight of global value chain theory then has been to explain the ability of powerful TNCs (referred to in this literature as "lead firms") to govern a chain through acts of coordination, usually without assuming direct ownership of production nodes within their supply chain.[6] The conceptualization of corporate power within the GVC literature, and the ability of lead firms to enlist states, second-tier firms, and even civil society organizations to reshape the institutional environment of the chain, provide a meso-level lens through which international political economy can be analyzed. This ability is referred to as value chain *governance*—how lead firms set, measure, and enforce the parameters under which others in the chain operate. GVC theory thus helps identify contemporary mechanisms of value appropriation and exploitation—and sometimes even opportunities for improvement through *upgrading* (Humphrey and Schmitz 2002). This is important, since the specific strategies of lead firms have been identified as key determinants of development processes operating at local, regional, and national scales (Coe and Yeung 2015).

The concept of upgrading has emerged as a critical mechanism through which to understand and promote development in the Global South. Gereffi (2005, 171) defined industrial upgrading as "the process by which economic actors—nations, firms and workers—move from low-value to relatively high-value activities in global production networks." There is often an assumed causal relationship between firm-level upgrading and the supportive role of lead firms willing to facilitate and encourage the upstream transfer of skills and knowledge, and this has made the upgrading concept particularly attractive to development practitioners (Neilson 2014). Such integration with GVCs, however, does not always deliver benefits to individuals within a region. The idea of "social upgrading" was thus introduced (Barrientos, Gereffi, and Rossi 2011, 324) as "the process of improvement in the rights and entitlements of workers as social actors, which enhances the quality of their employment." In Neilson (2019), I extended this notion further and into the realm of smallholders as "livelihood upgrading." I argued that while there are parallels between the subservient (exploited) position of labor within a firm and the position of ostensibly independent commodity-producing smallholdings, there are also several important points of difference, which are brought into sharper focus from a livelihood perspective. Given what we know about diversified rural livelihoods and the nature of smallholder embed-dedness within complex social environments, there is no reason to expect that smallholder integration into a GVC will necessarily deliver benefits in terms of livelihood upgrading for households (as also argued by Pegler 2015).

Explanations for the apparent persistence of smallholder farms and the still partial penetration of capitalist relations in farming across the Global South can also be partly explained in value chain terms. Put simply, it is in the commercial interests of large agrifood capital to concentrate on the more profitable down-stream nodes of the chain while outsourcing the riskier activity of primary pro-duction to smallholders. Indeed, there are important obstacles to investment by capitalist firms into agriculture, including the vagaries of agroecological produc-tion (pests, disease, climate, and the inherent limits in speeding up biological production times) and the social dynamics of smallholder production (including access to ancestral or customary lands at negligible cost and the ability to draw on unpaid household labor reserves). From the perspective of downstream capital, there are obvious advantages to refraining from direct investment in (inherently risky) farming and instead allowing smallholders to exploit themselves by using unpaid household labor (Watts 1994). Even though smallholders may retain ownership over, or at least access to, their fundamental means of production (land), they are deeply affected by their incorporation within commodity mar-kets through value chains. Lead firms govern suppliers in the chain through vari-ous acts of coordination, including through value chain sustainability programs in the coffee sector, in ways that improve their competitive market position and brand recognition, and so maximize surplus extraction.

It is true that the ability of lead firms to extract a surplus is often constrained by what Gereffi (1995, 113) referred to as the "institutional framework," or "how local, national, and international conditions and policies shape the globalization process at each stage of the chain." However, in my previous research with Bill Pritchard in the plantation districts of South India (Neilson and Pritchard 2009), with Niels Fold in the global cocoa sector (Fold and Neilson 2016), and with Albert Hasudungan in the Indonesian palm oil sector (Hasudungan and Neilson 2020), I have argued that it is necessary for GVC analysis to move beyond the institutional framework as something that GVCs are "framed within," toward one that is both external and internal to the chain. From this emerged the concept of

the institutional environment, which we argued to be "a pre-determining characteristic of the governance structures which subsequently emerge within the chain
and which, in turn, then act upon those arrangements in continual feedback"
(Neilson and Pritchard 2009, 56). The broader institutional environment is thus
co-constructed by lead firm strategies and their interactions with extra-firm actors
such as states, NGOs, and labor unions, as well as with place-specific cultural norms.

The concept of the institutional environment is core to my overall analytical framework and draws on theoretical developments in evolutionary economic
geography (Bathelt and Glückler 2014). It can also be traced back to North's
(1991, 97) presentation of institutions as "the humanly devised constraints
that structure political, economic, and social interaction. They consist of both
informal constraints (sanctions, taboos, customs, traditions, and codes of con-
duct), and formal rules (constitutions, laws, property rights). Throughout history, institutions have been devised by human beings to create order and reduce
uncertainty in exchange." North's approach was pivotal in establishing institutions (the "plays") as separate from organizations (the "players") and by clearly
identifying institutions as inclusive of both formal and informal constraints on
behavior. Bathelt and Glückler (2014) subsequently moved beyond an understanding of institutions as simply rules (whether informal or formal) toward one
based on how these rules unfold in practice in highly contingent ways. Such an
understanding is particularly helpful when considering, for example, land access
practices in Indonesia that are shaped by, but often deviate from, both formal
and customary rules. The institutional environment is both place-based (where
institutions coalesce in distinct constellations in particular geographies) and
multiscalar (intersected by rules and patterns of behavior forged by actors with
influence at local, regional, national and global scales). In this book, I will present
institutional environments comprising institutions that are fashioned by customary practices and traditions, ethics of land access, district and national-level laws,
routinized corruption and patronage, NGO development programs, corporate
sustainability and sourcing initiatives, payments for ecosystem service schemes,
and coffee-related quality conventions. I thus use the term "institutional environment" in a similar sense to McCarthy's (2006) "institutional arrangements" in his
study of the rainforest frontier in South Aceh. In McCarthy's case, these referred
to the interplay of customary *adat* practices, specific agroecological and social
contexts, and state interventions linked to resource control.

The work of North (1990) and others within the field of new institutional
economic history explains economic development as a path-dependent process.
Evolutionary economic geography takes this forward by explaining development
processes as the interplay over time of regional institutional settings and the
internal dynamics of industry structures, including the strategies of lead firms

within global value chains (Pike et al. 2009; Boschma and Martin 2010; Oro and Pritchard 2011). This requires taking a view of institutions as being embedded within deeper social practices expressed through traditions, belief systems, and cultural patterns of behavior that evolve slowly through time periods frequently stretching over centuries (Rafiqui 2008). I should emphasize, however, that there is nothing necessarily linear or inevitable about these developments. My presentation of institutional environments in rural Indonesia similarly takes such a long-term view, recognizing that routinized practices are slow to evolve and change, but I also reject notions that the present is necessarily held prisoner to the past. I will provide several examples where social movements, political upheavals, technological innovation, corporate strategies, consumer preferences, and other actor behaviors have been able to shift the structure of institutional environments.

Understanding Agrarian Change through Livelihoods and Value Chains

This chapter has situated the core theoretical concerns of the book within a history of scholarship that has attempted to understand the "agrarian question." I interpret this to be the question of how agrarian communities, where agricultural production was (at least until recently) a dominant livelihood activity and deeply embedded within traditional social structures, are transforming as they come under the broader influence of an industrializing society. Central to this endeavor is a concern to analyze the shifting role of farming within diverse livelihood strategies, and how this relates to landownership and land access. My entry point for considering land relations is informed by a concern for land as a livelihood resource. However, my approach also seeks to understand how rural communities are positioned within changing social structures, circulations of wealth, and patterns of extraction that extend well beyond the farm. There are two key aspects to this broader positioning. First, market-based capitalism is increasingly globalized, such that agricultural households are often integrated into systems of exchange where institutions are increasingly governed by lead firm strategies enacted along global value chains. Second, the twentieth century saw the rise of powerful nation-states across Asia, many of which were products of decolonization, and agrarian households and communities have had to renegotiate their positioning vis-à-vis these emergent states.

To pursue these aims, I develop a framework to understand contemporary agrarian transitions that, in the first instance, requires an appreciation of how institutional environments have evolved over time and have been more recently transformed under global capitalism. I have chosen to approach this aspect of my analysis from within a GVC theoretical framing to highlight the global-scale sets of influences through which capitalism is impinging on contemporary rural livelihoods. I hasten to add, however, that my application of GVC theory is strongly oriented toward an appreciation of how lead firm influences intersect with various nonfirm actors to co-construct institutional environments. I thus seek to avoid allegations of what I consider to be a tendency in this literature toward value chain determinism.

Such an appreciation of broader structural influences, I argue, is a necessary corrective to a bias within livelihoods research to focus on microscale processes and neglect the broader political economy of rural life. The key conceptual contribution I make to livelihoods theory is thus to examine how rural households are responding to evolving multiscalar institutional environments that are deeply permeated by power relations. I further make the argument that the current conjuncture of institutional environments has encouraged a particular livelihood strategy that I refer to as fortress farming, which I believe to be widespread. The cumulative impact of such strategies may be fundamentally reshaping processes of agrarian transition, and this holds important practical implications for contemporary rural development outcomes and the political and policy strategies likely to improve the lives of the rural poor.

AGRARIAN TRANSITIONS AND STRUCTURAL TRANSFORMATION OF THE INDONESIAN ECONOMY

> Typically, as an economy develops, agriculture's share of the economy declines. HPAEs (High Performing Asian Economies) with substantial agricultural sectors—Indonesia, Japan, Korea, Malaysia, Thailand, and Taiwan, China—have been making this transition more rapidly than other developing economies.
>
> —World Bank, *The East Asian Miracle* (1993)

The aim of this chapter is to commence the analytical task of positioning contemporary rural livelihoods and fortress farming within broader institutional environments and economic transformations. I pursue this by considering Indonesia's agrarian transition in its historical context by undertaking two lines of inquiry. First, I trace the incorporation of Indonesian agrarian communities within a colonial world economy through the cultivation of coffee, highlighting the evolution and persistence of institutional patterns over time. Second, I continue with this historical perspective into the postcolonial era by presenting the structural transformation of the industrializing Indonesian economy since independence and its effect on agrarian change. I open the chapter by examining the concept of "agrarian transition" and explore attempts to develop models for explaining the relationships between industrialization and rural change in East and Southeast Asia.

Agrarian Transitions

I am concerned with understanding changing rural livelihoods under conditions of contemporary agrarian transition, defined by De Koninck (2004, 286) as the "transformation of societies from primarily nonurban populations dependent upon agricultural production and organized through rural social structures, to predominantly urbanized, industrialized and market-based societies."[1] As I will

41

demonstrate, Indonesia is transforming in such a way, raising important questions about what this means for rural communities and their relationships with land. I follow this broader society-wide conceptualization of agrarian transition, which differs from yet builds upon the more specific rendering pioneered by Marxist agrarian scholars such as Terence Byres. Byres (1977, 1986, 1996) defined it as the specific set of processes through which a primarily agrarian society transitions from feudalism—or perhaps an alternative precapitalist mode of production—toward capitalist agriculture. Defining what constitutes capitalist agriculture is not easy, but an ideal form would be one where land, labor, and capital are all commodified to generate agricultural profit (and a surplus for accumulation). Byres (2016, 433) argued that "in societies that were overwhelmingly rural, it was, often if not always, in the countryside, in agriculture, that capitalism first, and in manifestly different ways, made progress." However, the implied inevitability of such a "transition" toward capitalist agriculture is problematic, and a key argument of this book is to show that approaches to farming and farmland in Indonesia remain highly varied.

A standard way of conceptualizing the transition to capitalist agriculture (according to Byres) was that societies either followed the Prussian pathway (capitalism from above, through the transformation of a landlord class of *Junkers* into capitalist farmers), the American pathway (capitalism from below, through the transformation of peasants into capitalists in the absence of feudalism), or an alternative English pathway (whereby tenant-farmers emerged as capitalists while paying ground rent to a landlord class). Byres (1986), however, acknowledged the great diversity of possible capitalist agrarian transitions, discussing later Asian alternatives presented by the historical cases of Japan, Taiwan, and South Korea. In these cases, Byres (1986) acknowledged that capitalist industrialization had occurred *without* the dominance of capitalist relations *within* agriculture. In postwar Japan, the semifeudal landowning class was weakened through land reform, and capitalist relations within agriculture were limited as farmers came instead under the influence of state monopoly capitalism (Itoh 1980). Similar observations are made for Taiwan and South Korea, where, also because of a generally progressive and American-facilitated land reform agenda, the postwar countryside became dominated by owner-cultivators on smallholdings alongside an absence or decay of a distinct landlord class (Studwell 2013). This, however, did not result in an American pathway to capitalist agriculture, as East Asia was instead characterized by the overbearing presence of a powerful, and often repressive, state (Amsden 1979).

The question of how capitalist accumulation in agriculture could and should contribute to broader industrialization of a national economy was a core concern of scholarship on agrarian transitions. Byres (1986) initially insisted that capitalist industrialization could not proceed without a contribution from the countryside, whereby an extraction of surplus from (capitalist) agriculture could be transferred and invested in urban-based industry. More recently, Studwell (2013) also assumes this to be necessary. This seems to imply the desirability of "urban bias" policies. Lipton (1977), however, severely critiqued policies that favor urban and industrial growth over rural development as being fundamentally flawed on both equity and efficiency grounds. While the World Bank's (1993) *East Asian Miracle* report suggested that resources were indeed transferred from agriculture to industry in the eight high-performing Asian economies (HPAEs),[2] it argued that this was relatively limited and that governments also invested in agricultural extension services and made heavy investments in rural development ("notably in Indonesia," it reports). According to this account, agricultural surplus was voluntarily transferred to industry through financial savings rather than overt urban policy bias.

The importance of prior agricultural accumulation has long been associated with mainstream ideas on the structural transformation of an economy—usually imagined and analyzed at a national scale. Productivity improvements in agriculture are often seen as a trigger to generate a surplus of food and other basic resources, freeing up labor and capital, which in turn can then be allocated toward "modern" sectors of the economy. Keijiro Otsuka has been a prominent advocate for linking such thinking with policies that encourage movement of workers out of agriculture in a way that enables consolidation of landholdings and ultimately a transition to more profitable larger farms (Otsuka, Liu, and Yamauchi 2016). There is, however, little evidence of land consolidation occurring on any meaningful scale within the smallholder sector of populous Southeast Asia (Rigg, Salamanca, and Thompson 2016).[3] Hart (2002, 200) similarly presented agrarian transitions in Taiwan and post-socialist China as "marked by rapid, decentralized industrial accumulation *without* dispossession from the land."[4] Zhan (2019) also argues that, in China, accumulation has largely occurred without dispossession in the countryside (or it has been associated with compensatory livelihood resources).

Bernstein (2009), moreover, emphasizes that capitalist accumulation within agriculture is far less important to national industrial development today given the opportunities to access capital from elsewhere in the global economy, including through global value chains. In Indonesia, large-scale resource extraction in the 1970s (especially timber, oil, and minerals, and to a lesser extent plantations) allowed an initial period of import-substitution industrialization, followed by a boom in manufacturing exports in the 1980s and 1990s (export-oriented industrialization). In both cases, foreign capital was critical, and industrialization occurred without a thorough prior transformation of the smallholder farm sector. Bernstein (2016) suggests that a transition to capitalist agriculture for later industrializers in the Global South appears to have been "thwarted," "stalled," or possibly "bypassed," driven by various combinations of capitalist and noncapitalist elements in the countryside.

Agrarian transitions are furthermore said to be "truncated" in the Global South when pathways for labor to move from agriculture to industry are absent (Li 2011; Du Toit and Neves 2014). Drawing primarily from ethnographic fieldwork in Indonesia, Li (2014, 4) has been critical of "transition narratives that posit an apparently natural evolution in which farming becomes more efficient and exclusive, and people whose labor is not needed on the land move into other sectors of the economy." This critique is further developed by Li (2017), where "the agrarian transition narrative" is linked to a "teleological narrative of unfolding and imminent development." Li (2017, 1249) explains, "These framings insisted that all the people of the world would—sooner or later—experience a natural progression from country to city, from farm to factory, and from low to high productivity work which would bring prosperity to all." Also based on fieldwork in Indonesia, McCarthy, McWilliam, and Nooteboom (2023b) critique "global narratives" of agrarian transition that assume the structural transformation of an economy will deliver improved living standards for all.[5]

Such narratives—"dangerously," in Li's view—reinforce a development myth that both perpetuates failed policies and stymies political mobilization by the rural poor. Instead, Li (2014) reports how remote highlanders in Sulawesi are inexorably drawn into capitalist relations and subsequently confront "land's end" as a result of being "expelled from agriculture." Rather than being absorbed in the off-farm economy, such individuals have become "surplus rural populations" (Li 2010), whose labor is surplus to the needs of capital and who are instead "left to die" without adequate institutional or social support. Li (2017, 1249) explains:

> This challenge is faced by about a billion people whose tiny incomes and low life expectancy confirm their limited relevance to capital at any scale; also by people who occupy land and use resources that bearers of capital want to acquire for large farms, logging, mines and so on, but whose labour is not needed for new uses that absorb few workers; and by people who occupy lands devastated by climate change or ecological ruin who can no longer survive in the old way, but for whom no new mode of livelihood has emerged in its place. Some of them have long been cast adrift, seeking work as migrants, or swelling the cities where they try to squeeze yet one more tray of goods for sale onto a crowded pavement, or survive in other creative but highly precarious and insufficient ways.

Her critique sees no Polanyian double-movement whereby socio-institutional responses might otherwise halt the excess of unregulated markets to prevent an agrarian crisis. A key concern in this book is to engage with such debates by exploring the social implications of society-wide agrarian transition in Indonesia's coffee-growing regions and to examine, more particularly, what this means for relationships with land. Are we likely to see the eventual dissolution of independent smallholding households? Will we see the development and dominance of capitalist agriculture in the countryside where all land and labor are commodified? If so, this could be occurring as part of a broader structural transition toward an advanced, industrialized, and urbanized economy, as envisaged by Otsuka, Liu, and Yamauchi (2016). Alternatively, such dissolution could be creating, as Davis (2007) suggests, a "planet of slums" where urbanization is increasingly disconnected from industrialization and economic growth, and a growing urban proletariat exists (barely) in vast shantytowns. Or are we in the midst of a specific set of intervening Polanyian countermovements, through evolving institutional environments, that is reshaping the contours of Indonesia's agrarian transition?

Development of Agricultural Export Economies: A Coffee-Flavored View

In considering the contemporary agrarian transition in Indonesia's coffee-growing communities, I will first contextualize the processes behind these developments within the much longer (colonial) integration of Indonesian agriculture within a system of global capitalism. I do this by presenting a brief historical sketch of export-oriented coffee production, which serves as a general case of agricultural commodity production, but it also identifies several specific, and resilient, institutional patterns.

Forced Cultivation of Coffee in the Indies

Coffee consumption became popular throughout the Ottoman Empire during the fifteenth and sixteenth centuries and across Western Europe in the seventeenth, with the first coffeehouse in London reportedly opening in 1652 (Ukers 1922). This was the first stage of the globalization of coffee. *Coffea arabica* is indigenous to the East African highlands and in the seventeenth century was produced exclusively in Ethiopia, Yemen, and on the Malabar Coast of India. The Dutch East Indies Company (Vereenigde Oostindische Compagnie, or VOC) became active in the Arabian-Persian-Indian coffee trade during the 1640s and recorded its first shipments of Yemeni coffee to Amsterdam in 1661 (Glamann 1981).

Meanwhile, the VOC had established Batavia on the northwest coast of Java as its eastern trading headquarters in 1619, wedged between the then dominant Javanese kingdoms of Banten to the west and Mataram to the east. By 1677, Mataram ceded its loose sovereignty over the intervening Preanger territories of West Java to the VOC, which soon after sought to extend its initial reliance on the spice trade toward alternative forms of agricultural extraction from these territories. The VOC began experimental coffee gardens near Batavia in 1699,[6] and soon it began requiring indigenous *bupati* (regents) in the Preanger hinterland to promote cultivation through an arrangement that became known as *Preangerstelsel* (the Preanger system). Commercial quantities were first delivered to the VOC in 1711, and by 1726 production was estimated at seventeen hundred tons,[7] allowing the VOC to control between half and three-quarters of the world coffee trade (Knaap 1986).

Polities in Banten and along Sumatra's east coast had already emerged in the sixteenth century, prior to VOC interventions, as important centers for the production and export of pepper (*Piper nigrum*)—a foreign crop introduced from India and exported to both Chinese and European markets (Reid 1988). Andaya (1993) describes how highly personalized trading systems in Sumatra, integrated within a framework of patronage relations, were coordinating upstream supply chains based around "gifts" provided to patrons in exchange for protection and rewards. In Preanger, the VOC appropriated the apical position within a similar system of nested patronage that extended back, through a system of mandatory crop deliveries, to peasant production (Breman 2015). Clients would deliver symbolic prestige services to their patrons (such as large retinues) as much as they would deliver material wealth (Kartodirjo 1972). Traditional patronage, however, was a labor-based, rather than a territorial, form of social organization, and disaffected peasants always had the option of fleeing to more remote forest regions if they found themselves unfavorably tied to a patron (Peluso 1992) or indeed a state (Scott 2009). This began to change under the VOC. Coffee plantings spread to nearby forests and eventually became semipermanent gardens, which the VOC claimed as property. The VOC, acting both as something like a global lead firm and a territorial power, delegated European "coffee sergeants" to increase control over production (Breman 2015). Output subsequently fluctuated throughout the eighteenth century in response to changing VOC policies of supply control through extirpation and forced expansion (figure 2.1).

Coffee was one of the only continuously profitable ventures for the VOC right up to the company's eventual bankruptcy in 1799, after which its territories were governed directly by arms of the Dutch government. The system of forced coffee deliveries, however, continued. In 1830, it evolved into the notorious *cultuurstelsel* (cultivation system) generally known by Indonesians today

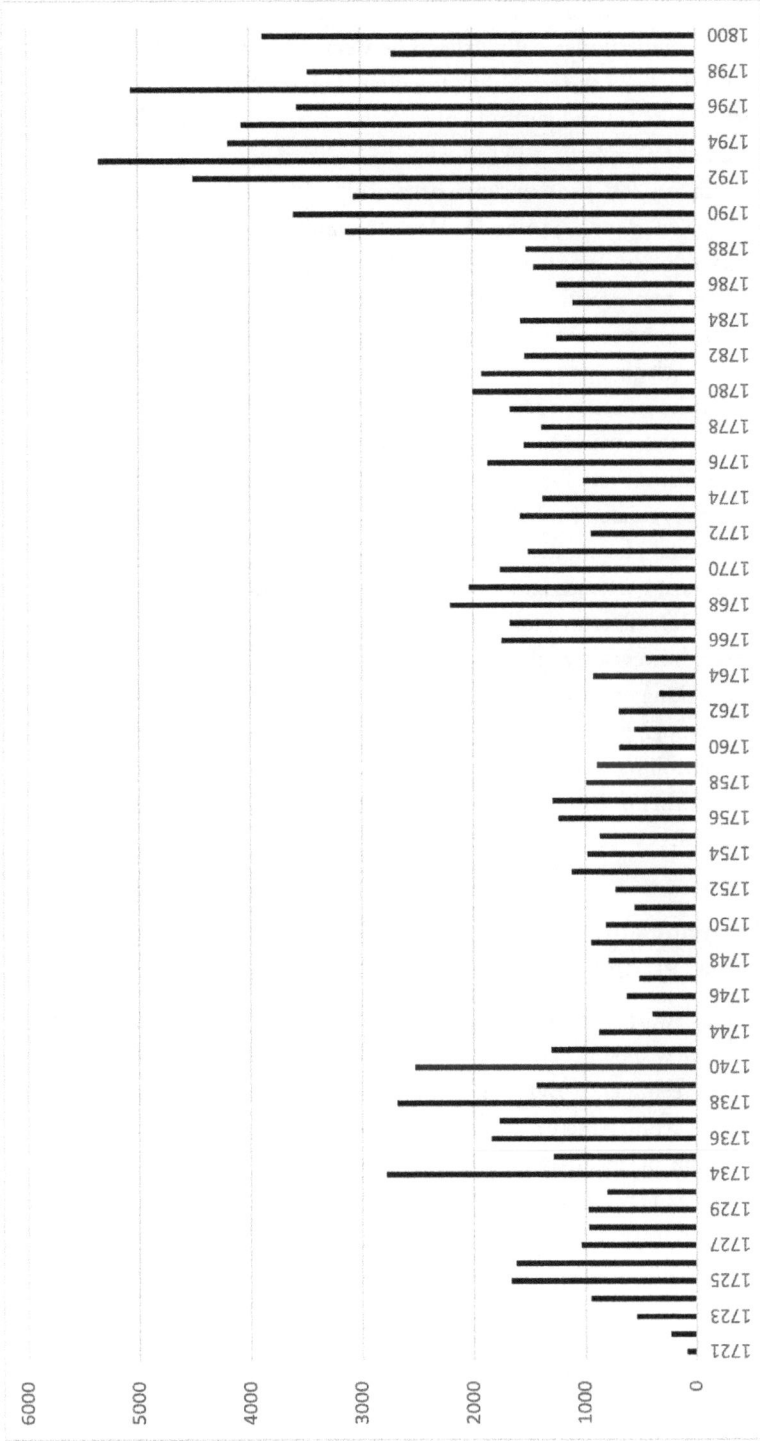

FIGURE 2.1. Tons of coffee supplied to the VOC by *bupati* under the control of Batavia.

Source: Breman (2015) based on De Haan (1910).

as *tanam paksa* (forced cultivation). Day (1904) estimated that 80 percent of government revenue under *cultuurstelsel* between 1840 and 1874 came from coffee. By the 1850s, a system of forced coffee deliveries also extended to the West Coast of Sumatra and parts of both northern and southern Sulawesi. The Dutch colonial state, exerting an influence more like a powerful firm (a role it inherited from the VOC) and in close partnership with a state-affiliated trading company, the Nederlandsche Handel-Maatschappij (NHM), thus used various modes of coercion and influence to reconfigure upstream institutional environments to extract profit. The systemic exploitation of the rural population by the *bupati* was conveniently ignored, as influentially described in an 1860 novel, *Max Havelaar, or the Coffee Auctions of the Dutch Trading Company*, written under the pen name Multatuli.

The colonial state, working closely with coffee traders, had grown dependent on extractive institutions for its own financial maintenance, and smallholder lives came to be regulated by their relations with state structures and state-linked actors. The impact of *cultuurstelsel*, however, was primarily felt on the island of Java. For the most part, alternative value chain structures emerged in the outer islands, to which I will return following a discussion on commercial plantations. The key point, however, was that the Netherlands East Indies (NEI) state acted like a profit-seeking company throughout this period, and it was able to do this successfully through its close cooperation with an indigenous elite that was more effective in controlling labor rather than being strictly feudalistic in terms of land control. Despite being enrolled in a global capitalist system through the coffee trade, smallholders were far from engaged in capitalist farming.

Capital Moving Upstream: The Rise of Commercial Plantations

A new agrarian law was issued in 1870, and this date is widely used to demarcate the beginning of a new "liberal period" in the East Indies, when private enterprise was to be afforded preeminence over smallholder compulsion. In fact, starting from the early eighteenth century, there had been various attempts by nonindigenous capital to directly assume the means of production on "private domain" lands (*particuliere landerijen*) along the north coast of Java. The 1870 Agrarian Law, however, with its seventy-five-year leases (*erfpacht*) on more favorable terms for capital, backed up by an increasingly powerful state, ushered in a new era of commercial investment. Estate-based coffee production on Java increased from nine thousand tons in 1869 to more than fifty thousand tons by 1939 (figure 2.2).

While coffee estates were concentrated in Java (table 2.1), the Sumatran highlands also attracted coffee-related plantation investment from around 1895,

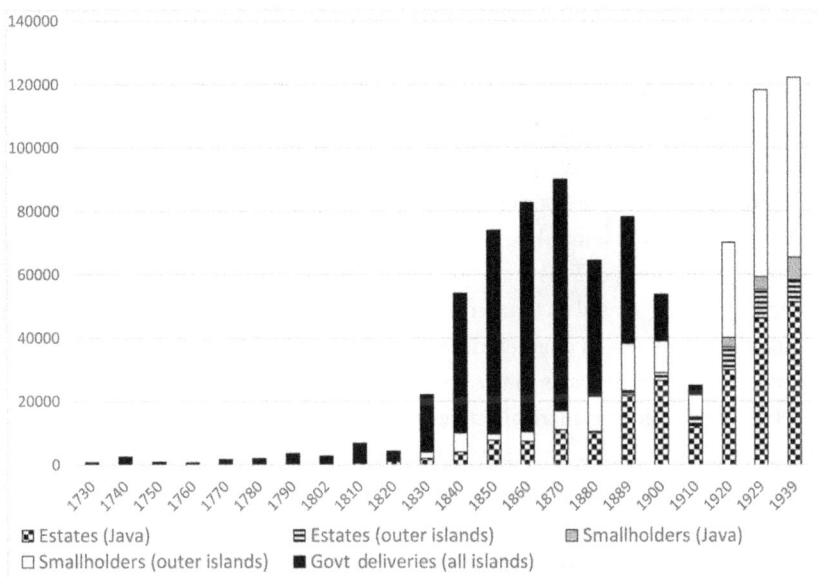

FIGURE 2.2. Contribution of different producer systems to total coffee production in the Dutch East Indies (tons).

Source: Creutzberg (1975); Breman (2015).

TABLE 2.1 Location of coffee estates in the Dutch East Indies (1932)

PROVINCE	PRODUCTION (METRIC TONS)	NUMBER OF ESTATES
Java	51,439	303
Lampung	2,751	14
Palembang	2,295	8
West Sumatra	1,491	21
Bengkulu	1,441	7
Manado	1,334	8
East Sumatra	1,061	5
Aceh	494	20
Sulawesi	270	11
Maluku	131	6
Tapanuli	6	3
Timor and Dependencies	1	9
Bali and Lombok	1	1

Source: Touwen 2001, table 49.

including in Rejang Lebong (Bengkulu), Pasemah (upland Palembang), and in Way Ratai, Way Galih, and Lake Ranau (Lampung) (Hoedt 1930; see also figure 7.1 in chapter 7). Through a series of mergers and acquisitions in the early twentieth century, individual estates became even larger, and estate output continued to increase until the outbreak of the Second World War (figure 2.2).

Colonial estates were dominated by merchant capital almost from the outset, including considerable holdings by the NHM trading company, with corporate head offices in Europe. This resulted in a production dichotomy between small-holders and these massive commercial leases, managed through corporate own-ership structures, which characterizes Indonesian agriculture today (rather than through feudal landlords as in the neighboring Philippines). While the founda-tions of large-scale commercial estates did not have lasting effects in the coffee sector itself, the influence of state-owned and state-supported corporate control over large swaths of Indonesian land came to dominate rubber and oil palm land-scapes, often dispossessing smallholders in the process. This can be traced back to these colonial institutions.

The corporate leases would, in theory, apply the latest scientific approaches to plantation agriculture to maximize productivity, and were supported by a collec-tive research effort, coordinated through the Besoekisch Proefstation in Jember, East Java (established in 1911, subsequently the Indonesian Coffee and Cocoa Research Institute, ICCRI). Touwen (2001) has argued, however, that there was very little dissemination of technologies between the large estate sector and smallholders during the colonial period, and that the broader impacts of coffee estates on outer island coffee smallholders were minimal. Indeed, the key centers of current Indonesian coffee production, and the ones I am most concerned with in this book, largely evolved beyond these corporate plantation enclaves.

Smallholdings in the Outer Islands

Coffee was quickly adopted by independent smallholders wherever institutional—and biophysical—environments were conducive, and where labor could be spared from subsistence-oriented agriculture. An early smallholder base emerged in the West Sumatran highlands, where Bastin (1965, cited by Kahn 1980) claims coffee was introduced by Bugis immigrants. Toward the close of the eighteenth century, American ships were arriving in Padang to buy coffee (thereby avoid-ing the VOC monopoly in Batavia), and this helped stimulate an export sector (Huitema 1935). The coffee trade flowed both west through the Padang port and east to the Malacca Strait (figure 2.3). Coffee cultivation was initially embraced by smallholder farms, where—unlike rice—its cultivation was not subject to lin-eage control by the Minangkabau nobility. This would be a familiar pattern else-where in Indonesia.

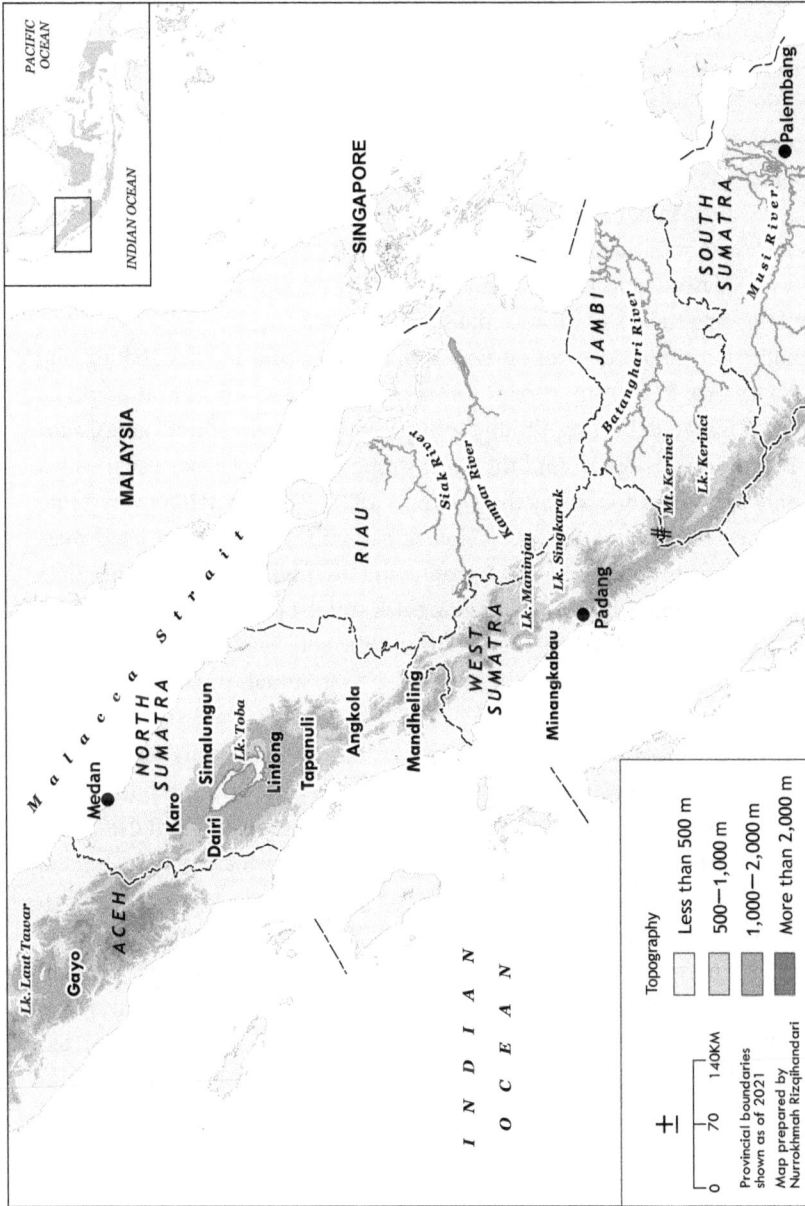

FIGURE 2.3. Coffee production regions in western Sumatra

This early period of independent smallholder production in western Sumatra was circumscribed as the Dutch consolidated political control of the region. Kahn (1980) described a process of "feudalization" in the Minangkabau economy under colonialism. The Dutch reinforced the power of local political elites, most evident in their support of customary (*adat*) chiefs against Muslim reformists during the Padri wars (1803–1837), and in return received tributes of pepper and coffee. This process, as in Java, involved the colonial regime relying on its superior military strength to enforce an extraction of surplus from peasant producers, and resulted in new social formations being imposed on peasant society. In the coffee regions of South Sumatra, Lampung, the Toba region of North Sumatra, South Sulawesi, and the eastern islands, however, independent production beyond the direct reach of the colonial state took hold.

Smallholder coffee cultivation was already occurring in Mandheling and Angkola (figure 2.3) from at least 1841, moving ahead of state attempts to implement forced deliveries. Production spread into further "free" areas, such as in Dairi (Sidikalang) around the northwestern shores of Lake Toba, which were only formally annexed by the Dutch in 1881. As production moved into new forested landscapes, access to land remained relatively open, land markets would have been minimal, and production methods extensive rather than intensive. At the start of the 1920s, Padang was still the principal Sumatran coffee port (Ukers 1922) before the orientation shifted to link in with the rapidly expanding infrastructure associated with the East Sumatra plantation sector (near Medan).

It was the region farther south, however, where Indonesia's largest center of coffee production would emerge, initially feeding into the port city of Palembang.[8] This city sits at the confluence of various river tributaries, with headwaters stretching up into an enormous hinterland, which includes upland communities such as Rejang, Pasemah, Semende, and Ogan, all on the eastern flanks of the Bukit Barisan range (see figure 7.1). Forced government deliveries were absent from this region, which became linked economically to Singapore rather than Batavia. According to Colombijn (2005), Dutch-built roads eventually enabled effective colonial territorial authority to be loosely asserted over the highland areas of Semende (in 1864) and Pasemah (1866). When a Brazilian policy of supply retention pushed global coffee prices up in the 1920s, Sumatran smallholders pounced on the opportunity, and the resulting boom established southern Sumatra as Indonesia's unrivaled center of coffee production. Touwen (2001, 296) emphasizes how smallholder export agriculture in Sumatra "grew rapidly with hardly any assistance from the government or the estate sector." The historical development of coffee in the Semende region of Sumatra is taken up in the chapter 7 case study.

The spread of coffee cultivation also occurred in the mountainous interiors of the eastern islands (including Sulawesi) via indigenous—sometimes Chinese—trade networks. Coffee was often the first major cash crop that linked these highland communities into a global system of trade. The VOC had maintained a permanent presence in the spice-trading city of Makassar, in Sulawesi, since its 1667 military conquest of the Gowa kingdom. The subsequent dispersal of both ethnic Bugis and Makassarese throughout the archipelago, and to the Malay peninsula, created an expansive *prahu*-based trading network that persisted well into the twentieth century (Sutherland 2015). These trading networks later helped link the eastern coffee-growing regions on Sulawesi, Bali, Sumbawa, and Flores with global trade systems, often via British Singapore rather than through state-linked Dutch traders. On the southwest peninsula of Sulawesi, coffee cultivation spread in advance of Dutch territorial control. The Toraja and Duri regions[9] of south-central Sulawesi were emblematic of a process of enrollment within coffee value chains without the direct influence of the colonial state (chapter 6).

Institutional Environments during the Colonial Period

The colonial-era experience of coffee demonstrates how smallholders became integrated within, and affected by, a global trading system that was always controlled by powerful downstream buyers. This was evident whether these buyers came to exert direct influence through state structures (as during *cultuurstelsel*) or through more independent trade linked to Singapore. Either way, downstream actors actively co-constructed local institutional environments that shaped processes of agrarian change, even if these were refracted through local social systems. Apart from the large, isolated, and foreign-owned plantation sector, it is difficult to identify these coffee farmers as engaged in capitalist agriculture. A midsize indigenous planter class was, and remains, noticeably absent.

A persistent theme in Indonesian economic historiography has been attempts to understand indigenous economic systems as primarily social rather than "capitalistic," with Boeke (1942) describing indigenous systems as "precapitalistic" in contrast to the exaggerated capitalist orientation of Dutch colonialism. This was always an oversimplification, as agrarian communities, most obviously in the pepper regions, had actively engaged in export agriculture well before European colonialism. Markets, however, were deeply embedded within social structures, and Day (1904) wrote of the strategic adjustments made by the VOC in response to persistent forms of indigenous social organization on Java.

Preangerstelsel and *cultuurstelsel* were operationalized through the *bupati*, who eventually came to be appointed by the Dutch, establishing a relationship where traditional aristocrats were operating as labor contractors to the VOC and NEI (Geertz 1963).

Boeke's (1953) "dual economy" thesis presented a traditional precapitalist society, with its communal orientation toward the social and religious community, being fundamentally incompatible with, and subordinated by, the capitalist society with which it was being brought into direct contact. The extent to which these supposedly communal characteristics stymied processes of agrarian class differentiation has, however, been actively, and contentiously, debated. Geertz (1963, 97) asserted that

> Javanese village society did not bifurcate, as did that of so many other "underdeveloped" nations, into a group of large landlords and a group of oppressed serfs. Rather it maintained a comparatively high degree of social and economic homogeneity by dividing the economic pie into a steadily increasing number of minute pieces, a process to which I have elsewhere referred to as "shared poverty." Rather than haves and have-nots, there were, in the delicately muted vernacular of peasant life, only *tjukupan* and *kekurangan*—"just enough" and "not-quite enough."

Geertz (1963), moreover, contrasted Java with the relative dynamism of smallholder commercial agriculture in the outer islands where land shortages were less acute and forest landscape dynamics prevailed. Other agrarian scholars took umbrage at Geertz's neglect of what they saw as widespread agrarian differentiation, especially on Java (Alexander and Alexander 1982; White 1983). There was, however, broad agreement that while a commercial orientation developed, technological progress in indigenous agriculture was constrained under colonial political economy. The effects of Dutch colonial policies on smallholder production contrasts with the Taiwanese experience under Japanese colonialism, where the colonial government actively (even forcefully) disseminated modern agricultural techniques, paving the way for subsequent agriculturally based accumulation (Amsden 1979). In Indonesia, capitalist energies were largely isolated in the commercial estate sector. In the coffee-growing regions of the outer islands, smallholders also had less interference from the colonial state. Finance, rather than technological advances, was the lifeblood that flowed through these value chains, and production remained smallholder-based, with minimal commodification of land and labor.

Relatively low population densities in the outer islands, combined with still accessible forestlands, meant that capitalist relations of production were the exception rather than the rule, despite a strong commercial orientation for production. Downstream influences thus interacted with very particular forest landscape dynamics to shape institutional environments of agrarian change. The establishment of coffee as an export crop commonly occurred through integration with tree-based landscapes associated with swidden farming (chapter 5). Control over land access and land use in these landscapes had been only rather loosely asserted by precolonial customary authorities and rarely constituted landlordism. Moreover, it has been argued by Scott (2009) that the swidden-based communities of Southeast Asia pursued a deliberate strategy of state evasion ("the art of not being governed") to maximize group freedoms. Indeed, state influence over forest landscapes in outer island Indonesia remained similarly tenuous well into the twentieth century, with individual landownership deeply circumscribed by social relations.

Indonesia's Transforming Economy Post-independence

When independence was declared in 1945, Indonesia had developed very little industrial capacity, with a weak indigenous capitalist class and a dependence on unprocessed exports of rubber, coffee, pepper, and petroleum. Agricultural production systems (at least in the coffee regions) were dominated by household-based smallholders, with a few isolated plantation enclaves owned by foreign merchant capital. The Indonesian economy was not miraculously transformed with independence. This politically momentous declaration event in 1945 was followed by a war of independence against the Dutch, ongoing struggles between rival political forces, regional rebellions, economic stagnation, and periods of mass violence. Kahn (1980, 11–13) described the immediate post-independence economy, and particularly that of the outer islands, as characterized by increasing "peasantization," in the sense that the bulk of productive output came to be generated by smallholders (farmers, fishers, petty traders, craftsmen) operating independently of the state. Although this peasantization involved enhanced self-provisioning of food and basic household items, it was also a commercial peasantry that continued to produce commodities, such as coffee, for the world market. Still, national coffee output was only one-eighth of its prewar peak in 1950 and, because of an initial neglect (and taxation) of traditional export industries during the 1950s, only reached prewar levels of production again in 1962 (McStocker 1987). The economic dysfunction and political uncertainty of the period did little to stimulate broad-ranging agrarian transition.

Prior to 1965, the Indonesian Communist Party (PKI) had considerable political influence and support, and this affected society-wide attitudes toward landownership and encouraged a general "land to the tiller" sentiment. With an eye on Java's rice-producing districts, an important series of land laws in the early 1960s were issued, including the Basic Agrarian Law (BAL), a Law on Sharecropping, and various regulations to implement land ceiling restrictions, land redistribution, and limits on share tenancy and absentee landlordism. The notion of a "social function of land," asserted in the BAL, provided legal impetus for this agenda. President Sukarno set the tone by proclaiming (in 1960) that "land is not for those who sit around and become fat and corpulent through exploiting the sweat of the people whom they order to till that soil" (cited by Bachriadi and Wiradi 2013, 40). Under Sukarno, the rural populist idea of "Marhaenism" was elevated to the official ideology of the Indonesian National Party (PNI), drawing on an apparent encounter Sukarno had with a smallholder farmer (Marhaen) near Bandung who fully owned his means of production yet was still oppressed by systemic forces.[10] This further helped create a powerful and persistent rhetoric in Indonesian politics of the smallholder owner-cultivator as a noble figure of resistance, whose interests were supposedly protected by the state.

Unlike in postwar Japan, South Korea, and Taiwan (Studwell 2013), however, land reform was only ever partially implemented, often through the "unilateral action" of PKI-affiliated peasant organizations, resulting in a volatile political situation in the countryside. Serious redistribution of land was then halted by the violence of 1965–66 when perhaps half a million communists, and alleged communist sympathizers, were killed by army-linked militias (Cribb 2001). Notwithstanding, the principles of owner-cultivation remained popularly embedded within Indonesian society and were rhetorically reinforced throughout the Suharto regime (Lucas and Warren 2013). Indeed, despite wide-ranging legal reform in other sectors, the 1960 BAL was never repealed (and remained in place in 2024). At least in the coffee regions of outer island Indonesia, much land has indeed remained in the hands of a multitude of smallholder owner-cultivators. Customary political control in the Indonesian islands was often focused on control over people as much as land or territory, and it is questionable whether this was comparable in a meaningful way with European landlordism, Russian serfdom, or the prewar landlords in Taiwan or Japan. At any rate, the real locus of unequal access to land in Indonesia came to be state control over forests and plantations, and the associated leases issued for logging concessions and mineral contracts (chapter 5).

The revolutionary impulses of the 1950s and 1960s did disrupt some exploitative feudal vestiges in the Indonesian countryside and ultimately (in the Suharto era) replaced them with a powerful, interventionist state. The upshot of these developments is that, despite land reform being jettisoned,

Indonesia does present some common features with Northeast Asia, with the presence of numerous owner-cultivator smallholdings operating household production units in the shadows of a powerful state. Indeed, I will describe (in chapter 3) how the traditional elites of premodern Indonesia have been largely incorporated within, and functionally replaced by, a feudalistic state, and this has moderated the influence of capitalist relations within agriculture in ways reminiscent of Taiwan (Amsden 1979). Overall, however, Indonesia did not follow a Northeast Asian agrarian transition trajectory whereby agricultural accumulation by emancipated smallholders provided the foundations for industrialization.

Industrialization and Agrarian Transition in Indonesia

The bloody rise to power of President Suharto in the mid-1960s was a trigger for a subsequent period of rapid economic growth. Like those in Northeast Asia, Suharto-era economic reforms did not follow a strict neoliberal economic playbook but rather involved an intervening "developmental state" engaged in selective industrial policy (Wade 2018). A series of investor-friendly reforms in the late 1960s, particularly in the forestry and mining sectors, initially stimulated growth. Robison (1986) described how the Indonesia state achieved high rates of accumulation primarily by promoting joint ventures between foreign (and ethnic Chinese) capitalists and Indonesian political elites, which nurtured the rise of an oligarchic indigenous industrial class of "bureaucratic capitalists." Oil export revenue was of central importance and allowed Indonesia to pursue a policy of import-substitution industrialization (ISI) throughout the 1970s. The global economic uncertainty of the early 1980s, culminating in the oil price crash of 1985, then triggered an economic crisis in Indonesia. Attention turned to manufactured exports (figure 2.4) as Indonesia came to be identified, alongside Malaysia and Thailand, by the World Bank (1993) as a so-called Newly Industrializing Economy (NIE), drawing workers out of farming through export-oriented industrialization (EOI). Figure 2.5 suggests the broader structural shifts in the Indonesian economy since 1960 during periods of both ISI and EOI, which contributed to the steadily declining share of agriculture and the more recent (relative) deindustrialization in favor of services.

During the 1970s and 1980s, Indonesia engaged with the Green Revolution in a way that was broadly pro-poor (Henley 2012; Timmer 2018) as it began reallocating resources toward rural development (Timmer 2004). Rises in farm productivity—concentrated in the rice sector and heavily subsidized by the state—were important in addressing poverty and improving welfare in rural Indonesia, but this did not mean that agriculture facilitated the accumulation

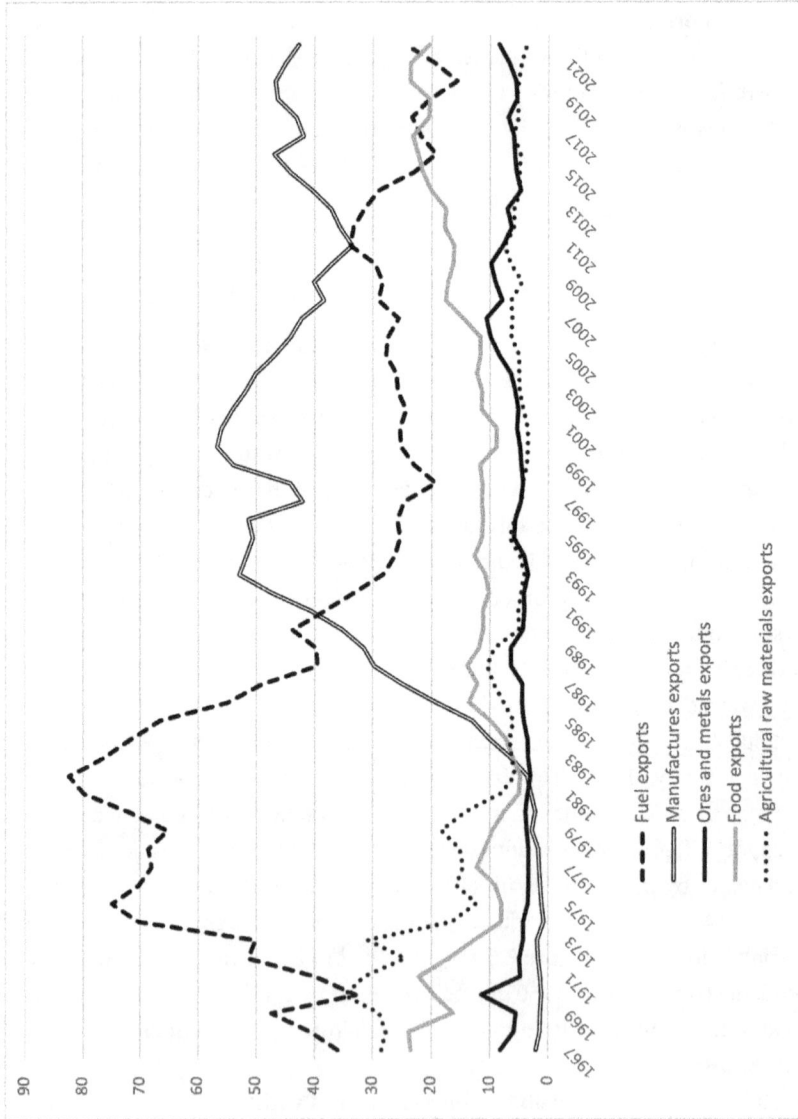

FIGURE 2.4. Shifts in sectoral contribution of Indonesian exports (% of merchandise exports, 1967–2022).

Source: World Bank 2024. (Note that "Food" includes beverages, tobacco, and vegetable oils.)

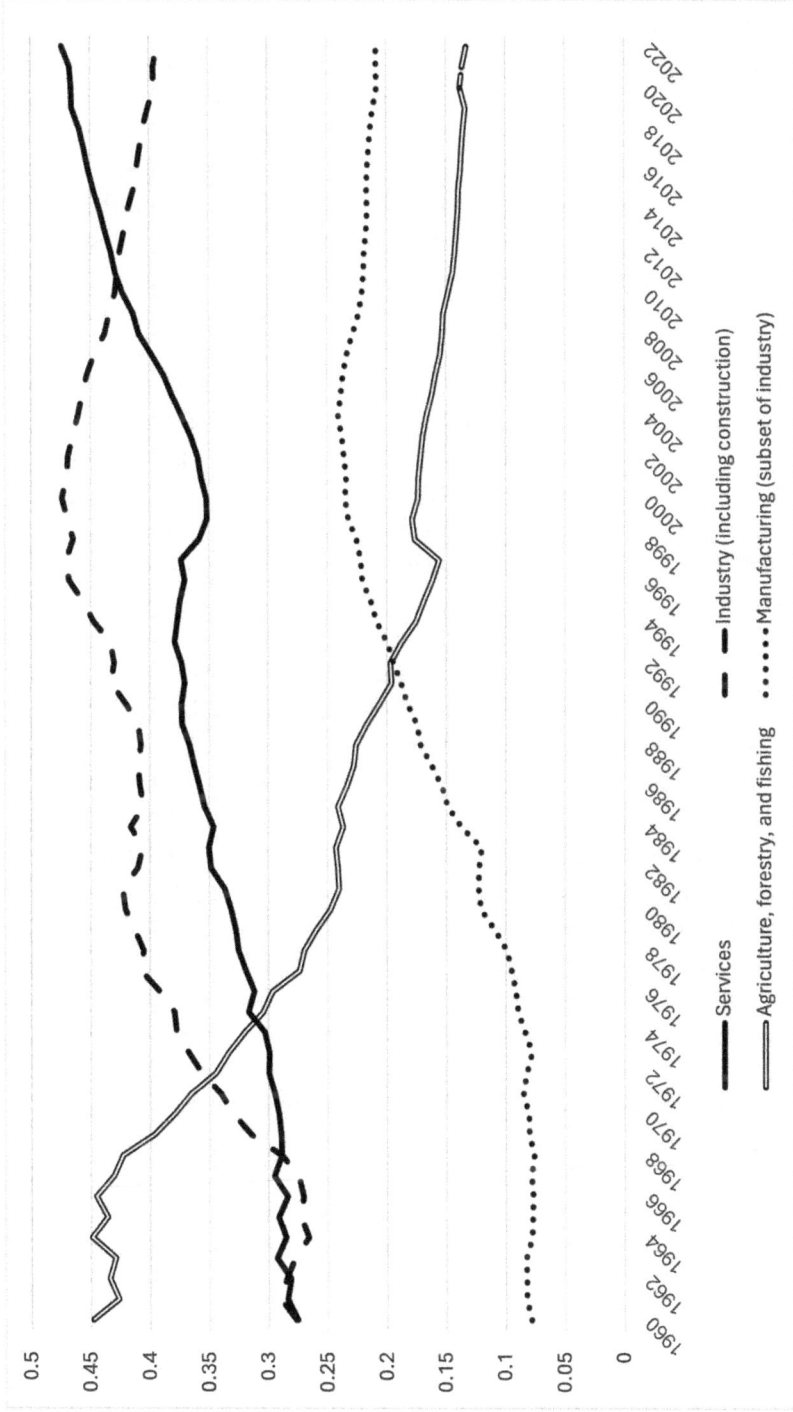

FIGURE 2.5. Structural transformation of the Indonesian economy (% of total value-added, 1960–2022).

Source: World Bank 2024.

of capital for national industrial development, as occurred in Northeast Asia. Capital for industry was instead accessed initially from oil (along with logging and mining) exports, and this encouraged the consolidation of extractive, rather than inclusive, institutions (drawing on ideas developed by Acemoglu and Robinson 2012). Indeed, many of the tycoons and business cronies of the Suharto regime who benefited from natural resource rents went on to themselves become industrialists (Robison 1986). Since the 1970s, agriculture, especially the food crop subsector (rice), has in fact benefited from a complex set of transfers from the nonagricultural sector. These have included investments in rural infrastructure (roads and irrigation); subsidies for fuel, credit, and fertilizers; price supports; and extension services (Booth 1988). Moreover, the supposedly dynamic export-oriented smallholder cash crop sector (dominated by rubber, cocoa, oil palm, and coffee) never experienced high levels of intensification and productivity improvements during this period (Booth 1988). In Taiwan and South Korea, extremely rapid industrialization and urban employment growth meant that the squeeze on agriculture had eased by the early 1970s, when rural development strategies began to be more significantly supported and subsidized by the state (Looney 2020). In the case of Indonesia, a reversal of urban bias of the Sukarno era (Penny 1971) occurred at an earlier stage of the industrialization process. As a result, Indonesia was already pursuing a policy of rural bias during Suharto's New Order (Timmer 1993).

The nature of Suharto-era rural development programs (further supported by international donors), however, meant that they disproportionately benefited larger farmers, and, on Java, this was associated with deteriorating conditions for rural labor (Hüsken and White 1989; Pincus 1996). These programs included "mass guidance" (*bimas*) that focused on achieving national self-sufficiency in rice, which Indonesia fleetingly achieved in the mid-1980s. This played an important part in maintaining more smallholders on their land (and involved in relatively low-risk rice farming) than might otherwise have been the case. Under Suharto, land reform (of a sort) was pursued only through the transmigration program, where landless villagers from Java and Bali were allocated two-hectare plots in the outer islands—frequently dismissing the customary claims of outer island communities already living there.

The extent of agriculturally driven class differentiation within smallholder communities during this period remains contentious. Li (2014) has described a process of land-based class differentiation in a cocoa-growing community in upland Sulawesi that essentially follows a classical Leninist model. She describes a process whereby "farmers able to accumulate land and capital prospered, and those who could not compete were squeezed out" (Li 2014, 2). White (2018, 1109), meanwhile, refers to rural differentiation and concentration of landholdings in

Java as "long-standing, established facts." Importantly, however, White (2018) suggests that land concentration in Java has not produced a class of large capitalist farmers, but rather a growing number of share tenants who rely on pluriactive livelihood strategies for survival.[11] Other observers of Indonesian agricultural development have been less convinced about agriculturally based class differentiation. According to Booth (1988, 253), "In spite of the undoubtedly 'top-down' nature of much of the rural development of the past two decades [1970s and 1980s], there is little support for a view that the New Order policies have witnessed a dramatic enrichment of those households controlling 'large amounts of land' (more than about 0.5 hectares of irrigated land), either relative to other rural households or relative to households in the nonagricultural sector." In the non-rice-growing Tengger highlands of East Java, Hefner (1990) also reported only a limited degree of land-based class differentiation despite expanding agricultural wage labor. Rather, Hefner reported the persistence of a "middle peasantry" (farm households that were neither accumulating land nor on the way to become landless workers). Outside of some intensive lowland rice regions, agriculturally driven class differentiation appears to have remained muted. In the outer islands (notwithstanding the growth of large plantations), the smallholder sector continued to be dominated by household-based owner-cultivators.

The Suharto-era manufacturing boom was to be prematurely interrupted by the 1998 Asian financial crisis—still the most important, and traumatic, event, both economically and politically, in Indonesia since the mid-1960s. Indonesia's economy contracted by 13 percent in 1998, and Suharto's thirty-two-year dictatorship was toppled as many Indonesians were plunged into poverty and hardship and left without a state-funded social protection system. In the immediate aftermath of the crisis, the agricultural sector provided a lifeline for some, and its share in the national economy briefly increased (figure 2.5). Tree-crop farmers in the outer islands producing export commodities, such as coffee, cocoa, palm oil, and rubber, even experienced "windfall" profits during the early stages of the crisis, as a result of devaluation of the rupiah (Ruf and Yoddang 2001). The decade following democratization in 1999 was then shaped by a China-fueled commodity boom, which triggered a decline in the export share of manufacturing (figure 2.4). This time it was coal, natural gas, palm oil, nickel, and copper that benefited from international commodity demand. Exchange rate depreciation following the 2008 global financial crisis, along with rising wages in China, then assisted the partial recovery of manufacturing exports since around 2010 (figure 2.4). Under President Susilo Bambang Yudhoyono (2004–2014), Indonesia commenced a policy of "downstreaming" in the commodity sector (resource-based industrialization) mainly by restricting exports of raw materials (Neilson et al. 2020). This policy was then further embraced as a core industrial policy under President Joko Widodo (2014–2024) and has successfully increased the value-added of select exports by attracting new investments in the processing of minerals like nickel and agricultural commodities like cocoa. To date, the policy has not, however, drawn workers away from farming to the same degree as earlier EOI policies.

Hill (2018) has presented Indonesia's past half century as an overall development success story, including significant advances in education, health, life expectancy, and poverty alleviation. Based on available data on social indicators (education, health, and poverty) for the Indonesian population since the 1980s, overall we observe a generally improving situation (table 2.2), even if many households feel themselves falling through the cracks (McCarthy, McWilliam, and Nooteboom 2023b) and remembering that national averages will inevitably mask inequalities. The twenty years up to the 2020 COVID-19 crisis were characterized by relative stability, economic growth of 5 percent per annum, and a gradually declining role for agriculture in the economy occurring at the same time as the lackluster expansion (but not absolute decline) of industrial activity and manufacturing.

Shifts in Employment

I now seek to understand how these broad processes of economic development are reflected in Indonesia's changing labor force. Admittedly, workforce data (Sakernas, the National Labor Force Survey) fails to capture more diverse income streams and the full complexity of multifaceted livelihoods in rural Indonesia, where levels of informality and pluriactivity are widespread, and social patronage

TABLE 2.2   Change in key social indicators in Indonesia (1980–2019)

SOCIAL INDICATORS	1980	1990	2000	2010	2019
% population >25 years completing upper secondary school	5.8	NA	NA	27.8	34.6[b]
% adult literacy	67.3	81.5	90.3[a]	92.5	95.6
Life expectancy (at birth) years	58	62	66	69	71
Infant mortality rate (per 1,000 live births)	85	61.8	41	28	20.2
% stunting (children <5)	NA	NA	42.4	39.2	30.5[b]
% poverty headcount at $3.20/day (2011 PPP)	NA	85.4	77.2	45	20.5
% poverty headcount at national poverty line	28.6	15.1	19.1	13.3	9.4

Sources: World Bank 2024; BPS 2022. Poverty rates for 1980 and 1990 taken from Booth (1993) based on official government estimates and Susenas data.
[a] Denotes 2014 data.
[b] Denotes 2018 data.
NA = not available.

and the politics of distribution critical. The Sakernas data presented here refers only to "primary source of income" for the individual. It, however, does provide an indicator of broad work opportunities, reflecting developments in the national economy.

The decline in agricultural employment share (meaning those reporting their primary income from farming) has been less emphatic than the decline in agriculture's share of national output, and the absolute number of individuals primarily employed in farming has been relatively constant (at around forty million) since 1990 (figure 2.6). Moreover, the number of individuals working in agriculture varies depending on work opportunities in the nonfarm economy. Sakernas data identifies the two most significant shifts between 1986 and 2020 as the increase in formal nonfarm employment (from a share of 21 percent to 40 percent) and the decline in self-employed farmers (from a share of 49 percent to 22 percent). The World Bank (2010, see also Aswicahyono, Hill, and Narjoko 2010), however, highlighted how Indonesia was affected by "jobless growth" during the period 2000–2010, associated with weak formal nonfarm job growth. Manning (2018) attributes this to the "resource boom" and strong commodity demand, such that manufacturing jobs stagnated (owing partly to so-called Dutch Disease, where an export boom in a particular commodity results in exchange rate appreciation and the declining competitiveness of other sectors). The problem of jobless growth was then less evident between 2010 and 2019, with service sector jobs drawing workers away from farming (Manning 2018). There are, of course, moments when such trends are reversed, and the agricultural sector again absorbed workers during the COVID-19 pandemic, with 2.7 million more Indonesians reporting farming as their primary income in 2020 than in 2019.

Self-employed household producers still dominate the agricultural workforce (the first three categories in table 2.3). There has, however, been a marked decline in unpaid household labor (often women) since 2000 and an increase in self-employed individuals (working alone). These indicators are consistent with off-farm livelihood diversification within the household. The moderate increase in agricultural laborers, as a share of the agricultural workforce, was due to the growth of large oil palm plantations, while the share of workers primarily employed as agricultural laborers on Java has declined. Nooteboom (2019) used longitudinal village data from Central Java to show how the share of rural laborers had declined in one village from 80 percent of rural working-age people in 1973 to 15 percent in 2014, and from 60 percent in 1992 to 25 percent in 2014 in another.

Manning and Purnagunawan (2016), meanwhile, attempted to determine whether Indonesia had reached a "Lewis turning point" whereby agricultural wages and labor productivity come to equal those in the nonagricultural sector.

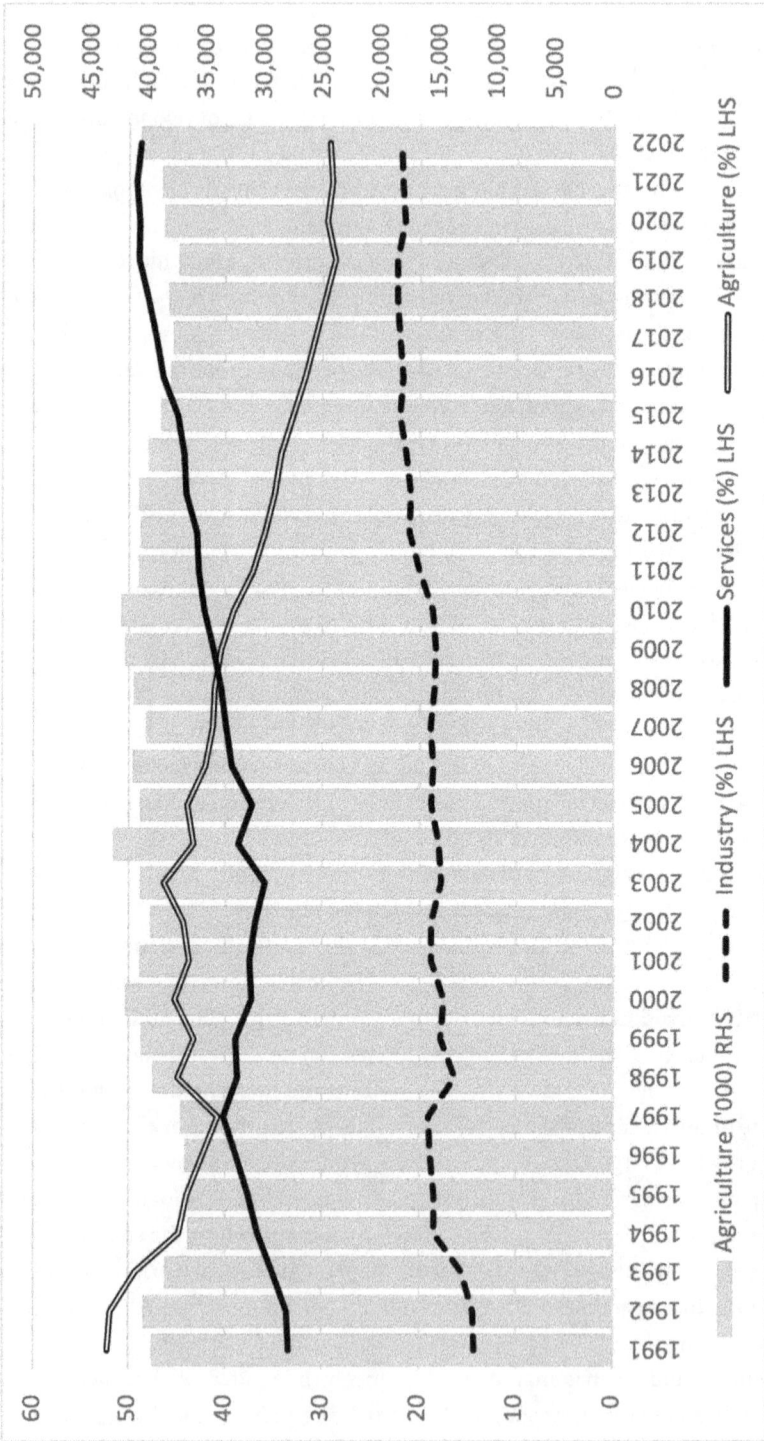

FIGURE 2.6. Sectoral share of employment, and absolute employment in agriculture, 1991–2022.

Source: World Bank 2024 (modeled ILO estimates); BPS 2024.

TABLE 2.3 Status of agricultural workforce (% of agricultural workforce)

WORK STATUS	2001	2010	2020
Self-employed with casual/household worker	37	35	33
Unpaid household worker	34	31	27
Self-employed	11	11	16
Self-employed with permanent worker	2	2	3
Casual laborer	9	15	13
Permanent laborer	7	6	9
Total size of agricultural workforce	39,743,908	42,825,807	38,956,801

Source: BPS 2024.

Lewis (1954) had divided low-income economies into a modern capitalist sector, dominated by industry, and a traditional subsistence sector, dominated by household farming, where the latter generated a constant supply of workers to the former until the turning point was reached. In their study, Manning and Purnagunawan (2016, 478) reported only marginally narrowing wage differentials between agricultural and urban construction workers, such that overall they "did not find evidence of a sustained transition similar to that experienced much earlier in the Northeast Asian economies." A Lewis turning point does not appear imminent, and in this sense Indonesia continues to be operating under a dual economy.

There are, of course, limitations in reading too much into such large-scale workforce datasets. Sakernas surveys recognize the very high number of self-employed Indonesians, especially in farming, and yet there is still a tendency to talk of these individuals as possessing agricultural *jobs*. Such a categorization is misleading, given what we know about how rural households draw on various capitals to construct a livelihood. This complexity is partially reflected in the decennial agricultural census (the most recent was 2023, although this was only partially available at the time of publication), which was enumerated by household units rather than individuals. There remained 28.4 million agricultural households across the country in 2023, thus constituting a 40 percent share of all households (BPS 2024), and this share has been relatively stable since the 2003 census. Given the falling primary employment rate in agriculture, this suggests an increasing incidence of part-time farming. Indeed, a full 36 percent of agricultural households (in 2018) identified nonfarm activities as their household's primary source of income (BPS 2019a).

These national trends inevitably mask far greater complexity at regional and local scales with Indonesia's long history of geographically uneven development. At the 2020 Population Census (BPS 2021a), 151 million of Indonesia's 270 million people were living on Java, such that trends in the outer islands can be hidden in national datasets. Agricultural households (as a share of all households) in West Java (which borders the capital, Jakarta) stands out as being well below the national average, while Nusa Tenggara Timur (with some of the highest poverty rates in the country) has a particularly high share of such households (table 2.4). The case studies of Toraja and Semende, discussed later in this book, are in the provinces of South Sulawesi and South Sumatra respectively, both of which have experienced a moderate decline in agricultural households.

The overall picture from this data is thus clear. While nonagricultural employment has grown in importance across Indonesia in recent decades, and nonfarm income is increasingly prominent within many agricultural households, low-intensity farming remains part of mixed livelihood strategies at the household scale, and smallholdings are not yet being abandoned.

Premature Deindustrialization?

These employment shifts were, for many years, driven by ongoing industrialization and growth in manufacturing. An important inflexion point, however, was reached in the Indonesian economy in 2013, when the contribution of services to the economy surpassed that of industry (figure 2.5). The category of "industry" here includes not only manufacturing but also mining, construction, and public utilities, while "services" includes trade, hospitality, transport, communications, finance, real estate, and personal services (including government spending on education and health). It is too soon to say whether this structural shift to services will be permanent, but it appears likely. It is common for a national economy to undergo (relative) deindustrialization and experience a long-term shift to services. Rodrik (2016), however, uses multicountry comparative data to show that later industrializing countries have been deindustrializing much

TABLE 2.4   Key characteristics of selected provinces in Java and the outer islands

	SHARE OF NATIONAL POPULATION (%)	SHARE OF INDONESIAN GDP (%)	AGRICULTURAL HOUSEHOLDS WITHIN PROVINCE (%)	
	(2020)[a]	(2019)[b]	2003[c]	2018[d]
West Java	18.4	13.2	41	25
East Java	14.7	14.6	63	47
South Sulawesi	3.3	3.1	55	50
South Sumatra	3.2	2.8	59	51
Nusa Tenggara Timur	2.0	0.7	85	70
Indonesia	100	100	55	41

Sources: [a] BPS 2021a, [b] BPS 2021d, [c] BPS 2003, [d] BPS 2019a.

earlier in the development process, so that these economies have not undergone "full industrialization." Rodrik explains this as due to the rapid development of globalized value chains, with constant outsourcing of intermediate products to cheaper production sites, along with labor-saving technological progress in manufacturing. Opportunities for later industrializers may also be further curtailed by the global trend toward resurgent protectionism over the last decade, while the impacts of climate change mitigation policies add further uncertainty to the future of manufacturing as an engine of growth. According to conventional economic analysis, the movement of low-skilled workers away from low-productivity farming to the technologically more dynamic (but still low-skilled) manufacturing sector is associated with increases in labor productivity (the fundamental argument made by Arthur Lewis). Rodrik (28) argues that "premature deindustrialization is not good news for developing nations. It blocks off the main avenue of rapid economic convergence [between urban and rural areas of a country] in low-income settings."

For Indonesia, a peak share of industrial output appears to have been reached in 2000, at 48 percent of GDP (figure 2.5). Given the stagnation of industrial employment in Indonesia (figure 2.6), and its relative (rather than absolute) declining contribution to the economy, reference to "deindustrialization" is perhaps stating the case a little too strongly. Employment shares in both manufacturing and industry have, however, been easily outstripped by employment growth in services, which eclipsed employment in agriculture in 2008 (figure 2.6). Table 2.5 further indicates the slow growth in industrial employment in Indonesia compared to South Korea. Recent decades could thus be described as a period of indeterminate industrialization in Indonesia during which manufacturing has neither boomed nor bust.

If Rodrik's basic proposition of premature deindustrialization is correct, and if it applies to Indonesia, as it apparently does, this has profound implications for the nature of contemporary agrarian transition. It is possible that the Lewis turning point will never be reached, which suggests the continued coexistence of a dual economy, as later industrializers become increasingly reliant on service sectors to deliver livelihoods to ex-farmers and part-time farmers. The reality in the Global South, where secure formal employment continues to be a privilege for a

TABLE 2.5 Growth in employment share in industry (Indonesia and South Korea)

	EARLIER EMPLOYMENT SHARE IN INDUSTRY (%)	PEAK EMPLOYMENT SHARE IN INDUSTRY (%)
Indonesia	11 (1977)	21 (2019)
South Korea	11 (1964)	37 (1991)

Source: International Labour Organization 2021.

minority, has indeed long been one where pluriactive livelihoods prevail. Recalling Chambers and Conway's (1991) plea to look beyond misguided "employment thinking" as outdated and flawed in low-income settings, full employment may indeed be an unrealistic policy goal for Indonesia. It may also be ultimately undesirable from an environmental perspective. Either way, assumptions about an agrarian transition that involves levels of manufacturing employment equivalent to earlier industrializing countries seem, at this moment, questionable.

Reconsidering Agrarian Transitions in Indonesia

In this chapter I have sought to analyze the unfolding agrarian transition occurring within Indonesia from a range of viewpoints, with a broader aim to contextualize changing rural livelihood opportunities. First, I presented the Indonesian experience in comparative perspective. While that experience shares some features with the experiences of Northeast Asia (notably the presence of an interventionist state, limits to the development of capitalist relations within agriculture, and shifts against urban bias), we also confront important differences. Comprehensive land reform was never implemented, and smallholder agriculture was never a platform for serious capital accumulation. Most importantly, however, globalization has meant that capitalist accumulation occurs at the scale of a world-system, where sites of production have become nodes within global value chains, such that industrialization does not necessarily depend on prior agricultural accumulation within the same country. This also has implications for deindustrialization as, compared to earlier industrializers, Indonesia now appears to be confronting a partial agrarian transition. Furthermore, considerable regional diversity exists within a country as large and diverse as Indonesia, where regions are inserted into the global economy in a myriad of ways, and it may be helpful to discuss agrarian transitions (in the plural).

I have applied a historical perspective to show how the coffee-growing regions of Indonesia were incorporated into the global economy during the colonial period through commodity chain structures driven by international buyers. On Java, this was supported by an exploitative state superstructure and forced deliveries, which had the effect of empowering, and enriching, traditional elites who eventually became incorporated into the state (discussed further in chapter 3). While a corporate plantation model emerged at this time (with important long-term ramifications in the noncoffee plantation sector), an independent smallholder production base developed beyond the direct reach of the colonial state in the outer islands. It developed in forest-based landscapes where land was relatively easy to access. By the early twentieth century, these smallholders were already incorporated into global value chains dominated by large trading companies, including NHM, but with particularly strong links to Singapore—often through Chinese intermediaries. Indonesian farmers were not supported by active government extension programs (unlike in colonial Taiwan and South Korea). These patterns continued after independence. Coffee-growing households became enrolled in a variety of global value chain structures that cocreated institutional environments that were, at times, oppressive and exploitative, but at other times favorable enough to stimulate smallholder investments of household labor on land they considered their own but often accessed without payment.

Global capital required local intermediaries to encourage smallholder production, and this created lucrative rents for some. The Dutch, for example, empowered the *bupati* as collectors under *Preangerstelsel* and *cultuurstelsel*. This tended to result in exploitative conditions being imposed on cultivators, as the powers of the state and capital combined. In the ensuing centuries, local elites have continued to seek ways to interpose between primary producers and global capital to capture rents, more recently appealing to the state to intervene on their behalf. Indeed, Agustono and Junaidi (2018) have argued for the continued influence of colonial-era structures in contemporary Indonesia, inferring that the desire to extract profits from smallholders still pervades government programs today.

The institutional environment of coffee farming also intersected with local social and political contexts, which varied considerably and are best examined through the case study approach pursued in later chapters. The coffee trade networks of outer island Indonesia, however, were characterized by the vibrant role of local collectors as intermediaries. Small amounts of capital often flowed along these networks to stimulate production by smallholder households, who remained ostensibly independent. The ongoing influence of global capital on Indonesian coffee smallholders will be the key theme picked up again in chapter 4 on global value chains. In the outer islands, a commercially oriented production base was characterized by petty commodity producers, whose basic subsistence was ensured by own rice production and drip-fed with capital from collectors. Coffee production in these smallholder regions, moreover, was highly dependent on access to land (often forest landscapes) that was regulated by customary community institutions (chapter 5). Broadly, this land was relatively accessible to most community members, and accumulation of land was primarily limited by labor availability.

Processes of industrialization across the broader Indonesian economy since the 1970s have had a further profound effect on the institutional environment of agrarian change. This drew upon capital accumulated primarily through oil wealth and channeled into import-substitution industrialization initially, and then later by participating in export-oriented, manufacturing-based global value chains. The combined effect was to draw labor away from the farm sector and into urban work, as reflected in shifting patterns of employment at the national scale over the last fifty years. At the same time, rural development programs (especially *bimas*) allowed (rice) farmers to pursue relatively secure, if not particularly lucrative, livelihoods in agriculture. The momentum of transition toward a thoroughly industrialized society appears to have more recently stalled—owing partly to the post-2000 rise of China as a global manufacturing powerhouse. As a result, the number of agricultural households has remained more or less constant, even though the dependence of these households on farming for their livelihoods has declined.

Looming large over these processes is, of course, the Indonesian state. This influence is evident both in its attempt to intervene in value chain structures linking smallholders with global coffee markets, and in its role in guiding the industrialization process. The state has also assumed a pivotal role in facilitating the accumulation and redistribution of resources. The next chapter develops further the role of the Indonesian state in co-constituting the institutional environment presented to Indonesian smallholders and so influencing livelihood strategies and processes of agrarian transition.

THE INDONESIAN STATE AND RURAL PATRONAGE

State patronage is central to understanding agrarian processes. It not only influences forms of extraction and accumulation, but also generates tensions and contradictions that constitute important sources of change and differentiation.

—Gillian Hart, *Agrarian Transformations* (1989)

This chapter examines the role of the modern Indonesian state in shaping the institutional environment presented to, and cocreated by, smallholders. The aim is to present the role of the state in encouraging (unintentionally), or at least facilitating, the emergence of fortress farming livelihood strategies. This requires first providing a biographical sketch of the Indonesian state, its origins, and its chief characteristics, many of which were inherited from its colonial antecedents. The key contribution in this chapter is to understand how the Indonesian state has functioned as an organization to accumulate and redistribute resources, and how this redistribution has commonly occurred through highly personalized patron-client relationships. In considering patron-client relationships in this chapter, I am largely following a definition provided by Scott (1972, 92), without the limiting gendered suggestions of the language: "a special case of dyadic (two-person) ties involving a largely instrumental friendship in which an individual of higher socioeconomic status (patron) uses his own influence and resources to provide protection or benefits, or both, for a person of lower status (client) who, for his part, reciprocates by offering general support and assistance, including personal services, to the patron." The state, or its constituent members, influences the lives of rural households by assuming the position of patron, and I will show how this has been further encouraged by the feudalization of the Indonesian state. I highlight how the state has commonly used specific projects (*proyek*) to reinforce patronage, and I will examine the effect this has had on livelihood resources and transforming social structures. From a household livelihood perspective, this entails treating state patronage as a form of social capital, which can be drawn on by select individuals to potentially enhance livelihood resilience and, in some circumstances, to even facilitate wealth accumulation. This process, however, almost necessarily involves the exclusion of others. The role of the state as a territorializing power is also critical, but I will discuss its role as the country's largest landlord in chapter 5.

Following an introductory vignette about state patronage from below in a coffee landscape, the chapter examines the birth and evolution of the Indonesian state, highlighting how characteristics inherited from the colonial period were then reshaped through the crucible of revolution (1945–1949), the Sukarno years (1949–1966), Suharto's New Order regime (1966–1998), and into the current post-1998 period of democratization sometimes referred to as *reformasi* or post-*reformasi*. While patronage has been important throughout these periods, the New Order was critical in establishing institutional norms (especially around *proyek*) that still resonate deeply today. The continued relevance of a "*proyek* mentality" to state patronage in the coffee sector—and ultimately to the distributed livelihoods associated with fortress farming—is then demonstrated through specific observations of village-level processing units and Geographical Indications. I highlight the interplay between these state programs and value chain structures, some reflecting continuities with the colonial era. Finally, I will introduce the rise of various social protection programs and community development projects that have become prevalent across rural Indonesia. These programs are recasting the livelihood resources available to households, and the social capital required to access them, in ways that are further contributing to fortress farming livelihoods within the context of a patronage-bound state.

A View of State Patronage from Below

In 2008, I visited a field site in northern Toraja, where government officials were encouraging the planting of coffee on a degraded slope covered mostly by pine trees and bracken fern. The project, funded as part of a national "coffee extensification" program, sought to increase the productivity of these hills, simultaneously improving incomes and preventing soil erosion. I accompanied a government official from the local agricultural office to the field site to observe the planting. Poorly maintained seedlings were being planted in shallow holes on denuded slopes with little or no topsoil, in the middle of the local dry season, and with no shade cover. The prospects for the seedlings looked grim. I asked the villager, Pong Salu, who had been paid to do the planting, whether he thought the seedlings would survive. He didn't—and similar skepticism was expressed by both the government extension staff and, more surprisingly to me, the program manager back in the district headquarters, who admitted that the program had been designed in Jakarta. None of these actors, however, seemed particularly unsettled by having to go through motions that all knew would likely result in failed project outcomes. Conversely, all seemed quite content with the process.

What this revealed to me was not just that poorly conceived development plans are delivered in a top-down manner with limited room for local adaptation (in itself true), but that this didn't really matter since the primary—unstated, but apparently widely accepted—aim of the initiative was the dispersal of *proyek* resources rather than project outcomes. All individuals along the state-derived resource distribution chain down to Pong Salu were benefiting from the arrangement as it was. As Li (2016, 83) explains, "After a project is over, no one expects to see a lasting result of the kind anticipated in the technical matrix that served to legitimate it. A successful project is one that generates a flow of revenue, and more projects."

Aspinall (2013, 30) defines the institution of Indonesian *proyek* as "a self-contained, collaborative, and funded activity intended to achieve a designated end and which is to be attained through at least the formal performance of a competitive process." Aspinall highlights how the *proyek* mode has flourished in the increasingly neoliberalized environment of post-*reformasi* Indonesia, where patrons compete—in a marketplace, as it were—to obtain the allegiance of clients. The *proyek* mentality is pervasive, and Aspinall (30) speaks of the "penetration of the *proyek* mode through virtually every sphere of social and political life," while the verb *diproyekkan* (to make into a project) has become common parlance. On the Torajan hillside, a redistribution of state resources was taking place, channeled through a very selective set of hands to be sure, without any serious regard for productive outcomes. Indeed, in this case, the project beneficiaries were invisible—all actors, including Pong Salu, were instead project implementers. Moreover, so deeply ingrained was this particular institutional form that it encounters very little opposition. It is simply the way much of rural Indonesia sees the operations of the state, and individuals have become habituated into seeking opportunities to participate in this pretense by enrolling themselves as clients to a patron-state rather than expecting, or demanding, effective service delivery. State patronage, moreover, has deep roots in Indonesia.

Birth and Evolution of the Indonesian State

To understand the centrality of patronage requires a deeper understanding of the institution that is the modern Indonesian state. Anderson ([1983a] 2006) reminds us that we need to keep in focus the hybrid character of any modern nation-state as being constituted by the state (*negara* in Indonesian, which includes the bureaucratic apparatus) and the "imagined community" of the nation (*bangsa*, as a social construction of "deep horizontal comradeship"). This is not to say that a state does not, at times, also act in the interests of either the nation or its citizens, or both, but that it is a mistake to automatically assume that it will. This distinction between *negara* and *bangsa* is particularly important in Indonesia, where the *bangsa* emerged in opposition to the Netherlands East Indies (NEI) state, but where the *negara* is an institutional continuation of its colonial predecessor. The character of the NEI is consequently fundamental to understanding the contemporary Indonesian state.

The NEI state emerged in the early nineteenth century from the decaying remains of the earlier, two-hundred-year-old institution that was the Dutch East India Company, the Vereenigde Oostindische Compagnie (VOC). The financial masters of the VOC chose a small, swampy outpost of the Bantenese pepper-trading sultanate as their Asian headquarters in 1619, renamed it Batavia, and set in train a series of events that eventually led to the modern city of Jakarta[1] controlling a state apparatus (*aparat* is the Indonesian term for the civil service[2]) stretching across some five thousand kilometers from Aceh to Papua. The VOC was not a nation-state but rather a company-state whose *raison d'être* was to deliver commercial profits to its owners and only secondarily to exert territorial control, although over time it assumed more and more statelike functions, such as imposing taxes, maintaining a military, concluding treaties, enforcing trade monopolies, and punishing lawbreakers. As it was de-linked spatially from the Dutch nation, self-aggrandizement of the VOC and its officials was always the priority.

Even with the formal dissolution of the VOC (in 1799) and the transfer of its territorial possessions to the Dutch colonial government, the NEI state pursued very similar extractive strategies throughout the nineteenth century, especially under *cultuurstelsel*, as presented in chapter 2. In 1899, the Dutch journalist-lawyer Coen van Deventer wrote an influential article in *De Gids*, titled "A Debt of Honour," in which he argued that the Dutch owed a moral debt to the Javanese for the unethical transfer of wealth to the Netherlands during *cultuurstelsel*. van Deventer was part of a movement that prompted the "Ethical Policy" after 1901, under which the NEI belatedly began to articulate its formally stated purpose in the Indies as improving native welfare. Despite this stated purpose, however, it never entirely abandoned its earlier extractive orientation nor its poorly disguised pursuit of self-interest. In the early twentieth century, state revenue continued to rely heavily on government-run monopolies and state-owned enterprises. These were estimated to constitute 57 percent of total NEI state revenue in 1900 and a still considerable 43 percent in 1928,[3] while a further 14 percent of total revenue in 1928 was obtained from import and export duties (Mansvelt 1976). State-owned enterprises remain important to state maintenance today. Much of this revenue was then spent, and continues to be spent, on the upkeep of the state itself, maintaining its investments, paying the salaries of the *aparat*, and ensuring political stability through selective redistribution and patronage.

The Japanese occupation (1942–1945) brought an effective end to the sovereignty of the NEI state, and Japanese armed forces seized control of the existing colonial state apparatus while allowing the multiple layers of native officialdom to continue functioning, more or less intact. In a desperate attempt to revive their flagging war effort, the Japanese also mobilized political forces among the Indonesian masses, thereby unleashing the vital energies of nationalism that would fertilize the seeds for future independence. Two competing states subsequently emerged during the war of independence (1945–1949) as the Dutch reasserted control of the colonial state, based in Jakarta, while Sukarno attempted to build a separate republican state from the Javanese cultural homeland of Yogyakarta (in close collaboration with Sultan Hamengkubuwono IX). Much of the early years following independence (proclaimed by Sukarno in 1945 and recognized by the Dutch in 1949) involved bringing together the competing factions of these two states. This, however, was a situation where the state had minimal control over economic resources, such that Anderson (1983b, 482) memorably described how the "postcolonial state glowed with the dim, fitful radiance of a klieg lamp powered by flashlight batteries."

This role of Sultan Hamengkubuwono IX hints at an important sociocultural aspect to understanding the modern Indonesian state. The colonial policy of indirect rule ensured that traditional aristocracies were initially preserved and then incorporated within the bureaucracy (the *priyayi* class in Java, which included the sultans and *bupati*), lending considerable social prestige to those working for the state. Particularly in many rural regions of the country today, where public-sector employment offers an attractive opportunity for a reliable income, the *aparat* constitutes an influential aristocracy—a class even—that embraces a semifeudal attitude toward the population, who are referred to in Indonesian political language as *rakyat*, the people, or *massa*, the masses. A degree of social distance between government *aparat* (together with influential social figures known as *tokoh*) and the *rakyat* is maintained and consistently reinforced through the adoption of elaborate, ritualized, state ceremonial behavior. Development interventions in rural Indonesia are grounded on such a separation between the *aparat*, who does the developing, and the *rakyat*, who is developed, even though initial entry to state membership is based more on social connections than on any inherent intellectual or technical capacity. When performing state ceremonies, the *aparat* uses a distinct, formalized government version of Bahasa Indonesia,[4] which further sets it apart from the *rakyat*. A formal bureaucratic form of the language has evolved that presents a degree of sophistication and refinement that can be difficult to master for everyday *rakyat*, while at the same time maintaining an uncanny capacity to remain apparently vacuous of tangible meaning and intent. In rural and regional Indonesia today, even after democratic reforms, such cultural forms assumed by the *aparat* continue to limit a genuine service delivery orientation within the bureaucracy.

The early years of Indonesian independence were devoted primarily to nation building and attempts to establish a functioning nationalist state. There were several contradictory forces at play. Sukarno initially drew support and legitimacy from his association with cultural figures such as Sultan Hamengkubuwono IX, continuing the colonial process whereby feudal elites were incorporated within state structures. At the same time, demands for land reform (particularly from the communists), Marhaenism (introduced in chapter 2), and "land to the tiller" campaigns encouraged a relatively equitable distribution of owner-cultivator smallholdings. Meanwhile, the nationalization of formerly Dutch-owned plantations in the 1950s, and their incorporation with the state-owned plantation company (Perseroan Terbatas Perkebunan Nusantara, PTPN), established the state itself as an influential managing landlord. This last development was furthermore consistent with the tendency for the new state to maintain the extractive political and economic institutions that it inherited from the colonial regime, and which continued to serve the interests of a bureaucratic elite. Penny (1971, 122) explained how: "Of course, the government of independent Indonesia was no longer in the hands of aliens, but its top people were a small elite, and they believed strongly that it was the peasants' duty to serve the state." Furthermore, the "originally small government elite expanded about seven-fold" (123), and the state had to extract ever-increasing surpluses from the *rakyat* to resource this expansion, given the absence of any meaningful industrial sector and the increasingly wanton disregard for economic stability. It did this through an initial policy of urban bias, including export taxation, price controls, and unfavorable exchange rates, such that by the end of the Sukarno presidency, coffee growers in South Sumatra were receiving only 38 percent of the international price for their coffee, and one kilogram of coffee was only enough to buy one kilogram of rice (Partosoedarso and Makmur 1968, cited by Penny 1971).

Following independence, the enlarged Indonesian state thus continued to be extractive, but it neglected to ensure adequate incentives and price stability to increase the resource base needed for this. The rise of Suharto's New Order in 1966 "is best understood as the resurrection of the state and its triumph *vis-à-vis* society and nation" (Anderson 1983b, 487). Anderson further stressed that, unlike Sukarno, Suharto had established his career from within the state (a son of a village official, he had attended training with the Dutch colonial army and joined the Japanese-controlled native forces known as PETA) and as such was well-primed to strengthen the state *qua* state, which he did extremely effectively, but with unrestrained violence. The authoritarian and fundamentally undemocratic New Order state (1966–1998) continued to be extractive, but it also made sure that the economy was growing sufficiently to ensure a healthy flow of resources to its supporters.

Patronage and *Proyek* in the Coffee Sector

Politically, Suharto's New Order concentrated on maintaining tight control over the rural population by pursuing a "floating mass" strategy in Indonesia's villages, where the state diverted the attention of the population away from so-called political distractions and toward the single-minded objective of economic development (*pembangunan*). A core approach here was for the state to distribute privileges, rather than rights, to the population. Hart (1989, 33) explains how the state pursued social control through the incorporation of traditional village elites into its machinery:

> Rural elites become, in essence, political and economic agents of the state in the countryside and are co-opted into the larger structure of power as preferred but dependent clients. Their access to subsidized credit, inputs, licenses, guaranteed prices, and so forth stems not so much from their ability to sway agricultural policy in their favor through direct influence, but rather from the services that they render to larger centers of accumulation by helping to police the countryside.

The democratization of Indonesia since 1998 has not significantly altered underlying patterns of patronage, as demonstrated through work by van Klinken (2009) on "patronage democracy" and Aspinall and Berenschot (2019) on "elections and clientelism," which emphasize institutional continuities with the New Order in this regard. The dispersal of resources via personalized clientelist networks for political benefit is considered so central by Aspinall (2013, 28) that he referred to it as "the most important glue of political relations in Indonesia." While patronage is now partly distributed via political parties, this has not seriously challenged the vital importance of access to the *aparat*, nor the importance of nonparty social organizations (such as farmer groups, cooperatives, and women's empowerment organizations) for distributing state resources to garner political support and obedience. Li (2016, 82) similarly links the *proyek* directly with state patronage: "Projects continue to serve as vehicles for channeling funds to favored members of the rural elite, and to discipline villagers who are told to wait patiently for state largesse to come their way. Hence, villages are awash with small projects sponsored by dozens of different national and transnational agencies that distribute free goats, sewing machines, water systems, and micro-credit schemes."

In *proyek* interventions by the state, the ethos that sustains such patronage involves a two-way interaction between patrons and clients. Indeed, Aspinall and Berenschot (2019, 251) emphasize how clientelist favors exist not only because politicians are willing to provide them, but also because clients (voters) demand them. Jakimow (2018) similarly describes a "moral atmosphere" of "development as a share" in Indonesia, drawing on the ubiquitous use of the expression *bagi-bagi* ("share it around") as a way of framing the moral acceptability of clientelism. The logic of *bagi-bagi* implies that access to project resources *in themselves* is often far more important than any benefits that might arise as a result of the project intervention. A similar observation was made, in rural Nepal, by Pigg (1992), who demonstrated how villagers saw tangible benefits from development projects accruing not from receiving project benefits, but from becoming involved in project implementation. In Indonesia, the *proyek* mentality has powerfully structured the relationship between the state and rural households.

The persistence of clientelistic practices, and the limitations of a public sphere independent of a patronage-bound state, are most pronounced in the outer islands and in the nonurban regions of Java. Indonesia's regional autonomy laws of 1999, which resulted in routine financial transfers from the central government to district government coffers through the "General Allocation Fund" (Dana Alokasi Umum), have further empowered programmatic decision-making at the local level and have brought state patronage networks much closer to the rural population (Hadiz 2004). It should be noted, however, that specific *proyek* are often undertaken by the state in partnership with NGOs, industry actors, and development agencies, and there has moreover been a tendency for the coffee-related interventions of these nonstate actors to become subsumed within the social structures established and maintained by state patronage.

Coffee Development Projects and Farmer Organizations

Writing in the 1980s, Booth (1984, 27) argued that "almost without exception, there has been little technological change in the production of any of the smallholder crops over the last fifty years; increases in production have been achieved by replicating existing technology over more and more land." While government development programs have never been a decisive factor in increasing the output of tree-crop smallholders, they have successfully enrolled rural households as clients of the state. Smallholders, in response to the removal of overt urban bias but otherwise independently of the state, increased coffee output nationwide to make an important contribution to export earnings throughout the 1970s and 1980s (figure 3.1).

This does not mean that the government did not implement coffee development projects. The first attempt at state support occurred under the third five-year development plan (1979–1984) with the "Rejuvenation, Rehabilitation and Expansion of Export Crops" project (Peremajaan, Rehabilitasi dan Perluasan Tanaman Ekspor, PRPTE). This was undertaken by the Directorate General of Estate Crops under the Ministry of Agriculture and followed, rather than initiated, smallholder expansion. The PRPTE included support for the "Coffee Intensification Project" (Proyek Intensifikasi Kopi, PIK), implemented through "Project Implementation Units" (Unit Pelaksanaan Proyek, UPP), which included agricultural extension and distribution of fertilizers, seedlings, and credit to smallholders. The government claimed that some thirty-four thousand hectares of coffee farms were rehabilitated through the PIK (Booth 1984), which would still have amounted to only 5 percent of the total smallholder coffee area at the time. While the PIK did not significantly raise productivity, it did embed the basic framework for delivering patronage support through *proyek*, which has proved to be an enduring social structure. Indeed, the term *upepe* (UPP) was still used by coffee-growing communities in the early 2000s to describe an entire programmatic approach, reflecting a focus on the creation of a client network linked to the state (rather than effecting productivity improvements).

Large multilateral development banks, such as the World Bank and the Asian Development Bank (ADB), were intimately involved in this process. They offered low-interest loans to implement projects that were commonly designed by the banks, who also provided technical oversight throughout implementation and so helped shape national and subnational institutions. For example, the World Bank was responsible for reforming Indonesia's agricultural research and extension system through a series of loans commencing in 1980,[5] and the ADB supported the Indonesian coffee sector through a series of four loans during the 1980s and 1990s.[6] These relatively large loans (up to 100 million USD), with generous terms such as 1 percent annual interest rates and grace periods of ten years, were provided to the central government but executed by government agencies such as the Directorate General of Estate Crops. This helped construct an institutional

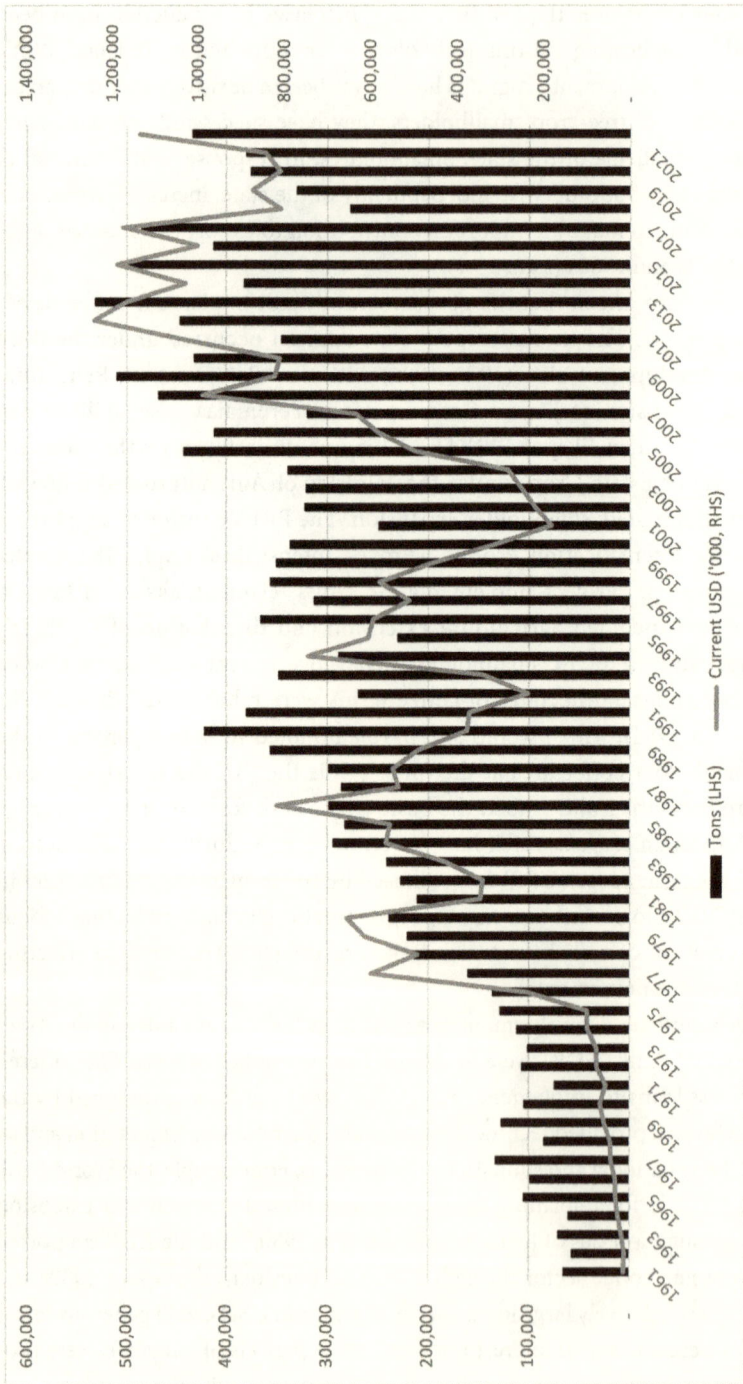

FIGURE 3.1. Indonesian coffee exports (volume and value, 1961–2022).

Source: FAO 2024.

environment whereby a patronage-laden *proyek* mentality emerged, with limited accountability for performance.

While there has been a thin presence of state institutions operating in the coffee sector, the Ministry of Agriculture and its Directorate General of Estate Crops (Ditjenbun) has generally assumed bureaucratic responsibility for these various projects and programs. Coffee, however, is far from the top priority within the ministry, which instead prioritizes food crops (rice, soybean, sugar, and corn), and coffee projects were never infused with a serious commitment to driving yield-increasing agronomic or technological improvements. In a North Sumatran village, Adi, a coffee farmer described the situation to me: "See what happens when you don't have any government support? Us farmers just do our own thing, guessing at what the best practice is. Everybody doing their own thing from their own experiences. We don't know the best way to grow coffee." Adi also complained that he would like to know whether insecticides could be used to control the coffee berry borer, but he did not know what to spray and when to spray. Indonesian coffee-growing households thus generally hold an extremely poor opinion of government extension services. Adi went on to ridicule them: "They just sit in their offices and wait for the afternoon roll call. I have never received any helpful advice and wouldn't trust it anyway."

Each year, however, Ditjenbun allocates a budget for the expansion and rehabilitation of smallholder coffee across the country, with funding provided for minor activities such as farmer training, seedling and fertilizer provision, and post-harvest processing equipment (often supplied by the Indonesian Coffee and Cocoa Research Institute—ICCRI). For example, in 2020, approximately 200 million IDR (13,000 USD) was allocated to North Toraja to rehabilitate four hundred hectares of Arabica, and 546 million IDR (36,000 USD) was allocated to South Sumatra to rehabilitate seven hundred hectares of Robusta (Ditjenbun 2021). In 2014, however, only 5 percent of Indonesian coffee-growing households reported receiving agricultural extension from the state (appendix table A1). For those who did, subsidized fertilizer was the most important. It seems inevitable that resources associated with government programs are captured by local elites acting in roles such as village heads, farmer group heads, cooperative leaders, or authorized fertilizer distributors.

Agricultural *proyek* are almost always delivered through the organizational form of a farmer group (*kelompok tani*), which generally consists of around thirty individual household representatives (mostly male "household heads" by default, although several women's groups have also been formed). *Kelompok tani* are found across all the coffee regions of Indonesia I have visited, although their performance is highly variable, and only 13 percent of coffee-growing households reported being a member of one (appendix table A1). Invariably, the Ministry of Agriculture established these groups as a structure through which *proyek* could be channeled. It is frequently commented that the groups are "only active when there is a government project [delivering resources]" (*cuman hidup asal ada proyek*). There are exceptions when a charismatic or motivated leader organizes labor-sharing days or monthly meetings to discuss agronomic issues and problems, but most groups are otherwise said to be "sleeping." It is rare for farmer groups to engage in the collective marketing of farm produce, although farmer group heads do sometimes operate as collectors (*tengkulak*). As conduits for patronage distribution, the farmer group leadership position offers both an opportunity for upward social mobility and access to state resources, and it has also become common for political parties to engage in "money politics" through the groups to mobilize vote banks. Private-sector sustainability programs also rely on these groups as the foundation for organizing farmers in their supply chains.

Development interventions with the explicit aim of "institutional strengthening" may also encourage the establishment of larger organizational forms such as farmer group confederations (Gabungan Kelompok Tani, GAPOKTAN), supported by the Ministry of Agriculture. Some may be formalized as rural cooperatives (Koperasi Unit Desa, KUD), involving further patronage from the State Ministry of Cooperatives. An alternative organizational form that focuses on small-business development, which I have observed in the coffee regions of Lampung and linked to Nestlé, is the Collective Business Group (Kelompok Usaha Bersama, KUBE), receiving patronage from the Ministry of Social Affairs. An explicit rationale for institutional strengthening is "cutting out the middleman" who is considered exploitative and usurious. However, such initiatives generally struggle to remain financially viable in competitive market environments. Furthermore, cooperatives were frequently mobilized as political vehicles during the Suharto regime and were associated with corruption and political control. Farmers, as a result, remain cautious of organizing under cooperative structures, and less than 1 percent of coffee-growing households reported being a cooperative member in 2014 (appendix table A1). Durable cooperatives in the Indonesian coffee sector are usually those able to manage a series of *proyek*-related supports from different state patrons, development agencies, NGOs, or downstream buyers (often motivated by corporate sustainability and certification programs).

The farmer groups and farmer cooperatives that do exist thus tend to be vertically oriented through patronage rather than representing the horizontal class interests of farmers. Indonesia's farmers have yet to organize into a coherent political force, and rarely have they successfully agitated for overtly pro-agriculture policies. Grassroots peasant unions were severely curtailed during

Suharto's New Order regime, and the post-*reformasi* emergence of peasant organizations, such as Serikat Petani Indonesia, has not significantly affected coffee-growing communities. Various manifestations of an Indonesian Coffee Farmer Association (Asosiasi Petani Kopi Indonesia, APEKI, or sometimes APKI) have been established, but with very little capacity to organize nationally. The absence of credible farmer representation in Indonesia contrasts with the situation in many Latin American countries, such as Colombia (Bentley and Baker 2000), and has meant that rural development programs and policies are rarely held accountable by farmer lobby groups. The following two sections will present specific examples of how rural social institutions interact "vertically" with the state to encourage resource flows into coffee-growing communities.

Patronage through Village-Level Processing Units

There was an excitable buzz in the air when I visited Balinese coffee-growing villages throughout 2005 and 2006. Traditional agricultural societies in Kintamani, known as *subak abian*, were assuming a key role in processing Arabica coffee into specialty coffee for high-end markets. A government official told me that 48 "product processing units" (*unit pengolahan hasil*, UPH) had been supported with government funding across the districts of Bangli, Buleleng, and Badung. These units would collect red cherries from individual farmers and, in small wet-processing mills built with government funding, remove the red skins, ferment the beans, dry the parchment coffee on purpose-built drying racks, and then stockpile in small storage sheds (figure 3.2). Many units had a hulling machine to remove the parchment. This process was labor intensive, and during one evening I counted some twenty villagers, men and women, painstakingly sorting out defective beans or else moving coffee manually through the factory. Pak Made, a leader at one of the *subak abian*, proudly proclaimed that his factory had increased employment from twenty-four to thirty that year. This was a remarkable labor allocation compared to fewer than ten people employed by a nearby privately owned factory that was centrally processing ten times the volume of coffee.

In addition to government funding, downstream buyers were providing the UPH with technical and financial support. In 2006, this was provided by the Indonesian subsidiary of Ecom Agro industrial, a major international trader from Switzerland. With the support of ICCRI, Ecom had signed a cooperation agreement with six *subak abian* to supply them with specialty coffee at a price determined by a formula related to the New York terminal price. In subsequent years, Ecom withdrew from Bali and was functionally replaced by a smaller

FIGURE 3.2.   Government-funded processing unit (UPH), Bali, 2011

specialty coffee roaster from Australia. The *subak abian* leader responsible for signing the agreement told me how the local government representatives had also wanted to be a signatory, but they had insisted on taking a commission and so were eventually excluded. The government staff apparently felt that it was their right to intercede between the farmers and downstream buyers based on their prior support for the UPHs.

The Kintamani project commenced in 2001 and became something of a model for coffee-based, village-level industrialization (UPHs) across Indonesia. In 2020, approximately eighteen billion rupiah (1.2 million USD) was allocated for forty-eight UPH units to be established for farmer organizations across seventeen Indonesian provinces (Ditjenbun 2021). The Kintamani project was based on what ICCRI researchers called a Mediated Partnership Model (MOTRAMED) and involved ICCRI staff training farmers to improve coffee quality, supplying seedlings and processing equipment (manufactured by ICCRI) and then facilitating trade relationships between producer organizations and downstream coffee buyers (Wijaya, Glasbergen, and Mawardi 2017). The legitimizing rationale for such interventions is one of village-level value-adding. Further support is sometimes provided to encourage the farmer organization to engage in coffee roasting as a cottage industry. The social unit responsible for such village-level processing has included farmer groups, farmer group federations, cooperatives, traditional agrarian structures (the *subak abian*), or collective businesses (KUBEs). Sometimes, new social structures were created by the intervention and the infrastructure itself, which are referred to simply as a UPH (as in Bajawa on Flores Island). Attempts are commonly made to establish some kind of collective ownership over the UPH, but influential individuals (local elites) routinely come to control these assets.

MOTRAMED interventions were pivotal in initially improving the quality of processing in coffee-growing locations such as Kintamani and Bajawa and for developing international market reputations for these origins. As applied in these two regions, the "partnership" aspect of MOTRAMED involved ICCRI brokering trade relationships with downstream buyers (exporters), who not only provided a market for the coffee but also provided important feedback and technical input about processing. The approach thus followed the basic value chain idea of "upgrading" in that engagement with downstream buyers can put firms on "potentially dynamic learning curves" (Gereffi 1999). State supports for village-level upgrading in these smallholder contexts, however, cannot be conceptualized in the same terms as firm-level upgrading in industrial sectors (Vicol et al. 2018). The UPHs are often led by charismatic individuals, who became the public face of the intervention (with both the state and the buyer) and the favored vehicles through which to funnel intervention funds. These organizations thus came to function as patronage networks controlled by these individuals.

Local elites can further leverage the connections created by value chain interventions to attract new resources and funding. In Kintamani, a subsidized credit program operated by the Bank of Indonesia had picked up the funding of *subak abian*, while I have observed international donors stepping in elsewhere. Maintaining the flow of (both public and private) funds becomes the modus operandi of the organization, rather than sustained value chain upgrading, and this has the additional effect of crowding out any political debate about improving agricultural livelihoods. It also focuses the attention of rural households on accessing patronage resources rather than maximizing productivity and so ultimately encourages fortress farming strategies. While farm-level upgrading interventions are presented as value-free technical and managerial responses to market opportunities, downstream buyers themselves have become unwittingly embroiled in local political projects aimed at consolidating prestige and reinforcing patronage. While the trade relationships tended to collapse after a few seasons, they are often outlived by the social structures they tap into.

The financial support of government agencies is a critical factor in the model, as it sustains the continued involvement of ICCRI (Wijaya, Glasbergen, and

FIGURE 3.3. Processing equipment delivered to a makeshift UPH site, South Sulawesi, 2015

Mawardi 2017). Notwithstanding the challenges UPHs face in remaining financially viable, the approach continues to receive considerable funding support, even in places where local capacity is minimal (figure 3.3). When I returned to Kintamani in 2018, very few of the UPHs were still functioning, and none were providing employment to large numbers of villagers. This example of village-level processing units demonstrates how a technical value-adding intervention has come to be subsumed within a broader logic of patronage.

Geographical Indications

Another example of how state-based patronage intersects with Indonesia's rural political economy is through the establishment of so-called Geographical Indications (GIs). GIs are a form of collective intellectual property where a place name associated with product quality is protected from geographical fraud through initial registration, legal protection, and subsequent monitoring. Place-based quality associations (such as "Toraja coffee") do indeed generate market premiums, such that restricting the use of the geographical signifier to legitimate users only, where a given quality is maintained, can increase prices and facilitate value capture within the producing region. GIs are consequently promoted by development agencies, NGOs, and the state to improve rural livelihoods in coffee-producing regions. In an online registry updated in 2023,[7] 138 GIs had been registered in Indonesia, including 48 for coffee, all of which were established as part of state-initiated and state-funded *proyek*. A comparative study of coffee-related GIs in Colombia, Thailand, and Indonesia (Quiñones-Ruiz et al. 2020) characterized the Indonesian process as being strongly "government-driven." GIs have now been established in all the major Arabica and Robusta producing regions of Indonesia.

I have been conducting research in the coffee-growing regions of Flores Island since 2007 and had the opportunity to observe the development of the Bajawa GI (in Ngada District) over the subsequent decade. In 2004, the district government of Ngada had begun working together with ICCRI on a quality-oriented MOTRAMED project that involved the establishment of a network of fourteen UPHs. This initiative led to discussions (also prompted by ICCRI) to establish a GI in late 2008. In Bajawa, as elsewhere, an important first step toward a GI was the establishment of a new social organization—the Bajawa GI Protection Society (Masyarakat Perlindungan Indikasi Geografis, MPIG, established in 2009)—which would coordinate and submit the GI application to the National Intellectual Property Office. Funding support for the MPIG, including a secretariat in a government building, was provided by the local Office of Estate Crops, and technical support was provided by ICCRI, which was responsible for the preparation of the "Book of Requirements" (a central part of the application). The Bajawa GI was approved in 2011, prompting the establishment of an MPIG cooperative and a district regulation (issued in 2016) to "protect" Bajawa coffee through the GI. An as-yet-unrealized aspiration expressed by the MPIG in Bajawa, and one shared by state-supported MPIGs elsewhere in Indonesia, is to develop a monopolized marketing arrangement (*jalur satu pintu*) for all coffee grown within the GI region. The MPIG was further financially supported by an Indonesian-Swiss Intellectual Property Project (ISIP-II) in 2017.

Through an impact assessment study of both the Bajawa GI and the Kintamani GI conducted in 2016, we found little evidence, and a limited likelihood, of livelihood improvements for coffee growers because of the GI (Neilson, Wright, and Aklimawati 2018). This was due to the inability of local institutions supporting the GIs to "strategically couple"[8] with the practices and strategies of downstream buyers. This misalignment belies a continued strong interest in promoting GIs by the Indonesian state. Rural livelihoods are embedded within a regional institutional environment that is oriented toward the promotion of GIs but not toward strategic coupling with lead firms. Rather, state interest is driven by attempts on the part of local elites to use GIs as a means to access state resources (a *proyek* mentality); attempts to create rent-seeking opportunities through a supply monopoly; opportunities to promote regional cultural identities linked to the construction of symbolic political power; and a nationalist desire to protect cultural and geographical property against foreign appropriation. The first three drivers of state interest in GIs, which in turn cocreate the institutional environment within which the GIs are embedded, are all satisfied at the point when the GI is formally registered. The GI does not actually need to be properly functioning, replete with complicated quality control, traceability, and monitoring mechanisms, for these outcomes to be realized. The establishment of GIs, and state interest in them, can be explained not by a commitment to value capture within the value chain, but by a commitment to a domestically oriented political economy and symbolic reinforcement of relationships between the state and rural populations. Again, an ostensibly technocratic value chain intervention has again been reshaped by local institutions to serve political objectives quite distinct from their formally stated intentions.

Social Protection and Community Development Programs

In many Indonesian villages today, a key feature stands out in contrast to twenty years ago. Many of the houses have plaques on them proclaiming the household to be recipients of various government-funded social protection programs (figure 3.4). Admittedly, many villagers complain that the process of determining program beneficiaries is distorted by village-level politics, with considerable discretion still held by the village head to determine recipient households (McWilliam et al. 2023). None, however, deny that regular payments are flowing into rural Indonesia from the national budget and performing an important role in propping up livelihoods.

The Indonesian state is thus reshaping the institutional environment within coffee-growing communities through such social protection programs. Following international trends more broadly, Indonesia has transformed its social protection system by moving away from subsidies of energy, credit, fertilizers, and food, toward direct cash payments for needy households and a universal health insurance scheme (McCarthy, McWilliam, and Nooteboom 2023a). A key moment in the development of Indonesia's current social protection system was the introduction of the subsidized rice program (known as Raskin) in the wake of the 1998 Asian financial crisis. This then evolved into an assortment of conditional and unconditional cash transfers, educational cash stipends, and a cash-for-work program (Holmemo et al. 2020).[9] The basic formula for these programs

FIGURE 3.4. A social protection recipient household receiving four kinds of assistance, South Sulawesi, 2022. The sign literally reads, "incapable family—recipient of social assistance."

is a targeted approach that attempts to identify poor households (increasingly under a unified poverty database) and makes direct payments, or provides non-cash assistance, as part of a social safety net. Much hinges on the ability to accurately target vulnerable individuals, and this process has been consistently identified as problematic and susceptible to capture by local patronage structures (McCarthy and Sumarto 2018; McCarthy, McWilliam, and Nooteboom 2023a). Nevertheless, by 2018, six billion USD (about 6 percent of the national budget) was being spent by the central government on these programs annually, which were designed to reach the poorest 15 percent of households, with the outcome that a household receiving all four of the major payments would collect 44 percent of median consumption levels from the state (Holmemo et al. 2020).

By 2019, the main social support program (reaching ten million of Indonesia's sixty million households) was the conditional cash transfer scheme "Family Hope Program" (Program Keluarga Harapan, PKH), with payments ranging between 50 USD and 500 USD per household per year, while the school scholarship program also reached eighteen million students in 2018 with payments of up to 80 USD per student per year. De-linked from a tax system that has low levels of personal income reporting, it is difficult to enact means-tested social protection, and this has instead led to "nested" implementation where community-based distribution principles are interwoven in state-driven systems (McCarthy and Sumarto 2018; Katiman 2023). In the Indonesian context, there has yet to be a shift toward what Ferguson (2013) referred to as *asocial* assistance—the possibility that state-based social protection payments become disembedded from personalized social relationships.

As a result of these programs, Indonesia was better placed to minimize the livelihood effects of the COVID-19 crisis compared to the disastrous effects of the Asian financial crisis twenty years earlier. While there have been serious issues of corruption with the Ministry of Social Affairs responsible for COVID-19 relief and ongoing reports of misallocations (Guritno and Prabowo 2021), the government was able to expand existing programs quickly both horizontally (including more beneficiaries) and vertically (by increasing the amount of support). A survey of more than twelve thousand households conducted in December 2020 found that 85 percent of all households (and 95 percent of the poorest quintile) had received at least one form of social assistance (UNICEF et al. 2021). Similarly, I assisted Enveritas, a coffee certification organization, with a mobile phone survey of 1,306 coffee-growing households in Aceh and North Sumatra in November 2020, where we found that 70 percent of these households had received government support during 2020. The capacity of the Indonesian state to continue facilitating such transfers depends, of course, on its ability to effectively access fiscal resources from other parts of a growing economy. The point, however, is that these programs, as argued by Ferguson (2013) in the context of southern Africa, are embedding Indonesia's rural poor in a new distributive political economy.

In addition to social protection supports at the household level, another important set of state programs has been implemented at the community level. These can be traced back to a World Bank initiative known as the Kecamatan Development Program (KDP), which commenced in 1997 as an attempt to involve communities in the design, management, and monitoring of small project grants. Bebbington et al. (2004) described the KDP as an attempt to develop social capital within communities by building bottom-up accountability, where rules were enacted regarding community consultation, needs identification, project design, and tendering. The program was considered sufficiently successful by the Indonesian government that, from 2007 until 2014, it was scaled up to reach some seventy thousand villages nationwide, renamed the National Program for Community Empowerment (Program Nasional Pemberdayaan Masyarakat, or PNPM), and funded from the national budget at a cost of around two billion USD annually, such that it was reportedly the world's largest community-driven development program by 2014 (Balachandran and Choi 2015). Principles of community-driven development funding were then embedded within the Village Law of 2014, resulting in the Village Fund (Dana Desa) program, which replaced PNPM and had a national budget of five billion USD in 2020. Much of this community development funding has been spent on infrastructure like roads, bridges, irrigation facilities, water supply systems, and school buildings, constructed by local contractors (who thereby benefit from programmatic distribution). Over time, however, noninfrastructural activities like education scholarships, revolving credit funds, and health service provisioning have assumed increased prominence. When the COVID-19 crisis struck Indonesia, Dana Desa funding was partially reallocated as cash-based social protection payments. The strict, process-based requirements inherited from earlier KDP and PNPM iterations have been relaxed over time, and the previously critical role of program facilitators has been weakened. Distribution mechanisms appear to be slowly gravitating back in alignment with an underlying logic of selective state patronage.

One final example of state-facilitated resource transfers into Indonesia's rural regions involves ecological fiscal transfers (EFTs). Indonesia has joined a growing number of countries experimenting with transferring public revenue from higher to lower levels of government based on performance against specific ecological criteria. The idea (described by Busch et al. 2021) is that local governments are compensated for the costs of protecting ecological services. Models have been developed to adjust General Allocation Fund (Dana Alokasi Umum, DAU) payments to subnational governments based on ecological performance. The first implementation of an EFT in Indonesia was from a provincial government (North Kalimantan) to districts in 2020 based on demonstrative reductions in forest fires, water quality, air quality, waste management, and an open space index (Busch et al. 2021). This program is introducing further resource flows into rural regions that explicitly promote nonproductivist land uses. Similar funding mechanisms have been proposed in international deliberations regarding carbon financing under REDD+ schemes.[10]

Together, social protection payments, community-driven development programs, and ecological transfers constitute considerable state-facilitated resource transfers into the rural regions of Indonesia. While Indonesia had already shed pronounced urban policy bias during the New Order regime, these recent transfers are different again, as they are not necessarily related to productivist agriculture (unlike, for example, fertilizer subsidies or irrigation infrastructure). Furthermore, some schemes do not assume that social need is a temporary situation brought about by job loss (like unemployment benefits). Rather, they suggest implicit recognition that alternative—or perhaps complementary—mechanisms of wealth redistribution may be now a required supplement to simply expanding productive capacity and creating formal jobs.

It would, of course, be naive to assume these transfers are equitably shared within Indonesian villages. Li (2008) reported how the KDP program was easily co-opted by local elites, was unable to seriously challenge entrenched social structures, and ultimately continued to exclude the most vulnerable individuals and households. Meanwhile, McCarthy (2020, 1091) argued that "while social assistance softens the sharp edges of poverty for some, the benefits are too small and distributed to too few to make a substantial difference to most nutritionally insecure households across the season, let alone provide pathways out of poverty. Social protection programmes function more as a means of helping the poor cope." There is indeed an important distinction between the role of such payments as a social safety net (coping) and a possible accumulation pathway. A related concern, raised by Ferguson (2015), is whether direct cash payments to rural households may contribute to a more fundamental restructuring of social relations between state and society whereby development is no longer considered a privilege that is gifted by the state, but rather becomes an entitlement based on citizenship. Indeed, while these cash-based payments schemes have been based on need, there have also been broader demands for similar payments based entirely on citizenship (a universal basic income), along with a trend toward delivering international aid through cash-based initiatives like GiveDirectly.

These programs have opened new avenues through which rural livelihoods are being supported by the state in contemporary Indonesia and have realigned the importance of social capital, as a livelihood resource at the household level, in contributing to livelihood resilience. The broader implications for farming and land relations of such developments, however, are not well understood. These programs may potentially prop up otherwise less competitive agricultural activities and contribute to smallholder persistence on the land (Rigg, Salamanca, and Thompson 2016). Alternatively, a more "densely woven" state social security system may remove livelihood precarity and so encourage farmers to abandon the social safety net of farming entirely. Meanwhile, McCarthy, McWilliam, and Nooteboom (2023c) suggest that such programs' individualized nature threatens to undermine community cohesion and existing informal social support mechanisms based on mutual help.

Social Capital and the Patronage State in Indonesian Coffee-Growing Communities

In this chapter I have argued that the Indonesian state has demonstrated little interest in meaningfully intervening directly in improving productivity in the coffee sector. This can be partly explained by the relatively small contribution that coffee makes toward total export earnings (around 0.5 percent) and to total agricultural output (around 1.3 percent by volume). In Indonesia's increasingly industrialized (and service-based) economy, coffee is not generally considered to be a crop of strategic economic importance and so not apparently worth the effort of serious policy attention. Unlike cocoa, rubber, palm oil, and timber, coffee was not identified as a "main economic activity" within the National MP3EI Masterplan (2011–2025).

This chapter has shown more generally, however, how the state has been a dominant force reshaping the institutional environments of rural Indonesia, particularly through politically mediated redistribution. The state does intermittently implement specific *proyek*, such as the occasional distribution of seedlings and fertilizers through farmer groups, establishing UPH processing units, Geographical Indications, and MPIGs. These interventions involve a one-off, or time-bound, distribution of resources to farmers or, more commonly, farmer representatives who are positioned as heads of cooperatives, farmer groups, or other organizations. These interventions have thus tended to empower local elites in a broad social sense rather than drive industry transformation and the adoption of high-productivity farm practices.

Despite their lack of impact on industry development, government *proyek* do reinforce vertically oriented patronage hierarchies stretching from state funding agencies through local rural elites to farm households, where political acquiescence is rewarded with resource allocations. The state further performs a significant role in the lives of rural Indonesians beyond sector-specific *proyek*, as highlighted through the implementation of community development programs and the rising importance of social protection payments. For many, privileged access to the distribution of such resources presents an attractive social resource (social capital) for enhancing livelihood resilience. Furthermore, this intersects with the fiscal relationship between the Indonesian smallholder and the state. In recent years, there has been little overt taxation by the state on the agricultural surplus in Indonesia, beyond an occasional export levy on selected commodities, *retribusi* sometimes paid to regional governments, and fairly minimal payments (usually not more than a few dollars per year) paid in land tax. Overall, however, these are insignificant compared to the various sources of development funding and social protection payments delivered to the rural population. At the same time, state resources are used to enroll rural households as clients, and elites continue to seek individual opportunities to extract the wealth created by smallholders, with state-based actors regularly expressing their concerns about farmers leaving villages for urban jobs.

Elements of path dependency exist in the behavior and institutional patterns of the Indonesian state and its functionaries. Indeed, Aspinall and Berenschot (2019) emphasized the serious challenges that confront attempts to break out of behavioral norms that are deeply entrenched in societal expectations and practices. In their analysis of political corruption in Indonesia, they further make the point that the perpetuation of clientelism can be considered a problem of collective action in the sense that even though both patrons and clients may eventually benefit from ending such practices, they each stand to lose individually if they reject them in a context where others continue to act clientelistically. Individuals have agency, but social institutions evolve only slowly.

The declining significance of coffee to the national economy has also helped create institutional environments dominated by global capital rather than domestic state structures. Indonesian government agencies do not generally possess the coffee-specific technical knowledge or expertise, nor the desire to develop such capacity, which might otherwise facilitate or drive industry development, or accumulation, based on productivity gains. One consequence is the increasingly influential role played instead by private-sector representatives of the global coffee industry (discussed further in chapter 4) in providing sectoral support in Indonesia, as these actors have a greater stake than do government agencies in ensuring long-term supply of coffee. The next chapter will show how these two forces are in fact strongly interwoven. The key implication for fortress farming that arises from this analysis of the state, and state interventions, is that a broader ethos of patronage and clientelism so pervades much of rural Indonesia today that entrepreneurial agriculture, as a livelihood strategy, has moved to the background. It makes little sense to make significant investments in on-farm productivity improvements when investments in maintaining social capital with patrons seem to provide greater security and greater opportunity.

GLOBAL CAPITAL AND THE ORGANIZATION OF COFFEE VALUE CHAINS

All firms or other units of production receive inputs and send outputs. The transformation of the inputs that results in outputs locates them within a commodity chain (or quite often within multiple commodity chains). In terms of the structure of the capitalist world-economy, commodity chains may be thought of as the warp and woof of its system of social production.

—Terence Hopkins and Immanuel Wallerstein, *Commodity Chains and Global Capitalism* (1994)

The previous chapter presented the ways that Indonesia's estimated two million coffee-growing households are embedded within an institutional environment linked to the Indonesian state. These households, however, are also petty commodity producers incorporated within a global value chain (GVC), which links them, ultimately, with coffee roasters and drinkers around the world. The various actors involved in the coffee industry—smallholders, large-scale plantations, village collectors, traders, mill operators, exporters, coffee roasting and processing companies, and cafés—are all embedded within this GVC, and the economic fortunes of these actors are sensitive to the changing dynamics occurring along the chain.

The GVC conceptual framework helps, in the first instance, to demonstrate how value is created and captured through an input-output structure. When examining the entire chain, it becomes clear that powerful actors within the chain create "rules of the game" that influence processes not only within their own value-adding node of the chain, but also shape dynamics elsewhere. In the GVC literature, these powerful actors are referred to as "lead firms" and the influence they exert as "value chain governance." The critical conceptual contribution of GVC theory has thus been to highlight the ability of lead firms to act at distance to maximize surplus value extraction without resorting to direct ownership of functions undertaken by other actors.

The institutional environments of rural Indonesia are thus dominated by the mutual constitution of programs, policies, and ethos of the state (chapter 3) together with the powerful influences of lead firms. Applying a GPN (global production network) analytical framework, with a firm-centric view of development processes, Coe and Yeung (2015) refer to this interaction as "extra-firm bargaining," as lead firms negotiate with, and influence, other social actors (including states). Within my analytical framework, these interactions are critical to understanding institutional environments. This chapter will introduce the value chain for Indonesian coffee, identifying value-adding processes and key sets of actors responsible for the journey from farm to café. I examine the strategies employed by lead firms to enable value capture and their implications for chain governance and institutional environments. The key aim of this chapter is to demonstrate how lead firm strategies, interacting with extra-firm actors, contribute to multiscalar institutional environments in Indonesia's coffee-growing landscapes. This, however, is a delicate analytical endeavor. On the one hand, I am attempting to correct accounts of agrarian change that ignore the influence of downstream agribusiness firms. On the other, I also refrain from "value chain determinism" whereby all rural development outcomes are seen as determined by the nature of value chain engagement.

Value-Adding Processes along the Coffee Value Chain

The value chain for coffee is largely additive, in that it involves adding value to a single raw material through processing up to the point of consumption (where sugar, milk, and flavorings can be added). This makes coffee a relatively simple case. Value, however, is also added through intangible quality construction linked to marketing, brand management and ethicality, and indeed by the ambience of cafés and restaurants. Table 4.1 presents a basic input-output structure for the global value chain for coffee and the key actors involved at each stage, which will be elaborated on in this chapter.

Farm Production

Ilham is a Robusta coffee producer living in the Muara Enim uplands of South Sumatra, whom I met in 2019. He is a forty-five-year-old Semende man whose family have been living in the region for generations and whose father also grew coffee before him. Ilham himself has been managing his two-hectare coffee farm for around twenty years. He estimates that he averages twenty hours per week

TABLE 4.1   Input-output structure for the global value chain for coffee

VALUE-ADDING PROCESS	KEY ACTORS INVOLVED
1 Agricultural production	· Smallholders · Planters · Corporate and state-owned estate plantations
2 Local collection and aggregation	· Petty traders · Producer organizations (cooperatives) · Company buying stations
3 Hulling	· Producer organizations (cooperatives) · Local entrepreneurs / regional traders · Multinational commodity trading firms
4 Export and trade	· National traders and exporters · Multinational commodity trading firms
5 Manufacturing and branding (coffee roasting by lead firms)	· Instant coffee manufacturers · Roast and ground (R&G) manufacturers · Specialty coffee roasters · Producing-country manufacturers (instant, R&G, specialty)
6 Retail and consumption	· Supermarkets and groceries (at home consumption) · Roaster-retailers · Cafés and restaurants · Hotels

working on the farm, and is sometimes helped by his wife, Heni, and their three children (between fifteen and twenty-one years old). He says that he and Heni own the farm, inherited from Heni's parents, although they do not possess a landownership certificate from the state.

Sumatran coffee farmers like Ilham have long adopted planting regimes linked to swiddening.[1] van Noordwijk et al. (2008) suggest that forest regeneration (rather than use of fire) should be the core defining feature of swiddening. While traditional swidden systems in Indonesia (known as *ladang*, or *ladang berpindah*) focused on food crops, Cramb (1993) referred to the widespread practice of planting a perennial cash crop following annuals as a "managed swidden fallow system." Swiddening seeks to benefit from various agroecological services (described as "forest rents" by Ruf and Lançon 2004), which include soil fertility regeneration, pest and disease control, suppression of weeds, and crop pollination. It is through processes of integration with swidden that Indonesia's forest landscapes have emerged, at different times, as major world producers of pepper, coffee, rubber, cacao, and palm oil. Utomo (1967, 296) describes the process of establishing coffee gardens in a swidden in central Lampung in the 1950s: "The Lampung peasant grows his coffee within the shifting cultivation system, he constantly opens new swiddens, which provide him with the necessary rice and food crops, while in his old clearings he cultivates coffee, which eventually gives him a steady crop. Old groves that do not yield well any more are abandoned and left fallow, to be opened again after a period of several years."

Ilham had already fallowed some of his coffee trees after perhaps eight years of production in a pattern of tree-crop shifting cultivation. He did this once his coffee yields started to decline and the management effort became too onerous. The coffee trees were still there, but they were no longer productive. In contrast, some of Ilham's fellow villagers had made greater investments of labor and capital on coffee plots located closer to the village, which had resulted in a more permanent garden (*kebun*) being established. Ilham still referred to "ladang kopi" rather than "kebun kopi." In other parts of southern Sumatra, Javanese migrants have applied more intensive farming techniques on *kebun*. Swidden practices also confound state governance. Byrareddy et al. (2019) found 44 percent of coffee trees in their southern Sumatra study were less than ten years old, compared to 28 percent in Vietnam, suggesting a more frequent cycle of replanting in Indonesia. These landscapes are commonly constituted by dynamic mosaics of clearings, plantings of annual food crops, agroforestry systems, and regrowth forests (figure 4.1). Indeed, Scott (2009) goes as far as to argue that swiddening even reflects a deliberate strategy by communities across Southeast Asia to avoid capture by state interests.

FIGURE 4.1. Swidden landscape in Sumatra, with coffee planting and fallows, 2018

The coffee tree depends on various agroecological relationships to produce fruit. This starts with flowering, which is weather induced, responding to the first rains following mild drought stress. Growing regions without a dry period may not experience this stress and so will have lower yields, while untimely rains cause flowers to fall prior to pollination, and irregular rains can prompt multiple flowering events and a staggered harvest (with higher labor costs). Research in Sulawesi has further found that a diversity of pollinators, which are more likely to be found near forest edges, can significantly increase fruit set (Klein 2009). Coffee cherries reach maturity around eight months after pollination. Coffee farms depend on a range of other agroecological services, such as soil rejuvenation through fallowing, use of nitrogen-fixing plants, nutrient recycling through the leaf fall of shade trees, the activities of soil microorganisms, and the insect and microbial control of various pests and disease (Perfecto and Vandermeer 2015). The coffee berry borer (*Hypothenemus hampei*, a tiny beetle less than two millimeters long) is the most destructive insect pest for coffee in Indonesia. Its natural enemies, such as the fungus *Beauveria bassiana* (De La Rosa et al. 2000) and the ant species *Azteca instabilis* (Perfecto and Vandermeer 2006), can be promoted to minimize crop losses. Ilham's coffee benefits from some of these services, which are encouraged by thinly interspersed shade trees. He explained, however, how his production levels were determined largely by weather patterns and by the prevalence of pest infestation (and the will of Allah), all of which he believed were largely beyond his control. Such agroecological relationships are being affected by climate change. Studies have suggested that climate change will reduce the area suitable for coffee globally by about 50 percent (Bunn et al. 2015), although Schroth et al. (2015) predict that Indonesia may be less negatively affected than some other regions. At any rate, concerns over how climate change will affect global coffee supply have been at the forefront of lead firm strategies to address sustainability (discussed later in this chapter).

Ilham applies a small dose of nitrogenous fertilizer (urea) twice per year, sometimes with an additional round of superphosphate. Indonesian coffee-growing households, however, have generally chosen to minimize fertilizer application. A comparative study of coffee farmers in Vietnam and southern Sumatra found the former to be applying more than five times the amount of fertilizers of the latter during the period 2008–2017 (appendix table A2). According to another national survey, around 50 percent of Indonesian coffee-growing households applied no synthetic fertilizer at all in 2014 (appendix table A3).

The broader point here regarding the low intensity of coffee production, and dependence on agroecological services, is that smallholders like Ilham have intentionally chosen to maximize yields per unit of labor effort, while minimizing capital investment, rather than maximizing yields per hectare. Ilham pruned his trees by removing suckers and secondary branches, and he keeps the farm clear of weeds by spraying herbicide three times per year. He manages this year-round work on the farm himself, while his family assists at harvest time, when he also casually employs other villagers. In 2019, his two hectares of coffee produced the equivalent of around eight hundred kilograms of green coffee. This contrasts with average coffee yields in Vietnam that regularly exceed two tons per hectare (Rigal et al. 2023). Ilham sun-dries these cherries directly at his farmhouse (*dangau*) for around two weeks before transporting them by motorbike along a concrete path (recently built by a PNPM project) to the village, where he takes them to a small processor who removes the skin and parchment, leaving him with so-called *asalan* coffee. This is known as natural processing (figure 4.2). In the Arabica-growing regions of Indonesia, farmers will de-pulp the cherries first (remove the red skin), ferment them overnight, wash and then dry the coffee for a few days while it is still encased in a hard white shell (known as parchment), and then sell to collectors. This is known as wet processing, and the growth of higher-valued "specialty coffee" markets has resulted in increased attention to

FIGURE 4.2.   Natural processing coffee in South Sumatra, 2014

this activity by downstream actors. Specialty coffee processing requires greater labor investment and higher risk (figure 4.3).

Local Collection and Aggregation

Ilham sells *asalan* coffee to the same village-based collector he has been using for years, who weighs the coffee and makes a cash payment. When scattered smallholders live in remote uplands, aggregation is necessary, and such first-stage collectors are critical conduits between smallholders and downstream markets (figure 4.4 and figure 4.5). In 2014, almost all coffee-growing households across Indonesia sold their coffee to local collectors and traditional markets (appendix table A4). Direct sales to coffee companies and cooperatives are rare. Various terms are used for these collectors, including *pengumpul*, *tengkulak*, or simply *kolektor*, some of which connote exploitation associated with pre-harvest credit provision, compulsory sales, and arbitrary price-setting (a system known as *ijon*). These relationships are complex and variable but generally assume a classic

FIGURE 4.3.   Hand-sorting specialty coffee, South Sulawesi, 2010

patron-client form, whereby farmers also look to collectors as potential benefactors. Collectors are frequently from within the community, quite possibly kin of the farmer, and may also manage their own farm. Petty commodity trade is a frequent, and relatively accessible, first step out of poverty for rural households who can accumulate sufficient capital, and is generally preferred to expanding or increasing farm production. Despite sometimes complaining of exploitation, farmers also frequently state their appreciation of collectors as financiers in a national context where less than 10 percent of farmers obtain any finance for coffee production (appendix table A5). Ilham described the ease and convenience of borrowing from his collector and how, since his collector lives in the village, credit can be provided quickly if there is an urgent need. While pre-harvest loans to coffee farmers have declined over the last twenty years, allegiance to a particular collector-patron is still a common risk-management strategy.

Throughout the 2019 harvest, Ilham was selling coffee for between 18,000 and 19,000 rupiah per kilogram (around 1.3 USD, when the ICO Robusta indicator price was equivalent to 1.6 USD). Despite recurrent claims to the contrary, traditional marketing chains in Indonesia are relatively efficient, with farmers

FIGURE 4.4. Collector weighing coffee in a Sulawesi market, 2005

FIGURE 4.5.   Collector measuring parchment coffee by volume in North Sumatra, 2005

receiving around 80 percent of the international price. The price that Ilham receives is largely determined by global supply and demand. The ICO Robusta indicator price later skyrocketed to 4.4 USD per kilogram in mid-2024 owing to an extended drought in Vietnam, generating windfall profits for Indonesian farmers. Coffee commonly takes around three years from planting to bearing fruit, and this can create a time lag between supply shortages, sending a price signal to farmers and new production coming to market, contributing to the characteristic price instability of the global coffee market (although this has recently been moderated somewhat by enhanced supply responsiveness in Brazil and Vietnam). Price variability between years and, sometimes, within seasons remains a serious risk for Ilham. He addresses this risk by minimizing inputs.

Village-level trading requires, first and foremost, access to capital, as small-holders generally demand payment on delivery (if not before). Over the years, I have come to know local collectors operating in the Torajan coffee markets, where they are known as *tengkulak*. Many grew up in Torajan coffee-growing villages, like Yohanes, who started collecting coffee in the 1990s after obtaining a loan from his brother, who was then working in Kalimantan. Other collectors I have met have accessed capital from prior agricultural accumulation, from using land certificates as collateral for a bank loan, or have accessed it from government programs (usually as a leader within a producer organization). Others have obtained it from downstream buyers, for whom they act as agents (sometimes known as *kakitangan*). Some traditional trade networks (figure 4.6) depend on an unbroken chain of such financing through three or four stages of aggregation through to export. For Yohanes, it is important that he maintains trust-based, but noncredit, relationships with downstream mills.

Groups of smallholders may cooperate to pool larger quantities of coffee and undertake collective marketing (this, however, is rare; appendix table A4). As described in chapter 3, state-funded development interventions have long supported the establishment of cooperatives with the aim of improving the "bargaining position" of farmers, so they can "escape from the clutches of the collector"—common refrains among NGOs and government officials. All too

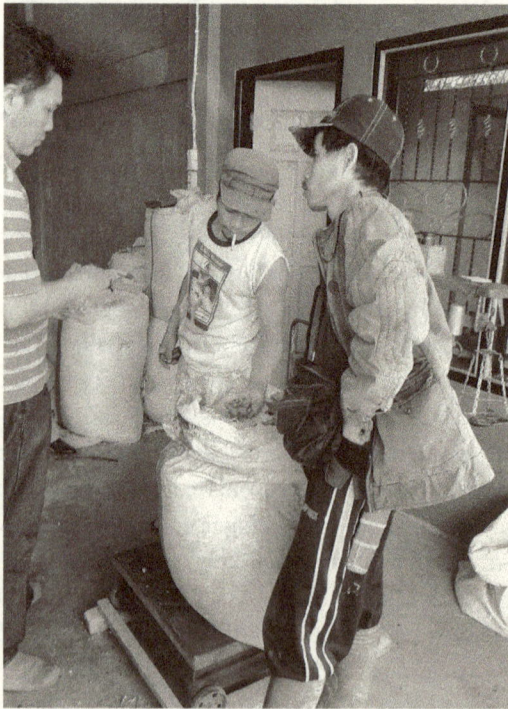

FIGURE 4.6. Farmer negotiating about quality and price with a trader, Sumatra, 2013

often, however, these interventions struggle to remain competitive once external support is withdrawn (Hartatri, Aklimawati, and Neilson 2019). Indeed, given the slender margins between collectors and the export market, there is little value-added to capture anyway. Patronage can also be provided to producer organizations by buyers, such as Nestlé, supporting KUBEs in Lampung. The introduction of sustainability standards (discussed later in this chapter) has also encouraged smallholders to work through cooperatives as preferred organizational structures. The Global Coffee Platform (GCP), for example, appealed to its private-sector members "to organize small-scale farmers to form cooperatives" in its 2016 *Vision 2020/2030—Call for Action*. Such interventions by buyers are locally influential but not yet widespread. Some international companies have also established buying stations to purchase directly from farmers, but these tend to be high-cost and need to be offset by value-adding through quality control, traceability, or symbolic value addition. More generally, coffee is moved along the chain by private traders with gradually increasing scales of aggregation until it reaches either an exporter or a domestic coffee roaster.

Coffee Milling, Export, and Trade

The first activity along the chain that requires a significant investment of fixed capital is milling, which involves the removal of the hard parchment with the use of specialized factory-made equipment (a huller). At its simplest, as in the case of Ilham in South Sumatra, it is a village business operating on a fee-for-service basis. In chapter 3, I described how, in Kintamani, producer organizations undertake this activity as part of a collectively owned business (supported by the state). Elsewhere, milling is undertaken by traders and so requires both fixed and operating capital. This milling function is particularly important in Arabica value chains, and some international firms have vertically integrated into it to better control quality (figure 4.7).

Most Indonesian coffee makes its way into the export market; USDA Gain Reports between 2014 and 2022 have estimated this share at around 60 percent of total production. Exporters maintain warehouses near containerized ports in places like Medan, Bandar Lampung, and Surabaya, where hulled beans are put through further processing by polishers (to remove a flaky "silverskin"), de-stoners, sorters, graders, and bagging machines. Access to low-wage workers is important for these exporters for activities like bean sorting (figure 4.8). The value chain is concentrated at this node, where profits depend on high turnover rather than high margins. Relationships between exporters and the state remain important, although less so now than during the pre-1989 international quota regime administered by the International Coffee Organisation (ICO, an

FIGURE 4.7. Foreign investment in an Arabica mill in North Sumatra, 2005

intergovernmental organization), when the state actively protected domestically owned exporters from foreign competition. Over the last thirty years, multinational trading firms have established a direct presence at these ports, and this node is now dominated by global firms like Neumann Kaffee, Ecom, Olam International, Louis Dreyfus, ED&F Man (Volcafe), Cofco, Sucafina, and Sucden (Nedcoffee). Indeed, as specialist supply chain managers with international experience, access to cheaper finance, and the ability to engage in futures trading on international exchanges, the five largest traders controlled an estimated 50 percent of total global coffee trade in 2021 (Panhuysen and Pierrot 2021). These traders have also consolidated their function as strategic partners of multinational coffee roasting firms by assuming greater responsibility for implementing sustainability programs and ensuring traceability.

The United States and Japan have been the most important destinations for Indonesian green coffee since the 1990s, with the importance of Malaysia and Egypt increasing over time (figure 4.9). The dominance hitherto of Western markets, with largely consistent approaches to supply chain practices, has contributed to the influence of organizational platforms like the Global Coffee Platform within Indonesia (discussed later in this chapter). However, shifting end-markets

FIGURE 4.8. Hand-sorting Arabica coffee for export, Java, 2011

(including the rising importance of domestic consumption within Indonesia) mean that perhaps half of Indonesia's coffee production now flows toward non-Western buyers.

Coffee Roasting

Coffee beans need to be roasted prior to consumption. At its simplest, this might involve a frying pan over a fire, but more sophisticated facilities characterize the industry to produce either soluble (instant) coffee or roasted coffee. "Artisanal" specialty coffee roasters can also be quite technically simple (figure 4.10). Although instant coffee is generally less expensive at the retail level and draws on lower-quality raw coffee beans, the process itself is capital-intensive and more technologically sophisticated (using techniques such as freeze or spray drying). Robusta coffee from Sumatra is generally sold into these lower-priced markets, while Indonesian Arabica finds its way into specialty markets. Conventional industry wisdom maintains that roasting requires advanced skills, even artistry, and this includes specialist cupping (tasting) capabilities. Commercial brands need to offer consistent-tasting coffees to consumers, which is achieved

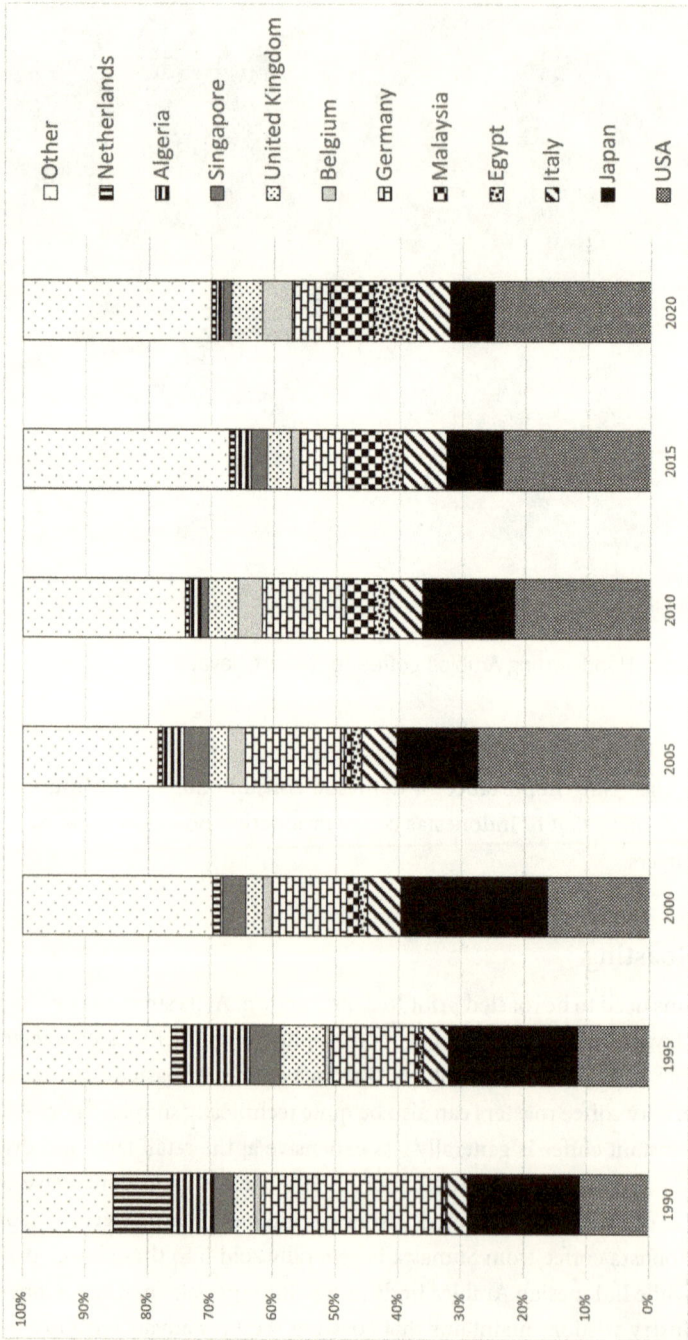

FIGURE 4.9. Major export destinations for Indonesian green coffee in terms of value (1990–2020).

Source: United Nations Comtrade 2024.

by carefully adjusting the composition of different origins (blending). Roasters thus require access to coffees from multiple origins, and the bulk of this sourcing, along with inventory and supply chain management, has long been outsourced to commodity traders (Ponte 2002).

Innovative product development also determines competitiveness at the roasting node. Ready-to-drink products like canned coffee and instant coffees premixed with sugar and creamer (sometimes known as "3-in-1") are popular in Indonesia and have been an important means of value capture for roasters. Increasingly popular prepackaged "coffee pods," which allow a convenient, mess-free, espresso-style experience in the home or workplace, were pioneered by Nestlé when the Nespresso brand was launched in 1986. This product segment has continued to grow, and similar products have been developed by other lead firms after 2012 (when Nespresso patents expired). Product development by roasters occurs alongside another key site of value addition—brand management. Indeed, according to Nestlé's 2018 financial report, expenditure on "marketing and administration" was 21.5 billion USD (a quarter of all outgoings) compared to just 1.8 billion USD on "Research and Development."[2] Effective brand management includes projecting an image as an ethically responsible firm ("Creating Shared Values," as Nestlé puts it),

FIGURE 4.10. An artisanal specialty coffee roaster in Sydney, Australia, 2023

actively contributing to a sustainability agenda, and disassociating the firm from allegations of social and environmental neglect. Nestlé (2021, 80) explains that "it's vitally important to translate the sustainability strategy into brand and business value or, over time, sustainability becomes just a cost to be managed."

As a result of the higher skill, capital, and technological requirements, roasting is the node where most value addition and capture occurs. It is also the node occupied by lead firms, whose corporate strategies reverberate throughout the chain and shape institutional environments and development prospects elsewhere, including in Indonesia.

Retail and Consumption

Coffee consumption generally occurs either in the home, the office, or in the hospitality sector (cafés, restaurants, bars, and hotels). Home consumption is reliant on retail sales from supermarkets and convenience stores and was responsible for between 65 and 80 percent of total global coffee sales by volume in 2017 (Samper, Giovannucci, and Marques Vieira 2017). Recent trends toward online coffee sales for home consumption (Shoup 2018 reported that coffee was one of Amazon's fastest growing product lines) have been associated with even greater product differentiation and enhanced origin-branding. Roasters generally supply coffee to the hospitality sector, sometimes offering a complete service that might include provision of branded sugar sachets, shade umbrellas, and espresso machine hire and maintenance. The meteoric rise of Starbucks in the 1990s (Clarke 2007), however, pioneered the phenomenon of roaster-retailer chains as out-of-home consumption emerged as a key site of value addition (Daviron and Ponte 2005). This is embodied in the personal interactions offered in the café environment, the specialist role of the barista, and the ambience of the space itself. The personalized world of cafés has been another important factor leading to ethical sourcing trends.

An essentially colonial pattern of international trade has been in place for centuries since European consumption began driving value chains back into Asia, Africa, and the Americas. The US eventually became the world's single most important consuming country. Europe and the US continued to dominate consumption well into the twentieth century, with Japanese consumption rising in the 1970s. More recent growth in global coffee consumption, however, has occurred more rapidly outside these traditional consuming markets. Figure 4.11[3] shows the rapid growth occurring within the producing countries themselves (led by Brazil, Indonesia, Vietnam, and the Philippines) and within nonproducing emerging markets across East Asia and the Middle East, such that leading roasters from these countries are also starting to drive chain governance.

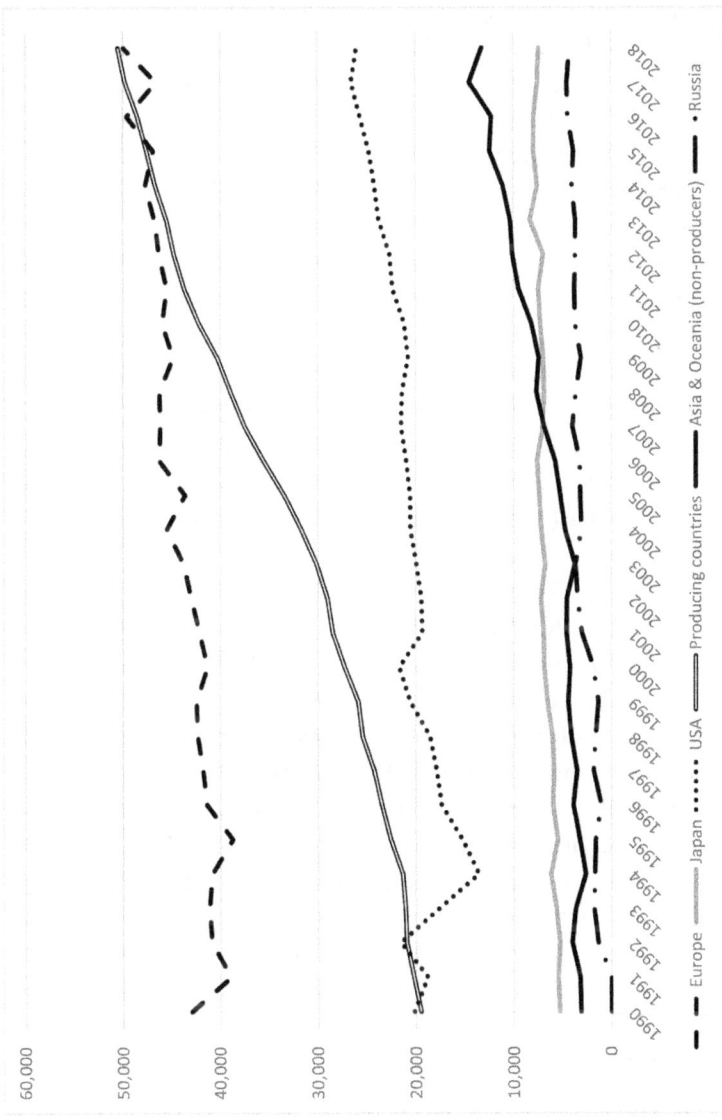

FIGURE 4.11. Changing global consumption of coffee (1990–2018) in thousands of sixty-kilogram bags.

Source: ICO 2020.

Governance of Coffee Value Chains and Lead Firm Strategies

The pioneering work of Stefano Ponte (2002) and Daviron and Ponte (2005) in analyzing the global value chain for coffee highlighted the role of global coffee roasters as lead firms who, since the collapse of the international quota system, have been "driving" chain governance (see also Talbot 2004).[4] Following a series of mergers and acquisitions, and increased financialization, two firms, Jacobs Douwe Egberts (JDE) and Nestlé, together had come to control a 20 percent share of the global coffee consumer market by 2020 (Panhuysen and Pierrot 2021). Their sourcing strategies have considerable influence over production dynamics in Indonesia. Lead firms pursue corporate strategies in response to the competitive pressures of global capitalism, and this has meant that, in the coffee sector, less-profitable functions like commodity sourcing and farm production are routinely outsourced. At the same time, lead firms are exposed to systemic environmental, social, and political risks, and this has driven firm strategies in relation to "sustainability." The resulting value chain governance structures then interact with extra-firm actors, like NGOs, states, development agencies, and worker unions, to co-construct multiscalar institutional environments in producing regions.

Multinational roasters have become influential within the ICO through a Private Sector Consultative Board (PSCB, established in 1999) and a Coffee Public-Private Task Force (in the ICO's International Coffee Council, established in 2019). Within Indonesia, owing to the relative weakness of coffee-related government agencies, lead firms co-construct institutional environments with fragmented elements of the Indonesian state. While large multilateral development banks, such as the World Bank and the Asian Development Bank, have delivered large coffee-related projects through the Indonesian state (chapter 3), international development assistance has increasingly adopted a "value chains for development" approach (Neilson 2014). Such an approach has the effect of enhancing the upstream influence of lead firms from donor countries. International institutions have thus intermeshed at the national and subnational levels, often through a myriad of North-South funding arrangements, and have tended to reinforce the agenda-setting role of lead firms. The 2015 establishment of the Sustainable Coffee Platform for Indonesia (SCOPI) by the Global Coffee Platform (GCP) is an example of this.

Lead firms also engage in extra-firm bargaining with globally active NGOs. The Specialty Coffee Association (SCA)[5] was established in 2017 through a merger between the Specialty Coffee Association of America (SCAA) and the Specialty Coffee Association of Europe (SCAE) and performs an influential role in setting global norms, protocols, standards, and industry culture. The US-based Coffee Quality Institute's "Q Program" has developed a global system of professional accreditations, while competition events such as the World Barista Championship and the Cup of Excellence confer credibility and industry clout for winners and finalists. A global coffee research agenda is set by a US-based industry-funded NGO, World Coffee Research, along with the Association for the Science and Information on Coffee (ASIC), which has considerable support from European industry actors like Nestlé and Illy. Finally, industry publications like *Roast*, *Global Coffee Report*, and *Perfect Daily Grind* provide platforms for constructing influential industry discourses. The key point here is to highlight the complex ecosystem of private organizations operating globally that create industry norms (institutions), which ultimately shape opportunities and constraints for Indonesian actors.

Industry norm-setting is important since institutional environments are also contested discursive fields. An example related to rural development discourse was an influential 2014 report titled *Indonesia: A Business Case for Sustainable Coffee Production*, by the US-based NGO TechnoServe, which purports to "take a business approach to reduce poverty." The report was prepared for the Sustainable Coffee Program (a precursor to the GCP) managed by IDH (the Dutch Sustainable Trade Initiative). The report stated that "Indonesia could become a net Robusta importer within 10 years . . . [and that] without Indonesia's export base, or the emergence of a new low-cost producer, the international coffee industry is likely to encounter a substantial supply gap in the next ten years" (TechnoServe 2014, 3). Ten years later, it should be noted, Indonesia continued to export a considerable volume of coffee. This report, however, helped galvanize action from lead firms concerned about losing an important commodity source region. The key theme of the report (page 2) was that "the international coffee industry has a rare opportunity to catalyze this change and invest in smallholder training. Boosting yields would address root issues in the sector, raise farmers' incomes by seventy percent, and improve the business case for supply chain actors to co-invest in sustainability efforts." TechnoServe identified what it called "active" coffee farmers and advocated support for these producers above others. A dominant discourse was thus constructed whereby a focus on improving yields was presented as being in the best interests of coffee producers, and, in this light, the report remained blind to fortress farming livelihood strategies. Related discourses are also constructed around the poverty-alleviating benefits of quality improvement programs, despite such assumptions breaking down on closer examination (Neilson, Hartatri, and Vicol 2019). Increasing yields, supply, and quality are, however, unquestionably in the best interests of lead firms. Extra-firm bargaining thus involves not only attempts by lead firms to influence various activities, projects, polices, approaches, and interventions of nonfirm actors, but to indirectly shape the broader discourses that frame what is considered inherently desirable for producer communities.

Outsourcing and Value-Adding through Domestic Roasting

Lead firms routinely outsource economic functions to strategic partners who have the capability to undertake those functions more efficiently. Brand management, product development, and coffee roasting were once so closely entwined that roasters could be referred to as "branded manufacturers." However, as branding becomes the core function of lead firms, we are witnessing some tentative moves toward the outsourcing of roasting. This is evident in the emergence of private-label roasting (or "toll roasting"), where coffee is roasted by one firm to be sold under a client's brand (Grant 2020). The global head of research and development from one of the world's largest branded coffee firms explained to me (in 2023) why his company was no longer involved in soluble coffee manufacturing: "It's too much effort. Why would we bother investing in factories around the world when companies like Olam can do it much better and cheaper than us?"

This is occurring both in high-end markets (for example, individualized blends for cafés and restaurants) and among cheaper soluble coffees and extracts. This is providing opportunities for Indonesian industrialists. The long-distance coffee trade was conventionally in green beans. Transporting roasted coffee is more expensive, requires greater care, and is more susceptible to quality deterioration, while effective branding requires intimate local consumer knowledge. As a result, roasting was conventionally located close to final consumption, thus limiting downstream value-adding within producing countries. This, however, is changing, and figure 4.12 shows the significant growth in the processed coffee trade.

The roasted coffee trade includes exports of globally branded products from the Global North. Producer countries, however, have also begun manufacturing and exporting lower-priced soluble coffees and coffee extracts. While the higher-end specialty markets require greater lead firm control over roasting, this is less so in the soluble sector. Value addition ("functional upgrading" in the GVC literature) has subsequently been picked up by multinational commodity traders like Singapore-based Olam International, which has built a soluble coffee plant in Vietnam and sells to commercial private-label customers. The rapid growth of bulk soluble exports from Indonesia (figure 4.13) has occurred primarily through investments by Indonesian industrialists, mainly for export to other Asian markets.

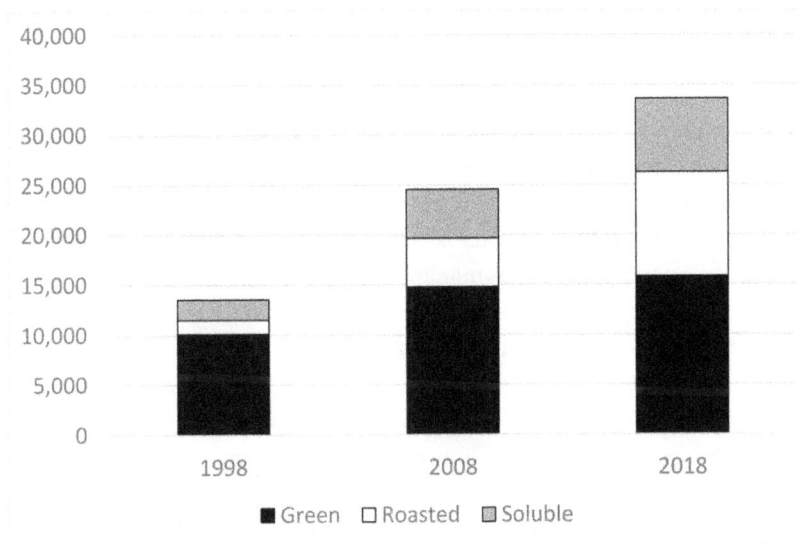

FIGURE 4.12. Share of international coffee trade by commodity form (million USD—current).

Source: United Nations Comtrade 2021.

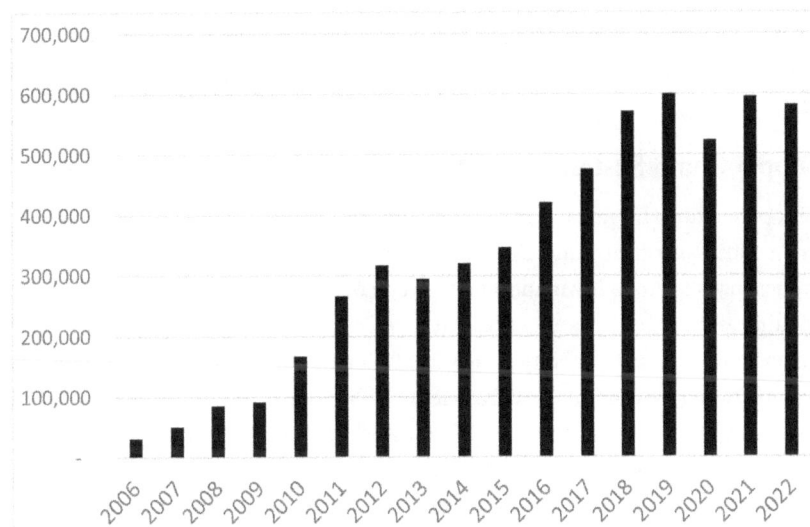

FIGURE 4.13. Value of Indonesian soluble (instant) coffee exports (in thousand USD, 2006–2022) (HS Codes 210211 and 210112).

Source: United Nations Comtrade 2024.

Indonesia's consumer market is also globally strategic for lead firms. Nestlé has a coffee manufacturing plant in Indonesia and is the foreign-owned company with the largest share of the Indonesian coffee market, estimated at 6.7 percent (by retail value) in 2022 (Euromonitor 2022). Indonesian-owned brands, however, remain dominant. Euromonitor (2022) estimated that five domestically owned companies (all Java-based) were responsible for 87 percent of Indonesian coffee retail value, with the Surabaya-based Kapal Api Group alone holding a 47.5 percent market share. Euromonitor (2021) reported Kapal Api to be the world's seventh-largest coffee company.

The Indonesian government identified downstreaming (*hilirisasi*), or domestic value-adding of raw materials, as a strategic development objective within its Economic Masterplan (2011–2025).[6] Taxes and bans on raw material exports have been imposed on other commodities (such as cocoa beans, rattan, and mineral ores like nickel) in recent years (Neilson et al. 2020). This prompted industrial interests within the Indonesian Chamber of Commerce (Kadin) to consider replicating the policy toward coffee (Bayu 2018). By 2024, however, the government had not pursued an interventionist coffee-related industrial policy. Indonesian firms have assumed control of value-adding functions anyway. Domestic café chains, such as Excelso (owned by Kapal Api) are competing alongside international chains, with Starbucks (2021) reporting to have 326 stores across twenty-two Indonesian cities in 2018. The growing influence of domestically owned coffee roasters within Indonesia has encouraged direct sourcing programs that offer unique opportunities for livelihood upgrading within producer communities (discussed below in the context of specialty coffee markets).

Supply Chain Sustainability Programs

Risk perceptions by global lead firms encouraged the rapid rise of "sustainability" as a central aspect of value chain governance (Grabs 2020). Ponte (2019) even argues that sustainability management is emerging as a fourth capitalist dynamic (adding to the three dynamics presented by Coe and Yeung 2015).[7] Certainly, the management of sustainability is decisively shaping lead firm strategies that are reconstituting institutional environments in Indonesia and in other producing countries. There exists a considerable supply risk from concentration of production within Vietnam and Brazil, resulting in initiatives to promote coffee cultivation elsewhere. Stefan Canz, global manager of Nestlé's Farmer Connect sustainability training program, explained why Nestlé had adopted sustainable sourcing strategies: "To be very honest. It's a very selfish approach because it's about ensuring supply. We have factories all over the world. Not only in Europe and the US, but also in the countries of production. So, if the production goes down, we are the first to suffer, it's as simple as that."[8] There is also the risk that climate change will affect supply, leading to initiatives to promote "climate-smart" farming, with the 2024 global Robusta shortage considered by some to be a harbinger of future supply vulnerability. Perhaps the greatest risk for coffee lead firms, however, lies in reputational damage and the need to disassociate brands from allegations of social and environmental abuses within their supply chains.

Lead firms began responding to broader societal pressures to be more sustainable, and fairer, by implementing stricter traceability measures during the so-called coffee crisis of 2000–2002 (Neilson and Pritchard 2007). This dovetailed with previous initiatives developed by NGOs to provide third-party certification for fair trade, organic, and shade-grown coffee. Initially, such schemes provided a means of product differentiation for lead firms, but they soon became embedded within broader supply chain management strategies, as firms committed to more generic sustainability labels like Rainforest Alliance, Utz Certified, and the 4C Standard (the Common Code for the Coffee Community). 4C was an industry-driven initiative, formerly owned by a member-based platform (the 4C Association) that included major global lead firms.[9] By 2015, up to 52 percent of global coffee production was thought to be third-party certified, making coffee the most certified agricultural commodity in the world (Grabs 2020). Certification standards provided clear ethical messaging to consumers while also driving enhanced upstream involvement by firms in producing regions.

In Indonesia, implementation of certification standards has involved large commodity traders developing a supply base of farmers, building or strengthening producer organizations, rolling out farmer training programs, preparing farmers for a third-party audit, facilitating the audit, and then maintaining traceability (this process is discussed further in chapter 7). Responsibility for implementation has thus fallen largely on traders, some of whom make proprietary-like claims over individual farms within their supply chain (figure 4.14). The willingness of traders to make these investments is dependent either on long-term purchasing commitments from roasters, or direct funding by roasters. The impacts of certification standards on producer livelihoods and environmental outcomes, however, have been widely debated within the industry and by researchers and have generally been disappointing (Bray and Neilson 2017, 2018; Oya, Schaefer, and Skalidou 2018; Neilson, Toth, Sari, et al. 2019; Garrett et al. 2021). Furthermore, the administrative burden can be overwhelming for some smallholder organizations (figure 4.15), such that reputational benefits accrue to lead firms while producers bear the costs.

Strategic decisions made by lead firms are central to the reach and impact of standards. In 2010, Nestlé launched its Nescafé Plan, which committed to having 70 percent of all Nescafé coffee supplies "responsibly sourced" and audited by

FIGURE 4.14. Coffee plot "claimed" by a value chain sustainability program (the sign reads "hunting forbidden"), 2009

FIGURE 4.15. Small cooperative overwhelmed with sustainability-related paperwork in Sulawesi, 2009

third parties by 2020 (much of this through 4C). The pendulum, however, may be swinging against third-party standards. For example, after steadily increasing their purchasing volumes of certified coffees from 2007, the German roaster Tchibo made the strategic decision in 2016 to reduce purchases of 4C coffee. As of March 19, 2020, their website explained,

> In 2016, we embarked on a new strategic path in our purchasing of green coffee grades validated according to the 4C base standard, because we believe that the basic requirements of the validation system for the 4C standard alone are no longer sufficient to further develop the supply chain across the board. . . . In the course of this, in 2016 we reduced our purchase volume of 4C-validated green coffee grades compared to 2015, and used the freed-up funds for "Mainstreaming Sustainable Coffee Production" and our supply chain programmes.

This retreat from third-party certified sourcing is not unique. According to its corporate website, as of August 18, 2020, JDE is working toward "responsibly sourced" coffee, which is broadly defined to encompasses an in-house corporate sustainability program (Common Grounds). This waning interest in third-party standards is driven by perceived inflexibility and high costs for a system that has had few proven social and environmental benefits. However, this trend, if sustained, should not be interpreted as a shift away from lead firm commitments to sustainability. Rather, new sustainability strategies are emerging. Irrespective of such trends, third-party standards have had widespread influence over the last two decades, with the lasting effect of stimulating far greater lead firm influence over institutional environments in producing regions (discussed further in chapter 7).

The strategy behind the apparent shift toward in-house corporate sustainability programs (such as JDE's Common Grounds and Tchibo's Joint Forces) has been to associate sustainability claims and commitments directly with corporate brand identities. Nestlé even has separate in-house programs for its two flagship brands: the Nespresso AAA Sustainable Quality Program and the Nescafé Plan. Great diversity exists among these in-house programs. JDE's Common Grounds has pursued what might be labeled a "project approach," where it makes specific investments in projects that are said to be tailored to the specific developmental needs of the producing region—through consultation with strategic suppliers and an "Origin Issue Assessment." While Common Grounds was initially developed in partnership with Rainforest Alliance, it is not a standard, and is only indirectly associated with supply chain purchasing. The JDE corporate website (August 18, 2020) explains, "Under *Common Grounds*, we source coffee, tea and palm oil that is either certified or verified or sourced from origins where JDE jointly addresses priority social and environmental challenges through impactful engagement with our suppliers and farmers." In Indonesia, four of the five Common Grounds projects presented on the JDE website in 2021 were implemented by four different global commodity traders. Common Grounds initiatives in southern Sumatra have focused on such issues as the capacity building of farmer organizations, agroforestry training, and deforestation-free coffee production. In 2020, JDE further partnered with one of its preferred suppliers to prepare and distribute hygiene kits, with reusable masks, soap, and a COVID-19 information kit. These initiatives are explicitly extending company influence "beyond the chain" and have begun actively rearranging the institutional environment in producer regions like Sumatra. Lead firms are also developing service delivery models for farmers, hoping to have greater influence over production processes to increase coffee supply. Nestlé's Farmer Connect program has already been discussed (it is operational in Lampung), while Starbucks has a similar, if smaller, initiative in North Sumatra through its Farmer Support Centers. Ecom, a commodity trader, has also developed its Sustainability Management Services (SMS) division to provide farmer services and to generate profits through input markets.

Third-party sustainability standards, in-house sustainability programs, supplier codes of contract, service delivery models, and firm-specific sustainability projects are important mechanisms through which lead firms manage risk and sustainability and, in so doing, are transferring resources back into producing regions. Irrespective of the effectiveness of such in-house projects in meeting their intended aims, they are reformulating the institutional environment presented to coffee smallholders, with effects that will be examined in later chapters.

Specialty Markets and Relationship Coffees

Starting in the 1990s, the global coffee sector experienced a pronounced turn to quality with the emergence of specialty coffee markets and the rise of large roaster-retailers like Starbucks. Rather than blending different origins to create a standardized product with brand names such as Nescafé or Moccona, the specialty sector celebrates the range of tastes offered by different producing regions (known as single-origin coffee). It is awash with place-based marketing and stories about roaster trips to farms. The Australian-based specialty coffee roaster Five Senses has been at the forefront of both using place-based marketing and developing relationships with Indonesian coffee growers for more than a decade. Like other specialty roasters, Five Senses frequently posts "Origin Trip Field Reports" accompanied by photos and anecdotes about relationships formed with farmers. The Five Senses website posted one such field report on December 4, 2017:

The aim for this trip was to visit our mill north of Lake Toba, taking in all the scenes and cultural differences along the way to best understand the unique and challenging Sumatran coffee production cycle. . . . These origin trips are an incredible chance to get up and close with the processing and relationships that make up our coffee supply. As a team we were able to witness the layers of production and difficulties often faced at the producing end of the supply chain. Some of the most enjoyable yet difficult times of these trips is understanding and talking through the hardships faced by the incredible people of Sumatra that supply to our Tiga Raja Mill partnership. . . . Here's a small selection of pictures that highlight our adventures, enjoy!

There is an indication here of how the production landscape provides an intangible service to these roasters, allowing them to capture value through symbolic quality construction. The governance of quality is fundamental to determining who benefits from product differentiation, and roaster-driven quality constructions have been able to appropriate place-related quality associations by using trademarks, vertical integration, and tightly coordinated supply chain controls (Neilson 2007). The paradox of booming specialty coffee consumption alongside a coffee crisis in producing countries was explained by Daviron and Ponte (2005) by the ability of lead firms to extract value from the symbolic and in-person attributes of coffee, including the use of place-based product differentiation, whereas producers' coffee was valued exclusively for its material attributes.

Indonesia's Arabica-growing regions have been prominent origins within this specialty sector, and this has allowed certain producing regions (like Toraja; see chapter 6) to demand higher prices (sometimes two to three times higher than Sumatran Robusta). In the case of Toraja, this involves the extensive marketing use of cultural imagery (*tongkonan* houses and their pictographs, figure 4.16). The ability of specialty roasters to present insider knowledge of origins, along with their heightened sensitivity to ethical claims, has led to what has become known in the industry as "relationship coffee," as discussed by Holland, Kjeldsen, and Kerndrup (2016), Hernandez-Aguilera et al. (2018), and, in Indonesia, by Vicol et al. (2018). The Five Senses mill in Sumatra is one such example. Roasters claim that these relationships are built around personal interaction, mutual trust, price transparency, a commitment to quality improvement, and a stated intention to improve the lives of coffee farmers. They can lead to higher prices for farmers, but they also enable firms to establish traceability, improve stability and reliability of supply, reduce or transfer risk, influence coffee production practices (and therefore quality), and achieve reputational and marketing goals (Holland, Kjeldsen, and Kerndrup 2016).

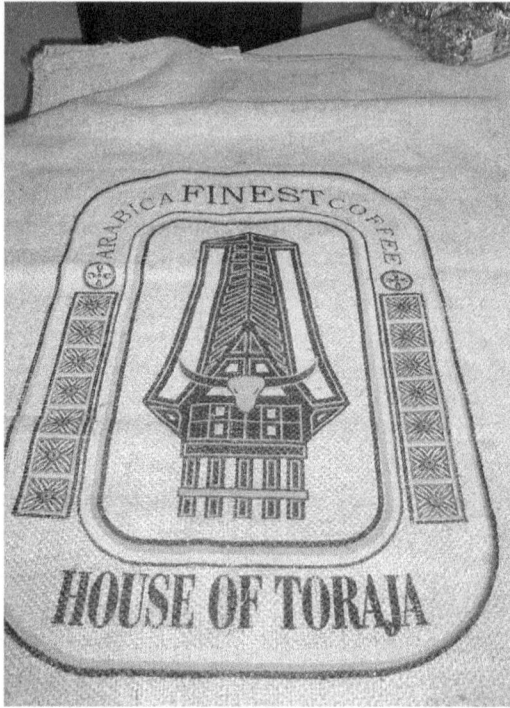

FIGURE 4.16. Downstream branding using Torajan cultural imagery, Surabaya exporter, 2011

Relationship coffees initiated by Indonesian specialty roasters may have even greater impact (figure 4.17). Since 2008, I have conducted action-research activities with Derby, a Jakarta-based roaster and green bean trader, who has established supply chains in various origins. Derby developed skills and knowledge by earlier working on a relationship between an Australian coffee roaster and a farmer cooperative in Sulawesi. His ability to regularly visit farmers, share meals, and joke together has facilitated a (so far) enduring relationship lasting ten years. This involves working with Petrus, a village-based processor, in the Bajawa region of Flores. In a familiar pattern repeated elsewhere, Petrus had himself benefited from being the head of a coffee processing unit (an UPH) supported by the local government, through which he learned how to process specialty coffee. Over time, Petrus added his own capital to the business, accessed occasional support from Derby, and then received support, in 2019 and 2020, from the German development organization GIZ. This processing unit has come to be effectively (and successfully) managed as a household business by Petrus. The relationship with Derby evolved from initial purchases of a few bags in 2010 (smaller volumes

FIGURE 4.17. Jakarta-based actors are setting up specialty supply chains in rural Indonesia, 2018

are made possible by the relative simplicity of domestic trade) through to more than twenty tons in 2019. Domestically oriented supply chain relationships have been profitable for local actors like Petrus across Indonesia, presenting opportunities for value capture for strategically positioned individuals who benefit from multiple forms of patronage (from downstream roasters, the state, and NGOs).

Relationship coffees do not involve third-party auditing, with (largely unverifiable) claims about community impact presented through online testimonies. With colleagues, I have examined livelihood impacts in three relationship coffee interventions in Bali, West Java, and South Sulawesi, where roasters facilitated an exchange of knowledge, technology, physical infrastructure, and financial capital to producer organizations. In each case, although the relationship was promoted as being with "farmers," it was actually with an organization controlled by local village elite (Vicol et al. 2018). Unsurprisingly, benefits are primarily captured by these elites, although farm-gate prices were also found to marginally improve. Rather than operating as firms, these producer organizations constitute part of the social matrix in rural Indonesia, where multifaceted patronage and mutual exchange obligations can be a critical component of livelihood resilience for clients, and a vehicle for accumulation for patrons. Several of the relationships we examined over an eight-year period broke down over time, even if the underlying social structures (the producer organizations led by charismatic individuals) endured. During the period of the relationship, however, a series of gifts, loans, skills, and material resources had been transferred to these local partners.

Industry Platforms, Partnerships, and "Landscape Approaches"

A report by the UNDP (O'Malley 2019, 3), titled *Value beyond Value Chains: Guidance Note for the Private Sector*, presented the case for "how companies can collaborate more effectively with governments in producer countries to create the enabling conditions for sustainable agricultural production." This suggests a final way that lead firm strategies are reconstituting the institutional environment in Indonesia's coffee regions—by supporting multi-stakeholder initiatives at the national and subnational levels. The 2016 merger of the 4C Association and IDH's Sustainable Coffee Program (SCP) to form the Global Coffee Platform reflected this trend. The GCP subsequently established numerous "country platforms" such as the Sustainable Coffee Platform for Indonesia (SCOPI).[10] The nationwide coordination, and direct support, of farmer training activities is a core activity of SCOPI, which claimed (on its website on June 30, 2021) to have trained twenty-three thousand Indonesian coffee farmers in 2019. Such initiatives provide opportunities for lead firms to engage in extra-firm bargaining with governments and development agencies in a way that more fundamentally reshapes local institutional environments, often with the explicit aim of encouraging a standardized suite of interventions (access to finance, high-yield production, use of agri-inputs, and quality improvement) aimed at constructing "professional, business-oriented farmers," according to the GCP website. The scope of the GCP is similar to, but larger than, International Coffee Partners, established in 2001 by eight family-owned coffee companies (including Lavazza and Tchibo). In its 2015 annual Sustainability Report, Tchibo (2015, 15) articulated its rationale for sector-wide approaches: "Instead of individualised supply chains, we will cover whole sectors of the local smallholders with a system of stocktaking and interventions, regardless of whether all smallholders in a given sector supply us with green coffee. To achieve this, we are currently looking for partners from all areas of society, both national and international: coffee farmers, green coffee traders, exporters, government agencies, nongovernmental organisations, science and academe, and funding agencies." As with JDE's Common Grounds program, Tchibo is seeking to work more collaboratively with a range of actors beyond its own supply chain in a strategy presented in terms of "stakeholder management."

Such strategies have more broadly come to be called "landscape approaches to sustainability." These take an area-based approach to reconciling tradeoffs among different actors with conflicting demands on resources (Kissinger, Moroge, and Noponen 2014; Sayer et al. 2015; Arts et al. 2017; ISEAL Alliance 2021; 1000 Landscape 2021). Landscape approaches were influenced by attempts to develop area-based climate change funding mechanisms to reduce emissions from deforestation and degradation, and to promote reforestation (so-called REDD+

programs) (Nepstad et al. 2013; Von Essen and Lambin 2021). Such schemes can be associated with new funding flows into commodity source regions that are contingent on the protection and provisioning of ecosystem services (carbon sequestration). This is an arena of dynamic institutional experimentation, where various landscape funding mechanisms are emerging (Minang et al. 2015).

By 2020, IDH furthered an agenda for landscape approaches to sustainable commodity sourcing through its concept of a "verified sourcing area" (VSA), which it described as an area-based mechanism to accelerate the production and uptake of sustainable commodities while developing impact assurances for buyers (IDH 2021). The aim is to develop markets for "landscape performance" through an online platform called SourceUp. The VSA approach develops "regional compacts" in commodity source regions involving local governments to identify regional sustainability priorities for aspects such as ecosystem protection, labor, and livelihoods (like the Common Grounds approach). Formalizing "land tenure" is also explicitly recognized as a target area within VSAs. The "compact action plan" identifies discrete projects to be financed through the mobilization of funds from commodity buyers.

The notion that lead firms can become directly involved in jurisdictional governance is potentially transformative, as their ability to reconstruct regional institutional environments is greatly enhanced. Bastos Lima and Persson (2020) identify an attendant risk of what they call "commodity-centric landscape governance" in the marginalization of local interests as the sustainability agenda becomes increasingly driven by lead firms. While landscape assurance schemes are still in their infancy, they have received strong support from lead firms and governments from the Global North. The development of VSAs, for example, has been funded by government agencies from Switzerland, Norway, Denmark, and the Netherlands, and a Global VSA Steering Committee has included representatives from PepsiCo, Mars, JDE, and Unilever.

Extra-firm Bargaining and Institutional Environments

In this chapter I have demonstrated how Indonesian coffee-growing households are integrated into a global value chain for coffee and so influenced by global lead firm strategies (firm strategies are summarized in table 4.2). These strategies, however, interact with various nonfirm actors to construct local institutional environments. Lead firms "bargained" with global NGOs (such as the Fairtrade Foundation, Rainforest Alliance, and Conservation International) in a process that resulted in a prominent agenda of supply chain accountability

TABLE 4.2 Lead firm strategies of upstream engagement in the coffee sector

LEAD FIRM STRATEGY	RATIONALE FOR STRATEGY	IMPLICATIONS AND OPPORTUNITIES FOR INDONESIA-BASED ACTORS	EXAMPLES IN INDONESIA
Outsourcing of processing	Minimize cost-capability ratio by seeking low-cost processors with preferential access to raw materials	Opportunities for value-added exports and development of industrial capacity	Growth in unbranded soluble coffee exports from various Java-based processors
Investments in processing in producing countries	Locate manufacturing plants close to both sites of production and growing consumer markets	Development of industrial capacity, employment, and technology diffusion. Risk of competition with domestic roasters.	Nestlé instant coffee factory in Lampung
Relationship coffees	Establish consumer reputation as possessing origin knowledge, control quality, create symbolic value	Opportunities for strategically located elites in producing regions to capture value and access resource flows	Domestic and international specialty roasters, like Five Senses and Derby
Third-party sustainability standards	Protect firm reputation against allegations of environmental and social neglect along supply chain	Cooperatives gain preferential market access, price premiums, and farmer training. Decreased producer control over farm practices.	-Rainforest Alliance -UTZ -4C -Certified Organic -Fairtrade
In-house sustainability programs	Assume greater control over ethical credentials and exert enhanced influence over producer regions	Farmer training, skill transfer, and development of social infrastructure.	-Supplier Code of Conduct (Lavazza) -Joint Forces (Tchibo) -Common Grounds (JDE Peet's)

| Service delivery models | Exert greater control over production processes, extract surplus through input markets, and increase coffee supply | Improved access to skills, technology, finance, and other resources. Possible shift toward entrepreneurial (capitalist) farming. | –Farmer Support Centers (Starbucks)
–Agriculture Services (Nestlé)
–Sustainability Management Services (SMS, Ecom) |
| Involvement in multistakeholder platforms and partnerships | Address landscape-level sustainability challenges and have a greater influence over the institutional environment through extra-firm bargaining | Encourages NGO and state investment in farmer training. Potential empowerment of local industry actors and stakeholders, but lead firms often perform agenda-setting roles. | –Global Coffee Platform
–Sustainable Coffee Challenge
–Various country coffee platforms (e.g., SCOPI in Indonesia)
–SourceUp/IDH Verified Sourcing Area (VSA) |

through certification standards and, ultimately, the internalization of this agenda within corporate sustainability programs. Lead firms have also bargained with consuming-country governments, who have financially supported the GCP agenda and IDH landscape initiatives, which are shaping rural development processes in Indonesia. Since late 2022, lead firms have further had to respond to European Union regulations on deforestation-free supply chains. Critically, I have demonstrated how value chain initiatives have become entwined with local institutions and social structures within rural Indonesia. Value chain initiatives have frequently been manipulated and reconstructed locally by deeply embedded social structures and a desire to access redistributive opportunities through patronage networks.

Sustainability initiatives have been at the forefront of value chain governance in the coffee sector, and initiatives to intervene in production processes have exerted contradictory pressures on rural households in Indonesia.

On the one hand, there are concerted attempts to promote "entrepreneurial farming." Indonesian coffee farmers have been encouraged to increase investments of labor and capital, obtain credit, expand production, and increase productivity. Lead firms have also sought to actively reconstruct the institutional environment at the national, regional, and "landscape" scale by enrolling state-based actors as extra-firm partners, stepping up their resourcing of agricultural extension programs, and promoting deforestation-free production. Some lead firms have even stated their preference for "non-serious farmers" to exit the sector. My analysis in later chapters will highlight the clear tension between such efforts and the prevailing livelihood strategies of rural households. Put simply, there is no guarantee that smallholder embrace of entrepreneurial farming would result in livelihood upgrading at the household level—although it might address the supply concerns of lead firms.

On the other hand, sustainability initiatives have also been associated with a transfer of resources along the value chain into producing regions (in parallel to the market-based purchasing of commodities). Lead firms have identified an additional element of risk and uncertainty from relying on market processes alone to ensure long-term supply (that is, by allowing coffee prices to increase in response to supply shortages). Resource transfers into producing regions have thus manifested themselves through such mechanisms as development premiums, social development projects, training activities and employment of agronomists, and the distribution of physical materials. While it is true that these initiatives are driven by imperatives for lead firms to ensure effective brand management, they are also an attempt to safeguard long-term supply. Such interventions are sometimes framed in terms of ensuring a "living income" for producers (something that is evidently not being achieved by relying solely on market processes).

Value chains, sometimes associated with development agency funding, are thus emerging as another axis along which new forms of redistribution are occurring. A further factor, then, determining rural futures and processes of contemporary agrarian change is the extent to which agrifood lead firms are willing to actively sustain people on the land through various resource transfer mechanisms alongside the value chain (beyond simple market processes). Such resource transfers interwoven with value chain structures are, however, inevitably refracted through intervening social systems. This will become apparent in the regional case studies presented in chapters 6 and 7, where local elites have been able to position themselves as village heads, cooperative managers, and preferred collectors in such a way that enables them to capture the benefits of these transfers.

Indonesian coffee farmers are part of a global value chain. Despite claiming ownership over their primary means of production (land), they are influenced and constrained by the strategies of lead firms. These strategies include initiatives with the stated intentions of improving producer livelihoods (often presented in terms of sustainability commitments), but these often assume a development vision based on entrepreneurial commodity production (Bray and Neilson 2018). This vision is resulting in attempts to encourage the penetration of capitalist relations into rural Indonesia and is effected discursively through narratives of "farming as a business" or "professional farmers." Although this may be at odds with fortress farming livelihood strategies, such initiatives have contributed resource flows into the coffee-producing regions of Indonesia. Improving supply sustainability for lead firms has, moreover, resulted in attempts to lock strategic source regions into agriculturally oriented development trajectories. Value chain governance structures are thus affecting dynamics of agrarian change in Indonesian coffee-growing communities by interacting with place-specific social institutions in surprising and contradictory ways.

INSTITUTIONS OF LAND ACCESS

> **What we call land is an element of nature inextricably interwoven with man's institutions. To isolate it and form a market for it was perhaps the weirdest of all the undertakings of our ancestors.**
>
> —Karl Polanyi, *The Great Transformation* (1944)

The ability of downstream capital (or indeed an extractive state) to capture value through the production of coffee as a commodity must, at some point, confront the complex set of institutions through which access to land is mediated. Land is an important factor of production (alongside labor and capital) necessary for the creation of value as manifest (in my case study) in the form of coffee beans. However, it is much more than that. Land is also the geographic space where living things, including humans, exist and so provides sustenance for life itself. Directly related to this life-sustaining character, and a key theme of this book, land is an important livelihood resource. In considering land as a livelihood resource, my concept of fortress farming also captures the importance of land as a source of social, cultural, and sometimes even spiritual refuge for individuals and communities. Land performs a critical role in sustaining social relations, which in turn can ensure access to social capital. Ferguson and Li (2018, 10) explain:

> Land (and housing) may serve as an anchor that draws in family members and encourages the multi-generational pooling of resources: care for the elderly; a place to go when injured, sick or unemployed; a site to gather in remittances to invest in house building or a small business; a demonstration of social status and creditworthiness, or value on the marriage-mart; and a place to bury family members, including migrants whose remittances earn them a proper, social funeral. Truly destitute

people are often those who are not only without productive work, but without a stable physical space in which to build and sustain social and affective ties.

To complete our understanding of the evolving institutional environment affecting contemporary agrarian change in Indonesia, this chapter examines specific institutions of land access. The cultivation of coffee relies, in the first instance, on the planting of a seed or seedling in a patch of soil and the care of that plant through to productive maturity. This banal statement, however, belies a much more complex set of social, cultural, and legal relationships with land. Social institutions inevitably arise to regulate both land access (the *ability* to derive benefits from land) and land as property (the *right* to benefit from it, commonly protected by the state) (Ribot and Peluso 2003).

I focus on the way land is simultaneously both a factor of (commodity) production and a livelihood resource. I explore the tensions these two understandings generate. While this first aspect might be considered a subset of the latter, there can be a tendency to assume that land should be treated exclusively, or primarily, as a factor of production and to disregard its broader function as a livelihood resource. This tendency, exemplified by several value chain interventions described in the previous chapter, creates a tension with individuals and communities who consider land a means to sustain social and physical life rather than simply a means to maximize production and productivity. While both experiences of land may be associated with the physical planting of coffee as a cash crop in a patch of soil, each manifests itself quite differently within changing livelihood strategies, and this has important implications for land-related policy and politics.

This dual character of land is of critical importance to fortress farming and, I suggest, for understanding contemporary processes of agrarian transition. My approach is consistent with the critique of mainstream economics (presented by advocates of a livelihoods perspective), which frequently assumes that problems of dearth can be overcome by increasing aggregate production of goods and services in society, or what Chambers and Conway (1991) referred to as the problem of "production thinking." A logical extension of production thinking is that land should be allocated to its most economically efficient use, often by constructing a market-based regime of access, which in turn has been used to justify the promotion of tradable individualized ownership rights in land (sometimes framed as "tenure security"). It has also justified the conversion of "unproductive" smallholder uses of land (for example, subsistence farming or low-intensity household production of coffee) toward large-scale commercial control of land. This is based on the concept of allocative efficiency and an assumption that it will result in the greatest good for the greatest number. Indeed, across Indonesia, the routine allocation of fishing rights, logging and mineral concessions, and plantation leases to commercial interests at the expense of community access is discursively justified based on enhancing aggregate production and efficiency. The resulting expropriation of resources can be devastating for livelihoods.

This chapter examines the various institutions that regulate social access to land for coffee production in Indonesia, ranging from national laws and state polices through to customary tenure and practices, and examines how these institutions intersect. Building on the importance of state-based patronage (chapter 3) and integration within a global value chain (chapter 4), this chapter thus completes my analysis of the multiscalar institutional environment shaping (and also responding to) livelihood strategies in Indonesia's coffee regions.

Legal Foundations for the Landlord State

At the time of independence, the Indonesian state inherited the Dutch legal system, with its inherent dualities between European and indigenous rights. Of central importance to land law, however, was the colonial notion of "free state domain" and the assumption that any land unencumbered by specifically designated European or indigenous rights was essentially the property of the state. Customary land tenure systems and territorial claims, which came to be known generically as *adat*, were consequently disregarded. According to von Benda-Beckmann (2019, 402–403), "the Domain Declarations enacted in the 1870s stipulated that all public rights were assumed by the colonial administration, including rights to land on which no 'private' or private-like rights rested. This land could be either governed by the government, for instance as forest land, or given out in private ownership, often for the establishment of plantations." This notion was challenged by Cornelis van Vollenhoven and the *adatrecht* school of legal theory at Leiden University in the early twentieth century, which argued for legal recognition of such rights as *hak ulayat*, the community right to avail over uncultivated customary lands (van der Eng 2016). However, despite further recommendations from a wide-ranging 1930 agrarian commission that the free state domain principle should be eliminated to ensure land access for community livelihoods, the fundamental principle of colonial state ownership persisted (Galudra and Sirait 2009).

Nor was the free state domain principle abolished at independence, with Article 33 of the 1945 Constitution stipulating that "the earth, water and the natural resources contained within them are to be controlled [*dikuasai*] by the state and used for the greatest possible prosperity of the people."[1] While the meaning of *dikuasai* here has been variously interpreted as "owned," "managed," "controlled," and "regulated," Butt and Lindsey (2008) have shown how decisions of the Constitutional Court have consistently upheld an interpretation of *dikuasai* that extends beyond mere regulation to suggest ownership. Hence, I refer to the "landlord state." Meanwhile, despite an evolving legal framework since 1999 (discussed below), *adat* rights have not yet been recognized under any common law, or native title, equivalent.

Furthermore, the 1960 Basic Agrarian Law (BAL) was drawn up during a time when Sukarno was promoting "Nasakom" (nationalism, religion, and communism) as a unifying political ideology, and so the BAL was strongly influenced by socialist values. BAL provided foundations for land law in the country and remains in place sixty years later, with land embedded as the property of the state. A somewhat ambiguous principle asserted within the BAL (Article 6), however, was that "all rights over land have a social function." This could be interpreted to insist that land should be managed in line with the more expansive notion of land as a livelihood resource. Unfortunately, this social function has, in practice, been used to justify forced government acquisitions (Bakker and Moniaga 2010). Furthermore, despite Article 5 of the BAL ostensibly asserting its foundations in *adat*, the law fundamentally adopted a system of land rights, inherited from the civil codes of continental Europe,[2] that weakened preexisting communal rights such as *hak ulayat* and strengthened the state right of control (Hooker 1978). These legal foundations provide the background to which the modern Indonesian state has come to assume feudalistic control over land. Narrative claims associated with these laws assert, naturally enough, that these rights are held on behalf of the Indonesian citizenry and are to be used for the benefit of the people, or the nation. In practice, this has meant that a state committed to achieving development (*pembangunan*) through economic expansion is likely to prioritize allocative efficiency over livelihood function.

The stated intention of promoting development has, for example, justified the allocation of plantation leases (*hak guna usaha*, HGU) to private and state-owned companies by the National Land Agency (BPN), usually for periods of twenty-five years and often to state cronies. This authority has proven to be lucrative for the state and its *aparat*, particularly with the rapid investment in oil palm over the last twenty years, which has expanded from 2.4 million hectares in 2000 to 6 million hectares in 2017 (BPS 2019c). While the recorded area of commercial coffee estates decreased from 27,801 to 23,186 hectares over the same period, HGU leases for coffee plantations can be locally important, and their role in the Toraja region will be discussed in chapter 6.

HGU leases are also held by the state-owned plantation company (Perseroan Terbatas Perkebunan Nusantara, PTPN), estimated to cover 1.18 million hectares across Indonesia (PTPN 2023), although coffee is a relatively unimportant part of its total portfolio compared to oil palm, sugar, and rubber (table 5.1). Almost all PTPN coffee estates are in East and Central Java, reflecting their colonial heritage, and these (like all PTPN estates) are managed centrally under a monolithic bureaucracy. The PTPN plantations constitute another important way in which the Indonesian state performs a landlord role, often in competition for land with local communities. PTPN was the product of the nationalization of Dutch-owned plantations (a process that commenced in 1957) due to tensions between the Netherlands and the Indonesian Republic over the political future of West Irian. Mackie (1962) described how 542 Dutch-owned estates (constituting 75 percent of all Indonesian plantations at the time) were nationalized as an important step in forging an economic basis for state control over productive resources. PTPN, however, was immediately plagued by problems of corruption and poor management as regional elites maneuvered to control these productive assets in an otherwise flailing economy. Article 33 of the Constitution not only ensures that all natural resources are to be *dikuasai* by the state, but Clause 2 also set out that "sectors of production which are important and affect the life of the people shall be controlled by the State," thereby justifying the manager-landlord role of PTPN. The management ethos on these plantations is one of paternalistic provisioning of livelihoods, schooling, and housing, and arguably maintaining environmental services, while at the same time offering opportunities for various individuals from the state *aparat* to earn off-the-book income from their privileged access to state resources, including from tourism. PTPN (2023) reported a net profit equivalent to around 380 million USD in 2022, when it employed a labor force of 122,215 workers. This formally reported profit is remarkably low, considering the extent of land-based assets at its disposal. The area of land controlled by the PTPN has not increased significantly over the last twenty years, and land conflicts between company estates and surrounding communities have even resulted in some formal reallocation of PTPN land to smallholders.

TABLE 5.1 Commodity share of planted area on PTPN plantations in 2022

CROP	SHARE (%)
Oil palm	62.4
Sugar	19.7
Rubber	14.2
Tea	2.6
Coffee	1.1
Cocoa	0.1

Source: PTPN 2023.

Within the coffee-producing Bukit Barisan mountain range, in the Pasemah highlands of South Sumatra, is the Gunung Dempo tea plantation. Spread across some six thousand hectares (only a quarter of which is planted with tea bushes), the plantation is managed by PTPN VII. Like most tea plantations, Gunung Dempo is visually stunning in the verdant green of its landscape, but the associated facilities have a rather moribund feel to them, with the leaf-processing factory emblazoned with the year "1929" in large letters above its main entrance. It looks as though little factory maintenance has been undertaken since that year. Rundown accommodations for tea pickers were located nearby. Visitors, however, are welcomed and can stay in either some newly built villas or in a restored Dutch-era bungalow. Tourism is just as important to company finances as productive output.

Smallholder coffee farms and horticultural production dominate the area surrounding the Gunung Dempo plantation; a local villager told me that the community had even successfully claimed and occupied a small portion of the plantation and converted it to vegetable farming during *reformasi*. Some of the nearby villages are populated almost entirely by ethnic Javanese, whose grandparents had been brought to the area to work the colonial plantation. One of these descendants explained to me how even more estates were established in the area before independence, but that in the 1950s Sukarno had encouraged workers to take over the land and cultivate it themselves. Such state support for reclamations can be fickle, however, as these same villagers were subsequently targeted for eviction in the 1980s, when a new forest boundary was delineated. The Indonesian landlord state has evolved from colonial-era institutions into an influential actor shaping land access arrangements across the country, often in direct competition with local communities, whose customary rights over land and territories are rarely recognized.

Negotiating Access to Forestry Land

Soon after the rise of Suharto's New Order regime, the Basic Forestry Law of 1967 was promulgated, in which the principles of the domains declaration encouraged an even more audacious land claim by the state, and one of particular importance to many swidden landscapes, such as those in the Bukit Barisan range. This law determined that the forestry zone (*kawasan hutan*) was controlled (again *dikuasai*) by the government as state forest (*hutan negara*), or what Peluso and Vandergeest (2001) called a "political forest." The extent of this area peaked at 75 percent of the total land area of Indonesia in the 1970s (Barber and Talbott 2003) but was estimated at around 63 percent in 2018 owing to subsequent de-gazetting and formal conversion to nonforest uses (MLHKRI 2018). The definition of *dikuasai* was determined (in Article 5 of the 1967 law) as the right to "regulate forest management in its broadest meaning"[3] and to determine legal relationships regarding use of the forestry zone, including the issuing of concessions to the private sector. The forestry zone, it should be noted, comprises both protected forest, including national parks, and production forest for timber extraction and potential conversion to agriculture, where production forest constitutes more than half the total forestry zone.

According to official government data (MLHKRI 2018), only 37 percent of the forestry zone is covered by primary forest, 31 percent is secondary forest, and the remainder (an enormous 32 percent) is either nonforest or planted with various tree crops. Although state control over this massive area is ever-tightening, the Forestry Department[4] had historically struggled to maintain effective authority over a territory that has always had extremely porous boundaries with community lands (like the *tanah marga* in Semende; see chapter 7). To address such spatial discrepancies, the central government pursued a "One Map" policy (Kebijakan Satu Peta) from 2010, soon after signing an ambitious REDD+ agreement, worth one billion USD, with the Norwegian government. By 2020, the policy was still said to be "inching toward completion," with many "wary of the project's lack of transparency and inclusiveness and whether the rights of indigenous communities are honored" (Aqil 2020). Conflicts between smallholder coffee growers and forestry officials are common, and competing claims remain mostly unresolved. These conflicts frequently assume the social form of agrarian communities asserting a moral claim to land being held (unjustly, in their opinion) by an essentially alien landlord—the state.

In 2019, in a coffee-growing village in Semende, I met with Pak Ridwan, the head of a local village forest users group (Lembaga Pemanfaatan Hutan Desa, LPHD), who was also a cousin of the current village head. We rode on a motorbike for about five or six kilometers into the nearby hills to the farming hut (*dangau*) of Pak Amin and Bu Ratna, a couple who I guessed were in their early sixties. They were packing dried coffee cherries into old rice sacks, to be transported back to the main village for sale. None of their four adult children were particularly successful in forging a prosperous nonfarm livelihood, and as a result the couple were largely dependent on the coffee harvest for their own sustenance. The government considered their coffee farm to be located within the national forest estate, although neither Pak Amin nor Bu Ratna was sure where community land (*tanah marga*) ended and forestry land (*tanah kawasan*) began. Even Pak Ridwan from the LPHD wasn't entirely sure. The landscape was a mosaic of coffee farms, regenerating fallows, and what looked like secondary forest. Pak Amin thought that much of the land had been initially cleared from primary forest perhaps fifty years ago.

Following sometimes violent attempts by forestry authorities to evict coffee growers throughout the Bukit Barisan range in the 1990s, the 1998 financial crisis and *reformasi* triggered another wave of "illegal" coffee farming as households sought refuge in these forest landscapes as a livelihood fortress. In 1999, a national-level coffee task force (Tim Kopi) proposed a more flexible policy toward coffee farming in the national forest estate, and this dovetailed with a new forestry law in 1999 (replacing the 1967 law). In the decade following *reformasi*, there had been little attempt by the government to exclude villagers like Pak Amin and Bu Ratna from using the land. In 2011, Pak Ridwan was then encouraged by district forest authorities to make an application for formal recognition of the land as a village forest (*hutan desa*), one of several emergent forms of community-based forestry in Indonesia. By 2015, a Ministry of Forestry decree established a *hutan desa* over 104 hectares on the outskirts of the village, with a thirty-five-year lease, formally held by the LPHD.

This lease had offered some certainty of access for Pak Amin and Bu Ratna, providing them with a defense against forced evictions (which still occurred occasionally, if sporadically, throughout the Bukit Barisan range) and allowing them to access free fertilizers and seedlings from a coffee development program being run by the district agricultural office. The path I rode along from the village was now mostly sealed with cement from a PNPM community block grant, and Bu Ratna was hopeful that electricity might even reach their *dangau* in the future. Despite their coffee farm being located within the forestry estate, its legitimacy was thus being increasingly recognized by the state. Pak Ridwan explained how, as LPHD head, he was responsible for allocating land within the *hutan desa* to village families, and that outsiders were excluded from accessing the land. He described it as a form of social security for villagers with limited livelihood alternatives. These *hutan desa* lands were thus functioning in a similar way to redistributed rice fields held by village heads as village welfare lands on Java (*tanah bengkok* or *tanah kemakmuran*), where public lands are "used for welfare purposes . . . rented under a more egalitarian arrangement to the landless and near-landless" (Ambarwati et al. 2016, 282). The *hutan desa* arrangement also constituted an explicit acknowledgment by the community that the land was state forestry land.

In Sumedang, West Java, I conducted research between 2015 and 2018 with a Forest Village Community Council (Lembaga Masyarakat Desa Hutan, LMDH) that had negotiated another form of community access to the forest estate. Here, and in various other sites across upland Java, coffee is planted as an understory crop in the shade of towering pine trees, eucalyptus and timber species such as *rasamala* and *suren*, all of which remain the property of a profit-generating state-owned enterprise, Perhutani. The forestry situation on Java is somewhat different from that of the outer islands. While the state acts as an institutionalized landlord in the outer islands through the Department of Forestry, on Java it performs this role through Perhutani, which managed 2.4 million hectares of nonconservation forestry land on Java in 2018 (or around 18 percent of Java's total land area) (Perhutani 2019).

Pressure on Perhutani to allow community access to this domain was intense in Sumedang after 1998 and culminated in unilateral occupation of forestry land and widespread timber "theft" by communities. Lukas and Peluso (2020) describe the political changes in Java's forests since 1998 as a "profound transformation." One manifestation has been the planting of coffee, which, in Sumedang, eventually came to be regulated through a community-based forest management agreement (Pengelolaan Hutan Bersama Masyarakat, PHBM) between Perhutani and the LMDH. Such agreements have been responsible for Java reemerging as an important coffee-producing island. The LMDH council is under the patronage (*binaan*) of Perhutani, which has supported coffee growing on the condition that the LMDH provides forest security and that farmers maintain specified densities of timber trees above the coffee. As the state regained effective political control of the areas from around 2004, it successfully enrolled the LMDH head in Sumedang (a charismatic man with locally influential social networks) as a state-sponsored client who determined who could access forestry land and who could not. He is also head of a farmer group federation (Perkumpulan Kelompok Tani) that had been supported since 2008 by various state-funded *proyek* to process and market specialty coffee.

Almost all forest rights holders in the Sumedang LMDH apply their own household labor to coffee, although sharecropping of coffee was prevalent on privately held land outside the Perhutani forest. The LMDH head claims that he allocates access to coffee land to fellow villagers based on need and willingness to farm it themselves. Indeed, there was some evidence that plots were allocated based on need. Many recipients were otherwise landless. Of the eighty-nine coffee farmers we interviewed in 2015 (randomly chosen members of a local coffee farmer organization), seventy-one only cultivated coffee in the Perhutani area, eleven privately held coffee land outside the forest area as well as accessing land in the Perhutani area, while 7 cultivated only privately held coffee land. Obedience to the state was also a factor in allocating access. The LMDH head explained that he would "never provide land to timber thieves or those that are disobedient [*nakal*]." The LMDH was formally required to share 15 percent of its coffee revenue with Perhutani as part of a profit-sharing agreement, although this was weakly enforced and seemed primarily aimed at ensuring community recognition of Perhutani's territorial claims. Nevertheless, during the period 2015–2018, the community was not yet agitating for any kind of formal land distribution but was content with having improved access rights to the forest.

I have observed a third institutional form of community access in the Sumber Jaya subdistrict in Lampung (Sumatra), which presents yet another case of negotiated settlement between the Forestry Department and coffee-growing households. Here, coffee cultivation was initiated by incoming Semende migrants in the late nineteenth century and then further developed by Sundanese migrants (from Java) in the 1960s and 1970s, only for farmers to be told in the 1980s that the area was a designated protection forest that provided hydrological functions for a downstream hydroelectricity plant (Suyanto et al. 2005; Verbist, Putra, and Budidarsono 2005; van Noordwijk, Leimona, and Amaruzaman 2019). Forestry reforms led to a 2001 ministerial decree allowing temporary use rights within a protection forest to be allocated under a community forestry program (Hutan Kemasyarakatan, HKm).[5] In Sumber Jaya, these rights were conditional on the maintenance of multistrata agroforestry systems, payment of royalties, and submission of annual reports. HKm rights are allocated to farmer groups for periods up to thirty-five years and were reported to already cover 35,719 hectares across Lampung by 2011 (Kaskoyo, Mohammed, and Inoue 2014). Individuals were motivated to join HKm programs because it provided formal recognition of their access rights and enabled them to receive various forms of government, private sector, and NGO assistance. Community access to the forestry zone (figure 5.1) has, moreover, been associated with increased rather than decreased tree cover (Suyanto et al. 2005; Verbist, Putra, and Budidarsono 2005). These communities have even been able to access ecological transfers from the downstream hydroelectric company for implementing land management practices that reduced sedimentation (Amaruzaman, Leimona, and Rahadian 2017). Despite the apparent ecological and social success of this HKm program, I was told in 2015 that coffee produced by HKm farmers was rejected from a supply chain sustainability program (Rainforest Alliance) because of concerns that the farms violated deforestation-free production requirements, as the coffee was grown in a "protection forest." HKm involves similar arrangements to the *hutan desa*, except that the license is issued to user groups (rather than linked directly to the village administration), and this meant reduced flexibility in periodically reallocating user rights.

At his election in 2014, President Joko Widodo made a commitment to reallocate 12.7 million hectares through these various community forestry programs across Indonesia, signaling a massive expansion from the 610,000 hectares reallocated under the preceding government (De Royer, van Noordwijk, and Roshetko 2018). By September 2019, at the end of Widodo's first term, this target had not been met. Even still, 3.4 million hectares had been

FIGURE 5.1. Community forestry area (HKm) planted with coffee, Lampung, 2013

reallocated by 2019, thus constituting a considerable expansion in community access to land in the forestry zone (Kurniasih et al. 2020). Excessive concern for meeting community forestry targets has meant that processes have been rushed and outcomes mixed, with a tendency toward weak community participation during preparation phases, top-down planning processes, and the empowerment of well-connected village elites at the expense of others (De Royer, van Noordwijk, and Roshetko 2018). Community forestry initiatives have, at the same time, also provided opportunities for communities to access external forms of support and resources, embedding them in patronage relations with NGOs, government agencies, firms, and research organizations, or what Kurniasih et al. (2020) refer to as "the networked nature of communities and the diverse actors . . . supporting them."

HKm, PHBM, and *hutan desa* arrangements, facilitating land access rather than landownership, also limit the extent to which land is directly exposed to market competition and therefore slow both speculative holdings and tendencies for concentration in ownership. Suyanto et al. (2005), for example, found that HKm arrangements in Lampung led to more equitable distribution of landholdings and income within the community, when compared to nearby freehold land. This is despite access to forestry lands requiring the approval of village-based elites who are themselves dependent for their authority on being vertically linked to higher levels of the state. It remains to be seen, of course, how secure such community access is in the long term, as it relies on continued good faith of the state to honor it even when (more powerful) competing interests threaten.

Customary (*Adat*) Land Rights

In 2019, the district government of North Toraja issued a decree on the recognition and protection of the rights of customary law communities (*masyarakat hukum adat*). This was supported by the Aliansi Masyarakat Adat Nusantara (AMAN, founded in 1999), which translates its name as the "Alliance for Indigenous Peoples of the Archipelago." AMAN claims that the Toraja decree was one of 149 similar district regulations on *adat* ("customary law and practice") that had been enacted by 2021, through which 786 *adat* communities had been legally recognized across Indonesia.[6] Such district-level recognition of customary law communities is the first step toward establishing legal claims over customary land. In 2022, supporters of the North Toraja decree, mostly traditional elites, were waiting for an implementing decree that would establish specific *adat* regions (*wilayah adat*), which it was hoped would allow resource claims to be legally acted upon in Toraja. A central aspiration in Toraja was that this would result in recognition of *adat* forests (*hutan adat*) involving a fundamental transfer of resource ownership—and hence the ability to regulate access and extraction—from the state to customary communities, as has occurred elsewhere in Indonesia.

Peluso and Vandergeest (2001) emphasized how the 1870 Domains Declaration, and the related state claim over the forest estate in 1967, were at odds with the prior view of land held by rural communities and customary rulers across Indonesia. Customary land rights were then generally disregarded within postcolonial Indonesia because they were considered a threat to the unitary state and a unified legal system, contained "feudalistic" elements, and were even alleged to perpetuate a neocolonial politics of "divide and rule" (De Royer et al. 2015). Furthermore, the notion of "indigenous people" has always been both contentious and problematic in multiethnic Indonesia, and while the term *masyarakat hukum adat* has now been recognized in Indonesian law, the state rejects the term "indigenous people" (arguing it is only applicable to colonial settler contexts). *Adat* itself is a diffuse term with multiple meanings and interpretations, and despite its association with indigenous authenticity, it is in fact a loan word from Arabic (Hooker 1978). In a general sense, and as used in daily language, *adat* captures not just, or even, the idea of "law," but a much broader notion of ever-changing customs and traditions embodied in such practices as wedding ceremonies and material culture (like dress). Therefore, it is closely associated with identity. Moreover, as highlighted by McCarthy (2006) in his study of *adat* institutions and resource management in southern Aceh's forest landscapes, the codification of *adat* as "customary law" involves a highly selective application of what were often highly fluid institutions. Nevertheless, AMAN has borrowed from a global discourse on indigeneity to become a nationwide movement of political significance. It claims to be one of the world's largest national movements to defend community resource rights and was founded in overt opposition to the state, even if it has more recently become enmeshed in networks of patronage with both international donors and the state (Arizona, Wicaksono, and Vel 2019).

AMAN has had successes in embedding *adat* in the Indonesian legal system. The last two decades have seen the legalization of such terms as "*adat* law communities," "*adat* forests," and "*adat* villages." The evolving *adat* legal framework has included an amendment to Article 18B of the constitution, and the previous extensive land claim by the Forestry Department was weakened by Constitutional Court Decision 35/PUU-X/2012, which ruled that *adat* forest could be claimed within the existing forestry zone and that the word "state" should be erased from articles in the Forestry Law. This was widely interpreted as a significant win for those struggling for customary ownership over forestlands. Soon after *reformasi*, the National Land Agency (BPN) also issued its first regulation for recognizing customary *adat* law communities (Minister of Agrarian Affairs Regulation No. 5/1999). This was followed by Regulation No. 9/2015 and No. 10/2016, facilitating collective freehold title (*hak milik komunal*), and No. 18/2021, facilitating customary rights to manage (*hak pengelolaan*). Such rights have provided a legal foundation for the BPN to incorporate customary tenure arrangements within the national cadastral register. While emergent forms of *adat* legal rights may yet struggle to prevent community dispossession when confronted by the forces of large-scale capital, these developments suggest a distinct re-embedding of land relations within social (rather than exclusively market-based) processes. This is creating opportunities to support the social, ritual, and kinship functions of land. It is possible, though certainly not inevitable, that this will result in enhanced access to land as a livelihood resource for rural households—even if the ethic of access is likely to be mediated by its embeddedness within Indonesia's prevalent networks of social patronage. I will return to the regulation of *adat* land within the Toraja and Semende case study chapters.

Formal legal structures and legal recognition of *adat*, however, do not represent the full extent of the influence of customary and other informal mechanisms in shaping land access institutions in Indonesia, with Kusters et al. (2007, 436) arguing that "it is not the legal status of tenure, but the perception of tenure security that is of significance in people's land-use decisions." The relatively limited capacity of the state to enforce and monitor the national forestry zone meant that de facto customary access rights (that is, *adat* practices recognized by the community but not the state) largely continued in the outer islands well into the 1980s and 1990s. The general pattern has been one whereby customary practices would prevail up to a point where these conflicted with more powerful resource-based commercial interests or a conservation agenda. In many coffee-growing regions, the integration of coffee plantings within tree-based swidden landscapes continued, even though land access rights were rarely recognized by the state. This lack of legal recognition, however, was only sometimes a problem, as explained by Kusters et al. (2007, 428):

> National laws and regulations are most often known locally only by government representatives and forest agents dealing with communities using these contested areas. These agents usually have nothing to gain in confronting locals when nothing other than respect of the top-down concept of state land ownership is at stake. In such situations most locals ignore the contested status of the land so that it may have little impact on their perception of land tenure security. However, when government supported projects claim land already controlled by local communities, the potential for conflict is highlighted and this inevitably leads to a growing feeling of insecurity regarding land tenure.

Here we gain a picture of institutions taking shape at the interface of law and practice. As the legitimacy and validity of laws are prone to local contestation, negotiated access often involves complex alliances between individuals, NGOs, and lower levels of government such as village administrations or national park authorities (Bakker and Moniaga 2010). Institutions of land access involve a complex, and partial, relationship between formal legal recognition and cultural norms. Within communities, access to land has often been regulated through highly dynamic institutions, often reflecting an "ethic of access," which Peluso (1996, 515) described as

> similar to the notion of a subsistence ethic (Scott 1976). However, for some resources, the ethic of access is driven by more than economics or subsistence rights and serves social, political, and ritual purposes as well, representing kinship, power relations, ritual harmony. Like other aspects of resource tenure, the ethic of access is a moment in a temporal zone of a larger property process—a dynamic concept rooted in

both common and individual experiences of history but affected by a myriad of social, political, and environmental factors. At any moment in time, the ethics of access to particular resources are influenced by the physical characteristics of a resource, especially its longevity and divisibility; the type of use of a resource (whether for subsistence or commercial purposes); the existence of some social meaning for the resource beyond economic value; and changes in social relations affecting the balance between group or individual resource control, political-economic factors such as the prices of products and the relative ease of marketing them, and environmental circumstances such as a resource's relative scarcity, substitutability, or spatial competition with other products.

van Noordwijk et al. (2008) similarly described an arrangement in Bungo District of Jambi (Sumatra) that followed an ethic of access, where areas of customary forest are maintained as "swidden reserves" (known locally as *sesap nenek*) in which land can be utilized by community members in times of need, as determined by the village leader. The land could be planted with dryland rice but not sold, pawned, or inherited, and the planting of commercial tree crops was forbidden, such that fallowed land returned to communal ownership. The soils were reasonably fertile and the land areas extensive, with one *sesap nenek* covering eight hundred hectares, such that this land was "the most important part of the social safety net in Muara Bungo" (27). This reserve has been maintained despite considerable commercial pressure on land in Jambi. A separate 2015 study into land acquisition pathways in the rubber and oil palm regions of Jambi, encompassing 1,681 plots of land, found that 18 percent of all plots were obtained by "direct appropriation" (likely claiming some ethic of access), 24 percent by intrafamily transfer, 7 percent through government programs (transmigration), and a full 49 percent by market purchases (Krishna et al. 2017). Market transactions for land outside the swidden reserves were thus already widespread in Jambi. Land acquired by direct appropriation was associated with "weak *de jure* property rights" but "high internal security" (Krishna et al. 2017). Importantly, this resulted in fewer subsequent land sales and generally lower land prices even if sold, which further enhanced community access.

Social mechanisms, including customary *adat* notions, whether recognized by law or not, thus constitute an important element of the institutional environment shaping land access regimes. I have highlighted how actual land-related practices are a complex outcome of intersecting norms, rules, and practice, often maintained in a tension that is continually renegotiated by various actors. Frequently, those practices pursued by community-based actors seek to establish some kind of ethic of access for households whose basic livelihood needs are land-dependent. Such an ethic is better facilitated when individual ownership and markets in land are restricted. This, however, is strongly contested by other actors, both situated within rural communities and without, whose interests are better served through more fluid land markets.

Accessing Lands for Coffee-Growing in Indonesia

While considerable institutional diversity exists in land access regimes across Indonesia's coffee-growing lands, there has been a general trend toward individualized claims over land as a salable commodity, increasingly backed up by state authority. The state has ultimate power to recognize individual property rights through registration by the National Land Agency, producing *hak milik* ownership certificates. The notion of individual landownership itself, however, conceals a broad array of institutional forms that includes (1) verbal recognition by others in the community of an individual's right over a plot based on accepted cultural norms, which we might broadly consider noncommunal customary tenure; (2) written recognition of a right, or land transfer, by village authorities, often in the form of a *surat keterangan tanah* (SKT), and sometimes countersigned by officials from the subdistrict (*kecamatan*); (3) land tax receipts (especially the *pajak bumi dan bangunan*, or PBB, a tax on land and buildings that has been in place since the 1980s), sometimes still known as *girik* following a colonial-era tradition on Java when village land tax registers were far more complete than the formal cadastre (van der Eng 2016); and (4) formal surveying and registration on the cadastral database, resulting in issuing a land certificate (land titling) based on a full ownership right (*hak milik*) from the BPN.

Hooker (1978, 118) described *hak milik*, introduced in the 1960 BAL, as "a radical departure from traditional Indonesian views on ownership," away from one that was oriented toward the recognition of labor effort and investment, but not permanent alienation, and loosely based on an ethic of access. *Hak milik*, however, has been strongly promoted by the Indonesian state and various international supporters. In 1981, the government introduced the National Agrarian Operation Project (PRONA), a program to subsidize the costs normally associated with land titling. PRONA was later financially supported by the World Bank and the Australian government under the Indonesia Land Administration Project (ILAP), the first phase of which was implemented from 1994 to 2001. At the last agricultural census (BPS 2013), however, still only 31 percent of the twenty-five million landowning farm households reported holding land under *hak milik*. By the end of 2019, BPN claimed that 54 percent of the estimated 126 million land plots (rural and urban) across Indonesia had been registered, with some 11 million plots registered in 2019 alone, and it aimed to register all plots by 2025 (BPN 2019). By 2022, the program was continuing to generate certificates and was known as PTSL (Pendaftaran Tanah Sistematis Lengkap, "Complete and Systematic Land Registration"). While these ambitious targets may yet prove illusory, with most of the remaining plots located in rural areas with complex access arrangements, it is remarkable that the share of registered plots has risen to this level from an estimated 20 percent of all registerable plots in 2000 (Slaats et al. 2009). Individual land registration appears to be gathering momentum, and in 2024, local BPN offices were under considerable pressure to meet registration targets determined by the central government.

The key arguments underpinning land registration are that legal certainty offers confidence for investment, reduces conflict, enables certificate holders to use their certificate as collateral against loans, and that it stimulates land markets in a way that improves allocative efficiency. It is said to unlock capital already owned by the poor (De Soto 2000). While some of these benefits are indeed likely to accrue to certificate holders, Hall, Hirsch, and Li (2011) emphasize how land registration also works to actively exclude others by making access rights more rigidly enforced and by more easily enabling transfers through market processes. Furthermore, Rigg (2019, 132) suggests that "the absence of formal titles, rather paradoxically, may have therefore helped *protect* smallholders from land accumulation by outside agents" on the basis that customary institutions often involved a land access regime that was difficult for outsiders to penetrate but which worked reasonably well for the needs of the local community.

The registration of coffee farms as *hak milik* has been relatively rare across the coffee regions I have studied (table 5.2), but it is slowly increasing. The relatively high rates in Enrekang (table 5.2) were a direct result of a PRONA initiative to expand registration there, and other areas have been more recently affected by the PTSL program. While actual registration was limited, the introduction of *hak milik* as a legal construct contributed to broader social acceptance of individualized claims over land in many coffee-growing regions. Across my field sites (table 5.3), access to land has most frequently been an inherited claim, with far fewer households purchasing their plots than in Krishna et al.'s (2017) Jambi study in oil palm and rubber landscapes. The buying and selling of coffee lands was so rare in the Toraja districts in 2008 that households were unable to estimate land prices. While "direct appropriation" of land for coffee farming has become less common over time, most Indonesian coffee farms were cleared from forest by current users or their parents. The nationwide SKB2014 survey asks farmers how their coffee land was originally cleared (*awal pembukaan lahan*), with less than a third stating that their land was purchased or converted from other crops (appendix table A6).

TABLE 5.2   Recognition of access claims to coffee land across Indonesia's coffee regions[a]

REGION	YEAR OF SURVEY	N	BPN *HAK MILIK* CERTIFICATES (%)	SKT / *GIRIK* / TAX RECEIPTS (%)	CUSTOMARY TENURE (%)	STATE FORESTS (%)
Semende	2015	1,478	7	31	62	
Simalungun, North Sumatra	2015	200	3	73	23	
Manggarai	2008	197	4	38	55	3
Ngada	2008	202	15	43	23	19
Tana Toraja	2008	65	0	98	2	0
North Toraja	2008	134	0	98	2	0
Enrekang	2008	197	47	14	37	1
North Toraja (2)	2008	66	15	85	-	-
Gayo	2008	135	20	58	21	1
Lampung	2008	122	16	62	16	5

Source: Author own surveys.

[a] Percentages may not add up to 100 because of rounding.

TABLE 5.3   Accessing coffee lands across Indonesia

DISTRICT (KABUPATEN)	YEAR	N	INHERITED (%)	PURCHASED (%)	DIRECT APPROPRIATION (%)
Simalungan	2015	217	76	23	1
Ngada	2008	207	62	16	22
Manggarai	2008	197	68	15	17
Tana Toraja	2008	65	100	0	0
North Toraja (nonfrontier)	2008	134	96	0	4
Enrekang	2008	197	82	15	3

Source: Author own surveys.

In 2008, I conducted field studies in three locations where coffee was being planted within predominately forest landscapes to examine institutions of land access. The sites included (1) the far north of Toraja, where small-scale land clearing was occurring in the vicinity of state-designated protection forest; (2) the districts of Tanggamus and West Lampung (both in Lampung Province), including along the perimeter of the Bukit Barisan Selatan National Park; and (3) in the Bener Meriah and Central Aceh districts in Gayo, where smallholders were expanding into protection forest, part of the Leuser Ecosystem Area. All three cases constituted landscapes that spanned across forestry zone boundaries.

FIGURE 5.2.   Forest clearing for coffee in protection forest, Toraja, 2008

All involved contested spaces whereby communities were actively challenging the forestland claims of the state and were acting "illegally" (figure 5.2). Each was a mosaic of primary forest, secondary forests, fallows (*belukar*), established tree-crop gardens, and annual food crop fields.

Despite their clear violation of formal forestry law, there was a widespread perception among farmers that they held a legitimate customary right to access these lands (an ethic of access) and that land was still considered easily accessible for those who needed it (table 5.4). Owing to higher rates of in-migration, the Lampung and Gayo sites were characterized by greater ethnic diversity than Toraja and associated with less-rigid customary access arrangements, higher rates of forest clearing, and the (tentative) emergence of land markets. In Gayo and Lampung, migrants would sometimes negotiate with local populations to access customary lands, with average prices for fallowed land (in 2008) equivalent to 1,300 USD per hectare across these two regions. Access to land in all three regions, however, was more commonly linked to labor outlays rather than market transactions.

While access to forest or fallowed lands was generally claimed by customary right, payments to village heads and subdistrict heads for this right were also widely reported. This reflects the ongoing interaction between customary

TABLE 5.4   Farmer attitudes to land availability in forest landscapes

REGION	N	CONSIDER LAND STILL EASILY AVAILABLE (%)	DO NOT PERCEIVE ANY RESTRICTIONS ON LAND ACCESS (%)	BELIEVE A CUSTOMARY RIGHT TO AVAIL EXISTS (%)
Toraja	66	47	23	98
Gayo	135	45	34	35
Lampung	122	25	25	51

Source: Author own surveys, 2008.

TABLE 5.5   Extent of land tax payments in forest frontier regions

REGION	PAYMENT OF A LAND TAX (% OF RESPONDENTS)	AVERAGE ANNUAL PAYMENT (USD)
Lampung	100	2.0
Gayo	81	3.4
Toraja	23	2.3

Source: Author own surveys, 2008.

and state modes of regulation. Meanwhile, many respondents reported making (extremely low) land tax payments to the state in the previous year (table 5.5), with the payment of a land tax long considered an initial step along a legal pathway toward individual ownership. (The amount of these nominal land tax payments had changed very little when I reviewed the district database in Toraja in 2022.) Despite individual claims made over crops planted in all three sites discussed above, however, ownership claims over the land itself were not always—or not yet—stridently asserted. In some instances, there was acceptance that individual access claims were not necessarily permanent and so did not constitute full ownership rights. Reallocations of land access rights, or evictions in the case of the national park, were often considered a legitimate risk borne by farmers, if fair and appropriate compensation was paid for loss of livelihood (that is, productive tree losses). As in the *damar* forests of Krui (Kusters et al. 2007), there is little evidence from these field studies for the assertion that lack of legal tenure discourages farmers from making long-term investments in farming. Indeed, land access, at least for the productive life of the crop, was perceived to be relatively secure despite the lack of legally recognized rights over land.

In 2014, Indonesia's coffee producers considered themselves, overwhelmingly, to be cultivating self-owned farms (appendix table A7). Fewer than 5 percent of outer island coffee producers rented their land (for payment) from landlords, although slightly more "rented for free," referring to situations when land owned by others is used without payment, which often occurs within extended family and patronage networks. This accounted for as many as 16 percent of farms in Lampung, but elsewhere was around 7 percent of coffee farms and highlights the widespread persistence of institutions providing informal land access (and social security) in many tree-crop-growing communities. This category of "rent for free" in the SKB2014 survey also includes various forms of sharecropping, which are reported in ST2013 (appendix table A8) and account for about half of the "rent for free" category. While standardized survey formats offer little opportunity to explain diversity in terms of local land access and management arrangements, the extent of sharecropping, renting of coffee lands, and management for a wage is limited (perhaps 5 percent of all coffee growers). This conforms with observations from my own surveys (table 5.6). Indeed, BPS (2014) found high levels of cultivating households working self-owned land across all major outer island export commodities including coffee (94.3 percent), cocoa (95.0 percent), oil palm (96.8 percent), rubber (91.1 percent), and coconut (94.6 percent).

Not only are Indonesian coffee smallholders largely cultivating what they consider to be their own land; they are also largely reliant on their own labor. An estimated 50 percent of all Indonesian coffee smallholders relied exclusively on household labor (an average of 2.2 unpaid workers per household), while the use of permanent paid workers was reported in less than 5 percent of cases (appendix table A9). The additional labor needs of the harvest are sometimes augmented with casual workers, but even these households still tend to rely "mostly" on unpaid household labor (table 5.7). I will explore labor relations on Semende coffee farms in more detail in chapter 7, but Indonesian coffee farms have been largely managed as household production units without a substantial wage relation, mostly without payment of land-rent, and mostly on inherited or directly appropriated land.

The tendency to rely on own-household labor is closely related to the average size of coffee smallholdings (one hectare, according to BPS 2013) and the observed clustering of farm sizes between 0.5 and 2.5 hectares (table 5.8). The capacity of the household unit to manage the farm, without reliance on permanent paid labor, limits the extent of the holding, with relatively few households accumulating coffee land beyond their household management capacity. This also reflects a key aspect of fortress farming, where land access supports livelihood resilience but accumulated capital is rarely invested back into farms employing capitalist relations of production.

In chapters 6 and 7 I will return to more localized analyses of land access, but the coffee-growing regions of Indonesia can be characterized as possessing highly diverse institutions of land access, many still linked to an ethic of access. Individualized ownership of coffee farmland in the form of registered *hak milik*

TABLE 5.6 Land status for coffee-growing lands in case study sites

REGION	YEAR OF SURVEY	N	COFFEE LAND OWNED BY CULTIVATOR (%)	CULTIVATES FAMILY/ CLAN LAND (%)	RENTED BY CULTIVATOR (%)	SHARECROPPED BY CULTIVATOR (%)	OTHER (%)
Semende (South Sumatra)	2019	1,208	57	33	7	3	0
Simalungun (North Sumatra)	2015	200	63	33	2	3	0
Sumedang (West Java)	2015	91	18	0	0	0	82 (PHBM)
Sidikalang (North Sumatra)	2012	209	96	3	1	0	0

Source: Author own surveys.

TABLE 5.7 Reliance on household and paid labor in three coffee-growing districts

LOCATION	YEAR (N)	USE ONLY UNPAID/ FAMILY LABOR (%)	MOSTLY HOUSEHOLD LABOR	MOSTLY PAID LABOR	USE PAID LABOR ONLY
Sumedang, Java	2015 (90)	36	54	7	3
Enrekang, Sulawesi	2014 (97)	49	48[a]		2
Simalungun, Sumatra	2016 (200)	27	48	18	8

Source: Author own surveys.

[a] The Enrekang survey simply asked whether households used (1) only household labor; (2) some casual labor; and (3) paid labor only.

TABLE 5.8 Coffee landholding sizes in study sites across Indonesia

REGION	YEAR OF SURVEY	N	AVERAGE COFFEE HOLDING (HA)	<0.51HA (%)	0.51–2.5 (%)	>2.5HA (%)
Simalungun, North Sumatra	2015	200	0.9	-	-	-
Manggarai	2008	197	1.4	23	62	15
Ngada	2008	202	0.8	50	47	3
Tana Toraja	2008	65	1.2	12	86	2
North Toraja (frontier)	2008	131	1.5	1	96	3
Enrekang	2008	197	1.3	16	79	5
Enrekang	2014	97	1.1	31	65	4
Gayo (frontier)	2008	135	1.7	2	86	12
Semende	2015	1589	1.9	6	85	9

Source: Author own surveys.

certificates is relatively rare even if it is increasing. Direct access to land in forested landscapes has been important to coffee-farming livelihoods, and the institutional arrangements facilitating such access are particular and often facilitated by negotiations with forestry departments. As a result of these diverse institutions of access, coffee growing regions are generally not yet characterized by high rates of problematic landlessness (in the sense of those wanting to farm being excluded from it). Not *all* households own their own farmland, but not all households wish to be engaged in farming, such that we need to treat the category of "landless households" carefully. Even studies that report the prevalence of landlessness in parts of Java also acknowledge a different situation in the outer island communities they have studied, where "almost all households [have] access to some farmland" (Ambarwati et al. 2016, 278).

Institutional Environments and Land Access

This chapter has demonstrated how Indonesian smallholder coffee production has been associated with a complicated set of land access institutions, shaped by the state, by community contestations, by customary arrangements, and by market processes. The specific agroecological embeddedness of coffee production, which is often integrated within tree-based landscapes, has profoundly influenced these institutions, as it results in negotiations with the landlord state. From the perspective of the state, it has proven difficult to successfully apply standard cadastral systems to tree-based swidden landscapes, but this has tended to enhance rather than hinder community access. The Indonesian state has assumed a powerful position as "landlord," sometimes actively engaged in production (the PTPNs), sometimes by issuing leases (HGUs), and sometimes by regulating community access to the political forest estate. While this position is far from uncontested, it generally embodies the logic of the patronage-bound state presented in chapter 3.

Across Indonesia, coffee continues to be cultivated predominately on lands other than those held under registered individual title (*hak milik*), even if there is significant and increasing pressure for individualization of formal land rights. Coffee production has resulted in conflicts with forestry authorities, but also negotiated outcomes, and this has often occurred in ways that facilitate fortress farming. These accommodated access arrangements can allow lands to be allocated to those households that need it most urgently as a livelihood resource. Community access to forestry land has, furthermore, not prevented households from accessing resource flows from development agencies, the state, and (in Sumber Jaya) from a downstream water user in return for the provisioning of ecosystem services.

Access to land for coffee is enabled by individualized land rights recognized by local administrations, negotiated outcomes with forestry departments, "illegal" occupation of lands, and lands regulated by customary norms. Land markets certainly exist, but these are circumscribed by social relations within communities and state interventions. This limits—but does not eliminate—the extent of speculative accumulation of land. In the next two chapters I will further show how, in comparison to wet-rice farming, tree-crop farming within swidden landscapes has been subject to far fewer restriction based on class and caste. Land access has been found to emerge and evolve in ongoing dialogue with underlying, yet dynamic, social structures and institutions. The multiscalar institutional environment shaping land access for coffee-growing households is thus constituted by the particular way these institutions interact and coalesce in particular places. To date, these dynamic institutional environments have generally enabled access to coffee-growing land as a social safety net (a fortress farming function). There are, however, cases where coffee-growing lands have become individual property and where market mechanisms, combined with capitalist pressures to maximize production, have resulted in households losing access to land. The key point, however, is that these latter processes are far from inevitable, and there continues to be considerable social resistance against attempts to construct entirely unregulated land markets ("the weirdest of all the undertakings of our ancestors").

Markets, of course, are not the only mechanism through which households may be excluded from accessing land, and we should be equally alert to the potential for exclusionary institutions to emerge through customary practices or an inability of households to successfully manage relationships with the state. Indeed, the various examples presented in this chapter have highlighted how access to land is frequently regulated by relations of patronage—both within communities and with the state. A further threat to livelihood-supporting land access institutions is the continued appropriation of large areas of land for resource developments. Not only can such arrangements, made in the interests of capital and economic expansion, involve the dispossession of existing land users, but they also threaten the longer-term capacity of rural landscapes to support fortress farming livelihoods. The tendency to assess the impacts of land-hungry developments in terms of formal job creation, easily quantifiable economic contributions, and tax revenue is doing considerable harm to the long-term ability of the institutional environment to protect livelihood resources.

FORTRESS FARMING IN TORAJA

Kurre! Kurre! Kurre!

Kurre Sumanga'na te padang tuo balo',

Mangkamo nasampa' rara' nene' mendeatanna

Te to ma'rapu tallang nabangunni banua

Saba' parajanna te tana tumbo kulau'

Napata bulaan to dolo kapuanganna

Te to ma'kaponan ao' umpate'dangi a'riri sanda pati'na

(Hail! Hail! Hail!

Hail to this soil, rich with blessings

Extolled exultantly as bearing good fortune by the divine ancestors

Of these descendants, numerous as bamboo culms, who built this house

Abundant be the blessing upon this prosperity-bringing soil,

Glorified with golden words by the divine forefathers

Revered as Lords by those present, whose group increases like bamboo clumps, who have erected the support poles cut to perfection.)

—Opening lines to the *Passomba Tedong* ceremonial invocation during the Torajan Merok feast (as transcribed by van der Veen 1965)

Rural livelihoods are shaped by the multitude of ways through which households and regions are embedded within an evolving national and global economy (chapter 2), relations with the state and state policies (chapter 3), incorporation within global value chains (chapter 4), and the highly dynamic, situated institutions of land access (chapter 5). I refer to these influences, collectively, as the institutional environment, and highlight both its multiscalarity and place-specificity. The aim of this chapter, then, is to show how the current conjuncture of the institutional environment has coalesced to encourage a particular livelihood strategy, fortress farming, in a particular place, Toraja. It is a case where cultural practices within the rural landscape are linked to a significant redistribution of resources through remittances. These practices occur alongside redistribution flowing through state-linked and value chain networks and are collectively shaping processes of agrarian change. Access to farmland, linked to one's position within the community, provides livelihood resilience through farming (increasingly as a fallback strategy), but I show how it can also facilitate access to other resource flows.

The Toraja highlands consist of two districts (*kabupaten*)—Tana Toraja and North Toraja, with capitals in Makale and Rantepao respectively—in the province of South Sulawesi, with a combined population of about 540,000 in 2020 (BPS 2021a). Rantepao is an eight-hour drive from the provincial capital of Makassar (figure 6.1). This extensive upland catchment ranges in altitude from six hundred to three thousand meters above sea level. Streams and tributaries flow through narrow valleys into the Sa'dan River,[1] which drains to the south through the Enrekang and Pinrang districts. Rain-fed *sawah* rice cultivation, on steeply terraced slopes and irrigated by simple stream diversions, has been practiced for centuries. It was a key factor allowing for relatively high precolonial population densities but coexisted with dryland swiddening (*ladang*) in adjacent forests. *Sawah* cultivation was probably introduced from neighboring Bugis society, with whom the Toraja maintain complex cultural relationships.[2] Torajan society, however, did not convert to Islam along with the Bugis in the seventeenth century but maintained earlier

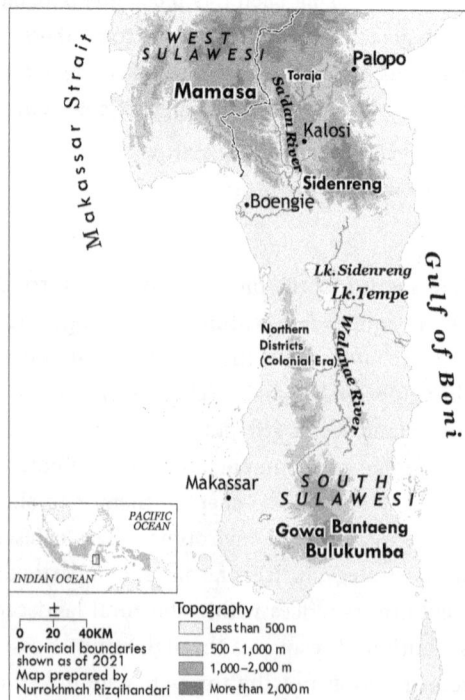

FIGURE 6.1. Map of the coffee regions of southwestern Sulawesi

Austronesian customs and rituals that were eventually integrated into a syncretic form of Protestantism in the twentieth century. This vibrant ritual life has been instrumental in encouraging remittance flows in the early twenty-first century.

In this chapter I will first present the historical context of Torajan integration with the global coffee economy during the nineteenth century and the rise of out-migration and a remittance economy in the late twentieth century, resulting in a dynamic agrarian transition. This then leads to an analysis of contemporary coffee value chain dynamics, where global lead firms have been active drivers of change. Toraja, however, is much more than just a production node in a global value chain, and I present Toraja as a highly multifunctional landscape. It is one where an émigré community "consumes" their homeland landscape through ceremonial participation (Neilson 2022). I then present how the institutional environment is shaped by land access regimes linked to customary practices (*tanah tongkonan*). While such *adat* institutions are distinctive to particular places and cultures, a detailed presentation of the *tana soa* land arrangements of Bajawa, or the *tanah huta* among the Toba Bataks, would have made the same fundamental point that land access is mediated by custom. I then present fortress farming livelihoods in some detail in the hamlet of Tondok Buntu as a response to this broader institutional environment.

Emergence of a Coffee-Producing Region

While the impact of coffee production for export was profound, it was not Toraja's first engagement with international trade. One of Southeast Asia's largest collections of fourteenth-century Gujarati textiles has been found in Toraja, where they have been preserved as ceremonial heirlooms (Barnes 2017). These highlands appear to have been the end destination in extensive trade networks—via the low-land court of Luwu (Palopo), across the archipelago, and into the Indian Ocean—in which they were engaged as suppliers of *damar* resins, rattan, rice, and leather hides (Waterson 2009). Despite their relative physical remoteness, it would thus be wrong to characterize the Toraja as historically isolated. Indeed, borrowing from the framework of Scott (2009), it seems more plausible to view Torajan society as having pursued a deliberate strategy of lowland Bugis state evasion and benefiting from the considerable "friction of terrain" afforded by their mountain home.

Ukers (1922) reported that coffee was first planted on Sulawesi in 1750,[3] while Sutherland (1983) identified a significant increase in coffee cropping in the "Northern districts" (the colonial territories directly north of Makassar; see figure 6.1) from around 1825. Coffee was only identified in the *Koloniaal Verslag* (Colonial yearbook) as being as an important agricultural product in the region in the 1830s. If coffee was grown in southern Sulawesi before the mid-nineteenth century, it was on a limited scale. Rather, coffee appears to have emerged as a key commodity following the 1847 declaration of Makassar as a free port, when it became a regional trading hub. High global prices in the 1850s were a potent trigger within Sulawesi and coincided with a decline in the Bugis textile industry (owing to European imports), thus pushing indigenous investment into export agriculture (Sutherland 2015). Coffee cultivation initially spread to the slopes of Bawakaraeng mountain, in the colonial districts of Bantaeng and Bulukumba, and then to the independent Bugis territories farther north. The famous British naturalist Alfred Russel Wallace (1869) stayed at a "small coffee plantation" owned by a Dutch-Indische farmer about two miles from Makassar in 1856, by which time he described coffee as a "chief product of the surrounding countryside."

According to the *Koloniaal Verslag*, 300 tons of coffee were exported from Makassar in 1852, increasing to 2,280 tons by 1862, but alternative Bugis trade networks linked directly to Singapore probably exceeded this volume recorded by the colonial state. Eastern Indonesia was embedded in a commercial system linked to Britain, India, and China rather than the Netherlands at this time. Until the 1920s, more than 60 percent of South Sulawesi's exports were foreign in destination, in the sense that they were non-Dutch and non-Indies (Sutherland 2015). By 1870, coffee was Makassar's dominant export commodity, when it was estimated to amount to 31 percent of export value (Sutherland 2015). The coffee trade was dominated by Bugis, Arab, and Chinese traders, where the latter two often formed alliances with traditional Bugis patrons, who encouraged extensive client networks to promote production in the interior. Sutherland (73) describes the gradual integration of the eastern islands into systems of global trade with relatively little state influence: "Commodity chains had linked beach barter to Makassar and global commerce for hundreds of years. This continuity with earlier times is not surprising, as East Indonesia was never fully colonised. Government penetration was limited, plantations few and far between, and the infrastructure poor."

The political consolidation of the Bugis territories, and the Dutch defeat of the Bone kingdom in 1860, further encouraged coffee expansion, such that an estimated peak of five thousand tons was being produced by some forty thousand households on "Government lands" in 1888 (*Koloniaal Verslag* 1890). During this time, coffee production expanded beyond Dutch influence into Toraja even though the colonial occupation of Toraja didn't occur until 1905. A Dutch coffee researcher, B. H. Paerels, spent more than two months studying Torajan coffee systems in 1922, claiming that "if I didn't go there, then it wasn't important to coffee." Paerels (1927) estimated that production commenced in Toraja from around 1850.[4] Torajan coffee was traded both west to Sidenreng and east to Luwu, with each lowland court vying for control of supply by the 1860s (Bigalke 2005). Colonial-era Dutch writers (Nobele 1926; van Lijf 1948) describe a volatile trading environment at this time where Sidenrengers would sweep through Torajan hamlets in violent gangs to monopolize supply. The Bugis court of Sidenreng was still independent of the Dutch at the time and traded through its archipelago-wide mercantile networks to Singapore and the Malaccan Strait from the port of Boengie (figure 6.1).

What we know about how coffee was initially incorporated into Torajan social and economic systems can be gleaned from colonial writers reporting more than a generation after the events. The first European known to have visited Toraja (van Rijn 1902) described how, in 1897, coffee was an established, welfare-improving commodity bought by Bugis traders, at markets they established, in exchange for cloth. Bigalke (2005) suggests that powerful Torajan headmen, such as the renowned national hero Pong Tiku, simply ensured security at highland markets and along trade routes, for which they applied informal taxes. Some traders also bought unharvested cherries from growers direct from the bush. Based on the Torajan nobility's general lack of control over production when the Dutch arrived, Paerels (1927) believed that coffee was probably introduced by the Bugis, bypassing village elites. The degree to which Toraja's rigidly hierarchical social system provided the structural foundations for commodity production and trade thus seems limited. There is little evidence for anything resembling the Prussian path to agrarian capitalism "from above."

Paerels (1927, 45) also highlighted the emancipating influence of coffee, which "makes the poor man rich and the rich man poor." He contrasted it with *sawah*, which remained under noble control, with production mediated through complex cultural and ritual practices. Instead, coffee began drawing peasants away from feudal control, as it did not require collective mobilization of labor. Coffee was integrated into dryland *ladang*, initially planted alongside rice, millet, corn, and beans, where *adat* institutions meant that ownership over the crop (rather than land) was retained by the labor that planted it. Coffee thus allowed Torajan smallholders to develop a degree of economic autonomy from local elites, who (according to Nobele) openly lamented their resulting loss of control over the lower castes. Moreover, Paerels estimated that Torajan coffee farmers were receiving 80 percent of the export price during the 1920s export boom.

Nobele (1926) described how his administration attempted to establish a coffee market and collection point in Makale after 1910 (ostensibly to maintain quality but probably to collect taxes). An attempt by the government to establish communal coffee gardens in Toraja (akin to *cultuurstelsel*) was rejected by Torajans and quickly abandoned (Paerels 1927). Efforts were also made to establish estate production during the colonial era, in Bolokon in west Toraja and at Pedamaran in the east, locations that were subsequently taken up as post-independence plantation leases (HGUs). The overall colonial influence on smallholder coffee production, however, seems to have been minimal.

At the turn of the twentieth century, market-oriented coffee production was embedded within Torajan livelihoods alongside the cultivation of rice, beans, cassava, and taro for own-consumption and supported by a lively handicraft industry (weavings, metalworks, carvings, pottery), some of which was sold into regional markets (Nooy-Palm 1979). Paerels (1927, 39) highlights, however, that "apart from some forest products such as *damar* resin and rattan, [buffalo] hides and some rice, it is thus coffee that is the first and most important export product, and the only product where we can expect an increase, and an important increase, in the future." Through coffee, Torajan smallholders emerged as petty commodity producers and began to be tentatively separated from feudal bonds to clan leaders. "Boengie" coffee, sourced from Toraja, developed a reputation as one of the most expensive in the Indies (Ukers 1922). By 1924, Torajan production was estimated to have already reached around eight hundred tons (Paerels 1927)—about the same as volumes in the early twenty-first century.

Based on anthropological fieldwork in the 1970s, Nooy-Palm (1979, 12) could still report that "since the turn of this century little change has taken place in how the Saʾdan Toraja support themselves," claiming that 90 percent of the economically active population were engaged in agriculture. While the district was still producing enough rice to feed itself, coffee was the chief cash crop, and "in a good coffee year the Toraja spend a large share of their coffee profits on major rituals" (Nooy-Palm 1979, 13). Indeed, the 1970s was a boom period for Torajan coffee, stimulated by a major investment in a five-hundred-hectare plantation and processing factory by Toarco Jaya (whose name is an acronym from Toraja Arabica Coffee), a wholly owned subsidiary of Key Coffee, a large Japanese coffee roaster. This encouraged wealthy émigré Torajan elites to collude with state agencies to obtain eight HGU plantation leases (issued by the National Lands Agency between 1988 and 1998) covering some six thousand hectares—mostly in the remote and underpopulated northwest of the district. Some of these leases were on lands specifically excised from the forestry estate through favorable deals with government *aparat* in the final decade of the Suharto regime (Ichsan 2017). In a particularly candid 2022 interview, a former high-ranking forestry official with close links to successive district governments shared with me how he was involved in a "game" whereby leases were issued with the specific purpose of being used as collateral for accessing bank credit rather than production. It was apparently unproblematic to then claim force majeure and to split the spoils with corrupt bank officials.

By the 1990s, it appeared as if Torajan coffee cultivation could eventually be dominated by the interests of large capital. However, this did not occur. Except for the Toarco Jaya estate and another granted to the Kapal Api Group (discussed below), these leases were either never fully planted or subsequently abandoned, and the HGU lease areas shown in figure 6.2 remain mostly undeveloped or revoked. During *reformasi*, communities surrounding the estates complained about unjust land appropriations, and in 2017 these underlying conflicts were still simmering (Ichsan 2017). Indeed, part of the rationale for the 2019 regional decree on *adat* communities (discussed in chapter 5), as described in the decree's general elucidation, was a desire to address past injustices associated with the "capitalist private sector" (*sektor swasta yang bermodal besar*). However, a broad-based protest movement to reclaim land never really developed and, to a large degree, proved unnecessary, given the general neglect of these estates (figure 6.3). Within at least one of the lease areas I visited in 2005, former plantation employees had divided up plots and were managing these individually. On others, there were no traces of managerial control at all. Despite corporate leases being issued

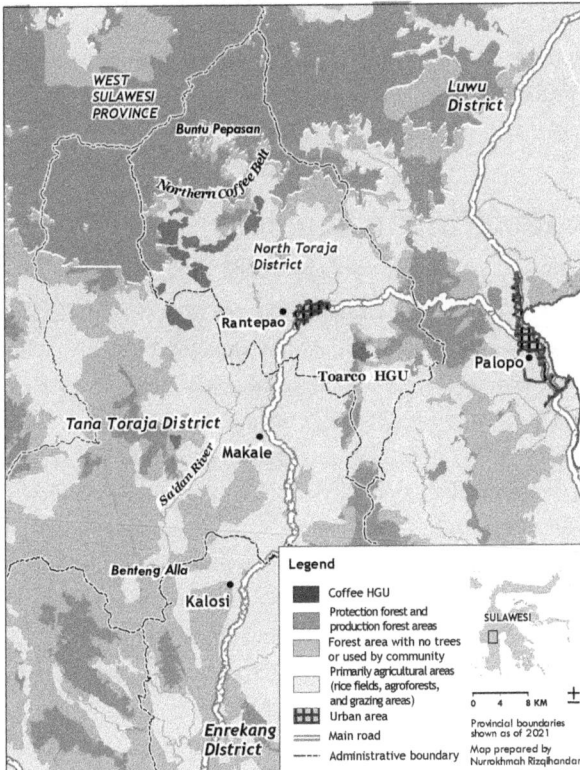

FIGURE 6.2. Land-use map of the Toraja districts

FIGURE 6.3.   Abandoned HGU estate in North Toraja, 2018

on paper, these lands were being treated by the community as fallowed land accessible based on an ethic of access under customary rights. Had the estates been commercially successful as productive entities, however, they might have triggered a significant land grab, jeopardizing long-term community access.

Rise of a Remittance Economy

Regional instability during the 1950s and 1960s, associated with the Darul Islam rebellion, made travel difficult and dangerous for non-Muslim Torajans, thus discouraging movement and migration. At any rate, the broader national economy provided few opportunities for rural migrants at that time (chapter 2). The manufacturing boom in neighboring Malaysia during the 1980s, however, was a critical trigger for Torajan out-migration, as it created shortages in the rural workforce in the plantation zones of Sabah, in Malaysian Borneo, many of which were backfilled by Torajans. Migration to Malaysia was particularly lucrative for low-skilled workers who labored on plantations, in logging camps, or in beauty salons. The expanding Indonesian urban economy of the 1990s also drew better-educated Torajans away from their homeland and into cities (including an influential community in Jakarta) and resource-rich peripheries. Malaysian migratory streams have since been eclipsed by Indonesian Papua (formerly Irian Jaya), especially following the 2001 Special Autonomy for Papua law, which had the effect of increasing wealth circulation within Papua. Torajans have been successful there, and elsewhere, in working in government and the military and by being active in politics and business.

Education was an important vehicle through which Torajans accessed these more lucrative opportunities. The quality of education is generally higher in Toraja than elsewhere in rural Sulawesi, due largely to Christian missionary activities in the early twentieth century (church organizations still support local schools and a university). Membership data of Torajan churches across Indonesia and Malaysia indicates that more ethnic Torajans may now live outside their homeland than in the two districts (De Jong 2013). Migrant success presaged significant changes for livelihoods and processes of agrarian change within Toraja.

As recently as 2001, government statistics still estimated that agriculture contributed 61 percent to the Torajan regional economy (BPS 2002). This declined spectacularly to 17 percent by 2017 (BPS 2018), while the contribution of "Trade" had increased from 9 percent to 23 percent and "Construction" from 4 to 16 percent.[5] According to the same source (BPS 2018), 65 percent of the working population living in North Toraja in 2017 was still primarily self-employed in agriculture, with the most important crops being rice and coffee (alongside livestock). According to Sakernas survey data (BPS 2019d), nearly half of these "primary farmers" identified a nonfarm secondary income (table 6.1). Meanwhile, 68 percent of those with nonagricultural primary incomes were also involved in farming as a secondary activity. This suggests a very high degree of part-time farming in Toraja. This reported dependence on agriculture, however, almost certainly overstates its importance to household livelihoods by this time, as official statistics consistently underestimate the role of remittances and informal redistribution.

TABLE 6.1 Pluriactivity in North Toraja (2019)

MAIN EMPLOYMENT	%	FARMERS WITH A SECONDARY NONFARM INCOME	FARMING AS A SECOND INCOME
Self-employed farmer (includes unpaid family member)	53.5	42.3%	
Agricultural labor	4.3		
Manufacturing	4.3		
Construction	6.3		
Wholesale or retail trade (includes mechanics)	9.4		
Transport	3.9		68.3%
Hospitality	2.2		
Government, health, and education	12.5		
Other	3.7		

Source: BPS 2019d.

Based on my own 2018 survey of ninety-nine households across ten Torajan villages,[6] 81 percent received remittances at least once from a family member in the last year, most often from children and spouses, but also from siblings, cousins, nieces, and nephews. Many households reported multiple remittance senders. The situation is thus like other parts of Southeast Asia, where Kelly (2011) has described rural development being increasingly reshaped by migration as the "household is stretched across space." Outside the main towns of Rantepao and Makale, the Torajan landscape still appeared quintessentially rural in 2024, dominated by rice fields and mixed agroforests of coffee alongside bamboo groves, sugar palm, various timber trees, *pinang* palm, betel pepper vines, fruit trees, and ornamental cordyline and crotons. This, however, like the "remittance landscapes" of the Philippines described by Deidre McKay (2003, 2005), belies a physical landscape profoundly shaped by migration and remittance flows.

Engagement with the Global Value Chain for Coffee

Prior to the 1970s, the effects of Torajan engagement with the global coffee economy were felt through remote market processes, with commodity-based pricing determined by global supply and demand, and an international quota system. This quota system, promoted by the United Nations Conference on Trade and Development, was operationalized by the International Coffee Organization (ICO) from 1962 until 1989. This helped keep global coffee prices artificially elevated, contributing to the 1970s production boom in Indonesia, but it also helped reshape the institutional context within Indonesia where export quotas were allocated to trading companies as political favors. These influences were transmitted to Torajan farmers through value chains coordinated by Makassar-based exporters. At this time, the market town of Kalosi (in Enrekang District, figure 6.2) emerged as an important coffee hub, with regional traders sending out collectors to the various highland markets to source beans. As elsewhere in Indonesia, this was often done by providing pre-harvest finance to lock in supply from household producers.

Downstream buyers later sought to intervene more directly in local production. Toarco Jaya initiated a community-based purchasing program, which by the 1990s was probably the most intensive upstream engagement by a foreign coffee company anywhere in Indonesia. It involved buying stations within coffee-growing villages, an active extension program, distribution of hand-powered pulping machines and fertilizers, demonstration plots, and the introduction

of disease-resistant planting material. It also involved an incentive-based purchasing system to improve quality. Ichsan (2017) claims that this program was
directly responsible for the commencement of coffee farming in the remote
northern village of Pulu-Pulu, now a key production center. Sometimes in partnership with the Japan International Cooperation Agency, Toarco has further
supported its investment with infrastructure development, such as roads, mini-
hydroelectricity plants, and bridges (figure 6.4). The result was the reinvigora-
tion of smallholder production in the 1980s and 1990s, supplying around four
hundred metric tons of coffee to the company mill by 2003.

In 1988, the Kapal Api Group obtained an HGU over 1,199 hectares in the
remote northwest of Toraja (the Sulotco estate at Bolokan). Like Toarco, Sulotco
was established at the site of a former colonial plantation. Estate production has
also been complemented by a community-based purchasing program, with the
roasted product sold through Kapal Api's premium Excelso range. The Toarco and
Sulotco estates are also exceptions in that they are owned by roaster lead firms,
and both claim to be operating at significant financial losses but maintaining

FIGURE 6.4.   Infrastructure built by international coffee company in North
Toraja, 2005

their estates because of their symbolic value (so-called "trophy assets"). Both feature in corporate promotional material. For example, in a section titled "Toraja (a Beautiful Experience)," the Sulotco website stated (in 2023),

> Visiting Sulotco coffee plantations, enjoying the beautiful mountain scenery at 1600 meters above sea level at Tana Toraja, experiencing humble and simple living in small villages, and participating in a cupping competition, Festival Barista, or Miss Coffee . . . these are attractions of a tourist destination that you should not miss. Especially, when combined with the opportunity to observe and experience the Toraja culture. Or visiting Toraja's traditional houses and unique cemetery that's well-known as "out of this world."[7]

The engagement of these firms with Toraja thus involves elements of landscape consumption (using the landscape as a resource for corporate storytelling) and appears to facilitate flows of corporate resources into production regions.

The international specialty coffee boom of the 1990s stimulated another significant investment in a major mill that became known locally as "the KUD" (it involved a partnership between a majority shareholder from the United States and a Rantepao-based cooperative, KUD Sane). The mill, which (like Toarco) buys wet parchment coffee from collectors and prepares green beans for export, became a major supplier to Starbucks. Starbucks claims that it had been "collaborating with the island's coffee growers since 1996" and that "Sulawesi coffee was on our original menu in 1971, and we have bought coffee from the region ever since."[8] By the mid-2000s, Starbucks was buying directly from the KUD; a local manager at the time estimated that Starbucks was absorbing 80 percent of mill throughput (around five hundred metric tons).

KUD Sane is not actually a cooperative of coffee farmers but rather maintains minor urban-based business interests in activities such as groceries and revolving credit, alongside being a mostly silent partner in the mill. The cooperative leadership, which has remained unchanged for decades, is dominated by an influential Torajan family and is further patronized by national political elites associated with the Indonesian Cooperatives Council (DEKOPIN).[9] In a familiar pattern, the cooperative leadership benefits from accessing patronage and resource flows from both state-linked actors and the global value chain. In return, Starbucks can claim to be sourcing coffee from a "cooperative," which is considered a preferred, ostensibly democratic, organizational form (recall the Global Coffee Platform's "call to action" in chapter 4 that said as much).

In partnership with KUD Sane, Starbucks had (by 2021) helped fund the building of fourteen "schools" on Sulawesi, including kindergartens, which the company claims have had a significant effect on community access to education.[10] It is noteworthy that the focus on kindergartens would also help free up parental labor to focus on coffee-growing. Community members are generally appreciative of such assistance and even proud of their village's association with an internationally renowned company like Starbucks.

Torajan farmers thus sell semiprocessed coffee to market-based collectors, who usually sell directly to one of these large mills (Toarco, Sulotco, and the KUD) with little support from state agricultural agencies. The chain here is short and relatively direct, farm-gate prices are high, at least relative to other Indonesian producers, and the major mills enforce a degree of supply chain traceability. By 2008, collectors started carrying identification cards issued by the mills that authorized them as preferred suppliers (known as *relasi*), who were gatekeepers of quality and responsible for ensuring farm-level conformance to sustainability program requirements (like Starbucks' CAFE Practices). As gatekeepers to the market, the *relasi* were significantly empowered by both sustainability requirements and quality-related control measures demanded by the value chain.

Torajan coffee has been particularly amenable to valorization by downstream actors, owing to the niche marketing of a highly distinctive coffee linked, for marketing purposes, to the uniqueness of Torajan culture. Starbucks has worked with the KUD to develop niche products, such as "Kopi Kampung" as a "Black Apron Exclusive." Such products draw on Torajan cultural imagery, notably the *tongkonan* (figure 6.5). In addition to supplying a physical product (coffee), the visual and cultural appeal of the Torajan landscape thus also provides an intangible service to downstream actors who use origin stories to generate value at the point of sale. Neumann Gruppe had earlier marketed green coffee in hand-carved barrels marketed as Kopi Tongkonan Toraja, at 50 USD per kilogram (in the early 2000s when ICO indicator prices were less than 2 USD). Neumann highlighted their relationship with a particular village community (a "relationship coffee") and claimed that "the coffee corresponds with the individuality of their culture in every aspect." Such sourcing activities do not generally stimulate a productivist approach to farming but do present opportunities for well-positioned community members to assume control of critical value-adding nodes in the chain. The strong market associations between place and quality also encouraged the development of a Geographical Indication, approved in 2013, driven by local state-based actors as a thus-far unsuccessful attempt to extract rent from these associations.

The influence of value chain dynamics on coffee production in Toraja is thus multidimensional. The earlier investments by Toarco were critical in encouraging farm-level coffee investments and instrumental in establishing an international reputation for "Toraja coffee." This has since triggered further value chain interventions, the cumulative impact of which has been to encourage smallholders to maintain coffee production in a context where household livelihood dependence on coffee has otherwise been waning. A possibly even more important impact from the various value chain interventions, however, has been the opportunities

FIGURE 6.5.   Torajan cultural imagery used by coffee roasters. *Photo:* Dreamstime.com © Antoni Halim (with permission).

for some individuals to position themselves strategically between downstream buyers and farmers as *relasi*, cooperative leaders, and brokers for relationship coffees. In this way, value chain interventions have become incorporated within prevailing social structures as a potential means to access resource flows.

Despite the powerful role of lead firm strategies throughout the value chain, this influence constitutes one of many factors shaping institutional environments within smallholder commodity-producing landscapes. As Kelly (2009, 460) reminds us, it is not enough "to seek explanations of regional development that focus solely on the multiscalar firm-based networks"—instead, he introduces the idea of a "global reproduction network." He argues that a singular focus on production rather than household strategies for reproduction can conceal the myriad forces driving rural development outcomes (Kelly 2013). This is certainly true for the institutional environment within Toraja that is strongly shaped by a distinct form of landscape multifunctionality.

Toraja as a Consumption Landscape

Toraja is a *multifunctional* rural landscape where agricultural production occurs alongside new patterns of redistributive livelihoods. It is a site of both production *and* consumption (Neilson 2022). What stands out compared to the emergence of a consumption countryside in the Global North (Marsden 1999), however, is that Torajan multifunctionality is not based around tourism or conventional leisure activities (although these activities exist too), but is enabled through a cultural entanglement between the émigré Torajan community and their homeland. It constitutes *intra-cultural consumption of a rural landscape* (Neilson 2022). This entanglement has important implications for the regional economy, attitudes toward coffee production, land relations, and ultimately for the rise of fortress farming.

Toraja is renowned across Indonesia for the scale of its funeral ceremonies (figure 6.6), which reflect Austronesian cultural influences associated with reverence for ancestors and the cultural importance of *tongkonan* kinship houses (as reflected in the epigraph that opened this chapter). These elements were central to a religious system known as Aluk To'dolo, and beliefs and practices have only been partly modified by Christianity. At their largest, in the case of a high-ranking noble, funeral ceremonies will involve years of planning following death, a weeklong series of main rites, catering for many thousands of guests, the construction of a temporary bamboo village, and the sacrifice of several hundred head of livestock. These rites are part of a broader cycle of ceremonial activity held to mark stages in rice cultivation, *tongkonan* and rice barn construction, weddings, and other events of social importance. Membership of an ancestral *tongkonan* provides an important source of identity for many, whether they live

FIGURE 6.6. Torajan funeral procession, 2018

in Toraja or elsewhere, and so helps construct powerful links between émigré Torajans and their homeland (Waterson 2009).

Attendance and participation in ceremonies are widespread and involve considerable resource redistribution. Some 80 percent of respondents from my 2018 ten-village survey had worked at a ceremony in the last year, about half of whom were paid in meat (from sacrificed livestock), cigarettes, and palm wine (although many were also "gifted" cash by patrons). The key type of work in the lead-up to ceremonies is the construction of bamboo structures (*lantang*) to receive guests, which is performed in a general spirit of mutual help (*gotong royong*) and often involves local work groups, known as *saroan* in North Toraja, or informally as *kobu*. *Saroan* usually have a clearly identified leader or patron (*ambe' saroan*) who is responsible for accessing, accumulating, and distributing resources among *saroan* members. During the ceremony itself, villagers work in butchering, food preparation, and the serving of food to guests, where labor is provided through both *saroan* and the PKK (Pemberdayaan Kesejahteraan Keluarga) women's groups (figure 6.7).

Cultural specialists can also earn a living from ceremonial services. Ritual poets (*tomina'a*, meaning "the knowledgeable one," figure 6.8) were being paid the equivalent of between 1,000 and 5,000 USD per ceremony in 2018, depending on their skill and reputation. The spiritual function of these poet-priests has been partially replaced by church ministers, but their presence is still considered

FIGURE 6.7.   Preparation and distribution of food at a 2018 ceremony

necessary to "create the right kind of mood at a ceremony," as a mourner once explained to me. Chanting dance troupes (*ma'badong*, paid around 1,500 USD, figure 6.9) and musicians (*pa'suling*, paid 500 USD) are paid either in cash or in live buffalo, and the increasing commercialization of such traditional roles has helped to reinvigorate interest in these arts. There are also exclusively commercial services including catering, sales of palm wine, electrical services and sound systems, water supply (often trucked in), decorators, and carvers. By far the greatest expenditure at a Torajan ceremony, however, is on livestock. Single buffaloes with highly desired markings (*tedong saleko* or *tedong bonga*) were being sold for as much as 50,000 USD in 2018 (but averaged around 2,000 USD for a standard gray buffalo). Several hundred may be purchased for the most extravagant funerals.

The funds required for funerals are immense. One Jakarta-based family estimated their total expenditure for a medium-size 2018 ceremony at 150,000 USD, at a time when annual Indonesian GNI per capita was only 3,530 USD. My rough estimate is that the total expenditure on ceremonies in North Toraja constitutes around 16 percent of the regional economy. Within Toraja, it is widely discussed how nearly all ceremonial funding comes from émigré Torajans. In this way, the Torajan rural landscape has become primarily a site of consumption, an economic parallel to leisure-oriented spending in multifunctional landscapes elsewhere. Toraja does attract domestic and international

FIGURE 6.8. A *Tomina'a* ritual poet reciting incantations in a megalith field, 2018

FIGURE 6.9.   *Ma'badong* dance troupe contracted for a funeral ceremony, 2018

tourists, but tourism activities are concentrated in Rantepao hotels and restaurants and at a limited number of village sites (*obyek wisata*), such that tourism's overall economic impact is minimal. Elsewhere in Indonesia, especially on Java, resource flows into rural regions are intimately related to domestic demand for leisure activities. The distribution of ceremonial spending in Toraja is much more spatially and socially dispersed (compared to tourism) and reaches every village in some way. Certainly, there is a degree of economic leakage of ceremonial spending (buffaloes need to be traded in from other districts), but overall, many ceremonial services and products provided are locally sourced, often through *saroan* and PKK groups. Demand for these activities is constantly re-created by their active promotion by those ceremonial "service suppliers" who benefit from ongoing resource flows. Émigré Torajans experience considerable social pressure to host extravagant funeral ceremonies and redistribute wealth, even if this means going into debt. While the scale of ceremonial economy in Toraja is unusual, the continued existence of ceremonially driven resource flows into cultural homelands is not unique. I have also observed similar processes in the coffee-growing regions of Bajawa, Kintamani, Semende, and Simalungun.

Toraja can also be read as a "remittance landscape" (McKay 2003), where the landscape effects of migration are manifest in a general disintensification of agriculture, but where farm activities linked to ceremonial use and local consumption persist. Small-scale pig and buffalo rearing are important and widespread household activities in North Toraja (figure 6.10). High-cost buffaloes are often reared on a profit-sharing basis, while pigs are overwhelmingly owner-reared (table 6.2). The rural landscape consequently consists of land dedicated to forage and fodder crops for these animals, often interspersed with agroforestry groves planted with bamboo (for ceremonial construction), sugar palms (for palm wine), and various timber species (for *tongkonan* and *alang* construction). While coffee is traded out of the region through global value chains, local ceremonial consumption of coffee is also significant and generates strong demand. Rice production is consumed locally.

A strong factor driving émigré Torajans to continue financing such ceremonial activity (alongside spiritual beliefs and the maintenance of social status) is that it reinforces personal identity linked to a distinct culture within multiethnic Indonesia. The Torajan rural landscape can thus be considered as delivering

FIGURE 6.10. Pigpens above coffee plot in North Toraja, 2017

TABLE 6.2 Extent of household-scale livestock rearing in North Toraja

	BUFFALO	PIG
Rear at least one (% of agricultural households)	40%	63%
Median number reared by each livestock-rearing household	1	3
Own only (% of livestock-rearing households)	51%	91%
Rear on profit-sharing basis only (% of livestock-rearing households)	41%	7%
Wage-based only (% of livestock-rearing households)	3%	0.1%
Own and profit share (% of livestock-rearing households)	5%	1%
Other	0.7%	0.2%

Source: BPS 2013 (N = 30,222).

a cultural service (providing a sense of purpose and meaning) to this broader community. An expressive example of this is evident in a video clip titled *Toraja Ethnic Music Project* produced by Allegra Choral Production, a collective of Torajan (and émigré Torajan) youth and released on YouTube on September 1, 2021, which has had more than forty-five thousand views within a month (figure 6.11).[11] The clip creatively presented an idyllic yet modern émigré perspective of their homeland, celebrating in an emotive way the physical and cultural landscape with which they and (judging by the numerous likes and comments) many other Torajans clearly identify. Identity-based cultural relationships are further manifested, through ceremonial funding, in various modes of "distributive labor," where sources of wealth are divided into "smaller and smaller slivers as they work their way across social relations of kinship, clientage, allegiance, and solidarity" (Ferguson 2015, 97). Social status and cultural meaning are conferred in return. While the cultural processes and economic pathways presented here are specific to Toraja, I suggest that such tendencies are likely to be widespread where rural homelands present opportunities for protecting and asserting cultural identities. Rural livelihoods, and the role of land within them, are transformed in the process.

FIGURE 6.11. An image from the Allegra Choral Ethnic Project, 2021. *Credit:* Seto Samben (Allegra Choral, with permission).

Accessing Land in Toraja

I have been visiting some of the same villages in the far north of Toraja since 1998, in what I call the "Torajan coffee belt" (mostly covered by the Buntu Pepasan subdistrict). Many of the forest-margin villages in this belt (figure 6.2) are tightly integrated into international specialty coffee chains (Key Coffee and Starbucks), and 75 percent of all agricultural households in Buntu Pepasan reported managing their own coffee farm in 2013 (BPS 2013). Land registration (*hak milik*) remains rare, although minimal payments of land tax (SPPT, Surat Pemberitahuan Pajak Terhutang), averaging 5,900 IDR (0.4 USD) per plot in 2021, are commonly paid. SPPT payments are made based on very rough land area estimates, with villagers estimating the extent of their coffee farm in terms of trees rather than hectares. Ichsan (2017) also describes how residents in Pulu-Pulu had never measured their coffee land. Land markets for coffee farms in these remote areas are generally absent. Figure 6.2 furthermore shows the large areas of land in the northern coffee belt cultivated or fallowed by the community despite being designated state protection forest.

In 1999 I met Bapa' Lia, who was planting coffee on what he considered ancestral land after losing his job in a factory outside Jakarta during the Asian financial crisis, and in 2003 I met with Simon, who had returned from Sabah after a crackdown on illegal migrants by Malaysian authorities, and who was also farming coffee. In 2018, when off-farm work in the Indonesian economy was more readily available, I found these coffee plots, which were a half-hour walk away from ancestral hamlets, abandoned to fallow, and some houses were unoccupied. New coffee plantings on land much closer to the hamlet, however, were still being maintained. During 2020, as COVID-19-induced social restrictions caused economic contraction, many workers and students again returned to their family villages in Buntu Pepasan to engage in farming. Household-scale coffee investments in Toraja are thus strongly determined by access to customary land and the lack of livelihood opportunities elsewhere in the economy.

At the onset of the colonial period in Toraja, the ownership of *sawah* was held individually and controlled by a hereditary elite (essentially a feudalistic noble caste) but with evidence of extensive sharecropping (Paerels 1927). The dryland *ladang* areas, however, had much broader "ownership," where profits were retained by the cultivator, which meant that coffee was one of the few crops where the "little man" (in Paerels's words) could obtain cash (or cloth) independently of the elites. This was important in a society where elite control over *sawah* was justified through genealogies that extended back to divine ancestors, a position that was constantly reinforced through ritual. These ancestors were said to have brought rice with them from the heavens and to have laid out the first fields, such that *sawah* is associated both with ancestor deities and the elite caste. Torajan society continues to be loosely structured into hereditary castes, the lowest of which (known as *kaunan*) once constituted a form of descent-based slavery, where entire families were dependent on an elite family or clan for their subsistence and who provided unpaid labor in return. It is therefore significant that coffee cultivation was apparently never subject to the same cultural controls or ritual activity as *sawah*. After more than a decade as the Dutch *controleur* in Makale, Nobele (1926) discussed not only how planters of perennial crops would retain ownership of the crop, but also how the land itself, upon fallowing, would revert to community ownership.

Access to this common land pool would be controlled by the institution of the *tongkonan*, which refers to both the ancestral houses and the genealogical associations that these houses represent. The *tongkonan* is thus much more than a physical residence in that it is also a symbol of social control over people and resources. Much of the agricultural land within the *tongkonan* territory is also referred to as *tanah tongkonan*, although claims of individual access (especially to *sawah*) are recognized within this. The continued association of individual plots of land to specific *tongkonan* has meant that the local Land Agency Office (BPN) has been generally reluctant to register such land individually as *hak milik*, implying de facto recognition of customary tenure. During the period 2016–2019, however, around a thousand *hak milik* certificates were issued by BPN annually in North Toraja, mostly in urban and peri-urban areas. The PTSL registration program (chapter 5) was also being rolled out in select villages during 2022. There is thus increasing pressure to register *tanah tongkonan* as individual *hak milik,* resulting in the progressive dismantling of customary tenure.

The 2019 regional decree on customary law communities (discussed in chapter 5) raises the potential for *adat* regulation to be legally reasserted over land (both *sawah* and dryland) where individual rights are recognized, such that rights over disposal would be limited by the *adat* law community. This would formalize existing customary practice, whereby outsiders find it difficult to purchase rural lands in Toraja, while also potentially limiting the bundle of rights usually associated with *hak milik*. The decree is very explicit about basing *adat* rights on "genealogical-territorial" ties, which, in the Torajan context, implies that *tongkonan* land is to be controlled by hereditary elites. There is already substantial overlap between *adat* and commercial and political elites at the district (*kabupaten*) level. Torajans sometimes use the term *tallu lalikan* (the three stones used for cooking in a hearth) as a metaphor for the shared power nexus between the Torajan church, *adat*, and government. Further empowering this leadership class holds attendant risks of marginalizing other groups. Indeed, Klenke

(2013, 165) highlighted how the Torajan nobility skillfully enrolled the state as a resource to consolidate their own political position, arguing that "indigeneity in the Toraja case serves as a means to again silence those who find it difficult to make political claims." The key point being, however, that the commodification of agricultural land in Toraja has been, and continues to be, circumscribed by *adat* structures, and this, together with the range of resource in-flows discussed earlier, has limited the growth of farming systems that might be considered either productivist or capitalist. While it is too early to assess the implications of the 2019 regional decree on *adat* recognition, its passage (and the passage of many others like it) does suggest a complicated, nonlinear, trajectory of land relations in rural Indonesia.

Accumulation of coffee-growing land is not readily apparent in the northern coffee belt, with coffee remaining a backyard crop on small plots close to village hamlets (figure 6.12). In 2013, 88 percent of coffee-growing households in Buntu Pepasan maintained fewer than one thousand trees (table 6.3). This reflects the prevalence of fortress farming strategies in a commodity-producing region, where access to coffee-growing land is relatively open to individuals with ancestral claims and who are willing to invest their own labor in establishing and maintaining a plot. Coffee-producing land remains fragmented but easily accessible (see also Ichsan 2017). Despite the extended history of commodity production for global markets, there is little evidence that coffee cultivation has driven processes of land-based agrarian differentiation in Toraja. This can be explained by local cultural institutions that restrict outsiders, underdeveloped coffee land

FIGURE 6.12.   Recently established coffee plot, North Toraja, 2018

TABLE 6.3   Distribution of coffee farm sizes (by trees) in Buntu Pepasan subdistrict, North Toraja

NO. OF COFFEE TREES	PERCENT OF COFFEE-GROWING HOUSEHOLDS
<100	25.5
100–999	62.4
1,000–2,999	9.5
3,000–4,999	1.6
>4,999	1.0

Source: BPS 2013.

markets, the persistence of customary access arrangements, the high degree of landscape multifunctionality, and the role that coffee performs within fortress farming livelihood strategies.

Two opposing forces are currently reshaping land access patterns in Toraja and elsewhere in Indonesia. The PTSL program is accelerating, with entire villages being mapped and landownership rigidly registered on a cadastre. In the long term, this threatens to undermine flexible access for those needing farming as a safety net. Meanwhile, efforts to strengthen the land management function of *adat* law communities may further empower traditional elites to control land access, but may also enhance the "social function of land" and potentially limit the full development of land as a commodity. Importantly, these processes are playing out at a time when the role of farming, as a source of accumulation, is in decline.

Rural Livelihoods in Tondok Buntu

I will now explore the intersection between remittances, ceremonial activity, land access, and coffee farming in a particular village hamlet (*tondok*) in North Toraja that I have been calling Tondok Buntu (figure 6.13). The hamlet abuts lower montane forest at around sixteen hundred meters altitude and is located not far from the locally well-known Sapan coffee market in what is considered the heart of the North Torajan coffee belt.

When I interviewed Mama Dewi in Tondok Buntu in 2018 (age forty-four, educated to junior high school), she was living with her aging grandfather in an ancestral *tongkonan* with a modified kitchen extension that relied on fuelwood. The household owned a motorbike, mobile phones, a ceramic squat toilet, and had an electricity connection, but no refrigerator. Mama Dewi is actively involved in the small Pentecostal church in the hamlet, and she is the head of the state-supported women's association (PKK). She estimated she had attended five

FIGURE 6.13. "Tondok Buntu," now largely populated by young children and the elderly, 2018

ceremonies in the last year, all of which helped build social capital. While she would consult her husband (Bapa' Dewi) on important financial investments, my observations over repeat visits suggest that Mama Dewi was primarily responsible for managing household finances. Bapa' Dewi had recently replanted around one hundred coffee trees, and Mama Dewi had sold around three hundred liters of parchment coffee that season to her regular buyer (*langganan*) at the market. That year, sales of parchment-encased coffee gave her a coffee income of around 400 USD. This was mostly used immediately for purchasing food items in the market (such as rice, sugar, canned fish, and instant noodles), or what Mama Dewi referred to as "kitchen money" (*seng dapo'*).

In 2018, all thirty-two resident households of Tondok Buntu cultivated their own coffee plot (ranging from around fifty to four thousand trees). The situation was reportedly similar in nearby Pulu-Pulu (Ichsan 2017). Households in Tondok Buntu sold between twenty and fifteen hundred liters of parchment coffee during each of the 2017 and 2018 harvests (around 3.5 liters of parchment are needed to produce one kilogram of green beans for export). Despite the relatively small volumes involved, all households in Tondok Buntu initially claimed that coffee was their most important source of cash income. Like most other house-holders in the hamlet, Mama Dewi had not obtained credit from a coffee buyer in the last year, although she felt that she could have if needed. Her household sold no other crops. Unlike most other coffee farmers in Tondok Buntu, Bapa' Dewi had pruned their trees himself that year, but (like other farmers) he didn't fertil-ize, although he did both cut weeds by hand and sprayed them (the widespread use of labor-saving herbicides in 2018 was a change from my earlier surveys in the northern coffee belt in 2008). Within Tondok Buntu, no paid labor was used for the coffee harvest or for crop maintenance, and there was no sharecropping of coffee land (in contrast to the situation with *sawah*). The fieldwork of Ichsan (2017) in Pulu-Pulu found some evidence of wages being paid on coffee farms, although harvest-sharing arrangements were more common. My ten-village sur-vey found sharecropping or renting of coffee land to be pursued by less than 5 percent of coffee-growing households.

In 2018 some households in Tondok Buntu had attended agronomic training organized by Toarco, and the hamlet was not part of Starbucks CAFE Practices program. However, the involvement of Toarco was reportedly still keenly felt in 2017 in Pulu-Pulu, where Toarco had established buying stations and rented land for a demonstration plot (Ichsan 2017). In Tondok Buntu too, attempts had been made by a village émigré (living in Kalimantan) to develop a specialty coffee chain with a Jakarta-based roaster, through the support of an international devel-opment agency. The initiative ultimately failed, but some financial resources and equipment were distributed during 2017–2019. In 2018, several coffee plots had been fallowed, and some outlying houses, built during a previous coffee boom, had also been abandoned, such that the "frontier" around the village was con-tracting rather than expanding. The remains of one of the HGU plantation leases from the 1990s, partially planted but now abandoned, can be found by a short walk higher into the hills behind Tondok Buntu.[12]

As was the case with around 40 percent of households in Tondok Buntu, Mama Dewi owned inherited *sawah* (Ichsan 2017 found 75 percent of households own-ing *sawah* in Pulu-Pulu). *Sawah* cultivation, however, generally requires labor recruitment beyond the household. Cash payments for labor in the rice fields (planting and harvesting) do occur, but these are less common than in-kind payment systems. In 2018 in Tondok Buntu, nearly half the resident villagers participated in an arrangement that allowed those participating in rice planting to take home a third of what they could later harvest (a high share by Indone-sian standards). Mama Dewi also helped planting and harvesting rice in other people's *sawah*. Elsewhere in Toraja (in the Tondon region), workers joining the harvest in 2022 could take home one-fifth of what they harvested (without being involved in planting) in a system known as *ma'kangkan*.

Despite Mama Dewi owning her own *sawah* and accessing further rice through share-harvesting, her rice stores lasted the household only six months. She accessed her remaining rice needs from the market or her Rastra allocation (a government social protection program). Her garden provided shallots, beans, bananas, cassava, choko, sweet potatoes, and chilies for direct consumption throughout the year. Neither Mama Dewi nor any other village resident reported skipping meals as a result of having no food, and only one household reported withdrawing children from school for lack of finances. In contrast, elderly villagers vividly recalled past times when food was scarce and individuals would go hungry. With small plots and double-cropping being at the mercy of seasonal rainfall, only 9 percent of North Torajan rice farmers reported actually producing a surplus of rice for sale in 2013 (only 1 percent reported a surplus in Buntu Pepasan, and none in Tondok Buntu). This is due to the small areas of *sawah* cultivated by each household, with 71 percent cultivating less than 0.3 hectare across Toraja (BPS 2013). While rice cultivation possesses cultural importance in Toraja, it has long since stopped being a source of wealth accumulation.

The number of *sawah*-managing households across North Toraja declined between 2003 and 2013, with some evidence of concentration in management (figure 6.14). Rather than indicating accumulation, this is related to out-migration, where migrants retain ownership over, but not management of, *sawah*. Sharecropping of *sawah* is widespread and often arranged within extended kin and patronage networks. One Torajan born and living in Jakarta explained to me how his inherited *sawah* would be cultivated by a cousin still living in Toraja, for which he received no rental payment or share of the harvest (many others, however, do claim a share). For these émigré Torajans, *sawah* ownership provides a tangible link to their ancestors. Despite widespread sharecropping, 78 percent of *sawah*-cultivating households across North Toraja reported owning at least some of the *sawah* they cultivated (BPS 2013). The majority of sharecroppers in Buntu Pepasan also own rice fields (BPS 2013). Unlike coffee farms, *sawah* fields are regularly bought and sold, pawned and leased.

Every morning, Mama Dewi would prepare feed for her two pigs. The previous year, she had sold one pig for the equivalent of around 200 USD and taken another three (of similar value) directly to ceremonies. More generally, however, only five households in the hamlet had sold a pig in the last year, while fifteen had taken at least one to a ceremony, which either constituted repayment of an earlier ceremonial debt or the opening of a new debt relationship in the circular ritual economy. Twenty-six of the thirty-two households had at least one pig at

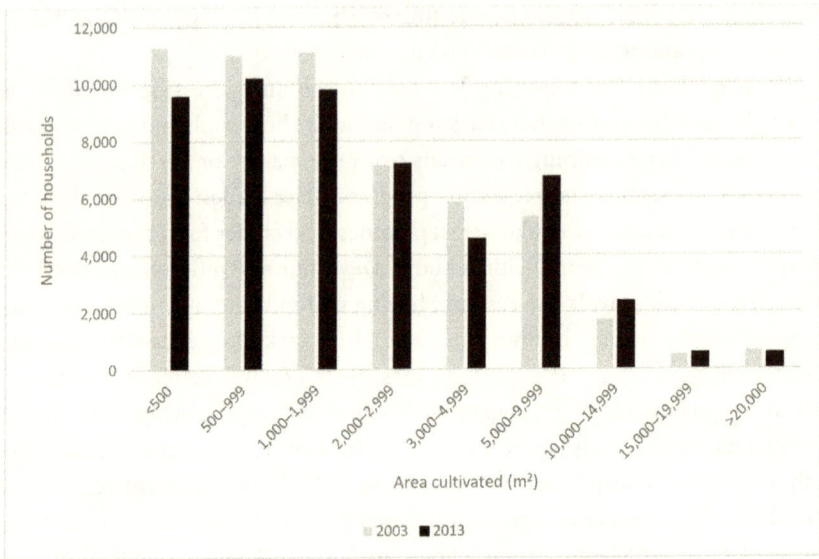

FIGURE 6.14. Size of *sawah* management in the Toraja districts.

Sources: BPS 2003, 2013.

the time of the 2018 survey, and Bapa' Dewi was one of six men in the hamlet then rearing buffaloes. Coffee and pigs were Mama and Bapa' Dewi's only source of agricultural income during the past year (a total equivalent to around 600 USD). A passion fruit boom, stimulated by a Toraja-based juice bottling industry, had occurred in Tondok Buntu during the mid-2000s (although farmers had since lost interest because of low prices). Toraja has thus shown signs of agricultural disintensification. Overall, there was one skilled wood-carver in the *tondok* (figure 6.15) and one driver in 2018. Locally earned income (whether farm or nonfarm) was in no way sufficient to sustain livelihoods.

Mama Dewi had six children, the eldest two of whom were working in Papua and Malaysia and who would occasionally send remittances to help with household living costs, while two were still in tertiary study (one in Rantepao and one in Makassar, funded by their older brother in Papua). The two youngest were attending local schools and living in Tondok Buntu. Mama Dewi's brother in Kalimantan also occasionally sent money for specific purchases (such as kitchen appliances and, in 2018, some mattresses) and for ceremonial contributions. Household structures are complex and multi-sited in village hamlets like Tondok Buntu. In a census of household members (defined as people sleeping under one roof, plus any nonresident spouse and children), about half were living

FIGURE 6.15. Wood-carver in Tondok Buntu working on a new *tongkonan*, 2018

elsewhere for work (*merantau kerja*), and the hamlet was primarily populated by children and the elderly, suggesting the important child-rearing service (social reproduction) provided by the rural landscape (table 6.4). Both men and women were involved in migration. Thirty of the thirty-two households received regular remittances to help with daily living expenditure (six from relatives other than spouse and children, suggesting the continued importance of extended kin networks), and twenty-two had received remittances specifically for ceremonial use in the last year. When I visited the hamlet in 2022, it was being converted into a ceremonial ground (ceremonial activity was vibrant across Toraja that year,

TABLE 6.4 Stretched households in Tondok Buntu (June 2018)

	LIVING ELSEWHERE		LIVING IN VILLAGE	
	NUMBER	SHARE	NUMBER	SHARE
<18 years	10	8%	38	33%
19–55 years	106	90%	47	41%
>55 years	2	2%	30	26%
male	60	51%	61	53%
female	58	49%	54	47%
Still studying	5		35	
Total	118		115	

Source: Author own survey (n = 32).

as rituals had been delayed by the COVID-19 pandemic). In her role as PKK head, Mama Dewi was responsible for preparing food for carpenters building the *lantang*. She and the carpenters were compensated for this, and meat from slaughtered livestock from a recent ceremony in a nearby village was being distributed through the hamlet. Across Torajan villages, meat is rarely bought from the market.

This redistribution of resources into Tondok Buntu through remittances is occurring alongside state-funded transfers. State supports had become prevalent in North Toraja even before they were increased further during the COVID-19 pandemic (especially through the reallocation of Dana Desa funds), with more than a third of all households receiving some kind of state support in 2019 (table 6.5). I found even higher rates of recipients in my 2018 census in Tondok Buntu. Ninety-four percent of households reported receiving food support payments (Rastra), and 38 percent received conditional cash transfers (PKH). While the amount of these transfers is relatively small, in combination with remittances and ceremonial redistribution it is helping to sustain and reproduce Torajan society to a greater extent than commodity production. Mama Dewi's household received government supports through both Rastra and PKH, as well as the school scholarships for the poor program (Program Indonesia Pintar), and the household was covered by the national health insurance program (Kartu Indonesia Sehat). In a study conducted during the 2020 COVID-19 pandemic, Williams (2020) described how state-based social protection supports in Toraja stepped in when ceremonial redistribution was disrupted by social distancing requirements. She emphasized how these state supports had become intertwined with both ceremonial patronage and party politics.[13]

TABLE 6.5 Government social protection programs in North Toraja (2019)

GOVERNMENT PROGRAM	HOUSEHOLDS RECEIVING SUPPORT (%)
Bansos Rastra (rice supports)	26
Program Keluarga Harapan (conditional cash transfers)	19
Kartu Keluarga Sejahtera holder (card to access food supports)	19
Program Indonesia Pintar (scholarship recipient)	23
At least one of the above	37

Source: BPS 2019e.

The regional government of North Toraja operated an annual budget of around 70 million USD in 2018, which is roughly equivalent to my estimate of ceremonial-based remittances. Of this budget, only 2.8 million USD was locally generated (Pendapatan Asli Daerah), while a full 55 million USD came from Regional Balancing Funds (Dana Alokasi Umum and Dana Alokasi Khusus) from the national budget (BPS 2021b). There is a sense in which the considerable government expenditures in rural regions like Toraja are another mechanism facilitating resource transfers across space, which provide redistributed livelihoods, either directly for government *aparat* or indirectly through opportunities for contractors to deliver *proyek*. As with other resource distribution networks, individuals seek to position themselves to benefit from these flows, often by inserting themselves strategically within patron-client relationships.

While many Torajans still produce agricultural products (especially for local consumption), the rural economy can be considered as shifting toward increasingly nonproductivist tendencies. The specific role of coffee income within Tondok Buntu household livelihoods has thus become that of providing seasonal cash income to meet basic consumption needs (*seng dapo'*). In this way, coffee income complements subsistence food production, food and cash distribution through ceremonies, and broader resource transfers to meet household consumption needs. Farm-based drudgery is calibrated against these needs and alternative opportunities. The result is that, in most circumstances, households in Tondok Buntu are not strongly motivated to allocate labor and capital to increase coffee production (although they have also not abandoned it entirely). Instead, they are content for coffee to provide additional cash income in a production system that can be readily managed by an aging workforce.

Fortress Farming in a Multifunctional Coffee Landscape

This chapter has presented a case of what I call fortress farming in a coffee-producing region that is heavily dominated by intra-cultural consumption of the landscape. The key elements of fortress farming presented here include the ability of farming to provide a safety net during personal distress or systemic crisis, how membership of the rural community and access to land confer protective, identity-based cultural meaning for individuals, and the way rural livelihoods are supported by various resource transfers from extra-local sources (thereby facilitating agricultural disintensification). Wealth accumulation through a productivist use of farmland is rare, and capitalist relations within farming are muted.

Farmland is instead embedded within a culturally imbued physical landscape that provides a livelihood refuge for community members and the diaspora. Farmland closer to urban centers and along main roads, however, is not insulated from commoditization for conversion to nonagricultural purposes such as residential and commercial uses, and as a speculative investment.

The buying and selling of coffee-growing land has remained remarkably uncommon, and most individuals have been able to access customary land for coffee-growing should they wish and should they have available labor resources within their household to manage it. Customary *adat* institutions support this by dissuading the commoditization of land but not preventing it entirely.[14] I have met with individuals who took up, or resumed, coffee farming after losing jobs elsewhere, many of whom considered coffee farming as affording temporary financial relief as a "fortress crop." This is made possible in Toraja by a combination of relatively low demand for farmland due to high rates of out-migration and the strength of customary land institutions. The situation for coffee differs somewhat from rice fields, which were frequently bought and sold, leased, pawned, and sharecropped, even though little Torajan rice is actually commoditized through the market. The reasons for this are as much cultural as they are economic, in that rice farming is associated with social status and cultural identity.

The extended engagement with the global coffee market has, however, reconfigured the immediate institutional environment for smallholders, and especially collectors and certain local elites. This has occurred through both market processes and through nonmarket value chain interventions by lead firms. Initiatives from within the value chain to promote coffee production have influenced decision-making at the farm level to continue growing coffee, but their influence also has its limits and is difficult to assess without the counterfactual of what would have happened in the absence of such initiatives. However, it is likely that value chain programs have had the effect of maintaining a considerable number of rural households engaged in petty commodity production who might have otherwise abandoned coffee entirely. Indeed, coffee is not unimportant for household livelihoods. It provides additional cash during the harvest that is used to buy items from the market for immediate household consumption and so can perform an important role for food security. Importantly, however, this engagement with the coffee value chain has not resulted in the emergence of capitalist farmers, or "agripreneurs" (in the language of some Indonesian government agencies). It has not triggered processes of agricultural modernization, land accumulation, and agriculturally driven class differentiation. These processes have been stymied by new patterns of non-land-based wealth accumulation and their distribution through the culturally mediated social networks discussed in this chapter. The value chain itself has also provided another flow of external resources for which local actors compete to access. In the case of Toraja, embedded as it is within specialty coffee markets that value place-based quality associations, the landscape provides a further service to lead firms who have used it to construct (symbolic) value and who have made investments to maintain supply.

While value chain initiatives have attempted to encourage households to increase resource allocation toward coffee production, these efforts intersect with other social structures to cocreate the local livelihood-shaping institutional environment. Instead of increasing coffee productivity, rural households preferentially attempt to position themselves within various patronage systems by providing services to patrons, often benefiting from multiple resource flows and distributed livelihoods. As a consumption landscape, Toraja provides cultural services to the diaspora, and this gives rise to a high degree of landscape multifunctionality. Remittances provide direct support for daily living expenses and are injected into the ceremonial economy, with significant multiplier effects for livelihoods more broadly. Distributed livelihoods were also evident through access to state welfare programs, involvement in government *proyek* or NGO initiatives, or even through employment as government *aparat*. The consequence of these various structures and processes in Toraja is fortress farming, where land is treated as a cultural and livelihood refuge for the community rather than a source of agricultural wealth accumulation. Instead, a nonproductivist style of farming prevails.

FORTRESS FARMING IN SEMENDE

Sangkan pandan bebuah paoh
Didalam kebun dide bebunge
Sangkan badan merantau jauh
Didalam dusun dide begune

Jiku lemak la sambal paoh
Makan dipaun nginak kesawah
Jiku lemak merantau jauh
Inga nga dusun nak balik tulah

(Why does the *pandan* give forth wild mango fruit?
In the garden it won't flower
Why must I leave my home [*merantau*]?
In the village I have nothing to do

I believe wild mango *sambal* is delicious
Eaten at the hearth gazing over the rice fields
I believed leaving home [*merantau*] would be pleasant
Remembering the village and longing to return)

—Opening lines from *Merantau Jauh* (a Semende song in the form of *pantun* verse, written by, and reproduced with permission from, Ilyas Albarsyah)

Southern Sumatra is the geographic center of Indonesian coffee production, where smallholders depend to a greater degree on cash crops for household income than in many other regions, while off-farm activities are less widespread. If Toraja is a coffee-growing region with advanced landscape multifunctionality, high remittance dependence, and integration with niche specialty markets, southern Sumatra is presented in this chapter as a bulk supplier of Robusta coffee where there is a higher livelihood dependence on commodity production. Yet even here there has not been a wholesale embrace of intensive production systems. Pluriactivity and migration are still evident, and land relations are heavily regulated through *adat*-related social institutions.

I first conducted field research in southern Sumatra in 2005 (in the Sumber Jaya region of Lampung), followed by a study of coffee-growing communities around the perimeter of Bukit Barisan Selatan National Park in 2008 (also in Lampung Province). Since 2012, I have conducted detailed field research in Semende (South Sumatra Province), and I will draw primarily on this Semende research in this chapter. I was part of a research team that, in partnership with SurveyMETER, a specialist surveying firm, coordinated three detailed household survey rounds in Semende (of 1,589 coffee-growing households) in 2015, 2017, and 2019. While the primary aim of these surveys was to assess the livelihood impacts of a value chain sustainability program, the survey work has also provided insights into livelihood strategies.

Semende is an upper catchment in the Musi River system on the eastern flanks of the forest-dominated Bukit Barisan mountain range, populated by a distinct ethnic group (Jeme Semende, sometimes written "Suku Semendo"). This group has also migrated in significant numbers to grow coffee farther south into Lampung Province (figure 7.1). There are three subdistricts (*kecamatan*) in Muara Enim District that make up the Semende homeland: Semende Darat Laut, Semende Darat Tengah, and Semende Darat Ulu (until 2002, Semende was administered as a single *kecamatan*). The total population in Semende was

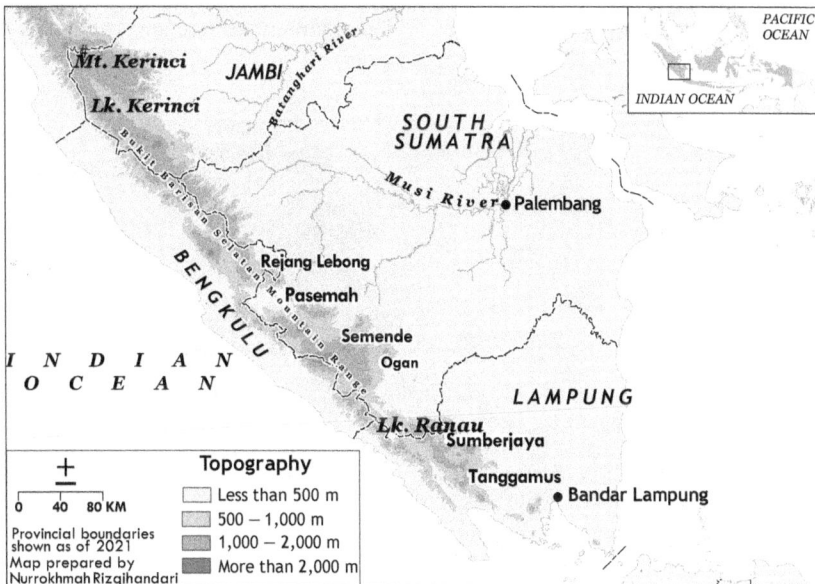

FIGURE 7.1. Coffee regions in southern Sumatra

42,510 in 2020 (much smaller than Toraja), and the districts are dominated by Islamic Jeme Semende (88 percent of coffee-growing households in our surveys), who speak a Malay-based language. There is also one small settlement of Javanese families in Semende who arrived in 2000 through the *transmigrasi* program.

The Semende landscape is dominated physically by coffee plantings, although, like Toraja, upland *sawah* has long been practiced, and coffee was similarly inserted into surrounding swidden-dominated forest landscapes. The Semende subdistricts are surrounded by forestry lands (figure 7.2). One Semende farmer explained to me that "since our ancestors, we have planted coffee and *sawah*. *Sawah* is our rice, but coffee provides us with salt." The coffee fields, on average larger than those in Toraja, are more distant from the village hubs (sometimes an hour on motorbike or several hours walking), and the Semende often build quite considerable farmhouses (*dangau*, figure 7.3) within their coffee fields for short-term stays.

Agriculture is a dominant sector in the Semende economy and is important for livelihoods. The Population Census (BPS 2010b) identified 87 percent of the Semende workforce with agriculture as their *primary* income (65 percent of whom identified coffee as their main agricultural activity), and the Agricultural Census (BPS 2013) reported 85 percent of households as agricultural households (91 percent of these cultivating coffee, almost all as owner-cultivators). There is no major township in Semende, but each village has a distinct center with a strip of *warung* and other home businesses and services, which generate off-farm income in petty trade, transport, and government service jobs (figure 7.4).

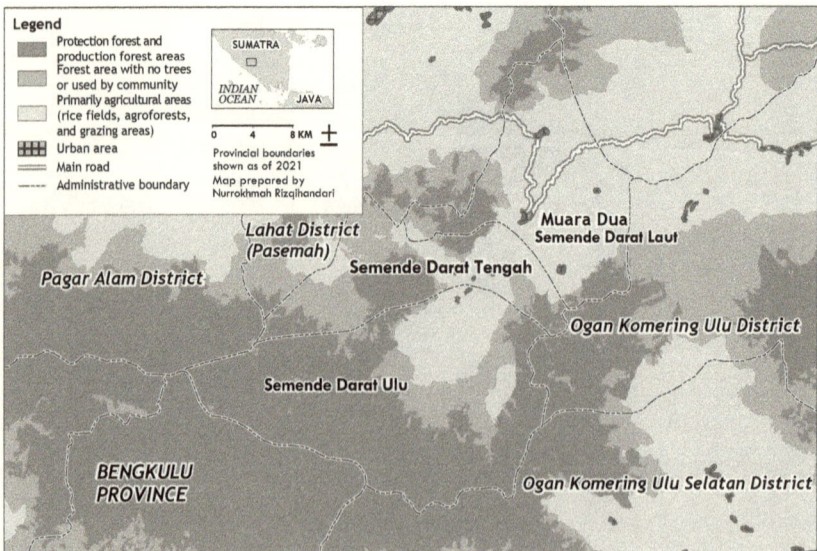

Legend

Protection forest and production forest areas
Forest area with no trees or used by community
Primarily agricultural areas (rice fields, agroforests, and grazing areas)
Urban area
Main road
Administrative boundary

SUMATRA
INDIAN OCEAN   JAVA

0   4   8 KM

Provincial boundaries shown as of 2021
Map prepared by Nurrokhmah Rizqihandari

Lahat District (Pasemah)
Pagar Alam District
Semende Darat Tengah
Muara Dua Semende Darat Laut
Ogan Komering Ulu District
Semende Darat Ulu
BENGKULU PROVINCE
Ogan Komering Ulu Selatan District

FIGURE 7.2.   Land use in and around the Semende subdistricts

FIGURE 7.3. Coffee farmer in front of a *dangau*, 2015

FIGURE 7.4. Typical Semende village center, 2019

The settlement pattern is more concentrated than the scattered *tondok* in Toraja, and these village centers (of which there were thirty-two in 2019) consist of a few hundred houses each and are usually immediately surrounded by *sawah*. The construction of a ninety-megawatt-capacity geothermal power plant has had considerable local impact in the Semende village of Segamit, with exploration commencing in 2012 and electricity generation in 2021. The project proponent claimed that around a thousand (mostly casual) workers would be needed during the peak construction phase (PT SERD 2018). This project, partially funded with a loan from the ADB, required the acquisition of 124.5 hectares of land, most of which was previously planted with coffee, and mostly within the forestry estate, with a smaller area on community land (PT SERD 2018). Compensation was paid to coffee-growing households both within and outside the forestry estate, and I didn't hear of serious community protest against the project or the land acquisitions, but clearly the area of land accessed by the community for coffee-growing in the village contracted significantly as a result.

As in the previous chapter on Toraja, I will start this presentation of fortress farming in Semende by providing a brief historical context to coffee production in the region, followed by an examination of how farm households are integrated into the GVC for coffee. As with Toraja, I will show how value chain interventions (especially corporate sustainability programs) contribute to the institutional environment affecting rural livelihoods. I then examine the institutions of land access, with a focus on customary tenure arrangements (*tunggu tubang*) and the introduction of village-based forestry agreements (*hutan desa*). These arrangements tend to support the prevalence of owner-cultivators, and I follow this with an analysis of labor allocations to farm activities, drawing principally on our empirical survey work. Despite the generally higher household dependence on farm income in Semende (compared to Toraja), I will then proceed to demonstrate how pluriactivity and migration are still key pathways for poverty alleviation, while a sense of a cultural homeland provides a fortress, a refuge, for émigré Semende.

Coffee Production in Southern Sumatra

The city of Palembang was likely the most important site of the maritime kingdom of Srivijaya, which Reid (2015) describes as a loose polity of rival river ports in the Strait of Malacca that hosted trade between India and China from the seventh to the thirteenth century. The city is strategically located near the strait and some fifty kilometers up the easily navigable Musi River, where it sits at the confluence of various tributaries with headwaters stretching up into an enormous hinterland, which includes the Semende homeland and other upland communities such as Rejang, Pasemah, and Ogan (figure 7.1). The Palembang court long maintained trade-based relations with these communities, which actively shifted between producing whatever commodity was most lucrative at the time (pepper, cotton, tobacco, and later coffee). Despite forced monopoly contracts signed with the VOC, much of the early trade in pepper (and subsequently coffee) was delivered to competitors to the Dutch in the strait—Chinese, European, Indian, and Bugis. The Palembang court came under Dutch control during the 1820s, but according to Andaya (1997, 190), "the flourishing trade of the nineteenth century, providing a firm basis for the transition into modern times, was far less a product of European endeavors than of pre-existing strengths which drew on the initiative and adaptability of indigenous society." When Palembang eventually emerged as the center of the East Indies coffee trade in the early twentieth century, it was thus building on a trading history stretching back more than a millennium.

As emphasized by Colombijn (2005), it was much easier for commodities to be transported downstream than for political control to be exerted upstream, and it would be decades before Dutch roads enabled effective colonial authority to be asserted over Semende. The colonial government never attempted to introduce forced coffee deliveries (*cultuurstelsel*) in these regions. Huitema (1935) presents a precolonial situation of banditry and extortion in the upper Musi catchment, coming to an end with colonial annexation in the 1860s, when Palembang production was estimated at around three thousand metric tons by 1879. Coffee production expanded rapidly in Semende because of heightened prices during the 1920s. This established the eastern slopes of the Bukit Barisan range as Indonesia's unrivaled center of coffee production—it has remained so ever since. In 1914, coffee from southern Sumatra contributed less than 1 percent of coffee exports across the Dutch East Indies, but fifteen years later, the area supplied 37 percent (Hoedt 1930).

Largely owing to the southern movement of Semende people in the late nineteenth century to places like Way Tenong, Robusta production also increased in Lampung, which still only produced seven thousand metric tons for export in 1932, compared to 30,000 tons from Palembang (Huitema 1935). It was not until the 1970s that Lampung rivaled South Sumatra as Indonesia's major coffee-producing province, eventually diverting the export trade away from Palembang to Bandar Lampung. The Dutch "colonization" program—a precursor to later transmigration—started supporting Javanese migrants to Sumatra in 1905, although attempts to provide extension and credit largely failed (MacAndrews 1978). In the 1930s, the government encouraged migrants through informal *bawon* arrangements (drawing on the traditional Javanese system of paying laborers with a share of the harvest), where new migrants worked for earlier settlers in exchange for food, housing, and a share of the harvest (MacAndrews 1978).

This system greatly increased migration rates such that, by 1961, up to 40 percent of the rural population of Lampung were Java-born (McNicoll 1968). Many of these settlers established communities that were involved in both independent coffee farming and wet-rice cultivation.

The 1920s boom involved an entirely new species as, following the ravages of leaf rust, the colonial authorities introduced rust-resistant Robusta plants from around 1907 (Cramer 1918, cited in Huitema 1935). Although this was the period of the so-called ethical policy, Touwen (2001, 296) emphasizes how such efforts were largely focused on Java, while smallholder export agriculture in Sumatra "grew rapidly with hardly any assistance from the government or the estate sector." Instead, Touwen argues, economic dynamism on Sumatra (referring to both rubber and coffee) was driven primarily by trade networks feeding into Singapore. Palembang was a major export hub, and commercially oriented smallholders were stimulated by the active upstream involvement of Malay and Chinese trade networks, within which credit relationships were vital. As in Toraja, a model of value chain actors interlinked by credit but otherwise independent of state-based political structures stimulated peasant entrepreneurs, who successfully shifted focus toward cash-cropping. In a later Lampung coffee boom in the 1950s, Chinese capital was still considered critical for financing Indonesian village traders in an environment that still had little direct agricultural support from the state (Utomo 1967).

Semende was estimated to be producing around 780 metric tons of Robusta alongside 114 tons of Arabica by 1927, but it was doing so through very extensive cultivation systems and little use of shade (unless intercropped with rubber or kapok), such that the productivity of gardens would start declining after around five years (Huitema 1935). Coffee trees were simply stumped to encourage regrowth. Coffee was integrated with swidden, and this extensive approach to cultivation was, at least in part, a response to natural conditions, with the soils in Semende being, in general, less fertile than in neighboring regions like Pasemah. Extensive coffee farming in Semende, however, brought this community into conflict with colonial forest authorities, who generally failed to understand or acknowledge traditional land management practices (Potter 2008). Coffee production in Semende was always smallholder-based and never attracted plantation investments, unlike Rejang (Bengkulu), Pasemah, and Lake Ranau (Lampung). It was also not a destination for colonial-era migration programs to Sumatra. In an environment of relative land abundance, extensive production systems, dominated by independent owner-cultivators, have prevailed, with little indication of emergent landlordism, and rarely did coffee displace food production (rice) entirely. The coffee-growing landscape of Semende is still characterized by a mosaic of *sawah*, new clearings, coffee farms, fallows, and forests (figure 7.5).

FIGURE 7.5.   New coffee planting on dryland *ladang* adjacent to wet-rice *sawah*, with forest landscapes in background, 2019

Value Chain Interactions in Semende

Throughout the 1980s, Semende came to be integrated into global value chains dominated by export firms based in Bandar Lampung and selling primarily to the US and European markets. Global industry dynamics at the time were dominated by the ICO regime, which led to the 1979 establishment of the Asosiasi Eksportir Kopi Indonesia (AEKI, replacing the earlier Sindikat Eksportir Kopi Indonesia) to directly manage the quota system within Indonesia. AEKI's establishment coincided with the introduction of a coffee export tax of 18 percent, which was ostensibly introduced to bring high coffee prices in line with other commodities and was earmarked as an industry development fund (De Graaff 1986). AEKI came to effectively own a "voluntary" export levy, enforced by the Ministry of Trade as a condition of export, and this lucrative tax farm was only withdrawn by the government in 2011.[1] Given the leading position of Bandar Lampung within national coffee exports, its AEKI branch came to be both influential and very well resourced.

AEKI focused on policy advocacy, promotion, and marketing (including frequent participation in international coffee expos), with minor attempts to deliver farmer support programs. AEKI established a farmer development center in West Lampung in 1999, although local famers were telling me in 2005 that it was already "useless" (*ngak ada gunanya*). Southern Sumatra was a key site for the "Coffee Intensification Project" (Proyek Intensifikasi Kopi, PIK, described in chapter 3), which included agricultural extension and distribution of fertilizers, seedlings, and credit to smallholders. Godoy and Bennett (1988), however, explained how up to half of these coffee farmers in South Sumatra discontinued or reduced chemical fertilizer application when PIK stopped providing credit in 1984.

Writing of the situation in the 1980s, De Graaff (1986, 290) reported that exporters in Sumatra "have little contact with the growers and have no first-hand knowledge of the factors affecting the quality of the 'asalan' [ungraded raw coffee] purchased." During its implementation, the ICO regime empowered AEKI to operate as a quota-allocating cartel, with only twenty-five exporters managing the bulk of exports nationwide, and with restrictions on the upstream involvement of international commodity firms (De Graaff 1986). This had the overall effect of suppressing prices for farmers. One estimate (McStocker 1987) was that the farm-gate price for coffee was around 60 percent of the export price in 1983, while another (De Graaff 1986) claimed it to be as low as 49 percent in 1981. Both estimates are far below my own observations (since 2005) of around 85 percent.

Since 1989, there has been a gradual displacement of domestic exporters (whose interests were supported by AEKI) by international commodity traders, who have controlled an increasing share of exports and who have coordinated upstream value chains more tightly (Neilson 2008). The first major engagement with southern Sumatran smallholders by an international coffee lead firm was by Nestlé, which built an instant coffee factory in Lampung in 1979. Nestlé Agricultural Services (NAS) was established in 1994, with a network of seven collection and training centers in the district of Tanggamus when I first visited in 2005. Nestlé agronomists would provide training in crop management and quality control and were generally well received by farmers. A comparative study of three different corporate training programs across southern Sumatra in 2017 identified the greatest level of support and satisfaction among those farmers involved in the Nestlé program (Bray 2018; Bray et al. 2023). The more remote regions of South Sumatra Province, however, including Semende, were beyond their direct reach. In 2005, Kraft was a major end user of southern Sumatran coffee, which it bought through arms-length relationships with exporters, including both foreign-owned commodity firms and Indonesian exporters. Traceability demands had yet to reach southern Sumatra in 2005, but Ecom had just started experimenting with upstream supports for farmer groups.

This situation soon changed with the release of a 2007 publication by WWF, *Gone in an Instant*, which highlighted coffee farming inside the Bukit Barisan Selatan National Park, where it was destroying habitat for critically endangered Sumatran tigers, rhinoceroses, and elephants. The report directly linked global brands with illegal habitat destruction. This dovetailed with the growing global interest by lead firms in voluntary sustainability standards at the time (Neilson and Pritchard 2007), which were then introduced to southern Sumatra from around 2008. In terms of volume, the Common Code for the Coffee Community (4C) became the most widely applied sustainability program; in 2016, seven different 4C-registered exporters based in Bandar Lampung had introduced 4C programs to southern Sumatran farmers. The coffee regions of Lampung, closer to the port and warehouse complex, were the first to be incorporated within 4C production units, but soon afterward firms began extending their reach farther afield into South Sumatra, and into Semende.

The introduction of 4C to Semende occurred in partnership with, and was financed by, one of the world's largest coffee firms, Mondelēz International (spun off from Kraft in 2012 and itself acquired by JDE in 2015). It was part of their corporate sustainability commitments under the in-house Coffee Made Happy initiative, although it was implemented by the trading firm Ecom. The arrangement whereby a major international roaster engages a commodity-trading firm to implement a farm-level development program on its behalf is, as discussed in chapter 4, widespread. Ecom built a small warehouse in Semende in 2012, followed by a farmer training center in 2014 (figure 7.6). By 2015, 141 farmer groups (a total of some three thousand households) were enrolled in the program, which covered around 50 percent of the coffee-growing households living in Semende, with an estimated production of three thousand metric tons. Many of these farmer groups (*kelompok tani*) had been created through previous government *proyek* but were reportedly nonactive when the value chain intervention commenced. Ecom (with support from Mondelēz) paid the cost of obtaining certification, including the cost of training farmers and undertaking audits. This was estimated, by Ecom, to be around 50 USD per farmer per year over the initial three-year life of the project.

The farmer training center consisted of a permanent brick building and demonstration gardens and was associated with recruitment of a team of local agronomists who managed the internal control systems (ICS) for the program, which focused on monitoring compliance with 4C requirements. Field officers, however, were referred to as both *agronomis* and *i-che-es* (ICS), suggesting their dual role in providing agricultural extension advice to farmers and in monitoring 4C compliance. By 2016, the initiative was directly employing a regional manager, six agronomists, and several security guards, most of whom were recruited from local villages. Ecom offered registered farmers between six and ten training

FIGURE 7.6.   Mondelēz-funded farmer training center in Semende, 2015

events per year (each lasting between three and four hours). Training, however, was not dependent on sales to the firm. The team of agronomists offered advice on fertilizers, composting, pruning, shade trees and cover crops, pest management, harvesting, and post-harvest handling. Ecom also sold subsidized berry borer traps and tarpaulins to farmers. Sometimes training was offered only to representatives of groups (the group leaders) in the expectation that the knowledge gained would be shared with other members, but often all farmers within groups were invited. The firm's agronomists undertook occasional farm visits, which were highly sought after by many of the enrolled farmers, and published a calendar that included monthly tree, pest, and soil management tips and which was widely distributed across Semende.

A period of intensive farmer training occurred during the process of preparing farmers for the 4C audit, and these tended to cover unacceptable practices, use of equipment, safety procedures, and quality assurance. Other training sessions were seasonally targeted so that relevant issues were addressed when they were most salient (such as quality control during the harvest and planting during the rainy season). The company's agronomists also provided internal audit support to review farm conditions and to ensure compliance with the standard. After completion of the training program, the company arranged for independent audits, and if the farmer group passed the audit (all did), the production unit received 4C certification valid for three years. To encourage farmers to participate in the production unit, Ecom offered a "certification premium" of 300 IDR/kg (around 3 US cents per kilogram), in addition to a quality premium, which varied but could reach 2,000 IDR/kg (20 US cents per kilogram). A subset of the farmers were subsequently "upgraded" to meet the more stringent Rainforest Alliance standard in 2014, for which no further price premium was paid.

The heads of farmer groups were encouraged to pool coffee from their members and deliver it to the company's buying station, prompting some of these group heads to eventually become collectors. At this point, it was intended that Ecom would integrate the farmer groups into their certified supply chain, providing them with regular updates on market prices (through mobile phone texts) and allowing them to sell coffee at the buying station with the associated premium. In practice, many farmers chose to sell to both Ecom and local traders, and integration of certified farmers within Ecom's supply chain only partially occurred. As it evolved, moreover, Ecom closed its Semende buying station in 2016, citing high logistical costs and a change in corporate focus associated with a general retreat from pursuing sustainability standards, although its sustainability team continued to provide support to the Farmer Training Center.

After their takeover of Mondelēz, JDE continued to provide financial support to the project, even though corporate branding shifted from Coffee Made Happy to Common Grounds. JDE referred to the Semende project as "improving smallholder coffee quality yields and productivity via the integration of women and youth in a family farming approach" and suggested that "a coherent farmer family-oriented message must be established in order to achieve higher productivity and quality results" (JDE 2021). By 2019, the intervention was no longer linked to a traceable supply chain, and in 2021 the JDE corporate website made no reference to 4C or Rainforest Alliance certification for its Semende intervention, but the JDE-funded training center was still being staffed by a reduced team of agronomists. I was informed that, in mid-2021 (as the delta variant of COVID-19 was having devastating impacts across Indonesia), the center was staffed by a single agronomist.

Thus, while the intervention was fairly intensive for a period, ultimately it tended to follow the basic pattern of an externally funded *proyek* (chapter 3), and this highlights the limitations of programs delivered along inherently labile supply chains. In 2019, a few months before JDE funding was scheduled to end its support, I attended a meeting of around twenty farmer group representatives that Ecom had convened to discuss an "exit strategy." The attendees were dressed in new T-shirts that identified them now as "crop doctors" who had become agents of Ecom's Service Delivery Model (SDM) team to provide agricultural supplies and financing to other farmers. There was discussion of forming a new organization, perhaps an association of farmer groups or perhaps a cooperative (a representative of the district government office made a presentation to explain how to do this), and there was also talk of how the network could position itself to access development initiatives being advanced through the Sustainable Coffee Platform for Indonesia (SCOPI). It seems likely that the organizational experience of working with Ecom, Mondelēz, JDE, 4C, Rainforest Alliance, and other organizations over an eight-year period provided the institutional foundations for this loose network of farmer group leaders to successfully access future coffee-based resource transfer mechanisms that might emerge. At the time of writing, the European Union Deforestation Regulation (EUDR) was shaping up as a likely driver of new traceability-related supply chain restructuring, with potential opportunities for the network.

This sustainability intervention thus had the primary effect of creating new social structures (or perhaps, more accurately, modifying preexisting farmer group structures) that enabled resource distribution, and which enhanced the social capital of farmer group leaders. This highlights the evolutionary nature of institutional environments. Leveraging their role as conduits of information and resources, some farmer group leaders have been able to reposition themselves as coffee collectors, while others are attempting to become input suppliers ("crop doctors") partnering with Ecom. Similar, but even longer-standing, networks have been constructed in Tanggamus District of Lampung with Nestlé's agricultural initiatives, linking farmers through farmer group heads and state-supported collective businesses (KUBEs) back to the company. Interviews with farmers participating in sustainability programs across southern Sumatra reveal generally positive perceptions about the programs, even if they didn't actually apply the training to their farms, or did so in a highly selective manner.[2] Community awareness was generally low regarding the type and key aims of sustainability program they were enrolled within (for example, 4C or Rainforest Alliance or a SCOPI initiative). The interventions were generally understood as an externally sourced *proyek*, through which some form of distributive economy might be possible. According to Bray et al. (2023), two-thirds of respondents surveyed from across five different sustainability programs reported receiving some form of material assistance from the programs (seedlings, tarpaulins, fertilizers, or pruning equipment).

Notwithstanding these social and material benefits from involvement in value chain sustainability programs, there is little evidence that the training activities resulted in significant changes in farm practices or yields. Our five-year study in Semende assessed the livelihood impacts on households enrolled in the 4C program against matched non-4C households (Neilson, Toth, Sari, et al. 2019). Farmers were expected to learn improved coffee-farming techniques, apply them, obtain higher coffee yields, and subsequently obtain higher incomes. Coffee yields, however, had not significantly changed after seven years of the program, and neither had implementation of productivity-improving practices. Some improved environmental practices, however, were observed (reduced use of banned pesticides and increased planting of shade trees), along with improved use of personal protective equipment and the use of tarpaulins to dry coffee (a quality-related improvement). We found that 4C-enrolled farmers had slightly higher income levels than nonenrolled farmers, with a lower propensity to be in poverty, but this was due to increased access to non-coffee-related income. Coffee growing in Semende did not become a professional, input-intensive, wealth-generating activity, although there have been increasing attempts from value chain actors to encourage such a transition.

It is significant that some of the farm practices that did change included those that were providing "services" and could be verified by the audit process. Indeed, the production landscape itself, once again, provides an intangible service to lead firms by offering an opportunity to deliver sustainability programs, which enables these firms to "sell" their ethical credentials to consumers. Other landscape services are also bundled together with coffee supply. Labeling initiatives for shade-grown coffee provide mechanisms for Payment for Ecosystem Service (PES) schemes along the value chain, where consumers pay a premium for the service of habitat provision by coffee producers. More recently, there has been a dovetailing of REDD+ funding schemes with supply chain sustainability standards to create "landscape approaches," often linked to lead firm strategies to become net carbon zero (von Essen and Lambin 2021). Resource flows are thus emerging to recognize the multiple ecological services provided by the production landscape (including carbon storage). For JDE, there has furthermore been a gradual de-linking of sustainability investments from direct supply chains, corresponding with a shift of the scale at which sustainability claims are made, from registering individual households (inherent to sustainability standards like 4C) to the landscape level. The key point is that resources are flowing into the coffee-growing regions of southern Sumatra through a range of "sustainability-related" projects and mechanisms, and this is intended to both ensure coffee supply and to compensate growers for a range of tangible and intangible services. These resource flows are increasingly occurring in parallel to actual supply chains along which coffee is priced as a commodity based on market processes. This, in turn, is reconfiguring the institutional environment and reshaping access to livelihood resources.

Accessing Land in Semende

Prior to the introduction of coffee in the nineteenth century, the Semende agricultural system was focused on rain-fed *sawah* and fishponds, and secondarily on swidden-based dryland rice (*ladang*), often intercropped with fruit trees such as durian. By 2015, however, coffee had become deeply embedded, and 95 percent of ethnic Semende coffee growers in our survey reported that their parents had been coffee growers before them. Similar to the Torajan situation in Buntu Pepasan, 76 percent of all agricultural households in Semende (BPS 2013) reported growing coffee in 2013, although the holdings tend to be larger, between one and three hectares (table 7.1). This compares to only 36 percent of agricultural households cultivating *sawah*.

Part of the reason that landholdings tend to be larger and more concentrated than in Toraja (which follows ambilineal inheritance) is an inheritance system of matrilineal primogeniture known as *tunggu tubang*. At its core, *tunggu tubang* is a system of indivisible and (in principle) inalienable inheritance whereby the eldest daughter (whose functional title is also referred to as the *tunggu tubang*) inherits family land, including rice fields, fishponds, heirlooms, housing, rice barns, and coffee farms, although she shares management responsibilities with her husband and male relatives (Salmudin 2012). *Tunggu tubang*, which can be literally translated as "to wait with a food container" (Hutapea and Thamrin 2009), is, however, more than just a system of inheritance. The term itself alludes to the responsibility that the *tunggu tubang* has in managing food production (in rice fields) and providing for the extended family ("waiting with a food container" if needed). Rice barns (*tengkiang*, figure 7.7) are inherited by the *tunggu tubang* and perform material and symbolic functions in food sharing across Semende. That a 2019 arts festival organized by the Muara Enim government was formally declared to be a "Festival Tunggu Tubang" could be seen as central to a broad conception of *adat* and at the core of what it means to be Jeme Semende.

TABLE 7.1   Distribution of coffee farm sizes in Semende

AREA OF COFFEE PLANTING (HA)	% OF ALL COFFEE-GROWING HOUSEHOLDS
<0.1	<1
0.1–0.2999	<1
0.3–0.4999	1.3
0.5–0.9999	7.1
1–1.9999	52.5
2–2.999	29.5
>2.999	8.6

Source: BPS 2013 (n = 5898).

FIGURE 7.7.   *Tengkiang* rice barns are a material symbol of *tunggu tubang* arrangements (2015 photo).

As *tunggu tubang* land cannot be sold, rights to it are essentially usage rights rather than ownership rights, and BPN had avoided issuing *hak milik* certificates on this land (this may have changed under the pressure of the recent PTSL accelerated land registration program). Almost all rice fields in Semende are held under *tunggu tubang* arrangements, as are about a third of coffee plots (according to our 2019 survey). Roughly another third of coffee plots are held under informal rights other than *tunggu tubang*. The median holding size for *sawah* was about a hectare and in 2018 produced an average of 2.7 metric tons of rice, using relatively intensive methods including hand tractors (figure 7.8). Annual household consumption of rice is around seven hundred kilograms. Rather than sold as surplus, what is not actually consumed by those in the household is said to be shared with the extended family, consistent with *tunggu tubang* responsibilities, or contributed to religious-cultural events (*sedekah*).

It is frequently emphasized by Semende informants that *tunggu tubang* rights are balanced with a series of responsibilities. These include food production, hosting and attending *sedekah* celebrations, looking after aged relatives or wayward youth, and providing informal social protection to extended family members experiencing hardship. Another expression used to refer to the *tunggu*

FIGURE 7.8. Use of hand tractor on a Semende rice field, 2019

tubang institution is *badah balek*, meaning "place to return to," and this hints at the wider social role of land as a refuge, whereby émigré community members have a place to stay when returning to their homeland. This extended family—known as the *apit jurai*—maintains a cultural identity that is intimately tied to its association with a particular *tunggu tubang* arrangement. The social role performed by *tunggu tubang* is quite similar to that observed in what is probably Indonesia's best-known matrilineal society, the Minangkabau of West Sumatra, where matrilineal primogeniture has long been associated with emigration by the male population. The situation among the Minangkabau in the 1920s observed by Schrieke ([1928] 1966, 141) is worth quoting at length for its contemporary resonance in Semende:

> Emigration often becomes more or less permanent, too, particularly in the case of small traders or of those who have, for instance, acquired land on the Malay Peninsula or have found a means of livelihood abroad. But even then the tie with the land of the emigrant's birth is not by any means entirely broken, thanks to his claim on the family property. If the self-exiled Minangkabauer feels a longing to return home, he knows, in most cases, that he will not be obliged to face the problem of earning

a living immediately, because, thanks to the family property, his family will supply him with food and clothes at least for a time. It is the family property, too, which has enabled many of the younger generation of the present day to make their way in the world, owing to the fact that from it money could be supplied to pay for their education or capital to start them in business. On the other hand the family profits from the earnings of the periodic, temporary emigrants, for the family also benefits from the earthly treasure collected by its members in foreign parts.

Indeed, as among the Minangkabau in the 1920s, the *tunggu tubang* provides a home base for the Semende *apit jurai*. This is important, since migration outside Semende offers no guarantees and can be a high-risk strategy. *Tunggu tubang* property is part of a support system, closely linked to webs of social relationships, that is not used to accumulate wealth but as a basis for livelihood security. *Tunggu tubang* also involves responsibility for hosting and attending *sedekah*, ceremonies such as multiday weddings, funerals, house initiations, and various other *syukuran* (expressing gratitude to God) for events such as a child's graduation, buying a new car, returning from the hajj, or recovering from illness. It is frequently commented on by the Semende, in a way that conveys mock frustration, how much time attendance at *sedekah* consumes. As in Toraja, but to a lesser extent, there is also a transfer of wealth from émigré Semende into the rural community to support ceremonial participation.

Also as in Toraja, *tunggu tubang* land is not considered simply as a productive asset but is rather imbued with patrimonial, cultural, and social value. Indeed, an argument against the continued adherence to these *adat* arrangements (made by some Semende, government officials, and by downstream coffee buyers) is that it does not sufficiently encourage the most productive use of the land since it inhibits land from being sold to "serious farmers." Based on field observations in 2002, Potter (2008, 185) described how "the large amount of temporarily unused rice land and simply vacant land in Semende villages was striking." Indeed, this continues to be the case and is partly related to *tunggu tubang* and partly to the prevalence of extended fallows in what is a predominately tree-crop-shifting cultivation system.

The Semende also recognize a customary form of territorial sovereignty, known as *marga*, considered to have existed prior to the establishment of both the colonial and republican governments and which was incorporated into the formal government administration until 1983, when it was replaced by the Kecamatan and Desa system (Salmudin 2012). Any uncleared land without private property rights, which is considered by the community to be outside the forestry estate, is called *tanah marga* (*marga* land, akin to *tanah ulayat* elsewhere).

According to Semende *adat*, fallowed lands (*belukae*) are still claimed by the original land-clearer, so that only their descendants could clear the fallow and assume planting rights. Territorial disputes between *tanah marga* and the forestry lands have been widespread since the 1967 Forestry Act. Determining the government-recognized forest boundary can be a challenge. I was once provided with a map, issued by the local Forestry Department itself, which showed three significantly different forest boundaries in Semende: the boundaries based on physical field markers, the boundaries based on Suharto-era forestry consensus mapping (Tata Guna Hutan Kesepakatan, TGHK), and the boundaries based on regional spatial planning maps. Such inconsistencies are well known across Indonesia and highlight the considerable challenges in determining the legal validity of community claims and land-use practices. In Semende, underlying issues related to forest boundaries have yet to be resolved. These tensions are exacerbated by the feeling among the Semende that they possess the institutional capacity through customary *adat* law to manage *marga* lands themselves. *Adat* rules regarding the permissibility of land clearing for swiddens and the existence of *rimboe larangan* (customarily protected forest) in Semende were presented by Potter (2008), while Martin et al. (2016) identified the persistence of a customary forest institution (*ulu ayek*) to ensure hydrological functioning associated with *sawah*.

In chapter 5 I introduced some recent negotiated compromises between the community and the Forestry Department, such as *hutan desa*, described in forestry regulations as "state forest not encumbered by previous rights/permits, which is managed by a village to improve general village welfare." While asserting the continued primacy of state rights, *hutan desa* has allowed improved community access to what are still considered customary *marga* lands in Semende. In one such *hutan desa* I visited in 2018, as described in chapter 5, land was being used to provide access to farmland for those community members with otherwise limited access to alternative livelihoods, and so facilitated a fortress farming function.

Such arrangements sit uneasily against supply chain sustainability requirements. A key constraint identified by Common Grounds (JDE 2021) is that "smallholders in the southern Sumatra Robusta sector often lack tenure security and have limited access to finance, extension services and other agricultural inputs" (that is, smallholders are not yet operating like capitalist entrepreneurs). JDE would quite clearly like to be able to reshape the institutional environment within southern Sumatra to encourage such a transition, which they believe will both improve livelihoods and enhance supply. The focus on supply sustainability remains central, and the willingness to engage with issues of "tenure security" is also significant. Only farmers with coffee plots outside contested forest zones were enrolled in the Semende sustainability programs, owing to uncertainty about whether *hutan desa* and HKm community forestry arrangements would violate deforestation-free clauses of 4C and Rainforest Alliance (similar exclusions from sustainability interventions also occurred in Sumber Jaya, Lampung). The Rainforest Alliance standard requires that "production activities do not degrade any protected area." Such requirements have been difficult to interpret in the highly dynamic community forest landscapes of southern Sumatra. Both *hutan desa* and HKm have been established within forestry lands classified as "protection forest" and so might be considered a protected area. There is a risk, therefore, that importing more rigid land-use classifications through value chain interventions and encouraging "tenure security" (if this is interpreted as individualized title) could lead to worsening conditions of access for fortress farming and worse environmental outcomes. The 2022 EU deforestation-free regulation is likely to face similar implementation challenges. A more likely scenario, however, is that the local institutional environment will respond, in a selective way, to reinterpret such value chain institutions through processes of contestation and eventually accommodation.

In addition to cultivating coffee in their homeland, Semende farmers performed a pivotal role during the 1950s and 1960s in stretching the coffee frontier farther south into Lampung, where they applied extensive swidden-style practices and where they came to be associated with forest clearing (Verbist, Putra, and Budidarsono 2005). This out-migration is frequently attributed to *tunggu tubang* by the Semende themselves (and also in the literature by Brechin et al. 1994 and Smith 1999), as the inheritance system left some without a direct land inheritance at a time when the off-farm economy offered few prospects. Fertility rates in South Sumatra were more than twice as high in the 1960s as they were in 2020, and direct demographic pressure on land has since eased somewhat as a result. The Semende are now more likely to migrate to urban areas in Muara Enim and Palembang than to open new forests. While the establishment of new coffee-related swiddens is still evident in the more remote villages of Semende (figure 7.9), including within *hutan desa*, government restrictions on further land expansion appear to be encouraging sedentary coffee cultivation near the more densely populated villages at the same time as more off-farm economic opportunities have emerged.

While certain families have greater prestige and larger landholdings than others, Semende society is not as rigidly stratified as Toraja. BPS (2013) reported that 96 percent of coffee farms were owner-managed in Semende (appendix table A10). Our own surveys from 2015 to 2019 revealed a similar dominance of owner-cultivators (table 7.2). Sharecropping and renting of land were both reported only very occasionally. Other arrangements exist, whereby landowners

FIGURE 7.9.   Land clearing in a Semende forest-margin community, 2015

TABLE 7.2   Land access arrangements for main coffee plot in Semende

LAND ACCESS ARRANGEMENT	% OF COFFEE-GROWING HOUSEHOLDS IN SURVEY
Cultivator owns all land	89
Cultivator rents all land	3
Cultivator sharecrops all land	4
Cultivator owns and sharecrops/rents land	1
Cultivator accesses other land for free	3

Source: Author own survey, 2019 (n = 1,302).

allow kin or other community members to manage coffee farms without any payment, although this may imply moral or social obligations that constitute enrollment into a patronage relation.

Markets for coffee land are more developed in Semende than in Toraja. In our 2017 survey, less than 3 percent of households (41 of 1,589 households) reported having acquired new coffee land in the preceding two years. Of these, 39 percent did so through market mechanisms (table 7.3), which is significant, but still a minority acquisition pathway. A still considerable 22 percent of new land acquisitions were reportedly through direct appropriations, indicating the continued importance of *marga* institutions and fallowed ancestral land as a livelihood resource. The remainder were inherited. Just as importantly, informal

TABLE 7.3   Manner of acquiring new coffee land in past two years in Semende

LAND ACQUISITION METHOD	%
New coffee land purchased or rented	39
New coffee land taken over from family (inherited or gifted)	27
Direct appropriation	22
Other	12

Source: Author own survey, 2017 (n = 41).

TABLE 7.4   Land status in Semende (2019)

LAND STATUS OF HOUSEHOLD'S MAIN COFFEE PLOT	%
Land certificate (*hak milik*)	10
Village-level recognition / informal sale deed (*Surat Keterangan Tanah or akte jual-beli*)	34
Ancestral land (*tanah warisan and tanah marga*)	14
Customary matrilineal tenure (*tunggu tubang*)	33
No evidence of ownership (*includes hutan desa access*)	8
Other	1

Source: Author own survey, 2019 (n = 1,208).

access regimes encourage land transactions to be conducted largely internally within the community, which dampens land prices and enhances community accessibility for those who need land. Our 2015 survey found 62 percent of coffee farms were held under the broad category of customary tenure with no written evidence (*tanah warisan*). In our 2019 survey, we examined this category in more detail and found a complex array of institutional forms of recognition (table 7.4). While only 10 percent of main coffee plots were registered with a BPN *hak milik* certificate, this had increased from 8 percent in 2015, and another 34 percent were held under individualized tenure recognized by village authorities (*surat keterangan tanah*). Customary tenure (especially *tunggu tubang*) and more flexible land access arrangements (including *hutan desa*), however, remained the most common land access institutions in 2019.

Laboring on Semende Coffee Farms

One case of sharecropping I observed in 2019 involved a 50–50 split of the harvest, with the cultivator (an unmarried twenty-something male) responsible for inputs such as fertilizers and herbicides. I was told, however, that it was increasingly difficult to find willing sharecroppers, since the arrangement was unappealing, given the available opportunities to either work off-farm or to easily access your own farm. Sharecropping, however, was common in rice farming.

TABLE 7.5   Labor in Semende coffee farms

INDICATOR	2015	2017	2019
Average weekly hours in coffee farming (median)[a]	15	23	16
Average weekly hours in agriculture (median)	21	28	19
Worked on own coffee farm (%)	-	-	99.7
Employs some casual labor (%)	40	48	52
Number of paid labor-days in year (median)	-	-	32 (9 female)
Number of workers employed in year (median)	-	-	4 (2 female)
Also worked as paid farm worker during coffee harvest (%)	-	-	16
Also worked as paid farm worker during non-coffee-harvest (%)	-	-	44

Source: Author own surveys.

[a] Averaged over the year for each respondent, but the median number of hours across all respondents is presented for greater clarity.

Almost all coffee smallholders, meanwhile, worked on their own farm, with the main household worker (usually male) estimating that he dedicated, on average, twenty to twenty-eight hours per week over the year (table 7.5). There was also considerable variation in own-labor allocation between years, with an extended dry season in 2017 (which caused lower yields) prompting higher labor allocation, suggesting that households were willing to increase their labor effort to meet a minimum level of consumption.

In addition to own-household labor, one in every two coffee smallholders also recruited casual workers for relatively short periods (usually for the harvest), with men recruited for longer than women (table 7.5). These farms continued, however, to operate fundamentally as household labor production units. Moreover, my informants suggested that reliance on non-household labor had declined over time. Today, this supplementary casual labor was generally recruited from within the Semende community and, given the small numbers involved, was informal and intersected with other social relationships in the village. During a peak harvest, however, this was sometimes supplemented by temporary migrant labor from surrounding districts. A considerable number of smallholders also worked (for a wage) on farms owned by other community members in addition to working on their own farm. Such workers included those whose own farms were temporarily unproductive because of recent replanting or fallowing, or were unemployed youth who had not yet established their own farm. It is difficult to identify a distinct farm laboring class working for landlords, or extensive class relations of production, in Semende. In one Semende village, we identified only 5 of the 130 resident households without access to farmland, and these 5 did not wish to be involved in farming, claiming that they preferred other vocations (*beda jurusan*) such as working as a mechanic or stall owner.

New coffee plantings in Semende frequently intersected with an individual's life course, being established soon after a new household was formed, with collective support from the extended family providing initial food supplies for the new couple (often by the *tunggu tubang*). Often the new plantings were on ancestral fallows or *marga* land. This coffee then reached peak productivity when the consumption needs of the household were greatest (when children are too young to contribute to the household labor pool) and when the plantings required minimal attention, aside from the harvest. At some point, often around ten years after planting, the farmer needs to decide whether to fallow the plot or, alternatively, to extend its productive life by increasing inputs of labor, fertilizers, or pesticides. This decision is determined by the livelihood needs of the household and the availability of alternative sources of income. In this sense, there is a kind of Chayanovian "demographic differentiation," where labor is allocated to the farm to the extent that it is necessary to meet the changing consumption needs of the household.

Elsewhere in southern Sumatra, at least in previous decades, the original owners sought a sharecropper to take over management at the point when the production starts to decline. In Lampung during the late 1950s, Utomo (1967) described how incoming Javanese could access land relatively easily in Lampung by taking over old swiddens from indigenous farmers, initially on a sharecropping basis. That started a process whereby Javanese migrants began to displace the indigenous Lampungese. It has been more common in Semende to simply allow the coffee farms to fallow and the soil to regenerate, ready for the next generation. The production system has adapted to the livelihood needs of the household rather than production relations responding deterministically to the commodity needs of the market. Furthermore, since maintenance costs of coffee plots were relatively low, owners often left the crop unattended and unharvested in a particular season if market conditions were poor or if more lucrative livelihood opportunities emerged off-farm. It could be relatively easily brought back into production the subsequent year. Shade tree management can also serve a similar purpose by being heavily pruned to improve yields in a particular season in response to external conditions (high prices) or household livelihood needs.

These conditions in Semende are not dissimilar to the symbiotic relationship between dryland rice farming and rubber cultivation in West Kalimantan, described by Dove (2011) as a dual household economy. Dove describes how Kantu Dayak households would switch their own labor to rubber tapping when market conditions were especially conducive, or when their household needs demanded it, or when the rice harvest failed, but at other times rubber could be left unattended without serious loss. Households appear to engage selectively, and largely on their own terms, with the rubber value chain, thus minimizing the encroachment of capitalist relations that might otherwise result in class differentiation among producers. The agroecological flexibility of rubber trees to withstand periods of neglect can also be observed, although perhaps to a lesser extent, in coffee. It is evident, however, that the ability of coffee farming to offer such protective fortress farming opportunities is fundamentally dependent on both the availability of land and the existence of relatively adaptive institutions of land access. In turn, land availability is also dependent on the ability of the wider economy to generate nonfarm livelihood opportunities for some born into the village community, even if they often retain multifaceted linkages with their cultural homeland.

Pluriactivity, Migration, and a Cultural Homeland

For many years, significant Semende out-migration was associated with coffee expansion throughout the Bukit Barisan range, where Semende became known as forest pioneers. Smith (1999) reported on a Semende coffee-growing community in a remote area of South Ogan Komering Ulu (one hundred kilometers from their home village) that had been cleared from forest in the 1970s. Like many other observers, he attributed that migratory event to *tunggu tubang*. Strong cultural and familial ties, linked to *tunggu tubang*, partially restrain the extent of out-migration for some (those inheriting *tunggu tubang*) while encouraging ongoing homeland links for others (the *apit jurai* extended family). Smith (1999) reported that links to their homeland were also important for initial food supplies. Nonagricultural migration among the children of Semende elites was also already apparent more than forty years ago (Tsubouchi 1980), and aspirations to escape relative rural poverty through migration remain strong. As with Torajans, homeland links are often maintained, and 12 percent of Semende households in our 2019 survey had received remittances in the previous year from an immediate family member (parent, child, or spouse). Sometimes migration is permanent, but often it is cyclical, and returnees can be motivated by either economic factors (such as a lack of success during *merantau*) or lifestyle (such as a former driver and his teacher wife I met in 2018, in their late fifties, who had just returned from Muara Enim city to pursue what they hoped would a more leisurely "kampong" lifestyle).

In addition to owning houses in the village itself, many households also own a "farmhouse" (*dangau*, figure 7.3) on their coffee plot, typically a relatively simple timber stilt structures but to which men in particular hold a degree of sentimental attachment, forming a key part of their "kampong lifestyle." While the *dangau* were initially built to enable work to be undertaken in relatively remote farm plots without the need for time-consuming daily foot journeys, many *dangau* can now be easily accessed by motorbike (often thanks to community infrastructure projects through the PNPM or Dana Desa programs). Yet, rather than falling into disuse, the *dangau* have become better quality in recent years as the community becomes more affluent (one such structure built in 2018 was said to cost a still affordable seven million IDR, or 600 USD). It was often remarked to me by Semende men that they would look forward to spending time in the *dangau* as a way of "refreshing" themselves from the daily routines of life in the village, a refuge where they could "yell and sing out loud" without disturbing neighbors. *Dangau* culture, along with a sustained interest in maintaining *tunggu tubang* arrangements, is also a common theme in popular songs and music, many of which are posted online on sites such as YouTube, with a considerable following. A key theme is to appeal to nostalgic sentiments within the émigré community.[3] For many Semende, their rural homeland also provides a space where cultural and religious values can be lived out, and as such, the village is frequently seen (as similarly described for Java by Nooteboom 2019) as a "better place," an ideal that is further strengthened by its being relatively pleasant, cheap, and relaxing. However, and with relevance for my argument regarding fortress farming, Nooteboom (129) qualified this by suggesting that "although living in rural areas is increasingly seen as a positive option, working in agriculture is less often seen this way."

In addition to coffee and rice farming, other forms of commercial farming were important sources of income for some Semende households, with 15 percent of coffee-growing households also maintaining durian trees, often as part of a managed swidden fallow, and selling the fruit. Higher-risk and higher-capital commercial vegetable production has also increased in Semende over the last decade (figure 7.10). While the number of households involved is still relatively few, the percentage share of the sample coffee-growing population growing chili commercially (the most common horticultural crop) increased from 4.5 in 2015 to 7.2 in 2017, and then to 9.3 in 2019.

In 2018 I spoke with Ibu Kurnia (then in her mid-fifties) in a small dirty hut filled with fertilizers, hand sprayers, and bottles of liquid pesticides, next to a field she owned that was laid out with long strips of black plastic to suppress weeds (figure 7.10). She had just invested 75 million IDR (6,000 USD) in chilies, shallots, and tomatoes, but highlighted the risks involved: "Horticulture is like gambling—sometimes you get lucky with a good crop and high prices, and sometimes you don't." Two male Sundanese workers from Lembang in West Java (a region well known for horticulture) were working for her in an arrangement she called *ngebandung*, referring to them as her "clients" (*anak buah*). The arrangement involved Ibu Kurnia paying for their meals and other costs

FIGURE 7.10. Vegetable farming in Semende, 2019

(and keeping a tab) and then splitting the profits of a single harvest with them after deducting their costs. The two *anak buah* had worked for her three years beforehand and had contacted her again to make the recent arrangement. Ibu Kurnia, and her Sundanese workers, were clearly treating these vegetables as a profit-generating business venture. At the same time, she owned half a hectare of coffee, but, unlike with the vegetables, she didn't apply fertilizers and had paid a casual worker 40,000 IDR a day to harvest the cherries that year. Such rural landscapes thus contain a patchwork of land-livelihood relationships. Ibu Kurnia was also a *tunggu tubang*, and it concerned her that neither of her daughters was living in Semende (of her four adult children, the eldest daughter traded vegetables in the neighboring district of Lahat, the second daughter worked in an optometrist shop on Batam Island, a son was working as an electrician at the geothermal plant in Segamit, while another son was unmarried and living with his older sister in Lahat). Ibu Kurnia ended our discussion by offering me lunch, saying "it's just a habit of being a *tunggu tubang*; you can't leave the house of a *tunggu tubang* hungry." Despite the obvious importance of vegetable farming in such cases, the majority of coffee-growing households in Semende identified coffee as their only source of agricultural income in 2019.

Even in a region otherwise dominated by agriculture like Semende, considerable pluriactivity exists beyond farming, and around one in every three coffee farmers also engaged in nonfarm income-earning activities outside the coffee harvest time (table 7.6). Around a third of this off-farm employment involved working with the local government administration on some form of government-related service delivery, but 52 percent involved casual labor in activities such as construction, transport, or retail. This work mostly involved remaining within Semende. In 2019, those households with off-farm income sources (as either labor or running a small business) tended to rely on it more than farming, such that average incomes from these sources were higher than coffee income (table 7.7). Non-remittance household income is significantly higher than in Toraja.

The main street of a Semende village consists of closely packed houses, mostly timber-framed, but increasingly made from plastered or tiled brick (figure 7.4). Many houses double as businesses—food and grocery stores (*warung*), clothes shops, mobile phone stores, shops for mechanics, cabinetmakers, music providers (for *sedekah* events), child-care centers, water purifier retailers, photocopiers, finance and insurance agents, coffee traders, agents for Islamic pilgrimages

TABLE 7.6 Non-coffee labor allocation of primary "coffee worker" within household

NON-COFFEE WORK	DURING COFFEE HARVEST	DURING NON-COFFEE HARVEST
Worked as laborer on others farms (%)	16	29
Worked as nonfarm labor (%)	14	30
Worked in own nonfarm business (%)	13	19
Worked in own non-coffee farm (%)	23	33

Source: Author own survey, 2019 (n = 1208).

TABLE 7.7 Household income sources

INCOME SOURCE	HOUSEHOLDS RECEIVING THIS INCOME SOURCE (%)	MEAN INCOME PER RECEIVING HOUSEHOLD FROM THIS SOURCE
		(million IDR)
Remittances	12	1.8
Government supports	37	1.7
Off-farm business	20	13.7
Off-farm labor	31	14.1
Agricultural income	100	11.1
Total household income		21.0

Source: Author own survey, 2019 (n = 1208, means are winsorized at 95%).

FIGURE 7.11. Village home businesses in Semende, 2015

(*umroh* and hajj), and tailors (figure 7.11). Like in much of rural Southeast Asia, such income-generating activities are often seen as complementary, and often preferable, to farming. The commercial viability of many of the services and products sold by village businesses in Semende is also strengthened by the enhanced spending power of households that benefit from various transfers and remittances. As in Toraja, many reported receiving state-funded social protection transfers (up to a maximum of 3.4 million IDR annually in 2019).

The specific role of coffee within household livelihoods was thus described by one farmer as a "livelihood reserve" (*kopi itu sebagai cadangan hidup*), or what I have been calling a fortress crop. Coffee is generally not viewed as an activity to generate wealth; I was frequently told "you can't get rich from coffee." In Semende (unlike Toraja), however, a good coffee harvest still allows households to save enough money for *umroh* (hajj), to buy a motorbike (even if on credit), or to educate children. Indeed, educating children was seen to be the key for the next generation to move beyond farming, while farming is frequently the fallback option for "those who didn't make it" (*orang yang ngak jadi*). Some Semende villagers explained to me how coffee was a good crop for older people (contrasting it with horticulture): "Coffee growing suits us old folk. . . . It doesn't need much labor."

Livelihoods and Value Chains in a Commodity Source Region

This chapter has presented how fortress farming manifests itself within the agricultural region of Semende, where production is dominated by a combination of household-labor coffee farms, *sawah*, and a more recent interest in horticultural production, and where access to land was influenced by a distinctive inheritance system known as *tunggu tubang*. Household investments of labor in establishing and maintaining coffee farms are far greater here than in Toraja, and coffee-related income is generally more important to household livelihoods as a result. Indeed, coffee cultivation has sustained a commercial orientation to livelihoods and land use for more than a century, and coffee production is still the most important driver of the regional economy. I have, however, emphasized how, even in this classic commodity source region, the commitment to intensive, profit-maximizing agriculture is moderated by complex livelihoods influenced by household-scale pluriactivity and various interregional resource transfers. Fortress farming is again evident, as households strive to meet their residual household consumption needs from coffee farming, as a "livelihood reserve," while wealth accumulation is pursued through alternative avenues. At the same time, a few individuals have invested in riskier high-value vegetable production, thereby engaging in a "stepping-up" livelihood strategy (Dorward 2009). Such agricultural entrepreneurs remain a minority. More households now depend on off-farm income and resource transfers (including remittances and state-based social protection payments).

Coffee growing in the region has been integrated, in an extensive manner, within surrounding forest-swidden landscapes, where it has been embedded in a form of tree-crop-shifting cultivation. This means that, in practice, fallowed land in more remote locations is often available for a new planting by the next generation. Coffee plantings closer to village hubs have tended to be managed more intensively, with attempts to regenerate soil resources, intercrop with fruit trees, and adopt a greater use of fertilizers, while outlying plots rely more on forest rents. The uncertainty over boundaries in Semende between *marga* community land and the state forest estate has created tensions, but many communities have negotiated these in such a way as to ensure that institutions allowing an ethic of access have often prevailed. While there is more evidence of expansion into forest landscapes in Semende compared to Toraja, overall demand for land is moderated by a number of factors, including slowing rates of population growth, the ability to access nonagricultural resources directly or indirectly through remittances and transfers, and a regulatory context that is starting to restrict expansion.

Livelihoods in Semende are also influenced by a persistent interest in maintaining cultural and social identities through local institutions such as *tunggu tubang, sedekah,* and the *dangau* culture, which constrain both the emergence of a self-regulating market in land and excessive accumulation. The system of matrilineal primogeniture further discourages fragmentation of inherited landholdings among siblings. Similar to the effect of the ceremonial cycle in Toraja, *tunggu tubang* helps create and maintain culturally meaningful relationships between those involved in farming in the Semende homeland and an émigré network. Here also, intra-cultural resource transfers for *sedekah* events can be observed, and life-course patterns are important, with émigré Semende sometimes returning to their homeland for retirement.

The last decade in Semende has also witnessed intervention by downstream value chain actors to promote coffee-related sustainability. The evolution of these interventions reflects broader trends in lead firm strategies across the coffee sector, which witnessed an initial embrace of third-party certification (4C and Rainforest Alliance), facilitating an arrangement whereby farmers become enrolled in value chain institutions. This created a resource distribution network that linked Semende farmers to global lead firms. Over time, the lead firm sustainability strategy shifted away from a focus on supply chain traceability and certification toward service delivery mechanisms and landscape-scale project interventions. This has included resource flows from lead firms associated with ensuring enhanced carbon sequestration and avoiding deforestation in this landscape. This reflects a broader, emergent trend whereby payments are made to producers through value chain structures for the provision of ecosystem services (to incentivize habitat protection, improve hydrological functioning, and encourage carbon storage).

The underlying social structures whereby individual farmers were enrolled as members of farmer groups, which were then linked to larger patrons (state-based actors, trading firms, development agencies, and lead firm training centers) were relatively stable throughout, although opportunities to access distributed resources (planting material, drying tarpaulins, price premiums, training, employment, and construction contracts) shifted over time. The series of value chain interventions I studied thus facilitated a flow of resources into the region for an eight-year period, while also consolidating the social capital of select households that might be useful to access further resource flows in the future.

These value chain interventions have also tried to promote a greater household focus on entrepreneurial coffee farming, which resulted in enhanced household investment in time and financial resources—for a period. Some farmers, often those without access to alternative income streams, tried increasing their production of coffee by applying the suggested practices (pest monitoring and control, regular fertilization, use of cover crops, and pruning). Ultimately, however, the more intensive production practices were broadly incompatible with prevailing livelihood strategies at the household scale and the current institutional environment in Semende. Subsequently, the intensity of the direct intervention subsided, and any significant long-term shift toward productivist agricultural practices has yet to occur. The effects faded away as they did following the end of the PIK government project in 1984. In contexts such as Semende where coffee production is generally considered (by rural households themselves) to contribute to livelihood resilience but not necessarily wealth accumulation, programs that promote a pathway out of poverty through increasing coffee-related investments are unlikely to be embraced. There remains little indication of a transition toward productivist farming (the exception being in horticulture), and land is not being accumulated by entrepreneurial farmers nor dominated by wage-labor farms. The size of holdings continues to be limited largely by the ability of the household to provide sufficient labor internally. It may be that, over time, the force of various value chain initiatives, particularly those at broader spatial scales, becomes sufficient to trigger a transition toward productivist farming. At this stage, however, fortress farming strategies, where households treat land as a multifaceted livelihood resource, prevail for the majority.

Conclusion

FORTRESS FARMING AND THE POLITICS OF LAND IN LATE-INDUSTRIALIZING COUNTRIES

> **But I will sing of your strength, in the morning I will sing of your love;**
> **For you are my fortress, my refuge in times of trouble.**

—Psalm 59:16

Understanding contemporary agrarian transitions in a late-industrializing country like Indonesia presents an analytical challenge. On the one hand, the importance of agriculture to the Indonesian national economy has fallen (from 45 percent of GDP in 1965 to 13 percent in 2022), the share of the workforce primarily engaged in agriculture has also declined (from 52 percent in 1991 to 29 percent in 2022), and the share of the population living in areas classified as urban has increased from 16 percent in 1965 to 58 percent in 2022. Such broad-brush indicators of deagrarianization suggest, perhaps, that this is an initial stage of a sustained agrarian transition away from farm-associated livelihoods. It might therefore be reasonable to expect that access to farmland is also becoming decreasingly important to contemporary livelihoods and that policies should encourage farm plots to be consolidated and managed by entrepreneurial farmers committed to raising productivity. Yet the absolute number of agricultural *households* in Indonesia has increased in each of the successive agricultural censuses between 1963 and 2023, and their proportion of all Indonesian households has also remained relatively stable, at around 40 percent since 2003. There is a paradox in that economic priorities are shifting away from agriculture while households remain attached to farmland. There has not been a significant shift toward farm consolidation within the sector, and Indonesian smallholders are not abandoning the land at any significant rate. Furthermore, not all households who remain attached to the land are compelled to embrace high-productivity farming to reproduce themselves, and the transformation of agriculture by capitalist

220

relations thus remains fragmented and incomplete. This raises profound questions about the nature of contemporary agrarian transition in Indonesia (and elsewhere), the future of rural livelihoods, relationships with land, and appropriate policies to manage agrarian change.

Fortress Farming as a Livelihood Strategy

For many of the Indonesian coffee-growing households encountered in this book, farming is now a residual economic activity, with which they engage to satisfy household consumption needs, but only rarely does it provide a pathway out of poverty through processes of accumulation. At the same time, and in contexts where this is possible, attachments to farmland are not severed completely. I refer to "fortress farming" to denote a livelihood strategy where *the household maintains access to farmland as a defensive strategy to enhance livelihood resilience, while actively tapping into resource flows from beyond the rural landscape.* Such a strategy is characterized by maintaining access to farmland as a livelihood safety net; diversifying income sources and nonfarm revenue streams at the household level; pursuing farm practices that minimize investments of capital and labor rather than maximizing yields; and retaining place-based attachments to land as a cultural refuge in the context of a rapidly changing society.

The existence of a defensive livelihood strategy like fortress farming should not detract from the evident diversity of strategies pursued by different individuals and households based on their specific circumstances. A recent examination of contemporary agrarian change across Indonesia (McCarthy, McWilliam, and Nooteboom 2023b) made the fundamental point that we are witnessing a range of agrarian change scenarios that evade simple generalizations. I have also met Indonesians investing in high-value horticulture, citrus, oil palm, and even coffee with the intention of accumulating wealth through these activities, and some have even succeeded. High-productivity rice farming can also be profitable, given the right conditions and infrastructural supports. Indonesian smallholders have enthusiastically embraced export agriculture during so-called commodity booms, alleviating poverty for some. However, profit-maximizing agriculture (let alone situations where land and labor are fully commodified) is not the only way that rural households engage with farming, it is far from inevitable, and it may not be the most widespread.

Under fortress farming scenarios, farming often generates some food for the household (with rice production prevalent in my case studies), while cash-cropping offers a relatively steady, if not always especially lucrative, income flow to meet basic consumption needs (the "kitchen money" described by Mama Lina in the preface). In times of crisis, moreover, access to farmland is critical for livelihood resilience. Smallholders in my research sites have, time and again, emphasized the importance of access to farmland during periods of both personal and systemic distress. At the time I was finishing this book, the world had only recently recovered from the COVID-19 pandemic. Not only was the pandemic a health disaster ending the lives of millions worldwide, with Indonesia affected particularly severely in July and August of 2021, but economic activity was dramatically curtailed because of social distancing requirements. Fortress farming provided a lifeline to many during this period, as it did during the 1998 Asian financial crisis, when a massive contraction of the economy caused urban job losses on an alarming scale. This safety net function of farming for livelihood resilience has yet to disappear in Indonesia, nor indeed elsewhere in the region, and periodic crisis events reinforce its importance.

Precarity and the less dramatic, but no less important, insecurity of contemporary off-farm livelihoods have further encouraged attachment to homelands and a desire to retain access to smallholdings (Rigg, Salamanca, and Thompson 2016). Given the inherent and growing uncertainties associated with processes of global economic and environmental change, a "safety first" approach to land access makes sense and may well be an enduring aspect of livelihood strategies across the Global South. Even in China, reforms to the *hukou* household registration system started in 2001 (and culminated in a major national reform in 2014) and were aimed at encouraging higher rates of urbanization; yet many rural residents have become reluctant to give up rural *hukou* and associated land rights because of the livelihood security this provides (Andreas and Zhan 2016). Residence in the rural community (or an ability to reside there) not only enhances livelihood resilience through the possibility of farm-based activities, but it can also further attract resource flows from the extended family, through government programs, international donors, rural tourism, NGOs, and downstream value chain actors. While state-based social protection programs are expanding in Indonesia (as they are elsewhere in the Global South), fiscal resources constrain the scale of such programs, and they have not yet replaced the safety net role of farming and have not yet resulted in the widespread abandonment of smallholdings. Such resources are likely to be further constrained in the future, as many parts of Asia are aging before they get wealthy, with profound implications for how social welfare can be provisioned. Indeed, these two safety nets (farm-based and state-supported) may be complementary; government transfers are supporting households to meet minimum welfare needs *and* remain attached to the land and involved in low-productivity farming.

There are traces of Chayanov's "drudgery-averse peasant household" (Ellis [1988] 1993) in Indonesia's contemporary fortress farming strategies, with their calibration between productive investments and household consumption needs. However, rural households across Southeast Asia are often highly motivated to improve their material circumstances by pursuing off-farm livelihood endeavors, and it is their off-farm success (or failure) that frequently determines agricultural effort (Rigg 2019 makes similar arguments in the context of Thailand). It is in this sense that investment in farming is often the dependent variable (and a residual activity) determined by the capacity to exploit opportunities in the nonfarm economy. This helps explain, in many cases, a reluctance to embrace high-productivity farming.

Many villagers who have pursued off-farm opportunities by migrating to urban areas, moreover, have retained relationships with rural homelands, frequently motivated by ancestral attachments, as I described in detail for both Toraja and Semende (but also evident in Simalungun, Kintamani, Bajawa, and other coffee regions across Indonesia where I have undertaken field research). In several cases, these relationships were intergenerational, with the children of migrants still owning farmland and returning intermittently—often to participate in ceremonial practices. The concept of fortress farming thus embodies not only a material safety net in a world of precarious work but also something of a cultural refuge, where place-based attachments to land and communities continue to offer a sense of identity to many. Whether this will continue to be the case in the long term, of course, is difficult to predict. Presently, however, many rural landscapes, and even rapidly changing ones, often provide what might be considered a cultural homeland service. The additional contribution I make in this regard, moreover, is that by staying attached to (and even maintaining) these landscapes, rural residents can benefit from emergent resource distribution networks. The case of Toraja highlighted how the drive to attain cultural meaning encouraged distinct patterns of persistent smallholdings, linked to the nonproductivist multifunctionality of rural space. As discussed in Neilson (2022), significant resource transfers were made by the Torajan émigré community, channeled through ceremonial commitments, and these underpinned processes of rural development and supported distributed livelihoods (a process I call *intra-cultural rural landscape consumption*). This was also evident, to a lesser extent, in the otherwise archetypical commodity-producing region of Semende and is likely to be driving similar distributive practices in other places.

Fortress farming was also associated with low-intensity coffee production systems in my research. Some coffee farmers have made more concerted attempts to increase yields than others, but overall we have not witnessed a sustained shift toward productivity maximization through either corporate plantations or increasing smallholder investments of capital and labor (see appendix A). In this sense, also, farming is a defensive fortress activity. While smallholder coffee yields have remained low (as they generally have for other tree crops), this is not necessarily a problem for the households involved, even though it is frequently presented as one by downstream buyers, governments, and development agencies. In the 1980s, Booth (1988) contrasted the yield increases in Indonesian rice production since the 1970s with the export-oriented cash crop sector, where yields had stagnated. She further suggested that yield increases would be necessary to maintain producer welfare in tree-crop regions. However, Indonesia's low-intensity coffee systems often reflect fortress farming livelihood strategies linked to livelihood diversification and diverse nonfarm resource flows, and this helps explain why welfare in many coffee-growing communities appears to be improving without yield increases. Neither is this necessarily a recent or unique phenomenon, with Brookfield (1972) writing on "disintensification" of farming in the Pacific in the 1970s. Nooteboom (2019) described a preference for labor-saving (and lower yielding) tree crops in rural Java since the early 2000s, in contexts where many household members had migrated for work (he associated this with increased tenure security for local elites and lost access to farm labor opportunities for others). Dove (2011) found that Indonesian rubber growers were tapping their trees primarily in response to household consumption needs rather than downstream market imperatives, and this was resulting in suboptimal yields.

In regard to the contemporary agrarian question of how rural communities and household livelihoods are being transformed under conditions of global capitalism, fortress farming does not presuppose the dominance or inevitability of capitalist relations, and class differentiation, *within* agriculture. To reiterate, I am referring here to capitalist relations, strictly defined, as the emergence of a landowning class employing capital and wage labor to maximize productivity and profitability. Indonesia's coffee-growing households are petty commodity producers, combining the class positions of capital and labor in a single household "enterprise," but this broad category still encompasses a considerable diversity of forms (Bernstein 1986). This diversity is generated by unique combinations of livelihood strategies pursued by households and the broader institutional environment these households find themselves embedded within. This environment has included attempts by downstream value chain actors (and indeed upstream input providers) to squeeze rents out of smallholder producers, but many of the fortress farming households described in this book have not responded by increasing productivity in accordance with the supply requirements of these firms.

The accumulation of coffee-growing land beyond the labor capacities of the household was relatively uncommon in my field sites, with the tendency toward accumulation further stymied by flexible regimes of land access, such as those available under customary tenure and community forestry arrangements. Sharecropping was evident but not widespread, and dependence on agricultural wage labor remains low (such observations are supported by the evidence from broader survey work across the country; see appendix A). Pervasive landlessness, in the sense of large numbers of individuals seeking land to farm themselves, has not emerged as a widespread problem in these regions, although it may be a problem elsewhere (White 2018 discusses ongoing landlessness in Java a decade ago). While Indonesia's coffee-growing communities are not an undifferentiated, homogeneous mass exhibiting "shared poverty," the readily apparent class and wealth differences in rural Indonesia are not necessarily created by agriculturally induced differentiation. They are more likely to be generated by uneven access to resource flows through patronage relations, and by off-farm work and business opportunities (a point already made in Hart, Turton, and White 1989). Furthermore, the notion of farmers as a social grouping with clearly identifiable class interests, or any conventional notion of class consciousness, is difficult to defend in Indonesia's coffee-growing regions. This explains why, despite the sheer size of the Indonesian "peasantry," it has been unable to coalesce into a meaningful political force and appears unlikely to do so in the future (a challenge recently discussed by White, Graham, and Savitri 2023).

Further research, of course, is required to determine just how widespread fortress farming tendencies are across the full range of Indonesia's agrarian landscapes, whether they may be found elsewhere in late-industrializing Southeast Asia (in Thailand, Vietnam, or perhaps the Philippines), and whether they can be observed further afield across the Global South. At the very least, aspects of fortress farming are not unique to my coffee-producing field sites. Reporting on the absence of either a productivist agricultural revolution or an agrarian crisis in rural Aceh, McCarthy (2020) describes households as "advancing sideways" or "muddling through" processes of agrarian change (apparently consistent with fortress farming). In Thailand, Rigg (2019, 195) found that "land remains an important component in rural livelihoods but less as a productive resource and more as a store of wealth, often for intergenerational transfer and as a safety net during times of crisis." The key point being that land relations are far more diverse and unpredictable than those anticipated by more linear accounts of the development process within capitalism. Such outcomes, I suggest, are intimately related to how social reproduction is occurring in unexpected ways through networks that extend well beyond the farm gate, and so require a deeper analysis of multiscalar institutional environments.

Institutional Environments in an Age of Global Value Chains

This book has demonstrated how livelihood strategies, such as fortress farming, are shaped by place-specific institutional environments that change slowly over time in a largely path-dependent manner. Despite elements of path dependency, I also wish to highlight how actor practices continually reshape this institutional environment, with these practices and strategies responding to a range of economic, social, political, ethical, and environmental pressures. These institutional environments are multiscalar structures that encompass local place-based norms and aspirations, regional and national policies, and the political practices of states and state-linked actors, and they are further shaped by the dynamics of global value chains that have their own internal logics of accumulation. My analysis in this book suggests a need to invigorate analyses of contemporary rural livelihoods with a deeper, and more nuanced, understanding of the institutional environment as partially constituted by global value chains and the strategies of lead firms in governing these chains.

Institutional environments are historically informed. Chapter 2 presented the specific political-economic structures through which coffee cultivation and trade were incorporated within agrarian communities across Indonesia during the Dutch colonial period. This generally involved planting coffee within forested landscapes, either integrated within tree-based swidden systems or on the outskirts of wet-rice production, such that commercialization of agriculture (through coffee) frequently proceeded alongside continued subsistence food production within these communities. This pattern has largely continued today and contrasts with many of Indonesia's oil palm landscapes where the material characteristics of the crop are such that the upstream penetration of large-scale capital along the value chain is far more pervasive and transformative (McCarthy 2010). Instead, many outer island smallholders who embraced coffee cultivation were able to partially remove themselves from rigid social structures associated with rice production and became instead integrated within trade-based patronage relationships (and largely independent of the colonial state). This pattern, where smallholders are intimately networked to global trade systems, has therefore long been a key element of livelihood-shaping institutional environments in Indonesia.

The colonial era of coffee production did, however, involve coercive state-based exploitation of the peasantry under *cultuurstelsel* (especially on Java), as well as corporate (nonindigenous) investment in plantations. The former contributed to persistent structures of patron-client relations between the state and rural communities (chapter 3) and, arguably, an ethos of antiproductivism among some

Indonesian smallholders. Colonial plantations, meanwhile, established a pattern of state-facilitated land grabbing by corporate entities, a continuing trend in the contemporary oil palm sector (Li and Semedi 2021). The late nineteenth- and early twentieth-century enthusiasm for large commercial plantations, however, ultimately fizzled out in the coffee-producing regions. In the emerging institutional environment of post-independence Indonesia, especially in the 1970s and 1980s, smallholders proved to be more competitive, and have remained so ever since. In the case of coffee (and indeed for other export crops like cocoa, rubber, pepper, and coconut), the overwhelming pattern became the persistence of household commodity producers reliant on family labor, with access to land regulated by a range of diverse institutions (informal and formal, as described in chapter 5). Many of these households now engage in what I call fortress farming. Also starting in the colonial era, Indonesia's coffee smallholders, especially those in southern Sumatra and the eastern islands, became intimately embedded in trade networks (value chain structures) where capitalist forces acted, at a distance, upon production landscapes.

Processes of global economic change since the 1990s have been influentially explained through the analytical frameworks of global value chains (refer to Ponte, Gereffi, and Reichert 2019) and global production networks (refer to Coe and Yeung 2015). These frameworks share a common understanding of *governance* as the global influence exerted on production processes by powerful lead firms (often transnational corporations). Such governance involves active coordination that differs both from direct ownership of productive assets and from simple reliance on spot markets (Gereffi, Humphrey, and Sturgeon 2005). In chapter 4, I demonstrated how this lead firm role in the global coffee industry was being performed by branded roasters like Nestlé, JDE, and Starbucks. Such firms have accumulated considerable power not only to capture agricultural surplus value through nonownership modes of governance but also to influence the institutional environments shaping livelihoods in producing regions. They have done this both directly, for example by requiring conformance to production standards, and indirectly, by enrolling state-based actors and NGOs as extra-firm partners. This influence is driven by their desire to control brand reputations, enhance supply sustainability, and improve product quality, with sustainability initiatives (including attempts to ensure a "living income" for household producers) looming large in any contemporary analysis of value chain governance in the sector (chapter 4).

An important factor determining processes of contemporary agrarian change and rural futures, therefore, is the extent to which agrifood lead firms are willing to actively sustain people on the land (to continue functioning as petty commodity producers). It is true that price signals will be sent to producers to increase supply when it falls below demand, but this results in considerable price and quality volatility for lead firms (and cycles of unacceptable living standards for producers that might ultimately affect long-term sustainability of supply and the ethical reputations of lead firms). In this book I have documented the emergence of a range of resource transfer mechanisms (initiated by lead firms, but often responding to broader social pressures) that operate through value chains *alongside* conventional market processes. In Toraja (chapter 6), this involved lead firm investments in infrastructure such as kindergartens, roads, and bridges, as well as the introduction of a corporate sustainability program (Starbucks's CAFE Practices). In Semende (chapter 7), this involved establishment of a team of agronomists initially linked to third-party certification schemes (4C and Rainforest Alliance), which subsequently became absorbed within JDE's Common Grounds program. Just as rural landscapes can provide a homeland service to an émigré community (thereby encouraging resource transfers), so too can these landscapes provide (nonproductivist) services to coffee roasters. This was apparent in the "origin stories" (presented in chapters 4 and 6) used by specialty roasters to add symbolic value to coffee at the point of sale. It was also evident in sustainability programs that encourage the provisioning of ecosystem services, such as habitat services through shade-grown coffee or carbon sequestration on coffee farms (enabling so-called carbon insetting). Such services assume even greater significance when ethicality and sustainability become arenas for product differentiation and value addition by lead firms (Ponte 2019).

Lead firms also engaged in processes of extra-firm bargaining within NGOs, development agencies, and local governments in Indonesia's coffee-producing regions to steer policies and encourage resource distributions to producers. Lead firm involvement in source-country initiatives under the Global Coffee Platform, like SCOPI (chapter 4), are emblematic of this strategy, through which lead firms have sought to mobilize state resources for activities such as agricultural extension and input subsidies. Similar processes of extra-firm bargaining to encourage resource allocations have also been evident (indeed even more prominent) in the Indonesian cocoa sector (Fold and Neilson 2016; Neilson, Pritchard, et al. 2018). This range of lead firm strategies, through their interactions with local actors, has thus reshaped local institutional environments in ways that encourage continued engagement with agricultural production but not necessarily a commitment to productivity enhancement. Source regions for commodities such as coffee may thus find themselves institutionally "locked in" to agricultural production, even as household livelihoods become more diverse. The institutional environment thus created has contributed to the prevalence of fortress farming livelihoods.

Value chain relationships, sometimes associated with donor funding, have moreover adhered to preexisting social structures to provide another axis of patronage. My historically informed analysis of the Indonesian state (chapter 3) highlighted not just its well-documented extractive nature but also its role in consistently reinforcing patronage relations within rural communities. The social structures through which state patronage was channeled to these communities became important institutional foundations for subsequent resource distribution by nonstate organizations (development NGOs and lead firms). This was most clearly demonstrated through the way state-formed farmer groups have been reactivated to facilitate third-party certification of sustainable farm practices. In southern Sumatra, moreover, coffee farmers did not find it functionally helpful to distinguish between private-sector sustainability programs and government *proyek*: from their perspective, each constituted a similar patronage relationship. Resource transfers delivered through both were contributing to redistributed livelihoods, unevenly accessed to be sure but still constituting important forms of social capital for strategically situated individuals.

I argued throughout this book that processes of rural development are interwoven with the value chain strategies of lead firms in increasingly complex ways. This suggests a need to invigorate analyses of contemporary rural livelihoods with a deeper, and more nuanced, understanding of institutional environments as partially constituted by global value chains. At the same time, notwithstanding the increasing upstream reach of powerful corporate influences, I have also demonstrated the need to contextualize these influences within local institutional complexity. There has been a tendency, prevalent among lead firms, development agencies, and NGOs alike, to overlook such complexity and livelihood diversity and to overestimate the impact of value chain initiatives (as argued in Neilson and Shonk 2014; Bray and Neilson 2018; Neilson 2019). The limited livelihood impact of voluntary sustainability standards in the global coffee sector (Bray and Neilson 2017) is partly related to the fact that rural households do not operate as profit-maximizing businesses, and partly due to the continued, misplaced, analytical foregrounding of production over redistributive processes. Indonesia's coffee-producing households are not *just* coffee farmers. I have highlighted how they are also, for example, members of farmer and forest user groups, citizens of the Indonesian state with certain rights and responsibilities, and community members involved in diverse forms of social reproduction. This book thus seeks to be a corrective to analytical accounts by some GVC theorists, NGOs, and development practitioners which suggest that opportunities for livelihood upgrading by smallholders are determined solely by value chain dynamics and corporate strategies of accumulation (refer to the review by Devaux et al. 2018). Such accounts are also integral, for example, to the underlying rationale of Fairtrade interventions. I have demonstrated how these dynamics can be important, but they also need to be more effectively contextualized within place-based development trajectories. Otherwise, such value chain determinism can instead be an impediment to understanding (and encouraging) broader processes of rural development.

It is, of course, an open question whether the institutional environments affecting Indonesia's rural regions that I have documented will continue to encourage livelihood strategies akin to fortress farming into the future. In particular, the potential for nonproductivist resource redistribution (through remittances, state-based social protection and community development programs, tourism, value chain mechanisms and payments for ecosystem services) is dependent on broader processes of wealth creation in the national and global economy, along with political motivations to redistribute this in some way.

Agrarian Transitions and Land in Late-Industrializing Countries

Fortress farming strategies intersect fundamentally with, and are mutually constituted by, broader structural transformation of the economy and the availability (or absence) of nonagricultural livelihood opportunities. As presented in chapter 2, large numbers of rural Indonesians have been drawn into urban employment, but not nearly as rapidly as in Northeast Asia, and the absolute decline of individuals involved in farm-based livelihoods has been moderate at best. Accounting for a regionally specific form of agrarian transition in East Asia, even one that deviates from classical accounts in Europe and North America, remains fraught. The key characteristics of agrarian transitions in Northeast Asia seem to have been an initial prevalence of smallholding agricultural cultivators who pursued rapid productivity increases facilitating the accumulation of capital for industrialization, even if capitalist relations *within* agriculture were subdued by the presence of a powerful, and overbearing, state (chapter 2). There are some parallels here with Indonesia, although productivity increases and farm-based accumulation in Indonesia were less obvious, and the postwar land reforms of Northeast Asia were never fully replicated. The discursive influence of Sukarno's *Marhaenisme* did, however, encourage an abundance of owner-cultivators, especially in the outer islands, where this was further facilitated by relatively open land access regimes in forest landscapes. Indonesian smallholders were then supported by various rural development schemes (especially input subsidies) during Suharto's New Order. The commitment to agricultural research and extension, however, especially in the tree-crop sector, was somewhat half-hearted and never sufficient to stimulate the productivity increases expected to allow significant on-farm accumulation.

Manufacturing-based industrialization took off in Indonesia during the 1980s and 1990s, fueled largely by foreign capital and oriented toward export markets, without the prior modernization of agriculture. A peak share of employment in manufacturing of 12.9 percent was reached in 2002 (remaining at this share ever since), compared to a South Korean peak of 27.8 percent (in 1989), from where it subsequently declined (Felipe, Mehta, and Rhee 2014). Future manufacturing growth in Indonesia, moreover, remains uncertain. Competition with China (and more recently Vietnam) has meant that growth in manufacturing jobs has been lethargic, with a general shift toward lower-paid service sector jobs. At the same time, the urgency of agriculturally driven poverty alleviation has been tempered, in part as a result of the various resource transfers presented in this book. Instead, many parts of the Indonesian countryside, including the coffee-growing regions I have visited, are drifting toward a nonproductivist multifunctionality without first undergoing a productivist revolution ("muddling through," in the words of McCarthy 2020). This then suggests a modern twist on the so-called dual economy thesis of Lewis (1954). In Indonesia, a dual economy has persisted, but the two sectors ("modern" and "traditional," to use Lewis's somewhat dated terms) have been bridged by interdependencies and a complex network of resource flows, which, paradoxically perhaps, have further entrenched an urban-rural divide in terms of labor productivity. This is consequently confounding standard analyses of economic development and limiting effective policymaking. While Indonesia may yet experience a long-term transition toward higher rates of industrialization and the eventual abandonment of smallholdings in the countryside, I remain skeptical at this point: such a transition should certainly not be considered inevitable.

The Indonesian state has been pivotal in shaping the institutional arrangements regulating land access, including through its landlord function (a product of the feudalization of the state) as described in chapters 3 and 5. The overt feudalistic exploitation of the peasantry through this landlord function, however, has been moderated by the demands placed on a modern nation-state, whose legitimacy has depended on ensuring a modicum of development (*pembangunan*) for its citizens. Where traditional feudal elites existed, they were commonly enrolled within state-based patronage systems, a process that commenced during the colonial period, with patronage subsequently being the cornerstone of rural class dynamics (Hart 1989).

Across Indonesia, coffee continues to be cultivated predominately on lands other than those held under formally registered individual title (*hak milik*) and on lands that were never purchased (refer to data presented in chapter 5 and appendix A). Instead, these lands were either directly appropriated based on a customary ethic of access, or inherited from others who did, or through specific arrangements with the landlord state (especially in the forestry zone). The extent of renting and sharecropping of land, and the value of taxes paid to the state, have also been limited, such that very little capital has been absorbed in the payment of ground rent (or in a capitalized form through a land price). Land markets remain circumscribed by social relations within communities and with the state, and this has limited—but has not eliminated entirely—the extent of agriculturally driven land accumulation.

My analysis of fortress farming has highlighted the limitations of a production-focused rendering of rural development. Conventionally, GVC and GPN approaches had emphasized processes of production (as suggested within the very term "global *production* network") and the associated notion of *upgrading* as being pivotal elements of successful regional economic development (discussed in chapter 1). Rather than an inevitable and necessary embrace of productivist agriculture, however, we instead observe the prevalence of non-productivist fortress farming at the household level. Recognizing the importance of evolving forms of resource redistribution thus presents a fundamental challenge to accepted ways of understanding processes of rural development. Efforts by lead firms to instill entrepreneurial farming among Indonesian coffee farmers have been largely unsuccessful to date (see Bray and Neilson 2018; Neilson, Toth, Sari, et al. 2019; and appendix A). Indeed, program implementers continually express their frustration that good agricultural practices are not being followed by farmers, prompting the common refrain "we need to change their mindset."

The key argument of this book, then, emphasizes the defensive livelihood function of land access and highlights how this has been divorced, at least in sites where fortress farming prevails, from productivist imperatives. I assert that by acknowledging these realities, we create space for a more diverse set of political possibilities in relation to debates over land in late-industrializing countries. Indeed, the ability of farming to operate as a livelihood fortress is fundamentally dependent on supportive institutional regimes of land access. My analysis argues that while Polanyian countermovements are evident, whereby societal processes have intervened in institutional environments to minimize the unregulated commodification of rural land and labor (or its effects), such outcomes are the result of active political struggles. Access to land in Indonesia's coffee regions has been enabled by a diverse array of institutional forms, including customary *adat* arrangements and agreements negotiated with forestry departments. Tree-rich landscapes have provided a lifeline for livelihood security, but this requires the emergence and maintenance of appropriate institutions. This is certainly not guaranteed, and highlights what I consider to be a key focus of contemporary political struggles over land. Fortress farming suggests there are advantages in maintaining a diverse range of land access regimes. Indeed, village administration lands (*tanah bengkok*) in Java, as well as community forestry lands in the outer islands, have been reallocated for welfare purposes to the landless and near landless to support livelihood resilience. Such institutional arrangements are dynamic, evolving opportunistically and responding to changing political circumstances and processes of economic and social change, but generally respond to an ethic of access (Peluso 1996).

A continued threat to land access for livelihood resilience is the appropriation of large areas of land for commercial activities and infrastructure projects, often justified in the "national interest." Highlighting the essential role of land for livelihood resilience thus helps support an alternative development narrative to counter the rationale of productivity-increasing land grabs. There is also significant, and increasing, pressure for the formal registration of individual land rights as property, as part of a broader capitalist transformation that seeks to create a commodity out of land while attempting to enhance productive capacity. Continued low rates of formal *hak milik* title to date, however, have tended to improve access to land as a livelihood resource rather than limit it. Value chain interventions seeking to "improve" land access regimes (as many do, as described in chapters 4 and 7) may be better off encouraging an ethic of access rather than the rigid (and more widespread) approach of promoting "tenure security," where this is pursued through individualized titling and smallholder exclusion from forestry zones. Paradoxically, given the way that coffee farming is embedded within multi-sited household livelihoods, formalization of land title may not even result in enhanced supply for lead firms. On the contrary, rigidifying individual landownership can decrease supply if it encourages speculative holdings rather than allowing more flexible access to those incentivized to pursue farming for livelihood resilience.

There are, meanwhile, important environmental impulses at play that are further reshaping the institutional environments driving processes of agrarian transition in novel ways. Demographic changes in Indonesia, including the moderate decline in the rural population, suggest easing pressures on forest and land resources to support livelihood resilience, but these resources will not be able to support continually expanding productive capacity and corporate land grabbing. A conventional development model has been one that seeks to address global poverty by ever-increasing production, industrialization, and consumerism, and the redistribution of accumulated societal wealth through "productive work." However, not only have there been structural limits in terms of formal job creation within a globalizing economy (owing to "premature deindustrialization"), but there are serious ecological consequences from continuing to pursue this model. As the full environmental costs are recognized, globally coordinated efforts to more effectively address the well-being of the world's rural poor (on a fundamentally resource-constrained planet) will be needed. Indeed, distributed livelihoods across a set of care-based activities, environmental stewardship roles, and cultural contributions, far more expansive than just conventional "productive work," are already emerging, albeit in a sporadic way. Chapter 4 discussed the design and emergence of payment mechanisms for rural communities through global value chains and how these have dovetailed with REDD+ initiatives to establish payment streams detached from orthodox ideas of rural productivism. Despite ongoing risks that such initiatives may result in new forms of land grabbing (Larson et al. 2013), shifts in household incentive structures to provide such landscape services are already reshaping rural livelihood opportunities (Blundo-Canto et al. 2018). Further consideration of the diverse mechanisms through which (global and national) wealth in the twenty-first century is being, and can further be, redistributed to these rural landscapes in the Global South for non-productivist activities may be necessary to ensure biophysical planetary limits are respected.

The notion of a singular agrarian transition occurring at the national scale is questionable, given the evident multiplicity of trajectories reported in different regions within diverse countries like Indonesia. Instances of dispossession and land grabbing by corporate interests may be occurring in some places, while elsewhere in the same country smallholders themselves might actively embrace commodity booms, and still elsewhere conservative farm practices, pluriactivity, and fortress farming may prevail. It should now be clear, however, that I do not associate the notion of agrarian transition with a particular, preordained structural transformation of a national economy, let alone one involving modernization of agriculture as a necessary platform for the broader development of capitalism. The development of productivist capitalist relations *within* farming is certainly not inevitable, inescapable, or inexorable. Many countries, like Indonesia, have urbanized and industrialized, such that agriculture is no longer the dominant economic sector. At the same time, the situation whereby a significant share of the population continues to rely on a combination of access to land and access to various resource transfers for livelihood resilience may be a more persistent feature of late-industrializing countries than sometimes imagined. This may even be a desirable outcome. If so, standard policy prescriptions to promote sustainable rural livelihoods will need to be adjusted accordingly.

STATISTICAL DATA ON INDONESIAN COFFEE PRODUCERS

Much of the data presented in this appendix is freely available at www.bps.go.id. Some was purchased in disaggregated form from BPS at https://silastik.bps.go.id and required some basic analysis. While these datasets are generally more reliable and professionally collected than those published by some other agencies, the BPS datasets need to be treated with some caution, especially considering methodological changes over time. Booth (2019, 10) suggests that BPS survey data "may be flawed because certain groups of households are undercounted or ignored altogether," and she is concerned that the considerable discrepancy between these datasets and the national accounts reflects underreporting or undersampling in the household surveys. Furthermore, some surveys (notably Susenas) involve a lengthy questionnaire where respondents can be further expected to experience fatigue affecting the quality of responses. Other surveys (such as the ST questionnaires) are more concise. Any survey questions that involve lengthy recall of information beyond a few weeks also need to be treated with caution.

TABLE A1 State support for coffee-growing households in major coffee-growing provinces (percentage of all coffee-growing households)

PROVINCE	RECEIVE ANY FORM OF STATE SUPPORT	RECEIVE STATE SUPPORT OTHER THAN SUBSIDIZED FERTILIZERS	RECEIVE STATE AGRICULTURAL EXTENSION	MEMBER OF A COOPERATIVE	MEMBER OF A FARMER GROUP
Aceh	10.4	7.5	5.4	2.8	20.3
North Sumatra	36.2	2.2	6.4	0.3	8.4
South Sumatra	15.3	0.7	1.2	0.1	7.8
Lampung	9.8	0.7	6.3	0.4	14.5
South Sulawesi	23.5	2.4	8.8	0.8	18.8
All	19.9	2.0	5.3	0.6	13.1

Source: BPS 2014.

TABLE A2 Fertilizer applications by coffee farmers in Vietnam and Indonesia

INDICATOR OF APPLICATION	INDONESIA	VIETNAM
Applications per year (median)	2	4
Apply urea (% of farmers)	80	100
Apply blended NPK (% of farmers)	68	79
Apply superphosphate (% of farmers)	5	98
Apply potassium chloride (% of farmers)	0	98
Apply organic compost (% of farmers)	96	81
Annual average urea applications (kg/ha)	70–180	400–800
Annual average NPK applications (kg/ha)	60–100	1000–1400
Annual average TSP applications (kg/ha)	65–100	400–800

Source: Byrareddy et al. 2019.

TABLE A3 Fertilizer application among Indonesian agricultural households whose main crop is coffee

PROVINCE	APPLY SYNTHETIC FERTILIZER (%)	APPLY UREA (%)	APPLY NPK (%)	AVERAGE APPLICATION UREA (KG/HA/YEAR)	AVERAGE APPLICATION NPK (KG/HA/YEAR)
Aceh	39	27	18	135	139
North Sumatra	78	59	40	139	121
South Sumatra	50	43	17	193	86
Lampung	51	40	21	245	195
South Sulawesi	43	35	10	147	84

Source: BPS 2014.

TABLE A4   Main coffee marketing channels across Indonesia

PROVINCE	ALL TO COLLECTOR (%)	ALL TO LOCAL MARKET (%)	ALL TO CO-OP (%)	ALL TO COMPANY (%)	SOME TO COMPANY (%)	MIXED SALES (%)
Aceh	89	7	<1	<1	<1	3
North Sumatra	81	9	1	<1	3	6
South Sumatra	85	4	<1	<1	1	8
Lampung	81	10	<1	<1	<1	8
South Sulawesi	77	7	0	1	1	15

Source: BPS 2014.

TABLE A5   Coffee farmer integration with credit markets

PROVINCE	NO CREDIT FOR COFFEE PRODUCTION (%)	CREDIT FROM BANK (%)	CREDIT FROM COOPERATIVE (%)	INTEREST-FREE CREDIT (INCL. COLLECTORS) (%)	OTHER (INCL. FAMILY SUPPORT) (%)
Aceh	90	<1	<1	7	1
North Sumatra	95	<1	<1	3	<1
South Sumatra	86	<1	<1	11	1
Lampung	87	<1	0	10	2
South Sulawesi	95	<1	<1	4	<1

Source: BPS 2014.

TABLE A6   Coffee land originally cleared (from secondary or primary forest)

PROVINCE	N	LAND ORIGINALLY CLEARED (%)
Aceh	1,028	51
North Sumatra	1,951	74
South Sumatra	2,557	82
Lampung	2,499	54
South Sulawesi	2,068	69
All major coffee provinces	10,103	68

Source: BPS 2014.

TABLE A7   Land status of coffee lands in major coffee-growing provinces

PROVINCE	N	SELF-OWNED (%)	RENT LAND (%)	RENT "FOR FREE" (%)
Aceh	1,028	91.6	1.7	6.7
North Sumatra	1,951	89.5	1.6	8.9
South Sumatra	2,557	90.1	5.3	4.6
Lampung	2,499	80.4	3.8	15.8
South Sulawesi	2,068	91.3	0.8	7.9
All provinces (includes Java)		79.8	6.5	13.7

Source: BPS 2014.

TABLE A8   Management status of coffee lands in selected districts

REGION	SELF-OWNED LAND (%)	SHARECROPPED (%)	MANAGE FOR WAGE (%)
Semende (2013)	97.1	3.7	0.1
North Toraja (2013)	93.6	4.3	2.1
Tana Toraja (2013)	94.6	3.7	1.7
Indonesia (2018)	94.3	5.6	0.1

Sources: BPS 2013; BPS 2019a.

TABLE A9   Reliance on household and paid labor in major coffee-growing provinces

PROVINCE	N	USE ONLY UNPAID / FAMILY LABOR (%)	AVERAGE NUMBER OF UNPAID / FAMILY WORKERS	USE PERMANENT WORKERS (%)
Aceh	1,028	46.6	2.2	4.3
North Sumatra	1,951	59.1	2.3	1.5
South Sumatra	2,557	48.0	2.1	2.9
Lampung	2,499	45.6	2.1	4.8
South Sulawesi	2,068	59.6	2.5	1.6
All major coffee provinces	10,103	51.8	2.2	3.1

Source: BPS 2014.

TABLE A10   Management arrangements for coffee farms in Semende

MANAGEMENT ARRANGEMENT	PERCENT OF ALL COFFEE-GROWING HOUSEHOLDS
Owner-manager only	96
Sharecropper only	3
Owner-manager and sharecropper	1
Manage for a wage only	<1
Other combination of management arrangements	<1

Source: BPS 2013 (N = 5898).

THE SUSTAINABLE LIVELIHOODS FRAMEWORK

Figure B.1 provides a schematic presentation of the relationship between the various elements presented throughout the book by refining earlier visualizations of Sustainable Livelihoods Frameworks (figure 1.1, based on Scoones 1998 and Carney 1999). While I am sympathetic to the critiques made by Natarajan et al. (2022) of earlier frameworks, their highly relational reformulation has (to my mind) lost some of the utility of those earlier frameworks. My modifications are therefore more moderate.

My modifications are fourfold. First, figure B.1 takes what Scoones (1998) called "Institutions and Organisations" and Carney (1999) called "Transforming Structures and Processes" and develops this analytically as "the Multiscalar Institutional Environment," which I place directly adjacent to the broader livelihood context. This seeks to embed the institutional environment within longer-term trends, histories, and geographies in a partially path-dependent way. It is rare that actor interventions can act directly on these broader contexts. However, the institutional environment is more dynamic and can be altered by political interventions, programs, policies, and practices. The other key contribution here is to insert the influential role of lead firm strategies and global value chains within the institutional environment and to make a claim for GVCs as being an integral component within such contemporary multiscalar processes.

Second, figure B.1 retains the asset pentagon as a helpful way of thinking through resource access at the household or individual level. This seeks to

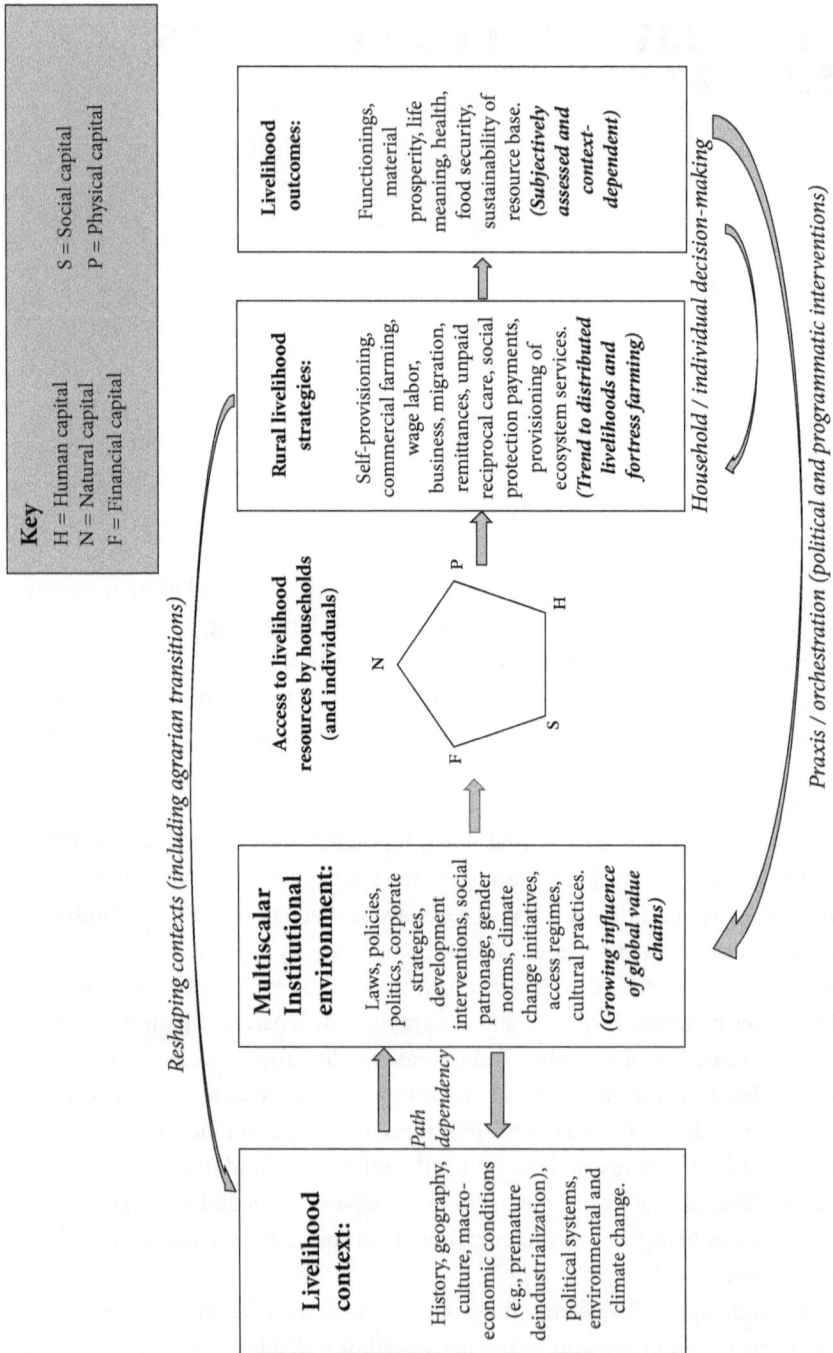

Key

H = Human capital   S = Social capital

N = Natural capital   P = Physical capital

F = Financial capital

Livelihood context:

History, geography, macro-economic conditions (e.g., premature deindustrialization), political systems, environmental and climate change.

Path dependency

Multiscalar Institutional environment:

Laws, policies, politics, corporate strategies, development interventions, social patronage, gender norms, climate change initiatives, access regimes, cultural practices. **(*Growing influence of global value chains*)**

Access to livelihood resources by households (and individuals)

N   P   H   S   F

Rural livelihood strategies:

Self-provisioning, commercial farming, wage labor, business, migration, remittances, unpaid reciprocal care, social protection payments, provisioning of ecosystem services. **(*Trend to distributed livelihoods and fortress farming*)**

Livelihood outcomes:

Functionings, material prosperity, life meaning, health, food security, sustainability of resource base. **(*Subjectively assessed and context-dependent*)**

Reshaping contexts (including agrarian transitions)

Household / individual decision-making

Praxis / orchestration (political and programmatic interventions)

FIGURE B.1. A refined schematic for understanding contemporary livelihoods maintain the people-centered focus of the original framework. However, in contrast to earlier framework, I have repositioned the asset pentagon to the right of the institutional environment to emphasize how access to resources is predetermined by the institutional environment and associated power relationships. This positioning also captures the idea of bounded agency, as households and individuals make decisions about livelihood strategies based on the resources at their disposal set within a particular institutional and political environment. Natarajan et al. (2022, 11) removed reference to these assets on the basis that it "predisposes the framework to a tacit acceptance of capitalism." I do not entirely agree with this assertion and have demonstrated in this book how the inclusion of nonfinancial capitals at the household, or individual, level is analytically useful to appreciate noncapitalist livelihood pathways.

Third, figure B.1 identifies a particular livelihood strategy (fortress farming) as emergent in various places as a response to both cultural and material aspirations of individuals within communities, given their institutional context. I developed this livelihood strategy conceptually in the second substantive section of the conclusion.

Fourth, I retain a distinct focus on "livelihood outcomes," although I have altered the otherwise positive rendering of outcomes suggested by earlier models, acknowledging that livelihoods may in fact deteriorate over time. Natarajan et al. (2022), in contrast, have removed this distinction, claiming that "the original Livelihood outcomes element obscures the turbulence of livelihoods" and "implies a certain finality that does not correspond to experience." I agree that livelihoods are certainly in flux, and I capture this notion by inserting the direct feedback loop between outcomes and strategies. I believe it is important to consider outcomes separately (appealing back to Amartya Sen's work on functionings and development as freedom), as it keeps the end goal of context-dependent human flourishing and sustainability firmly in focus. I would like to think that this accommodates the disparate ways that individuals, households, and communities seek life meaning, commonly expressed through culture. Importantly, figure B.1 provides a feedback link from outcomes to the institutional environment (rather than a feedback loop to the asset pentagon, as in the UK's Department for International Development framework, figure 1.1). This highlights the mediating role of institutions and political structures in determining individual access to resources and maintains the idea of bounded agency. Earlier models are rightly criticized for a belief that interventions could be made directly to build up household-level assets rather than intervening in the institutions of power. After assessing livelihood outcomes, individual households will inevitably refine their own livelihood strategy. In addition, there is always the possibility of political action (and programmatic interventions) to reshape the institutional environment. This revised framework should therefore hold some purchase on praxis (action oriented toward changing society). It is commonly the institutional environment, rather than the asset pentagon of the household, where praxis should be focused. By better understanding the institutional environment, we can identify specific sites where orchestration (borrowing from Abbott and Snidal 2010) may be possible and more likely to be effective.

Terms and Abbreviations

ACIAR The Australian Centre for International Agricultural Research

adat Customary values, rules, and norms of behavior

ADB Asian Development Bank

AEKI Asosiasi Eksportir Kopi Indonesia (Association of Indonesian Coffee Exporters)

agricultural household Defined by the 2013 Indonesian Agricultural Census as those where "at least one household member undertakes an agricultural activity partly or wholly aimed to be sold or bartered"

alang Carved Torajan rice barns

AMAN Aliansi Masyarakat Adat Nusantara (Alliance for Indigenous Peoples of the Archipelago)

aparat State apparatus / state employee in Indonesia

apit jurai A term for extended family in Semende, associated with *tunggu tubang* land tenure arrangements

asalan Ungraded green coffee beans

bangsa The Indonesian nation

Beasiswa Siswa Miskin Educational cash stipends, later becoming **PIP** (**Program Indonesia Pintar**), implemented by the Indonesian government

belukar (belukae in Semende) Secondary forests and fallows

bimas Mass guidance programs providing agricultural extension and input subsidies, especially prominent during the New Order regime (1966–1998)

BLT Bantuan Langsung Tunai (unconditional cash transfer program implemented by the Indonesian government)

BPN Badan Pertanahan Nasional (National Lands Agency)

BPNT Bantuan Pangan Non-Tunai (Non-cash Food Assistance), subsidized rice for the poor program implemented by the Indonesian government

BPS Badan Pusat Statistik (Indonesia Statistics Agency)

bupati Regent, and head of district (***kabupaten***) below the level of province. In precolonial Java, the *bupati* were highest level of Javanese lord beneath the monarch, whose position was preserved throughout the Dutch period.

cultuurstelsel Forced cultivation scheme by the Netherlands East Indies government that was most thoroughly implemented from 1830 to 1870, within which coffee was the preeminent crop

Dana Alokasi Umum General Allocation Fund fiscally transferred from the national budget to regional governments

Dana Desa Village-level funding mechanisms (a successor to the **KDP** and **PNPM** community development programs)

dangau A farmhouse in Semende

desa Administrative village

domein verklaring Domain declarations of the 1870s and 1880s through which the colonial state effectively claimed ownership over all uncultivated lands in the East Indies

dikuasai "To be controlled" (with reference to resources such as land) but ranges in meaning from "ownership" to "regulate"

Ditjenbun Directorate General of Estate Crops, within the Indonesian Ministry of Agriculture

FAO Food and Agricultural Organization of the United Nations

FOB Free on Board, price of export goods prior to shipping

4C Common Code for the Coffee Community, an industry-led supply chain sustainability standard

GAEKI Gabungan Eksportir Kopi Indonesia (Indonesian Coffee Exporters Association)

GCP Global Coffee Program, an initiative of Western donor countries, international NGOs, and lead firms in the coffee sector

giling basah Wet-milling process where coffee is hulled prior to drying as green beans

GI Geographical Indication, a form of collective intellectual property through which a place name associated with a particular product originating in that place is legally protected

GPN Global production network

GVC Global value chain

hak milik Formal state recognition of individual ownership of land through a land registry

hak ulayat The community right to avail over uncultivated customary lands

HGU Hak Guna Usaha (Commercial Right to Use), given to large-scale plantations, usually for a period of twenty-five years

hutan Forest

hutan adat Legally recognized customary forest

hutan desa Village forest, where state forest is managed by the local village administration

Hutan Kemasyarakatan (HKm) Community-based forestry programs, where state forest is leased to user groups with conditions attached to tree density

Hutan negara State forest; land (forested and unforested) claimed by the state

ICA International Coffee Agreement, administered by the ICO, associated with quotas between 1962 and 1989

ICCRI Indonesian Coffee and Cocoa Research Institute, based in Jember, East Java

ICO International Coffee Organization, an intergovernmental organization based in London and established under the auspices of UNCTAD

ICRAF World Agroforestry Research Centre, part of the CGIAR (Consortium of International Agricultural Research centers), with an affiliate office in Indonesia

IDH Sustainable Trade Initiative (development NGO with considerable support from the Dutch government)

IDR Indonesia rupiah (national currency)

ijon System of interlocked markets where a collector provides pre-harvest finance to a farmer

jalur satu pintu "One-door pathway," or a single-desk trading system

JKN Jaminan Kesehatan Nasional (universal health insurance scheme of the Indonesian government)

kabupaten Indonesian district (sometimes referred to as regency)

KDP Kecamatan Development Program, a community-driven development program initiated by the World Bank, which later became the **PNPM**

Kecamatan Subdistrict level of government, and administrative level between the *kabupaten* and *desa*

kelompok tani Farmer groups, usually established with patronage from the Ministry of Agriculture

kepala dusun Administrative head of the subvillage hamlet (*dusun*)

Koloniaal Verslag Colonial yearbooks for the Dutch East Indies issued as government reports during the period 1852–1939

Koperasi / KUD Koperasi Unit Desa (Village Unit Cooperatives) supported by the Ministry of Cooperatives and Small and Medium Enterprises in 2023

KUBE Kelompok Usaha Bersama (Collective Business Groups) supported by Ministry of Social Affairs in 2023

ladang Swidden dryland farm systems or semipermanent gardens

LMDH Lembaga Masyarakat Desa Hutan (Forest Village Community Councils, common on Java for managing use allocations of **Perhutani** land)

Marhaenism Sukarnoist ideology of the "working poor" who own their own means of production

masyarakat adat Also called *masyarakat hukum adat*, refers to a customary law community (sometimes considered akin to "indigenous peoples")

merantau Migratory experiences

MOTRAMED "Mediated Partnership Model" of coffee development promoted by **ICCRI**, involving quality improvement linked to value chain engagement

MPIG Masyarakat Perlindungan Indikasi Geografis (**GI** Protection Society, established to manage a GI)

negara state

NEI Netherlands East Indies colonial government (1800–1806, 1816–1949)

Nek honorific used in Toraja for grandmother or grandfather, or elderly person

New Order Authoritarian regime headed by President Suharto from 1966 to 1998

NGOs Nongovernmental organizations

NHM Nederlandsche Handel-Maatschappij, the Netherlands Trading Society, a private company established in 1824 and sometimes considered the successor to the **VOC**, which worked closely with the **NEI**

pasar Indonesian market

patih Vice-regent during the colonial period

PBB Pajak Bumi dan Bangunan, a tax on land and buildings

pembangunan Development (especially as embraced as a government ideology under President Suharto)

Pemda Pemerintah Daerah, regional governments (usually refers to the district-level, but can also be provincial)

pengumpul Individual-as-collector (of agricultural products)

perahu Timber sailing ship (now motorized) widely used by Bugis and Makassan traders

Perhutani Perusahaan Hutan Negara Indonesia, a state-owned forest enterprise on Java

petani Peasant, farmer

PHBM Pengelolaan Hutan Bersama Masyarakat (Community-Based Forest Management Agreements)

PIP Program Indonesia Pintar, a school scholarship scheme implemented by the Indonesian government

PKH Program Keluarga Harapan, the flagship conditional cash transfer program for families, implemented by the Indonesian government

PNPM Mandiri Program Nasional Pemberdayaan Masyarakat Mandiri (National Program for Community Empowerment), implemented by the Indonesian government

preangerstelsel A system of mandatory coffee deliveries enforced by the **VOC** in western Java (Preanger) as a precursor to *cultuurstelsel* (approximately 1700–1830)

priyayi The traditional aristocracies of Indonesia, especially on Java

PRONA National Agrarian Operation Project, with a mission to provide *hak milik* certificates to landholders

proyek Government projects ostensibly aimed at improving public welfare but often controlled in practice by patronage interests

PRPTE Peremajaan, Rehabilitasi, dun Perluasan Tanaman Ekspor (Rejuvenation, Rehabilitation, and Expansion of Export Crops), government program in the 1980s

PTPN PT. Perkebunan Nusantara, the state-owned plantation companies, initially known as PPN (Perusahaan Perkebunan Nusantara)

RA Rainforest Alliance, a voluntary sustainability standard

rakyat The people

Raskin Subsidized rice for the poor program by the Indonesian government

Rastra Beras Sejahtera, a successor of **Raskin**, implemented by the Indonesian government

reformasi The democratization of Indonesia since 1998

retribusi Levies paid to regional governments as a local tax

rijksdaalders Currency used during the **VOC** period

RPN PT. Riset Perkebunan Nusantara, a quasi-state organization whose role is to provide research support for the large state-owned plantation sector (**PTPN**s)

Sakernas Survei Angkatan Kerja Nasional (National Labor Force Survey), now undertaken twice yearly

saroan Small work groups in the Torajan community through which patronage is distributed

sawah Wet-rice field, either rain-fed or irrigated

SCOPI Sustainable Coffee Platform for Indonesia, international donor-funded public-private partnership, with funding from **IDH** and support from the Global Coffee Platform

SDMs Service delivery models, especially those developed by **IDH** and the private trader ECOM to deliver services (including inputs) to farmers

sedekah Cultural-religious celebrations (in Semende)

seng dapo' An expression used in Torajan community, meaning "shopping money for the kitchen"

Serikat Petani Indonesia Indonesian mass peasant organizations (linked internationally to La Via Campesina)

sertifikat tanah A land certificate issued by the **BPN** Land Agency (*sertifikat hak milik*)

sifat kampungan "Villageness," implies a degree of backwardness

SKB (Survei Rumah Tangga Usaha Perkebunan) Estate Crop Household Economic Survey, conducted following the Agricultural Census

SKT Surat Keterangan Tanah, written recognition of individual's rights over a plot by village authorities and sometimes countersigned by higher levels of government such as the *Kecamatan*

SMS Sustainability Management Services, input services division of Ecom Agroindustrial

SP (Sensus Penduduk) The decennial Population Census, most recently undertaken in 2020

ST (Sensus Pertanian) The decennial Agricultural Census, most recently undertaken in 2023

Statistik Kopi Annual Coffee Statistics, published by **BPS** based on data from the Ministry of Agriculture

subak abian Customary farmer groups responsible for managing Balinese dryland agriculture

Susenas Survei Sosial Ekonomi Nasional (annual national socioeconomic survey)

SUTAS (Survei Pertanian Antar Sensus) Inter-Census Agricultural Survey, first undertaken in 2018

tanah marga Ancestral land without private property rights, as found across several Sumatran ethnic groups

tanam paksa "Forced cultivation," enforced in the Netherlands East Indies during *cultuurstelsel*

tengkulak Individual-as-collector, often acts as financier in contexts where access to formal finance is otherwise limited

tondok Scattered village hamlets in Toraja generally consisting of between one and fifteen *tongkonan*

tongkonan Torajan ancestral houses, which also act as a symbol of social control over both people and resources

transmigrasi A national resettlement program by the Indonesian government, usually involving the migration of people from Java and Bali to the outer islands

tunggu tubang Matrilineal system of land inheritance in Semende, South Sumatra

UNCTAD United Nations Conference on Trade and Development

UPH Unit Pengolahan Hasil, local village-based processing units managed by producer organizations (usually supported by the Indonesian state)

UPP Unit Pelaksanaan Proyek (Project Implementation Unit), used by large agricultural development programs to distribute fertilizers, credit, and other farm inputs during the Suharto regime

USD United States dollars

VOC Vereenigde Oostindische Compagnie (Dutch East Indies Company, 1602–1799)

VSA Verified Sourcing Area, a landscape-level sustainability assurance scheme developed by **IDH**

Notes

PREFACE

1. "Mama Lina" or "Indo Lina" refers to Lina's mother in the Torajan naming system. "Pong Arno" or "Bapa Arno" refers to Arno's father, while "Nek Tomas" is Tomas's grandmother or grandfather. Elsewhere in the book, I will also use the Indonesian honorifics "Pak" (father) and "Bu" (mother). These and other names used in the book are pseudonyms, as is the place Tondok Buntu. Places at the subdistrict level (*kecamatan*) and higher are actual place names.

INTRODUCTION

1. Elson (1997, xix–xx) here defines the peasantry as "rural groupings of people whose primary orientation, both economic and social, was towards a broad participation in simple, relatively unspecialized, household-based, subsistence agricultural production, who shared notions of social and economic life beyond their specific community, and who stood in relations of subordination to a more powerful class of claimants outside their sphere."

2. In Indonesia, a designation of "urban" (*perkotaan*) or "rural" (*pedesaan*) is formally applied to the village administrative unit (*desa* or *kelurahan*), but with a definition that has changed over time. According to BPS (2010a), it is based on a scoring system that considers (1) population density; (2) employment in agriculture; and (3) the presence of specific facilities, such as a kindergarten, junior or senior high schools, a market, a shopping center, cinema, hospital, entertainment facilities (hotel, billiards hall, nightclub, massage parlor and salon), and the percentage of households with access to telephones and electricity.

3. See, for example, in Indonesian, https://www.merdeka.com/uang/pandemi-covid-19-sebabkan-banyak-pekerja-kota-kembali-ke-desa-untuk-menjadi-petani.html; https://www.liputan6.com/lifestyle/read/4406237/makin-banyak-anak-muda-terjun-jadi-petani-di-masa-pandemi-covid-19; https://mediaindonesia.com/ekonomi/390364/sektor-pertanian-tetap-jadi-primadona-di-masa-pandemi-covid-19.

4. *Merantau* is a term originating from the Minangkabau region of West Sumatra that means something like "to leave one's birthplace and seek fortune in the wider world."

5. Swidden is a Scandinavian word meaning "land cleared by burning" and has been defined as a "land-use system that employs a natural or improved fallow phase, which is longer than the cultivation phase of annual crops, sufficiently long to be dominated by woody vegetation, and cleared by means of fire" (Mertz et al. 2009, 261). It is generally preferred to the term "slash-and-burn," which holds negative connotations.

6. Such coffee/*sawah* landscape mosaics can be found in the Dairi, Toba, Simalungun, Semende, Ogan, and Minangkabau regions of Sumatra and in the Mamasa, Toraja, and Gowa regions of Sulawesi, in Kintamani and Pupuan in Bali, and in the Manggarai regions of Flores.

1. AGRARIAN CHANGE AND LIVELIHOODS IN A WORLD OF GLOBAL VALUE CHAINS

1. Byres (1986) presented three possible renderings of the agrarian question: the question of how essentially noncapitalist agriculture and peasant communities would develop and evolve within a capitalist society (Kautsky's concern in part 1 of *Die Agrarfrage*); the question of what role agriculture could and should perform with respect to accumulation for industrial development (with specific reference to socialist states); and the political question posed by European Marxists in the late nineteenth century of how to seize power in countries with large peasant populations. Framed in this way, my concern in this book is primarily with the first formulation of the question, which appears to me to be the only one with continued contemporary relevance. When considering the possible insights that can be gained from classical agrarian studies, however, we should be alert to White's (1989, 17) reminder that the political agenda that motivated writers like Lenin, Kautsky, and Chayanov had a considerable influence over their method of analysis.

2. Li (2014, 8) provides a shorthand definition for "capitalist relations" as "the ensemble of relations characterized by private and unequal ownership of the means of production (land, capital), a group of nonowners compelled to sell their labor, and the use of capital to generate profit under competitive conditions." She further explains: "Competition means that the owners of capital must seek profit to generate more capital to invest simply to reproduce themselves as they are, that is, as owners. To the extent they succeed, their accumulation squeezes others out, entrenching and sometimes deepening the unequal ownership with which the cycle began." This rendering of capitalist relations thus highlights processes of classical "class differentiation," although White (1989) had suggested a need to consider "agrarian differentiation" more broadly to be sensitive to the diverse ways that differences may emerge within rural populations, including through processes of "surplus extraction" beyond the wage relation (such as rents, sharecropping, taxes, terms of trade for commodities and inputs, interest, illegal protection rackets), in addition to the bifurcation into landlords and laborers. My analysis in this book suggests limited penetration of capitalist relations, according to Li's stricter definition, within Indonesian coffee production systems, but leaves open the possibility for broader processes of agrarian differentiation suggested by White.

3. This contrasts with what Bernstein (2006) calls the "agrarian question of capital," which he claims had been effectively resolved by the 1970s. Bernstein (452) bases this argument on the observation that *"predatory landed property had largely vanished as a significant economic and political force by the end of the 1970s.* This was one marker of the end of the agrarian question of capital on a world scale" (italics in the original).

4. Johnson, in turn, built on the earlier work of Gaventa (1995) and initially introduced a fourfold categorization—natural, human, social, and economic capital. The idea of physical capital, including infrastructure and physical goods, was later differentiated from economic or financial capital.

5. Ferguson uses the example of a windshield washer at traffic lights to highlight the sometimes-slight distinction between a service (which the washer ostensibly provides) and pressing for a distributive claim (which is what the washer is actually doing). Distributive labor thus ranges from pickpockets and thugs, to requests for sending remittances, to conventional service sector jobs (restaurant waiters, performing musicians, and government clerks). It also includes demands from the citizenry for social support payments from the state. Elsewhere, Ferguson (2013, 169) challenged the supposition that people make their livelihoods by being "productive" and meeting their own or others' needs, which he claims "has never been an adequate account. In no modern industrial society does the number of people directly engaged in productive labor come anywhere close to accounting for the entire population."

6. In this book, I will use the term "supply chain" when referring to the specific chain of suppliers providing inputs for a particular buyer, and "supply chain management" for the specific way a firm procures inputs, while the term "value chain" is reserved for analytical usage referring to broader industry structures.

2. AGRARIAN TRANSITIONS AND STRUCTURAL TRANSFORMATION OF THE INDONESIAN ECONOMY

1. Byres (1996, 27) defined an agrarian transition as the occurrence of "those changes in the countryside of a poor country necessary to the overall development of capitalism and its ultimate dominance in a particular national social formation." This definition makes it explicit that the market-based society is envisioned at the national scale. More problematically for my purposes in this book, however, Byres suggested that the overall development of capitalism was dependent on changes (capitalist transformation) in the countryside.

2. These HPAEs were identified by the World Bank as being led by Japan, followed by the four "tiger economies" of Taiwan, Hong Kong, Singapore, and South Korea, and then by the so-called Newly Industrializing Economies (NIEs) of Malaysia, Thailand, and Indonesia.

3. By populous Southeast Asia I refer to Indonesia, Myanmar, the Philippines, Thailand, and Vietnam, all of which have populations in excess of fifty million and rural population shares of at least 40 percent in 2020 (and incidentally, all have had long-term annual economic growth rates averaging above 5 percent between 2000 and 2019).

4. This was contrasted against "accumulation by dispossession," as described by Harvey (1982, 2003), who associates this with the ongoing expulsion of peasant populations following commodification of land and labor, the conversion of collective property rights into individual property, and the appropriation of land by repressive states.

5. While I am sympathetic to these critiques, I do not share the concern that use of the term "agrarian transition" itself necessarily implies either urban employment, or indeed improved livelihood outcomes, *for all*. I use the term, as defined by De Koninck (2004), to describe the broad transformation of a society, recognizing of course that this will involve a range of "agrarian change scenarios" in different local contexts and for specific individuals in those contexts (McCarthy, McWilliam, and Nooteboom 2023b). As I see it, describing and analyzing the local implications of (national scale) agrarian transitions remain important tasks of agrarian studies scholars.

6. According to Ukers (1922), the first coffee plants were introduced to Java from Malabar in 1696, at the instigation of Nicolaas Witsen, then burgomaster of Amsterdam, but were destroyed in a 1699 earthquake, and this encouraged Henricus Zwaardecroon (later to be governor-general) to import new cuttings from Malabar that same year, from which cultivation spread.

7. Volumes of coffee are commonly described in the literature in terms of "pikol," meaning something like a "shoulder load" and which varied somewhat. For consistency, throughout this book, I have converted these measurements to metric tons based on a conversion of one standard "pikol" as equivalent to 61.8 kilograms.

8. Today, "Palembang" refers to the capital city of South Sumatra Province, but in the colonial period "Palembang" referred to the entire administrative area coinciding with today's province. To avoid the anachronism, I use "Palembang" for the larger area when referring to the colonial period.

9. Communities who currently use the "Toraja" ethnic identifier are now located exclusively in the Tana Toraja and North Toraja districts, although very closely related languages are also spoken elsewhere, including in the neighboring Enrekang District,

where the vast majority of the population are now Muslim and identify themselves as ethnically "Duri."

10. The encounter, well known in Indonesia, was described in detail by Sukarno (1957) in a speech before the Indonesian National Party. "I came across a man hoeing the field," Sukarno related, "and I asked him: 'Brother, who owns this field?' 'I own it' he said. And so he participated in ownership of the means of production, owning that rice field. 'And the hoe, who owns that?' 'I own it.' 'These tools, who owns these?' 'I own them.' 'But brother, you live in poverty?'. . . I asked him 'What is your name?' 'I am Marhaen.'" Sukarno used the term to refer to all poor Indonesian common people, including workers, peasants, fishermen, poor clerks, stall vendors, cart drivers, and chauffeurs (or loosely, Bernstein's "classes of labor").

11. Geertz (1963) had similarly argued that the mechanism for sharing productive capacity (and output) in Java was also through sharecropping, which he considered to be flexible and locally adaptable, allowing a form of "work spreading."

3. THE INDONESIAN STATE AND RURAL PATRONAGE

1. In 2024, Indonesia was in the process of building a new capital city, Nusantara, on the island of Borneo.

2. As an insight into the character of the *aparat*, it is revealing that Indonesia has a specific law (Undang-Undang No. 5, 2014, tentang Aparatur Sipil Negara) that sets out the responsibilities of the *aparat* (Article 23) to (a) be faithful and obedient to Pancasila, the 1945 Constitution of the Republic of Indonesia, the Republic of Indonesia, and the legitimate government; (b) maintain the unity of the nation; (c) implement policies formulated by government authorities; (d) comply with the provisions of legislation; (e) carry out official duties with devotion, honesty, awareness, and responsibility; (f) demonstrate integrity and be an exemplar in attitude, behavior, speech, and action to every person, whether on duty or not; (g) maintain state secrets and only share state secrets in accordance with the requirements of legislation; and (h) be willing to be placed anywhere within the entire territory of the Republic of Indonesia.

3. These "utilities" also incurred costs, but even if their net revenue is calculated as a share of total state revenue, it accounts for 38 percent in 1900 and 21 percent in 1928 (Mansvelt 1976, table 4).

4. Anderson (1966) observed an earlier *Javanisation* of Bahasa Indonesia, which assumed the Javanese language peculiarity of having multiple registers reflecting class positions and was borrowing Sanskritized vocabulary in a process he referred to as *kramanisation*.

5. These included the Agricultural Extension Project I and II (1980–1993, 70 million USD), the Agricultural Research Management Projects (ARMP I and ARMP II, 1990–2000, 98 million USD), the Decentralized Agricultural and Forestry Extension Project (DAFEP, 2000–2004, 18 million USD), and Farmer Empowerment through Agricultural Technology and Information (FEATI, 2007–2013, 93 million USD).

6. These included the National Estate Crop Protection Project (1984–1991, valued at 41.0 million USD); the Tree Crop Smallholder Development Project (1992–2000, 87.6 million USD); the Sulawesi Rainfed Agriculture Development Project (1995–2004, 26.8 million USD); and the Integrated Pest Management for Smallholder Estate Crops Project (1997–2006, 32 million USD).

7. "E-Indikasi Geografis," DJKI (database managed by the Directorate General of Intellectual Property Rights within the Indonesian Ministry of Law and Human Rights), https://ig.dgip.go.id/.

8. The notion of strategic coupling is presented by Yeung (2016) within the global production network (GPN) framework as a multiscalar phenomenon that can give rise to processes of regional development. It occurs at the intersection of global linkages through GPNs and regional institutions when economic actors in a specific territory can capture enhanced value within a competitive production chain by "holding down the global."

9. Raskin later became Rastra, and then Bantuan Pangan Non-Tunai (BPNT), followed by Bantuan Langsung Tunai (BLT) in 2005 during a major subsidy reform policy. The flagship conditional cash transfer program for families (Program Keluarga Harapan, PKH) was introduced in 2007, educational cash stipends (Beasiswa Siswa Miskin, later Program Indonesia Pintar, PIP) in 2013, and a Cash-for-Work program (Padat Karya Tunai, PKT) in 2017. Further cash payments related to COVID-19 were introduced in 2020. A helpful overview of these programs is provided in UNICEF et al. (2021).

10. "Reducing Emissions from Deforestation and forest Degradation" (+ refers to afforestation). This in the generic term for a range of ecosystem payment schemes that seek to financially incentivize land managers to maintain or increase carbon stocks stored in landscapes, often involving payments made *not* to engage in deforestation.

4. GLOBAL CAPITAL AND THE ORGANIZATION OF COFFEE VALUE CHAINS

1. See the definition provided in endnote 5 in the introduction, which highlights the key role of burning.

2. The Nestlé report is available at https://www.Nestlé.com/investors/annual-report (values converted from Swiss francs). The specific allocation for "Advertising" in 2018 was estimated at 7.3 billion USD (Guttmann 2020).

3. "Europe" refers to imports to the European Union (ICO member and nonmember countries) plus Norway, Switzerland, and the UK, minus reported volumes of "re-exports." "Producing Countries" refers to "Domestic Consumption by all exporting countries." "Asia and Oceania" refers principally to nonproducing countries in this region but includes countries like China and Australia, which do actually produce coffee.

4. Grabs and Ponte (2019) have more recently suggested that, following the 2008 global financial crisis, the coffee GVC entered a new governance phase, which they refer to as "diversification and reconsolidation," following the "liberalization" phase from 1989 to 2008. Diversification and reconsolidation refers to an initial sell-off of coffee roasting investments by diversified (and publicly listed) multinationals like Kraft and Sara Lee, which eventually led to the emergence of a private equity firm, JAB Holding (later Jacobs Douwe Egberts, JDE), as a global leader, competing alongside longtime frontrunner Nestlé. I would argue, however, that this latest governance phase appears to be characterized by far greater continuity with the pre-2008 situation than this periodization might suggest, and many of the trends associated with this third phase (as presented in tables 3 and 4 in Grabs and Ponte 2019, 12–15) are actually "continuing" from the pre-2008 situation.

5. In 2021, SCA claimed to have close to ten thousand members and chapters in more than thirty countries (SCA 2021).

6. The *Masterplan for Acceleration and Expansion of Indonesia's Economic Development 2011–2025* (MP3EI) was subsequently endorsed by President Joko Widodo after his election in 2014. The Ministry of Industry had earlier identified the development of a "Coffee Processing Industry Cluster" as strategically important to national development objectives (Ministerial Regulation No. 115/M-IND/PER/10/2009). Ditjenbun (2021) identifies the downstream processing of plantation crops as one of its three strategic development priorities.

7. Work undertaken within a GPN analytical framework (Coe and Yeung 2015) has sought to identify the causal drivers of particular organizational platforms and the specific strategies of lead firms in response to the competitive pressures of global capitalism. Coe and Yeung present these pressures in terms of (1) optimizing cost-capability ratios, which result in core competencies being maintained within the firm, while other functions and logistical aspects of supply chain management are outsourced to strategic partners; (2) responding to market imperatives, including growth opportunities in emerging markets (in the coffee sector, this equates to the establishment of manufacturing plants within these countries); and (3) enforcing financial discipline, with a large share of the world's coffee manufacturing now exposed to shareholder pressures.

8. This was a public online event, "Sustainable Coffee Dialogues Launch," hosted by USAID Green Invest Asia and the Global Coffee Platform (GCP), held on October 6, 2021. Available at https://www.youtube.com/watch?v=M3ADXTPfoWQ.

9. In 2018, however, the 4C Association was formally split to form the Global Coffee Program, while Coffee Assurance Services, a private body, came to own and manage the 4C Standard.

10. According to its website on June 30, 2021, other country platforms have been established under the GCP in Brazil, Colombia, Honduras, Kenya, Nicaragua, Peru, Tanzania, Uganda, and Vietnam.

5. INSTITUTIONS OF LAND ACCESS

1. Original text: "Bumi dan air dan kekayaan alam yang terkandung di dalamnya dikuasai oleh negara dan dipergunakan untuk sebesar-besarnya kemakmuran rakyat." In this sense, *dikuasai* is somewhat intermediate between the threefold classification by Hall (2013) of state control over land as territory, regulation, and property.

2. More specifically, the Dutch legal system imported into the Indies was based on the Napoleonic Code of 1804, which had as an explicit aim to modernize written legal codes and remove any vestiges of feudalism embedded within customary or common law principles.

3. Original text: "Mengatur pengurusan hutan dalam arti yang luas."

4. The Forestry Department is the state institution historically responsible for its management, although in 1967 it was under a Directorate General of Forestry within the Department of Agriculture, and since 2014 it has been part of the Ministry of the Environment and Forestry.

5. De Royer et al. (2018, 169–170) identify an early 1995 ministerial decree on community forestry (Hutan Kemasyarakatan) as simply being "aimed at mobilizing forest communities to rehabilitate degraded forestland." Kusters et al. (2007, 430) describe the 1998 designation of a community-managed *damar* forest in the Krui region of Lampung within the state forest zone "as a 'breakthrough' as it was the first time the Indonesian government had acknowledged local user rights on state forest land."

6. "Tema KMAN VI Resmi Ditetapkan pada RPB AMAN," AMAN's official website, published November 23, 2021: https://www.aman.or.id/news/read/tema-kman-vi-resmi-ditetapkan-pada-rpb-aman.

6. FORTRESS FARMING IN TORAJA

1. In the past, anthropologists would refer to the "Sa'dan Toraja" to distinguish them from other ethnic groups in the highlands of Sulawesi also referred to as "Toraja." However, only the inhabitants of the area covered by the administrative districts of Tana Toraja and North Toraja now self-identify as "Toraja."

2. While the language spoken in Toraja is distinct from the Bugis, Mandar, and Makassan spoken in the lowlands, all languages are considered part of the same South Sulawesi subgroup of the Western Malayo-Polynesian group of Austronesian languages, and so hint at a common ancestry (Blust 2013). Torajan oral literature includes several of the same stories contained in the *I La Galligo* epic manuscripts that offer a remarkable window into the pre-Islamic Bugis cultural world, and Waterson (2009) cites a sixteenth-century Portuguese description of Bugis funeral rights that are strikingly like those in Toraja today. Some of the oldest genealogies in Toraja can be traced back twenty-eight generations, which is broadly contemporaneous with the *musu' selleng* Bugis-Makassan wars that led to Islamic conversion of the Bugis courts between 1608 and 1611 (Pelras 1985, 109). It seems likely (as suggested by Reid 2015) that an important migration event to Toraja occurred in response to Bugis Islamization, preserving selected cultural traditions, and which broadly follows the pattern described by Acabado et al. (2019) for the Ifugao in response to the Spanish conquest of lowland northern Luzon.

3. No reference was provided by Ukers for this claim, and it may refer to the northern Minahasan peninsula near Menado.

4. While Bigalke (2005) speculated that coffee may have found its way into Toraja centuries earlier, the evidence for this seems to be weak. The suggestive evidence is based on linguistic analysis (the Torajan word for coffee, *ka'a*, is derived through the Bugis from the Arabic, *qahwah*, rather than through the Dutch, *koffie*) and on the records of a single Dutch planter in the 1920s who claimed to have found trees that were two to three hundred years old.

5. This 2017 data is from the North Toraja district, which split off from the Tana Toraja "mother district" in 2008. The 2001 data refers to the unsplit district. However, similar trends are also evident in the remaining Tana Toraja district in 2017, when agriculture contributed 25.8 percent, trade 16.9 percent, and construction 12.8 percent to GDRP.

6. The results of two separate household surveys are reported in this section: ninety-nine households across ten villages in 2018 where every third house in a transect was selected, and a complete enumeration of all thirty-two households living in a single hamlet in 2019 ("Tondok Buntu").

7. "Toraja (a Beautiful Experience)," Sulotco, accessed April 10, 2023, https://toraja.coffee/Coffee-Toraja.

8. "Sulawesi Coffee from Indonesia at Starbucks," Starbucks Stories & News, published March 28, 2016, https://stories.starbucks.com/stories/2016/starbucks-sulawesi-single-origin-coffee/.

9. "Hadiri Rapat Tahunan Koperasi Sane, Nurdin Halid Jelaskan Soal BUMdes," Merdeka.com, April 7, 2018, https://www.merdeka.com/peristiwa/hadiri-rapat-tahunan-koperasi-sane-nurdin-halid-jelaskan-soal-bumdes.html.

10. According to "Building Schools, Building Coffee," Starbucks Reserve, www.starbucksreserve.com/en-us/articles/building-schools.

11. This clip can be viewed at "Medley Toraja Folksong—Toraja Ethnic Project," Allegra Choral Production YouTube Channel, published September 1, 2021, https://www.youtube.com/watch?v=4WwjdZVq0OY.

12. The owner of this HGU, living in Australia, emailed me in 2019 seeking advice on how to restart production on the estate. By 2022, nothing on the ground had changed. In 2024, I was also approached by a Torajan man asking my advice about reinvesting in another abandoned HGU. Despite my overall presentation of these HGUs as currently dead, it seems they could still have an afterlife.

13. During 2020, and based on "Facebook ethnography," Williams also reported a retreat to own-consumption farming in Toraja, particularly vegetables and root crops (sweet potato, cassava, and taro), undertaken in part by redundant workers and students returning to villages.

14. Elsewhere in Toraja, I have heard stories of *tongkonan* land being registered by individuals as *hak milik* with BPN and the certificate being promptly used as collateral for a bank loan.

7. FORTRESS FARMING IN SEMENDE

1. AEKI still maintained offices in Jakarta and across Indonesia in 2022, but its post-2011 financial viability has been severely diminished. Disaffected AEKI members in East Java established a rival industry association in Surabaya in 2011, the Indonesian Coffee Exporters Federation (Gabungan Eksportir Kopi Indonesia, GAEKI). GAEKI has obtained some degree of state patronage, particularly within the Ministry of Trade, and has represented the Indonesian coffee industry at some international events, including the ICO. Currently, neither AEKI nor GAEKI is financially supported by a mandatory industry levy.

2. In a study of farmer perceptions of five different sustainability initiatives across Lampung and South Sumatra, Bray et al. (2023) found overwhelmingly positive attitudes to such issues as "impact on family" and "increased price transparency" because of the initiatives.

3. See, for example, "Tunggu Tubang," Zefri Oi YouTube Channel, published March 19, 2013, https://www.youtube.com/watch?v=ruY4--OHibQ; or "Tunggu Tubang—Lagu Daerah Muara Enim," Karim Bani YouTube Channel, published May 7, 2011, https://www.youtube.com/watch?v=ffpzofP5kBA; or "Merantau Jauh—Gitas Tunggal Semende," Ilyas Channel, published July 7, 2020, https://www.youtube.com/watch?v=SeLRQDm5YuI (used in epigraph opening this chapter).

References

Abbott, K. W., and D. Snidal. 2010. "International Regulation without International Government: Improving IO Performance through Orchestration." *Review of International Organizations* 5:315–344.

Acabado, Stephen B., Jared M. Koller, Chin-hsin Liu, Adam J. Lauer, Alan Farahani, Grace Barretto-Tesoro, Marian C. Reyes, Jonathan Albert Martin, and John A. Peterson. 2019. "The Short History of the Ifugao Rice Terraces: A Local Response to the Spanish Conquest." *Journal of Field Archaeology* 44 (3): 195–214. https://doi.org/10.1080/00934690.2019.1574159.

Acemoglu, Daron, and James A. Robinson. 2012. *Why Nations Fail: The Origins of Power, Prosperity, and Poverty.* New York: Crown.

Adams, Kathleen M. 2006. *Art as Politics: Re-crafting Identities, Tourism, and Power in Tana Toraja, Indonesia.* Honolulu: University of Hawai'i Press.

Agustono, Budi, and Junaidi. 2018. "The Dutch Colonial Economic Policy: Coffee Exploitation in Tapanuli Residency, 1849–1928." *Kemanusiaan* 25 (2): 49–71. https://doi.org/10.21315/kajh2018.25.2.3.

Alexander, Jennifer, and Paul Alexander. 1982. "Shared Poverty as Ideology: Agrarian Relationships in Colonial Java." *Man,* n.s.: 597–619.

Amaruzaman, Sacha, Beria Leimona, and N. P. Rahadian. 2017. "Maintain the Sustainability of PES Program: Lessons Learnt from PES Implementation in Sumberjaya, Way Besay Watershed, Indonesia." In *Co-investment in Ecosystem Services: Global Lessons from Payment and Incentive Schemes,* edited by S. Namirembe, B. Leimona, M. van Noordwijk, and P. Minang, 1–9. Nairobi: World Agroforestry Centre (ICRAF).

Ambarwati, Aprilia, Ricky Ardian Harahap, Isono Sadoko, and Ben White. 2016. "Land Tenure and Agrarian Structure in Regions of Small-Scale Food Production." In *Land and Development in Indonesia,* edited by John F. McCarthy and Kathryn Robinson, 265–294. Singapore: ISEAS.

Amsden, Alice H. 1979. "Taiwan's Economic History: A Case of Étatisme and a Challenge to Dependency Theory." *Modern China* 5 (3): 341–379.

Andaya, Barbara W. 1993. *To Live as Brothers: Southeast Sumatra in the Seventeenth and Eighteenth Centuries.* Honolulu: University of Hawai'i Press.

Andaya, Barbara W. 1997. "Adapting to Political and Economic Change: Palembang in the Late Eighteenth and Early Nineteenth Centuries." In *The Last Stand of Asian Autonomies,* edited by Anthony Reid, 187–215. London: Palgrave Macmillan.

Anderson, Benedict. 1966. "The Languages of Indonesian Politics." *Indonesia* 1:89–116.

Anderson, Benedict. (1983a) 2006. *Imagined Communities: Reflections on the Origin and Spread of Nationalism.* New York: Verso Books.

Anderson, Benedict. 1983b. "Old State, New Society: Indonesia's New Order in Comparative Historical Perspective." *Journal of Asian Studies* 42 (3): 477–496.

Andreas, Joel, and Shaohua Zhan. 2016. "Hukou and Land: Market Reform and Rural Displacement in China." *Journal of Peasant Studies* 43 (4): 798–827.

Andriesse, Edo, and Anouxay Phommalath. 2012. "Provincial Poverty Dynamics in Lao PDR: A Case Study of Savannakhet." *Journal of Current Southeast Asian Affairs* 31 (3): 3–27.

Aqil, A. Muh. Ibnu. 2020. "Concerns of Transparency, Inclusivity Raised as One Map Nears Completion." *Jakarta Post*, September 4. www.thejakartapost.com/news/2020/09/04/concerns-of-transparency-inclusivity-raised-as-one-map-nears-completion.html.

Arizona, Yance, Muki Trenggono Wicaksono, and Jacqueline Vel. 2019. "The Role of Indigeneity NGOs in the Legal Recognition of Adat Communities and Customary Forests in Indonesia." *Asia Pacific Journal of Anthropology* 20 (5): 487–506.

Arrighi, Giovanni. 1973. "International Corporations, Labor Aristocracies, and Economic Development in Tropical Africa." In *Essays on the Political Economy of Africa*, edited by Giovanni Arrighi and John S. Saul, 105–151. New York: Monthly Review.

Arts, Bas, Marleen Buizer, Lumina Horlings, Verina Ingram, Cora van Oosten, and Paul Opdam. 2017. "Landscape Approaches: A State-of-the-Art Review." *Annual Review of Environment and Resources* 42:439–463.

Aspinall, Edward. 2013. "A Nation in Fragments: Patronage and Neoliberalism in Contemporary Indonesia." *Critical Asian Studies* 45 (1): 27–54.

Aspinall, Edward, and Ward Berenschot. 2019. *Democracy for Sale: Elections, Clientelism, and the State in Indonesia*. Ithaca, NY: Cornell University Press.

Aswicahyono, Haryo, Hal Hill, and Dionisius Narjoko. 2010. "Industrialisation after a Deep Economic Crisis: Indonesia." *Journal of Development Studies* 46 (6): 1084–1108. https://doi.org/10.1080/00220380903318087.

Bachriadi, Dianto, and Gunawan Wiradi. 2013. "Land Concentration and Land Reform in Indonesia: Interpreting Agricultural Census Data, 1963–2003." In *Land for the People: The State and Agrarian Conflict in Indonesia*, edited by Anton Lucas and Carrol Warren, 40–92. Athens: Ohio University Press.

Bakker, Laurens, and Sandra Moniaga. 2010. "The Space Between: Land Claims and the Law in Indonesia." *Asian Journal of Social Science* 38 (2): 187–203.

Balachandran, N., and N. Narae Choi. 2015. *2014 PNPM Support Facility (PSF) Progress Report*. Jakarta: PNPM Support Office. https://www.dfat.gov.au/sites/default/files/indonesia-pnpm-support-facility-progress-report-2014.pdf.

Barber, Charles Victor, and Kirk Talbott. 2003. "The Chainsaw and the Gun." *Journal of Sustainable Forestry* 16 (3–4): 131–160. https://doi.org/10.1300/J091v16n03_07.

Barnes, Ruth. 2017. "Indian Cotton for Cairo: The Royal Ontario Museum's Gujarati Textiles and the Early Western Indian Ocean Trade." *Textile History* 48 (1): 15–30. https://doi.org/10.1080/00404969.2017.1294814.

Barrientos, Stephanie, Gary Gereffi, and Arianna Rossi. 2011. "Economic and Social Upgrading in Global Production Networks: A New Paradigm for a Changing World." *International Labour Review* 150 (3–4): 319–340. https://doi.org/10.1111/j.1564-913X.2011.00119.x.

Bastin, J. Sturgus. 1965. *The British in West Sumatra (1685–1825)*. Kuala Lumpur: University of Malaya Press.

Bastos Lima, Mairon G., and U. Martin Persson. 2020. "Commodity-Centric Landscape Governance as a Double-Edged Sword: The Case of Soy and the Cerrado Working Group in Brazil." *Frontiers in Forests and Global Change* 3 (27): 1–17. https://doi.org/10.3389/ffgc.2020.00027.

Bathelt, Harald, and Johannes Glückler. 2014. "Institutional Change in Economic Geography." *Progress in Human Geography* 38 (3): 340–363.

Bayu, Dimas Jarot. 2018. "Kemenperin Dorong Penerapan Bea Keluar Flat 15% untuk produk Agro." *Katadata*, February 23. https://katadata.co.id/yuliawati/berita/5e9a56031737c/kemenperin-dorong-penerapan-bea-keluar-flat-15-untuk-produk-agro#google_vignette.

Bebbington, Anthony, Scott Guggenheim, Elizabeth Olson, and Michael Woolcock. 2004. "Exploring Social Capital Debates at the World Bank." *Journal of Development Studies* 40 (5): 33–64.

Bentley, Jeffery W., and Peter S. Baker. 2000. "The Colombian Coffee Growers' Federation: Organised, Successful Smallholder Farmers for 70 Years." Agricultural Research and Extension Network Paper No. 100, 1–9.

Bernstein, Henry. 1986. "Capitalism and Petty Commodity Production." *Social Analysis: The International Journal of Social and Cultural Practice* 20:11–28.

Bernstein, Henry. 2006. "Is There an Agrarian Question in the 21st Century?" *Canadian Journal of Development Studies / Revue canadienne d'études du développement* 27 (4): 449–460.

Bernstein, Henry. 2009. "V. I. Lenin and A. V. Chayanov: Looking Back, Looking Forward." *Journal of Peasant Studies* 36 (1): 55–81.

Bernstein, Henry. 2010. *Class Dynamics of Agrarian Change.* Halifax, NS: Fernwood.

Bernstein, Henry. 2016. "Revisiting Agrarian Transition: Reflections on Long Histories and Current Realities." In *Critical Perspectives on Agrarian Transition: India in the Global Debate*, edited by B. B. Mohanty, 95–119. London: Routledge.

Bernstein, Henry, and Carlos Oya. 2014. "Rural Futures: How Much Should Markets Rule?" Working paper, International Institute for Environment and Development (IIED), London.

Bigalke, Terance. 2005. *Tana Toraja: A Social History of an Indonesian People.* Singapore: NUS Press.

Blundo-Canto, Genowefa, Vincent Bax, Marcela Quintero, Gisella S. Cruz-Garcia, Rolf A. Groeneveld, and Lisset Pérez-Marulanda. 2018. "The Different Dimensions of Livelihood Impacts of Payments for Environmental Services (PES) Schemes: A Systematic Review." *Ecological Economics* 149:160–183.

Blust, Robert. 2013. *The Austronesian Languages.* Canberra: Australian National University Press.

Boeke, Julius H. 1942. *The Structure of Netherlands Indian Economy.* New York: International Secretariat, Institute of Pacific Relations.

Boeke, Julius H. 1953. *Economics and Economic Policy of Dual Societies, as Exemplified by Indonesia.* New York: International Secretariat, Institute of Pacific Relations.

Booth, Anne. 1984. "Survey of Recent Developments." *Bulletin of Indonesian Economic Studies* 20 (3): 1–35.

Booth, Anne. 1988. *Agricultural Development in Indonesia.* Sydney: Asian Studies Association of Australia / Allen & Unwin.

Booth, Anne. 1993. "Counting the Poor in Indonesia." *Bulletin of Indonesian Economic Studies* 29 (1): 53–83. https://doi.org/10.1080/00074919312331336341.

Booth, Anne. 2002. "The Changing Role of Non-farm Activities in Agricultural Households in Indonesia: Some Insights from the Agricultural Censuses." *Bulletin of Indonesian Economic Studies* 38 (2): 179–200. https://doi.org/10.1080/0007491 02320145048.

Booth, Anne. 2019. "Measuring Poverty and Income Distribution in Southeast Asia." *Asian-Pacific Economic Literature* 33 (1): 3–20. https://doi.org/10.1111/apel. 12250.

Boschma, Ron, and Ronald Martin, eds. 2010. *The Handbook of Evolutionary Economic Geography.* Cheltenham, UK: Edward Elgar.

Bourdieu, Pierre. 1977. *Outline of a Theory of Practice.* Cambridge: Cambridge University Press.

BPN (Badan Pertanahan Nasional). 2019. *BPN Laporan Kinerja 2019.* Jakarta: BPN. https://www.atrbpn.go.id/unduh/laporanKinerja2019.pdf.

BPS (Badan Pusat Statistik). 2002. *Kontribusi PDRB di Tana Toraja*. Rantepao: Badan Pusat Statistik Kabupaten Tana Toraja.

BPS. 2003. *Sensus Pertanian 2003 (ST2003)*. Jakarta: Badan Pusat Statistik.

BPS. 2010a. *Peraturan Kepala Badan Pusat Statistik Nomor 37 Tahun 2010 tentang Klasifikasi perkotaan dan Pedesaan di Indonesia*. Jakarta: Badan Pusat Statistik. https://sirusa.bps.go.id/webadmin/doc/MFD_2010_Buku_1.pdf.

BPS. 2010b. *Sensus Penduduk 2010 (SP2010)*. Jakarta: Badan Pusat Statistik.

BPS. 2013. *Sensus Pertanian 2013 (ST2013)*. Jakarta: Badan Pusat Statistik.

BPS. 2014. *Survei Rumah Tangga Usaha Perkebunan 2014*. Jakarta: Badan Pusat Statistik.

BPS. 2018. *Toraja Utara Dalam Angka 2017*. Rantepao: Badan Pusat Statistik Kabupaten Tana Toraja.

BPS. 2019a. *The Result of the Inter-census Agricultural Survey (SUTAS) 2018*. Jakarta: Badan Pusat Statistik. https://www.bps.go.id/publication.

BPS. 2019b. *Statistik Kopi 2018*. Jakarta: Badan Pusat Statistik. https://www.bps.go.id/publication/2019/12/06/b5e163624c20870bb3d6443a/statistik-kopi-indonesia-2018.html.

BPS. 2019c. *Plantation Commodity Statistics*. Jakarta: Badan Pusat Statistik. https://www.bps.go.id/subject/54/perkebunan.html#subjekViewTab4.

BPS. 2019d. "Data Mikro: Survei Angkatan Kerja Nasional (Sakernas) Februari Data." Micro data available at https://silastik.bps.go.id.

BPS. 2019e. "Data Mikro: Survei Sosial Ekonomi Nasional (Susenas) 2019." Micro data available at https://silastik.bps.go.id.

BPS. 2021a. *Sensus Penduduk 2020 (SP2020)*. Population Census. Jakarta: Badan Pusat Statistik.

BPS. 2021b. *Realisasi Pendapatan Pemerintah Daerah (Ribu Rupiah), 2016–2018*. Rantepao: Badan Pusat Statistik Kabupaten Toraja Utara. https://torutkab.bps.go.id/.

BPS. 2021c. *Statistik Kopi 2020*. Jakarta: Badan Pusat Statistik. https://www.bps.go.id/publication/2021/11/30/b1b6cf2a6aad1ee2d8a4c656/statistik-kopi-indonesia-2020.html.

BPS. 2021d. *Gross Regional Domestic Product of Provinces in Indonesia by Industry 2016–2020*. Jakarta: Badan Pusat Statistik.

BPS. 2022. "Produk: Statistik Menurut Subjek." https://www.bps.go.id/id/statistics-table?subject=521.

BPS. 2023. *Sensus Pertanian 2023 (ST2023)*. Jakarta: Badan Pusat Statistik.

BPS. 2024. "Labour—Statistical Data." Based on SAKERNAS survey. Jakarta: Badan Pusat Statistik. https://www.bps.go.id/en/statistics-table?subject=520.

Bray, Joshua G. 2018. "Sustainability Programs, Livelihoods and Value Chains in Southern Sumatra, Indonesia." PhD diss., University of Sydney. https://ses.library.usyd.edu.au/handle/2123/20293.

Bray, Joshua G., Bustanul Arifin, Hanung Ismono, and Jeffrey Neilson. 2023. "Sustainability Standards and Social Network Development: Indonesian Coffee Farmers' Unpredictable Impact Pathways to Achieving a Living Income." *Die Erde—Journal of the Geographical Society of Berlin* 154 (3): 112–122.

Bray, Joshua G., and Jeffrey Neilson. 2017. "Reviewing the Impacts of Coffee Certification Programmes on Smallholder Livelihoods." *International Journal of Biodiversity Science, Ecosystem Services & Management* 13 (1): 216–232.

Bray, Joshua G., and Jeffrey Neilson. 2018. "Examining the Interface of Sustainability Programs and Livelihoods in the Semendo Highlands of Indonesia." *Asia Pacific Viewpoint* 59 (3): 368–383.

Brechin, Steven R., Surya Chandra Surapaty, Laurel Heydir, and Eddy Roflin. 1994. "Protected Area Deforestation in South Sumatra, Indonesia." *George Wright Forum* 11 (3): 59–78.

Breman, Jan. 2015. *Mobilizing Labour for the Global Coffee Market: Profits from an Unfree Work Regime in Colonial Java*. Amsterdam: Amsterdam University Press B.V.

Brookfield, Harold C. 1972. "Intensification and Disintensification in Pacific Agriculture: A Theoretical Approach." *Pacific Viewpoint* 13 (1): 30–48.

Bunn, Christian, Peter Läderach, Oriana Ovalle Rivera, and Dieter Kirschke. 2015. "A Bitter Cup: Climate Change Profile of Global Production of Arabica and Robusta Coffee." *Climatic Change* 129 (1): 89–101.

Busch, Jonah, Irene Ring, Monique Akullo, Oyut Amarjargal, Maud Borie, Rodrigo S. Cassola, Annabelle Cruz-Trinidad, et al. 2021. "A Global Review of Ecological Fiscal Transfers." *Nature Sustainability* 4:756–765.

Butt, Simon, and Tim Lindsey. 2008. "Economic Reform When the Constitution Matters: Indonesia's Constitutional Court and Article 33." *Bulletin of Indonesian Economic Studies* 44 (2): 239–262.

Byrareddy, Vivekananda, Louis Kouadio, Shahbaz Mushtaq, and Roger Stone. 2019. "Sustainable Production of Robusta Coffee under a Changing Climate: A 10-Year Monitoring of Fertilizer Management in Coffee Farms in Vietnam and Indonesia." *Agronomy* 9 (9): 1–19. https://doi.org/10.3390/agronomy9090499.

Byres, Terence J. 1977. "Agrarian Transition and the Agrarian Question." *Journal of Peasant Studies* 4 (3): 258–274.

Byres, Terence J. 1986. "The Agrarian Question, Forms of Capitalist Agrarian Transition and the State: An Essay with Reference to Asia." *Social Scientist* 14 (11–12): 3–67.

Byres, Terence J. 1996. *Capitalism from Above and Capitalism from Below: An Essay in Comparative Political Economy*. Hampshire, UK: Palgrave Macmillan.

Byres, Terence J. 2016. "In Pursuit of Capitalist Agrarian Transition." *Journal of Agrarian Change* 16 (3): 432–451.

Carney, Diane. 1999. *Livelihoods Approaches Compared*. London: Department for International Development.

Carney, Diane. 2002. *Sustainable Livelihoods Approaches: Progress and Possibilities for Change*. London: Department for International Development.

Chambers, Robert, and Gordon Conway. 1991. "Sustainable Rural Livelihoods: Practical Concepts for the 21st Century." IDS Discussion Paper 296, Institute of Development Studies, Brighton, UK. https://opendocs.ids.ac.uk/opendocs/handle/20.500.12413/775.

Chayanov, Alexander V. (1925) 1966. "Peasant Farm Organization." In *A. V. Chayanov on the Theory of Peasant Economy*, edited by Daniel Thorner, Basile Kerblay, and R. E. F. Smith, 29–269. Manchester: Manchester University Press.

Clarke, Taylor. 2007. *Starbucked: A Double Tall Tale of Caffeine, Commerce, and Culture*. New York: Little, Brown.

Coe, Neil M., Martin Hess, Henry Wai-Chung Yeung, Peter Dicken, and Jeffrey Henderson. 2004. "'Globalizing' Regional Development: A Global Production Networks Perspective." *Transactions of the Institute of British Geographers* 29 (4): 468–484.

Coe, Neil M., and Henry Wai-Chung Yeung. 2015. *Global Production Networks: Theorizing Economic Development in an Interconnected World*. Oxford: Oxford University Press.

Colombijn, Freek. 2005. "A Moving History of Middle Sumatra, 1600–1870." *Modern Asian Studies* 39 (1): 1–38. https://doi.org/10.1017/S0026749X04001374.

Creutzberg, Piet, ed. 1975. *Changing Economy in Indonesia: The Export Crops 1816–1940*. Amsterdam: Royal Tropical Institute.

Cramb, Robert A. 1993. "Shifting Cultivation and Sustainable Agriculture in East Malaysia: A Longitudinal Case Study." *Agricultural Systems* 42 (3): 209–226.

Cramb, Robert A., and John F. McCarthy, eds. 2016. *The Oil Palm Complex: Smallholders, Agribusiness and the State in Indonesia and Malaysia*. Singapore: NUS Press.

Cramb, Robert A., Carol J. Pierce Colfer, Wolfram Dressler, Pinkaew Laungaramsri, Quang Trang Le, Elok Mulyoutami, Nancy L. Peluso, and Reed L. Wadley. 2009. "Swidden Transformations and Rural Livelihoods in Southeast Asia." *Human Ecology* 37 (3): 323–346.

Cramer, Pieter J. S. 1918. *De groote landbouw in Zuid-Sumatra* 20. Weltevreden, Java: Zuid-Sumatra Landbouw- en Nijverheidsvereeniging.

Cribb, Robert. 2001. "Genocide in Indonesia, 1965–1966." *Journal of Genocide Research* 3 (2): 219–239.

Daviron, Benoit, and Stefano Ponte. 2005. *The Coffee Paradox: Global Markets, Commodity Trade and the Elusive Promise of Development*. London: Zed Books.

Davis, Lance, and Douglass North. 1970. "Institutional Change and American Economic Growth: A First Step towards a Theory of Institutional Innovation." *Journal of Economic History* 30 (1): 131–149.

Davis, Mike. 2007. *Planet of Slums*. London: Verso.

Day, Clive. 1904. *The Policy and Administration of the Dutch in Java*. Kuala Lumpur: Oxford University Press.

de Graaff, Jan. 1986. *The Economics of Coffee*. Wageningen, Netherlands: Pudoc.

de Haan, F. 1910. *Priangan: De Preanger-Regentschappen onder het Nederlandsch bestuur tot 1811*. 4 parts. Batavia: Bataviaasch Genootschap van Kunsten en Wetenschappen.

de Haan, Leo, and Annelies Zoomers. 2005. "Exploring the Frontier of Livelihoods Research." *Development and Change* 36 (1): 27–47. https://doi.org/10.1111/j.0012-155X.2005.00401.x.

de Jong, Edwin. 2013. *Making a Living between Crises and Ceremonies in Tana Toraja: The Practice of Everyday Life of a South Sulawesi Highland Community in Indonesia*. Leiden: Brill.

De Koninck, Rodolphe. 2004. "The Challenges of the Agrarian Transition in Southeast Asia." *Labour, Capital and Society* 37 (1/2): 285–288.

De La Rosa, W., R. Alatorre, J. F. Barrera, and C. Toriello. 2000. "Effect of *Beauveria bassiana* and *Metarhizium anisopliae* (Deuteromycetes) upon the Coffee Berry Borer (Coleoptera: Scolytidae) under Field Conditions." *Journal of Economic Entomology* 93 (5): 1409–1414. https://doi.org/10.1603/0022-0493-93.5.1409.

de Royer, Sébastien, Meine van Noordwijk, and J. M. Roshetko. 2018. "Does Community-Based Forest Management in Indonesia Devolve Social Justice or Social Costs?" *International Forestry Review* 20 (2): 167–180.

de Royer, Sébastien, L. Visser, G. Galudra, U. Pradhan, and M. van Noordwijk. 2015. "Self-Identification of Indigenous People in Post-independence Indonesia: A Historical Analysis in the Context of REDD+." *International Forestry Review* 17 (3): 282–297.

de Soto, Hernando. 2000. *The Mystery of Capital: Why Capitalism Triumphs in the West and Fails Everywhere Else*. New York: Basic Books.

Devaux, André, Maximo Torero, Jason Donovan, and Douglas Horton. 2018. "Agricultural Innovation and Inclusive Value-Chain Development: A Review." *Journal of Agribusiness in Developing and Emerging Economies* 8 (1): 99–123.

Ditjenbun (Directorate General of Estate Crops, Indonesian Department of Agriculture). 2021. "Rencana Strategis (Renstra) Direktorat Jenderal Perkebunan Kementerian Pertanian Republik Indonesia 2020–2024." http://ditjenbun.pertanian.go.id/info-publik/rencana-strategis/.

Ditjenbun. 2024. "Rencana Kinerja Tahunan 2020, Annual Work Plan 2020." https://ditjenbun.pertanian.go.id/info-publik/rencana-kerja-tahunan-rkt/.

Dorward, Andrew. 2009. "Integrating Contested Aspirations, Processes and Policy: Development as Hanging In, Stepping Up and Stepping Out." *Development Policy Review* 27 (2): 131–146.

Dove, Michael R. 1993. "Smallholder Rubber and Swidden Agriculture in Borneo: A Sustainable Adaptation to the Ecology and Economy of the Tropical Forest." *Economic Botany* 47 (2): 136–147.

Dove, Michael R. 2011. *The Banana Tree at the Gate*. New Haven, CT: Yale University Press.

Du Toit, Andries, and David Neves. 2014. "The Government of Poverty and the Arts of Survival: Mobile and Recombinant Strategies at the Margins of the South African Economy." *Journal of Peasant Studies* 41 (5): 833–853.

Eaton, Charles, and Andrew W. Shepherd. 2001. *Contract Farming: Partnerships for Growth*. Rome: Food and Agricultural Organisation of the United Nations. http://www.fao.org/3/y0937e/y0937e00.pdf.

Ellis, Frank. (1988) 1993. *Peasant Economics: Farm Households and Agrarian Development*. 2nd ed. Cambridge: Cambridge University Press.

Ellis, Frank. 1998. "Household Strategies and Rural Livelihood Diversification." *Journal of Development Studies* 35 (1): 1–38.

Elson, Robert. 1997. *The End of the Peasantry in Southeast Asia: A Social and Economic History of Peasant Livelihood, 1800–1990s*. London: Palgrave Macmillan.

Euromonitor. 2021. *Hot Drinks 2020: Coffee*. London: Euromonitor International. http://www.portal.euromonitor.com.

Euromonitor. 2022. *Passport: Coffee in Indonesia*. London: Euromonitor International. http://www.portal.euromonitor.com.

Fane, George, and Peter Warr. 2009. "Indonesia." In *Distortions to Agricultural Incentives in Asia*, edited by Kym Anderson and Will Martin, 165–196. Washington, DC: World Bank.

FAO (Food and Agriculture Organization). 2014. *The State of Food and Agriculture: Innovation in Family Farming*. Rome: Food and Agriculture Organization.

FAO. 2020. *World Food and Agriculture—Statistical Yearbook 2020*. Rome: Food and Agriculture Organization of the United Nations. https://doi.org/10.4060/cb1329en.

FAO. 2024. "FAO Statistical Datasets." http://www.fao.org/faostat/en.

Felipe, Jesus, Aashish Mehta, and Changyong Rhee. 2014. "Manufacturing Matters . . . but It's the Jobs That Count." Asian Development Bank Economics Working Paper Series No. 420, Asian Development Bank, Manila. https://www.adb.org/sites/default/files/publication/149984/ewp-420.pdf.

Ferguson, James. 2013. "Declarations of Dependence: Labour, Personhood, and Welfare in Southern Africa." *Journal of the Royal Anthropological Institute* 19 (2): 223–242.

Ferguson, James. 2015. *Give a Man a Fish: Reflections on the New Politics of Distribution*. Durham, NC: Duke University Press.

Ferguson, James, and Tania Murray Li. 2018. "Beyond the 'Proper Job': Political-Economic Analysis after the Century of Labouring Man." PLAAS Working Papers 51, Institute for Poverty, Land and Agrarian Studies, University of the Western Cape, Cape Town. https://repository.uwc.ac.za/handle/10566/4538.

Fold, Niels, and Jeffrey Neilson. 2016. "Sustaining Supplies in Smallholder-Dominated Value Chains: Corporate Governance of the Global Cocoa Sector." In *The Economics of Chocolate*, edited by Mara P. Squicciarini and Johan Swinnen, 195–212. Oxford: Oxford University Press.

Galudra, Gamma, and Martua Sirait. 2009. "A Discourse on Dutch Colonial Forest Policy and Science in Indonesia at the Beginning of the 20th Century." *International Forestry Review* 11 (4): 524–533.

Garrett, Rachael D., Samuel Levy, Florian Gollnow, Leonie Hodel, and Ximena Rueda. 2021. "Have Food Supply Chain Policies Improved Forest Conservation and Rural Livelihoods? A Systematic Review." *Environmental Research Letters* 16 (3): 033002. http://dx.doi.org/10.1088/1748-9326/abe0ed.

Gaventa, John. 1995. "The Political Economy of Land Tenure: Appalachia and the Southeast." Paper commissioned for the Who Owns America? Land and Resource Tenure Issues in a Changing Environment Conference, Land Tenure Center, University of Wisconsin–Madison, June 1995.

Geertz, Clifford. 1963. *Agricultural Involution: The Process of Ecological Change in Indonesia.* Berkeley: University of California Press.

Gereffi, Gary. 1994. "The Organization of Buyer-Driven Global Commodity Chains: How US Retailers Shape Overseas Production Networks." In *Commodity Chains and Global Capitalism*, edited by Gary Gereffi and Miguel Korzeniewicz, 95–122. Westport, CT: Praeger.

Gereffi, Gary. 1995. "Global Production Systems and Third World Development." In *Global Change, Regional Response: The New International Context of Development*, edited by Barbara Stallings, 100–142. New York: Cambridge University Press.

Gereffi, Gary. 1999. "International Trade and Industrial Upgrading in the Apparel Commodity Chain." *Journal of International Economics* 48 (1): 37–70. https://doi.org/10.1016/S0022-1996(98)00075-0.

Gereffi, Gary. 2005. "The Global Economy: Organization, Governance, and Development." In *The Handbook of Economic Sociology,* 2nd ed., edited by Neil J. Smelser and Richard Swedberg, 160–182. Princeton, NJ: Princeton University Press.

Gereffi, Gary, John Humphrey, and Timothy Sturgeon. 2005. "The Governance of Global Value Chains." *Review of International Political Economy* 12 (1): 78–104.

Glamann, Kristof. 1981. *Dutch-Asiatic Trade 1620–1740*. Den Haag, Netherlands: Martinus Nijhoff 's-Gravenhage. https://doi-org.ezproxy1.library.usyd.edu.au/10.1007/978-94-009-8361-8_10.

Glaser, Barney G., and Anselm L. Strauss. (1967) 1999. *Discovery of Grounded Theory: Strategies for Qualitative Research*. London: Routledge.

Godoy, Ricardo, and Christopher Bennett. 1988. "Diversification among Coffee Smallholders in the Highlands of South Sumatra, Indonesia." *Human Ecology* 16 (4): 397–420.

Grabs, Janina. 2020. "Assessing the Institutionalization of Private Sustainability Governance in a Changing Coffee Sector." *Regulation & Governance* 14 (2): 362–387. https://doi.org/10.1111/rego.12212.

Grabs, Janina, and Stefano Ponte. 2019. "The Evolution of Power in the Global Coffee Value Chain and Production Network." *Journal of Economic Geography* 19 (4): 803–828. https://doi.org/10.1093/jeg/lbz008.

Granovetter, Mark. 1985. "Economic Action and Social Structure: The Problem of Embeddedness." *American Journal of Sociology* 91 (3): 481–510.

Grant, Tasmin. 2020. "Becoming a Private Label Specialty Coffee Provider." *Perfect Daily Grind*, April 30. https://perfectdailygrind.com/2020/04/becoming-a-private-label-specialty-coffee-provider/.

Grigg, David B. 1975. "The World's Agricultural Labour Force 1800–1970." *Geography* 60 (3): 194–202.

Guritno, Tatang, and Dani Prabowo. 2021. "Korupsi Pengadaan Paket Bansos Covid-19, Saksi Ungkap Aliran Dana untuk Anggota BPK dan Pejabat Kemensos." *Kompas, June 8.* https://nasional.kompas.com/read/2021/06/08/10384201/korupsi-pengadaan-paket-bansos-covid-19-saksi-ungkap-aliran-dana-untuk?page=all.

Guttmann, Agnieszka. 2020. "Nestlé: Advertising Spending Worldwide 2015–2018." *Statista*, January 8. https://www.statista.com/statistics/286531/Nestlé -advertising-spending-worldwide/.

Hadiz, Vedi. 2004. "Decentralization and Democracy in Indonesia: A Critique of Neoinstitutionalist Perspectives." *Development and Change* 35 (4): 697–718. https://doi.org/10.1111/j.0012-155X.2004.00376.x.

Hall, Derek. 2013. *Land.* Cambridge: Polity.

Hall, Derek, Philip Hirsch, and Tania Murray Li. 2011. *Powers of Exclusion: Land Dilemmas in Southeast Asia.* Singapore: NUS Press.

Hart, Gillian. 1989. "Agrarian Change in the Context of State Patronage." In *Agrarian Transformations: Local Processes and the State in Southeast Asia*, edited by G. Hart, A. Turton, and B. White, 31–52. Berkeley: University of California Press.

Hart, Gillian. 2002. *Disabling Globalization: Places of Power in Post-apartheid South Africa.* Berkeley: University of California Press.

Hart, Gillian, Andrew Turton, and Ben White, eds. 1989. *Agrarian Transformations: Local Processes and the State in Southeast Asia.* Berkeley: University of California Press.

Hartatri, Diany Faila Sophia, Lya Aklimawati, and Jeffrey Neilson. 2019. "Analysis of Specialty Coffee Business Performances: Focus on Management of Farmer Organizations in Indonesia." *Pelita Perkebunan* 35 (2): 140–155. https://doi.org/10.22302/iccri.jur.pelitaperkebunan.v35i2.382.

Harvey, David. 1982. *The Limits to Capital.* London: Verso.

Harvey, David. 2003. *The New Imperialism.* Oxford: Oxford University Press.

Hasudungan, Albert, and Jeffrey Neilson. 2020. "The Institutional Environment of the Palm Oil Value Chain and Its Impact on Community Development in Kapuas Hulu, Indonesia." *Southeast Asian Studies* 9 (3): 439–465.

Hefner, Robert W. 1990. *The Political Economy of Mountain Java: An Interpretive History.* Oakland: University of California Press.

Henley, David. 2012. "The Agrarian Roots of Industrial Growth: Rural Development in South-East Asia and Sub-Saharan Africa." *Development Policy Review* 30 (S1): s25–s47.

Hernandez-Aguilera, J. Nicolas, Miguel I. Gómez, Amanda D. Rodewald, Ximena Rueda, Colleen Anunu, Ruth Bennett, and Harold M. van Es. 2018. "Quality as a Driver of Sustainable Agricultural Value Chains: The Case of the Relationship Coffee Model." *Business Strategy and the Environment* 27 (2): 179–198.

Hill, Hal. 2018. "Asia's Third Giant: A Survey of the Indonesian Economy." *Economic Record* 94 (307): 469–499.

Hoedt, T. G. E. 1930. "Indische bergcultuurondernemingen voornamelijk in Zuid-Sumatra: gegevens en beschouwingen." PhD diss., H. Veenman & Zonen, Wageningen.

Holland, Emil, Chris Kjeldsen, and Søren Kerndrup. 2016. "Coordinating Quality Practices in Direct Trade Coffee." *Journal of Cultural Economy* 9 (2): 186–196. https://doi.org/10.1080/17530350.2015.1069205.

Holmemo, Camilla, Pablo Acosta, Tina George, Robert J. Palacios, Juul Pinxten, Shonali Sen, and Sailesh Tiwari. 2020. *Investing in People: Social Protection for Indonesia's 2045 Vision*. Jakarta: World Bank Indonesia. https://www.worldbank.org/en/country/indonesia/publication/investing-in-people-social-protection-for-indonesia-2045-vision.

Hooker, Michael Barry. 1978. *Adat Law in Modern Indonesia*. Oxford: Oxford University Press.

Hopkins, Terence K., and Immanuel Wallerstein. 1994. "Commodity Chains in the World-Economy prior to 1800. Commodity Chains: Construct and Research." In *Commodity Chains and Global Capitalism*, edited by G. Gereffi and M. Korzeniewicz, 17–20. Westport, CT: Praeger.

Hugo, Graeme. 1977. "Circular Migration." *Bulletin of Indonesian Economic Studies* 13 (3): 57–66.

Huitema, W. K. 1935. *De bevolkingskoffiecultuur op Sumatra: Met een inleiding tot hare geschiedenis op Java en Sumatra*. PhD diss., H. Veenman & Zonen, Wageningen. https://edepot.wur.nl/51615.

Humphrey, John, and Hubert Schmitz. 2002. "How Does Insertion in Global Value Chains Affect Upgrading in Industrial Clusters?" *Regional Studies* 36 (9): 1017–1027.

Hüsken, Frans, and Juliette Koning. 2006. "Between Two Worlds: Social Security in Indonesia." In *Ropewalking and Safety Nets: Local Ways of Managing Insecurities in Indonesia*, edited by Juliette Koning and Frans Hüsken, 1–26. Leiden: Brill.

Hüsken, Frans, and Benjamin White. 1989. "Java: Social Differentiation, Food Production, and Agrarian Control." In *Agrarian Transformations: Local Processes and the State in Southeast Asia*, edited by G. Hart, A. Turton, and B. White, 234–265. Berkeley: University of California Press.

Hutapea, Yanter., and D. Tumarlan Thamrin. 2009. "Tunggu Tubang sebagai Upaya Mempertahankan Sumber Daya Lahan Berkelanjutan." *Jurnal Balai Pengkajian Teknologi Pertanian Sumatra Selatan* 5:348–362.

Ichsan, Syaukani. 2017. *Dinamika Pertanian Komoditas Kopi: Dataran Tinggi Toraja*. Bogor: Sajogyo Institute. https://sajogyo-institute.org/dinamika-pertanian-komoditas-kopi-dataran-tinggi-toraja/.

ICO (International Coffee Organization). 2020. *Historical Data on the Global Coffee Trade*. London: International Coffee Organization. https://www.ico.org/historical/1990%20onwards/PDF/1a-total-production.pdf.

IDH. 2021. "SourceUp Policy: Draft of Consultation." https://www.idhsustainabletrade.com/approach/sourceup.

Ilbery, Brian, and Ian Bowler. 1998. "From Agricultural Productivism to Post-productivism." In *The Geography of Rural Change*, edited by Brian Ilbery, 57–84. Harlow, UK: Addison Wesley Longman.

International Labour Organization. 2021. "ILOSTAT: Wages and Working Time Statistics." https://ilostat.ilo.org/topics/wages/#.

ISEAL Alliance. 2021. "Credible Assurance at a Landscape Scale: A Discussion Paper on Landscape and Jurisdictional Assurance and Claims." https://www.isealalliance.org/about-iseal/our-work/landscape-assurance.

Itoh, Makoto. 1980. *Value and Crisis: Essays on Marxian Economics in Japan*. New York: Monthly Review and Pluto.

Jakimow, Tanya. 2018. "A Moral Atmosphere of Development as a Share: Consequences for Urban Development in Indonesia." *World Development* 108:47–56.

Jakobsen, Thomas Saetre. 2018. "From the Workplace to the Household: Migrant Labor and Accumulation without Dispossession." *Critical Asian Studies* 50 (2): 176–195.

JDE. 2021. "Common Grounds: Where We Work." https://www.jacobsdouweegberts. com/siteassets/sustainability/common-grounds/2018-projects-overview.pdf.

JDE Peet's. 2021. "JDE Peet's NV Annual Report 2020." https://www.jdepeets.com/ corporate-responsibility/our-progress/.

Johnson, Craig A. 1997. "Rules, Norms and the Pursuit of Sustainable Livelihoods." IDS Working Paper 52, Brighton. https://opendocs.ids.ac.uk/opendocs/ handle/20.500.12413/3355.

Kahn, Joel S. 1980. *Minangkabau Social Formations: Indonesian Peasants and the World-Economy.* Cambridge: Cambridge University Press.

Kartodirjo, Sartono. 1972. "Agrarian Radicalism in Java: Its Setting and Development." In *Culture and Politics in Indonesia*, edited by Claire Holt, 71–125. Ithaca, NY: Cornell University Press.

Kaskoyo, Hari, Abrar Juhar Mohammed, and Makoto Inoue. 2014. "Present State of Community Forestry (Hutan Kemasyarakatan/Hkm) Program in a Protection Forest and Its Challenges: Case Study in Lampung Province, Indonesia." *Journal of Forest and Environmental Science* 30 (1): 15–29.

Katiman. 2023. "Village Politics, Ritual Distribution and the Problem of Beneficiary Mistargeting in Central Java." In *The Paradox of Agrarian Change: Food Security and the Politics of Social Protection in Indonesia*, edited by John F. McCarthy, Andrew McWilliam, and Gerben Nooteboom, 326–348. Singapore: NUS Press.

Kautsky, Karl. (1899) 1988. *The Agrarian Question.* Vol. 1 (*Die Agrarfrage*). London: Zwan.

Kelly, Philip F. 2009. "From Global Production Networks to Global Reproduction Networks: Households, Migration, and Regional Development in Cavite, the Philippines." *Regional Studies* 43 (3): 449–461.

Kelly, Philip F. 2011. "Migration, Agrarian Transition, and Rural Change in Southeast Asia: Introduction." *Critical Asian Studies* 43 (4): 479–506.

Kelly, Philip F. 2013. "Production Networks, Place and Development: Thinking through Global Production Networks in Cavite, Philippines." *Geoforum* 44:82–92.

Kissinger, Gabrielle, Mark Moroge, and Martin Noponen. 2014. "Private Sector Investment in Landscape Approaches: The Role of Production Standards and Certification." In *Climate-Smart Landscapes: Multifunctionality in Practice*, edited by Peter A. Minang, Meine van Noordwijk, Olivia E. Freeman, Cheikh Mbow, Jan de Leeuw, and Delia Catacutan, 277–293. Bogor, Indonesia: ASB Partnership for the Tropical Forest Margins.

Klein, Alexandra-Maria. 2009. "Nearby Rainforest Promotes Coffee Pollination by Increasing Spatio-temporal Stability in Bee Species Richness." *Forest Ecology and Management* 258 (9): 1838–1845.

Klenke, Karin. 2013. "Whose Adat Is It? Adat, Indigeneity and Social Stratification in Toraja." In *Adat and Indigeneity in Indonesia: Culture and Entitlements between Heteronomy and Self-Ascription*, edited by Brigitta Hauser-Schäublin, 149–165. Göttingen: Göttingen University Press. http://books.openedition.org/gup/179.

Knaap, Gerrit J. 1986. "Coffee for Cash: The Dutch East India Company and the Expansion of Coffee Cultivation in Java, Ambon and Ceylon 1700–1730." In *Trading Companies in Asia: 1600–1830*, edited by J. van Goor, 33–50. Utrecht: HES Uitgevers.

Knigge, LaDona G. 2017. "Grounded Theory." In *International Encyclopedia of Geography: People, the Earth, Environment and Technology*, edited by Douglas Richardson et al., West Sussex, UK: Wiley-Blackwell. https://doi. org/10.1002/9781118786352.wbieg0339.

Koentjaraningrat. 1967. "A Survey of Social Studies on Rural Indonesia." In *Villages in Indonesia*, edited by Koentjaraningrat, 1–29. Ithaca, NY: Cornell University Press.

Koloniaal Verslag (various years, 1852–1890). The Hague: Ministry of Colonial Affairs of the Netherlands.

Krishna, Vijesh V., Christoph Kubitza, Unai Pascual, and Matin Qaim. 2017. "Land Markets, Property Rights, and Deforestation: Insights from Indonesia." *World Development* 99:335–349.

Kurniasih, Heni, Rebecca M. Ford, Rodney J. Keenan, and Barbara J. King. 2020. "A Typology of Community Forestry Approaches in Indonesia: Implications for External Support to Forest Communities." *International Forestry Review* 22 (2): 211–224.

Kusters, Koen, Hubert De Foresta, Andree Ekadinata, and Meine van Noordwijk. 2007. "Towards Solutions for State vs. Local Community Conflicts over Forestland: The Impact of Formal Recognition of User Rights in Krui, Sumatra, Indonesia." *Human Ecology* 35 (4): 427–438.

Larson, Anne M., Maria Brockhaus, William D. Sunderlin, Amy Duchelle, Andrea Babon, Therese Dokken, Thu Thuy Pham, et al. 2013. "Land Tenure and REDD+: The Good, the Bad and the Ugly." *Global Environmental Change* 23:678–689.

Lewis, W. Arthur. 1954. "Economic Development with Unlimited Supplies of Labor." *Manchester School* 22 (2): 139–91.

Li, Tania Murray. 2007. *The Will to Improve: Governmentality, Development and the Practice of Politics*. Durham, NC: Duke University Press.

Li, Tania Murray. 2008. "Social Reproduction, Situated Politics, and the Will to Improve." *Focaal* 2008 (52): 111–118.

Li, Tania Murray. 2009. "Reading the World Development Report 2008: Agriculture for Development." *Journal of Peasant Studies* 36 (3): 591–661.

Li, Tania Murray. 2010. "To Make Live or Let Die? Rural Dispossession and the Protection of Surplus Populations." *Antipode* 41:66–93.

Li, Tania Murray. 2011. "Centreing Labor in the Land Grab Debate." *Journal of Peasant Studies* 38 (2): 281–298.

Li, Tania Murray. 2014. *Land's End: Capitalist Relations on an Indigenous Frontier*. Durham, NC: Duke University Press.

Li, Tania Murray. 2016. "Governing Rural Indonesia: Convergence on the Project System." *Critical Policy Studies* 10 (1): 79–94.

Li, Tania Murray. 2017. "After Development: Surplus Population and the Politics of Entitlement." *Development and Change* 48 (6): 1247–1261.

Li, Tania Murray, and Pujo Semedi. 2021. *Plantation Life: Corporate Occupation in Indonesia's Oil Palm Zone*. Durham, NC: Duke University Press.

Lipton, Michael. 1977. *Why Poor People Stay Poor: A Study of Urban Bias in World Development*. London: Temple Smith.

Long, Norman. 2001. *Development Sociology: Actor Perspectives*. New York: Routledge.

Looney, Kristen E. 2020. *Mobilizing for Development: The Modernization of Rural East Asia*. Ithaca, NY: Cornell University Press.

Lowder, Sarah K., Marco V. Sánchez, and Raffaele Bertini. 2021. "Which Farms Feed the World and Has Farmland Become More Concentrated?" *World Development* 142:105455.

Lucas, Anton, and Carol Warren. 2013. *Land for the People: The State and Agrarian Conflict in Indonesia*. Athens: Ohio University Press.

Lukas, Martin C., and Nancy Lee Peluso. 2020. "Transforming the Classic Political Forest: Contentious Territories in Java." *Antipode* 52 (4): 971–995.

MacAndrews, Colin. 1978. "Transmigration in Indonesia: Prospects and Problems." *Asian Survey* 18 (5): 458–472.

Mackie, James A. C. 1962. "Indonesia's Government Estates and Their Masters." *Pacific Affairs* 34 (4): 337–360.

Manning, Chris. 2000. "Labour Market Adjustment to Indonesia's Economic Crisis: Context, Trends and Implications." *Bulletin of Indonesian Economic Studies* 36 (1): 105–136.

Manning, Chris. 2018. "Jobs, Wages, and Labor Market Segmentation." In *Indonesia: Enhancing Productivity through Quality Jobs*, edited by E. Ginting, C. Manning, and K. Taniguchi, 29–67. Manila: Asian Development Bank. https://www.adb.org/publication/indonesia-enhancing-productivity-quality-jobs.

Manning, Chris, and Raden Muhamad Purnagunawan. 2016. "Has Indonesia Passed the Lewis Turning Point and Does It Matter?" In *Managing Globalization in the Asian Century*, edited by Hal Hill and Jayant Menon, 457–484. Singapore: ISEAS.

Mansvelt, W. M. F., ed. 1976. *Changing Economy in Indonesia: A Selection of Statistical Source Material from the Early 19th Century up to 1940*. Vol. 2, *Public Finance 1816–1939*. The Hague: Martinus Nijhoff.

Marsden, Terry. 1995. "Beyond Agriculture? Regulating the New Rural Spaces." *Journal of Rural Studies* 11 (3): 285–296.

Marsden, Terry. 1999. "Rural Futures: The Consumption Countryside and Its Regulation." *Sociologia Ruralis* 39 (4): 501–526.

Martin, Edwin, Didik Suharjito, Dudung Darusman, Satyawan Sunito, and Bondan Winarno. 2016. "Tunggu Tubang and Ulu Ayek: Social Mechanism of Sustainable Protected Forest Management." *Journal of Tropical Forest Management* 22 (2): 85–93. https://doi.org/10.7226/jtfm.22.2.85.

McCarthy, John F. 2006. *The Fourth Circle: A Political Ecology of Sumatra's Rainforest Frontier*. Stanford, CA: Stanford University Press.

McCarthy, John F. 2010. "Processes of Inclusion and Adverse Incorporation: Oil Palm and Agrarian Change in Sumatra, Indonesia." *Journal of Peasant Studies* 37 (4): 821–850.

McCarthy, John F. 2020. "The Paradox of Progressing Sideways: Food Poverty and Livelihood Change in the Rice Lands of Outer Island Indonesia." *Journal of Peasant Studies* 47 (5): 1077–1097.

McCarthy, John F., Andrew McWilliam, and Gerben Nooteboom, eds. 2023a. *The Paradox of Agrarian Change: Food Security and the Politics of Social Protection in Indonesia*. Singapore: NUS Press.

McCarthy, John F., Andrew McWilliam, and Gerben Nooteboom. 2023b. "Understanding Agrarian Change Scenarios of Agricultural Development, Income Diversification, Food Poverty and Nutritional Insecurity in Indonesia." In McCarthy, McWilliam, and Nooteboom, *Paradox of Agrarian Change*, 5–27.

McCarthy, John F., Andrew McWilliam, and Gerben Nooteboom. 2023c. "Conclusions and Implications: Paradoxes of Agrarian Change and Social Protection." In McCarthy, McWilliam, and Nooteboom, *Paradox of Agrarian Change*, 408–422.

McCarthy, John F., and Mulyadi Sumarto. 2018. "Distributional Politics and Social Protection in Indonesia: Dilemma of Layering, Nesting and Social Fit in Jokowi's Poverty Policy." *Journal of Southeast Asian Economies* 35 (2): 223–236.

McKay, Deirdre. 2003. "Cultivating New Local Futures: Remittance Economies and Land-Use Patterns in Ifugao, Philippines." *Journal of Southeast Asian Studies* 34 (2): 285–306.

McKay, Deirdre. 2005. "Reading Remittance Landscapes: Female Migration and Agricultural Transition in the Philippines." *Geografisk Tidsskrift–Danish Journal of Geography* 105 (1): 89–99.

McMichael, Philip. 2013. *Food Regimes and Agrarian Questions*. Halifax, NS: Fernwood.

McNicoll, Geoffrey. 1968. "Internal Migration in Indonesia: Descriptive Notes." *Indonesia* 5:29–92.

McStocker, Robert. 1987. "The Indonesian Coffee Industry." *Bulletin of Indonesian Economic Studies* 23 (1): 40–69.

McWilliam, Andrew, John F. McCarthy, Gerben Nooteboom, and Naimah Talib. 2023. "Social Protection and the Challenge of Poverty in Indonesia." In McCarthy, McWilliam, and Nooteboom, *Paradox of Agrarian Change*, 65–86.

Mertz, Ole, Christine Padoch, Jefferson Fox, Rob A. Cramb, Stephen J. Leisz, Nguyen Thanh Lam, and Tran Duc Vien. 2009. "Swidden Change in Southeast Asia: Understanding Causes and Consequences." *Human Ecology* 37 (3): 259–264.

Minang, Peter A., Meine van Noordwijk, Olivia E. Freeman, Cheikh Mbow, Jan de Leeuw, and Delia Catacutan, eds. 2015. *Climate-Smart Landscapes: Multifunctionality in Practice*. Nairobi: World Agroforestry Centre (ICRAF).

MLHKRI. 2018. *Status Hutan dan Kehutanan Indonesia 2018*. Jakarta: Kementerian Lingkungan Hidup dan Kehutanan Republik Indonesia. https://www.menlhk.go.id/site/download.

Multatuli. (1860) 1995. *The Coffee Auctions of a Dutch Trading Company*. Translated by R. Edwards. London: Penguin Classics. Originally published as *Max Havelaar, of de koffi-veilingen der Nederlandsche Handel-Maatschappy* (Amsterdam: J. de Ruyter, 1860).

Natarajan, Nithya, Andrew Newsham, Jonathan Rigg, and Diana Suhardiman. 2022. "A Sustainable Livelihoods Framework for the 21st Century." *World Development* 155 (July): 105898.

Neilson, Jeffrey. 2004. "Embedded Geographies and Quality Construction in Sulawesi Coffee Commodity Chains." PhD diss., University of Sydney. https://ses.library.usyd.edu.au/handle/2123/9222.

Neilson, Jeffrey. 2007. "Institutions, the Governance of Quality and on-Farm Value Retention for Indonesian Specialty Coffee." *Singapore Journal of Tropical Geography* 28 (2): 188–204.

Neilson, Jeffrey. 2008. "Global Private Regulation and Value-Chain Restructuring in Indonesian Smallholder Coffee Systems." *World Development* 36 (9): 1607–1622.

Neilson, Jeffrey. 2014. "Value Chains, Neoliberalism and Development Practice: The Indonesian Experience." *Review of International Political Economy* 21 (1): 38–69.

Neilson, Jeffrey. 2019. "Livelihood Upgrading." In *Handbook on Global Value Chains*, edited by Stefano Ponte, Gary Gereffi, and Gale Raj-Reichert, 296–309. Cheltenham, UK: Edward Elgar. https://doi.org/10.4337/9781788113779.00026.

Neilson, Jeffrey. 2022. "Intra-cultural Consumption of Rural Landscapes: An Emergent Politics of Redistribution in Indonesia." *Journal of Rural Studies* 96:89–100.

Neilson, Jeffrey, Angga Dwiartama, Niels Fold, and Dikdik Permadi. 2020. "Resource-Based Industrial Policy in an Era of Global Production Networks: Strategic Coupling in the Indonesian Cocoa Sector." *World Development* 135:105045. https://doi.org/10.1016/j.worlddev.2020.105045.

Neilson, Jeff, Diany Faila Sophia Hartatri, and Mark Vicol. 2019. "9 Myths about Coffee Farmer Development: A Closer Look at 'Relationship Coffee' in Indonesia." *Roast*, January–February, 53–62.

Neilson, Jeffrey, and Bill Pritchard. 2007. "Green Coffee? The Contradictions of Global Sustainability Initiatives from an Indian Perspective." *Development Policy Review* 25 (3): 311–331.

Neilson, Jeffrey, and Bill Pritchard. 2009. *Value Chain Struggles: Institutions and Governance in the Plantation Districts of South India*. West Sussex, UK: Wiley-Blackwell.

Neilson, Jeff, Bill Pritchard, Niels Fold, and Angga Dwiartama. 2018. "Lead Firms in the Cocoa–Chocolate Global Production Network: An Assessment of the Deductive Capabilities of GPN 2.0." *Economic Geography* 94 (4): 400–424.

Neilson, Jeff, and Felicity Shonk. 2014. "Chained to Development? Livelihoods and Global Value Chains in the Coffee-Producing Toraja Region of Indonesia." *Australian Geographer* 45 (3): 269–288.

Neilson, Jeff, Russell Toth, Niken Sari, Joshua Bray, Manann Donoghue, Bustanul Arifin, and Hanung Ismono. 2019. *Evaluation of the Impacts of Sustainability Standards on Smallholder Coffee Farmers in Southern Sumatra, Indonesia.* London: ISEAL Alliance. https://www.evidensia.eco/resources/37/.

Neilson, Jeff, and Josephine Wright. 2017. "The State and the Food Security Discourses of Indonesia: Feeding the Bangsa." *Geographical Research* 55 (3): 131–143.

Neilson, Jeffrey, Josephine Wright, and Lya Aklimawati. 2018. "Geographical Indications and Value Capture in the Indonesia Coffee Sector." *Journal of Rural Studies* 59:35–48.

Nepstad, Daniel, Silvia Irawan, Tathiana Bezerra, William Boyd, Claudia Stickler, João Shimada, Oswaldo Carvalho, et al. 2013. "More Food, More Forests, Fewer Emissions, Better Livelihoods: Linking REDD+, Sustainable Supply Chains and Domestic Policy in Brazil, Indonesia and Colombia." *Carbon Management* 4 (6): 639–658. https://doi.org/10.4155/cmt.13.65.

Nestlé. 2021. "Our Sustainability Journey: Ten Years of the Nescafé Plan." https://www. Nestle.com/sites/default/files/2021-01/sustainable-journey-ten-years-nescafe-plan-2021-en.pdf.

Nobele, E. A. J. 1926. "Memorie van overgave betreffende de onder-afdeeling Makale van den aftredenden Gezaghebber bij het Binnenlandsche-Bestuur." *Tijdschrift voor Indische Taal-, Land-en Volkenkunde* 66 (1): 1–144.

Nooteboom, Gerben. 2003. *A Matter of Style: Social Security and Livelihood in Upland East Java, Indonesia.* Nijmegen, Netherlands: Radboud University.

Nooteboom, Gerben. 2019. "Understanding the Nature of Rural Change: The Benefits of Migration and the (Re)creation of Precarity for Men and Women in Rural Central Java, Indonesia." *Trans—Regional and—National Studies of Southeast Asia* 7 (1): 113–133. https://doi.org/10.1017/trn.2019.3.

Nooy-Palm, Hetty. 1979. *The Sa'dan-Toraja: A Study of Their Social Life and Customs.* Vol. 1, *Organization, Symbols and Beliefs.* Dordrecht: Springer.

North, Douglass C. 1990. *Institutions, Institutional Change, and Economic Performance.* Cambridge: Cambridge University Press.

North, Douglass C. 1991. "Institutions." *Journal of Economic Perspectives* 5 (1): 97–112.

O'Malley, Charles. 2019. *Value beyond Value Chains: Guidance Note for the Private Sector.* New York: United Nations Development Programme. https://www.greencommodities. org/content/gcp/en/home/global-initiatives/v2b.html.

1000 Landscape. 2021. "1000 Landscapes for 1 Billion People: Strategy for Scaling Sustainable Landscape Solutions for People and Planet." https://landscapes.global/ wp-content/uploads/2021/04/1000L-strategy-for-scaling-sustainable-landscape-solutions-for-people-and-planet.pdf.

Oro, Kohei, and Bill Pritchard. 2011. "The Evolution of Global Value Chains: Displacement of Captive Upstream Investment in the Australia–Japan Beef Trade." *Journal of Economic Geography* 11 (4): 709–729.

Otsuka, Keijiro, Yanyan Liu, and Futoshi Yamauchi. 2016. "The Future of Small Farms in Asia." *Development Policy Review* 34 (3): 441–461.

Oya, Carlos, Florian Schaefer, and Dafni Skalidou. 2018. "The Effectiveness of Agricultural Certification in Developing Countries: A Systematic Review." *World Development* 112:282–312.

Paerels, B. H. 1927. *Agronomische beschrijving van de koffiecultuur in de zuidelijke Toradjalanden Mededeelingen van de Afdeeling Landbouw No. 11*. Batavia: Departement van Landbouw, nijverheid en Handel.

Paerels, B. H. 1949. "Bevolkingskoffiecultuur." In *De landbouw in de Indische archipel*, edited by C. J. J van Hall and C. van de Koppel, 89–119. The Hague: NV Uitgeverij W. Van Hoeve.

Panhuysen, Sjoerd, and Joost Pierrot. 2021. *Coffee Barometer 2020*. Arlington, VA: Conservation International. https://coffeebarometer.org/.

Partosoedarso, Moeljono, and Amris Makmur. 1968. "Tata Produksi dan Niaga Kopi di Indonesia." Bogor: Agro-Economic Survey of Indonesia.

Pegler, Lee. 2015. "Peasant Inclusion in Global Value Chains: Economic Upgrading but Social Downgrading in Labour Processes?" *Journal of Peasant Studies* 42 (5): 929–956.

Pelras, Christian. 1985. "Religion, Tradition and the Dynamics of Islamization in South-Sulawesi." *Archipel* 29 (1): 107–135.

Peluso, Nancy Lee. 1992. *Rich Forests, Poor People: Resource Control and Resistance in Java*. Berkeley: University of California Press.

Peluso, Nancy Lee. 1996. "Fruit Trees and Family Trees in an Anthropogenic Forest: Ethics of Access, Property Zones, and Environmental Change in Indonesia." *Comparative Studies in Society and History* 38 (3): 510–548.

Peluso, Nancy Lee. 2017. "Plantations and Mines: Resource Frontiers and the Politics of the Smallholder Slot." *Journal of Peasant Studies* 44 (4): 834–869.

Peluso, Nancy Lee, and Peter Vandergeest. 2001. "Genealogies of the Political Forest and Customary Rights in Indonesia, Malaysia, and Thailand." *Journal of Asian Studies* 60 (3): 761–812.

Penny, David H. 1971. "The Agro-economic Survey of Indonesia: An Appreciation." *Indonesia* 11:111–130.

Perfecto, Ivette, and John Vandermeer. 2006. "The Effect of an Ant-Hemipteran Mutualism on the Coffee Berry Borer (*Hypothenemus Hampei*) in Southern Mexico." *Agriculture, Ecosystems & Environment* 117 (2–3): 218–221. https://doi.org/10.1016/j.agee.2006.04.007.

Perfecto, Ivette, and John Vandermeer. 2015. *Coffee Agroecology: A New Approach to Understanding Agricultural Biodiversity, Ecosystem Services and Sustainable Development*. London: Routledge.

Perhutani. 2019. *2018 Perhutani Annual Report*. Jakarta: Perhutani. https://perhutani.co.id/laporan/.

Pigg, Stacy Leigh. 1992. "Inventing Social Categories through Place: Social Representations and Development in Nepal." *Comparative Studies in Society and History* 34 (3): 491–513.

Pike, Andy, Kean Birch, Andrew Cumbers, Danny MacKinnon, and Robert McMaster. 2009. "A Geographical Political Economy of Evolution in Economic Geography." *Economic Geography* 85 (2): 175–182.

Pincus, Jonathan. 1996. *Class, Power and Agrarian Change: Land and Labour in Rural West Java*. Basingstoke, UK: Macmillan.

Polanyi, Karl. (1944) 2001. *The Great Transformation: The Political and Economic Origins of Our Time*. Boston: Beacon.

Polanyi, Karl. (1957) 2011. "The Economy as Instituted Process." In *The Sociology of Economic Life*, edited by M. Granovetter and R. Swedberg, 3–21. New York: Routledge.

Ponte, Stefano. 2002. "The 'Latte Revolution'? Regulation, Markets and Consumption in the Global Coffee Chain." *World Development* 30 (7): 1099–1122.

Ponte, Stefano. 2019. *Business, Power and Sustainability in a World of Global Value Chains.* London: Zed Books.

Ponte, Stefano, Gary Gereffi, and Gale Raj-Reichert, eds. 2019. *Handbook on Global Value Chains.* Cheltenham, UK: Edward Elgar.

Popkin, Samuel L. 1979. *The Rational Peasant: The Political Economy of Rural Society in Vietnam.* Berkeley: University of California Press.

Potter, Lesley. 2008. "Production of People and Nature, Rice and Coffee: The Semendo People in South Sumatra and Lampung." In *Taking Southeast Asia to Market: Commodities, Nature, and People in the Neoliberal Age,* edited by J. Nevins and N. L. Peluso, 176–190. Ithaca, NY: Cornell University Press.

Pritchard, Bill, Mark Vicol, and Rosemary Jones. 2017. "How Does the Ownership of Land Affect Household Livelihood Pathways under Conditions of Deagrarianization? 'Hanging In,' 'Stepping Up,' and 'Stepping Out' in Two North Indian Villages." *Singapore Journal of Tropical Geography* 38 (1): 41–57.

PTPN. 2023. "Continue to Grow: Towards a Sustainable Business." *Perkebunan Nusantara Annual Report 2022.* https://holding-perkebunan.com/laporan-tahunan/.

PT SERD. 2018. "Environmental and Social Impact Assessment Report (ESIA): INO Rantau Dedap Geothermal Power Project (Phase 2)." Project Number 50330–001, prepared by PT Supreme Energy Rantau Dedap (PT SERD) for Asian Development Bank, South Sumatra. https://www.adb.org/sites/default/files/project-documents/50330/50330-001-eia-en.pdf.

Pye, Oliver, and Jayati Bhattacharya, eds. 2013. *The Palm Oil Controversy in Southeast Asia: A Transnational Perspective.* Singapore: Institute of Southeast Asian Studies.

Quiñones-Ruiz, Xiomara F., Thilo Nigmann, Christoph Schreiber, and Jeffrey Neilson. 2020. "Collective Action Milieus and Governance Structures of Protected Geographical Indications for Coffee in Colombia, Thailand and Indonesia." *International Journal of the Commons* 14 (1): 329–343.

Rafiqui, Pernilla S. 2008. "Evolving Economic Landscapes: Why New Institutional Economics Matters for Economic Geography." *Journal of Economic Geography* 9 (3): 329–353.

Razavi, Shahra. 2009. "Engendering the Political Economy of Agrarian Change." *Journal of Peasant Studies* 36 (1): 197–226.

Reid, Anthony. 1988. *Southeast Asia in the Age of Commerce, 1450–1680.* Vol 1, *The Lands below the Winds.* New Haven, CT: Yale University Press.

Reid, Anthony. 2015. *A History of Southeast Asia: Critical Crossroads.* West Sussex, UK: Wiley-Blackwell.

Ribot, Jesse C., and Nancy L. Peluso. 2003. "A Theory of Access." *Rural Sociology* 68 (2): 153–181.

Rigal, Clément, Duong Tuan, Vo Cuong, Bon Le Van, Hoang quôc Trung, and Chau Thi Minh Long. 2023. "Transitioning from Monoculture to Mixed Cropping Systems: The Case of Coffee, Pepper, and Fruit Trees in Vietnam." *Ecological Economics* 214:107980.

Rigg, Jonathan. 2001. *More Than the Soil: Rural Change in Southeast Asia.* Harlow, UK: Pearson Education.

Rigg, Jonathan. 2005. "Poverty and Livelihoods after Full-Time Farming: A South-East Asian View." *Asia Pacific Viewpoint* 46 (2): 173–184.

Rigg, Jonathan. 2006. Land, Farming, Livelihoods, and Poverty: Rethinking the Links in the Rural South. *World Development* 34 (1): 180–202.

Rigg, Jonathan. 2019. *More Than Rural: Textures of Thailand's Agrarian Transformation*. Honolulu: University of Hawai'i Press.

Rigg, Jonathan. 2020. *Rural Development in Southeast Asia: Dispossession, Accumulation and Persistence*. Cambridge: Cambridge University Press.

Rigg, Jonathan, Albert Salamanca, Monchai Phongsiri, and Mattara Sripun. 2018. "More Farmers, Less Farming? Understanding the Truncated Agrarian Transition in Thailand." *World Development* 107:327–337.

Rigg, Jonathan, Albert Salamanca, and Eric C. Thompson. 2016. "The Puzzle of East and Southeast Asia's Persistent Smallholder." *Journal of Rural Studies* 43:118–133.

Robison, Richard. 1986. *Indonesia: The Rise of Capital*. ASAA Series. Sydney: Allen & Unwin.

Roche, Michael, and Neil Argent. 2015. "The Fall and Rise of Agricultural Productivism? An Antipodean Viewpoint." *Progress in Human Geography* 39 (5): 621–635.

Rodrik, Dani. 2016. "Premature Deindustrialization." *Journal of Economic Growth* 21 (1): 1–33.

Ruf, François, and Frédéric Lançon. 2004. "Innovations in the Indonesian Uplands." In *From Slash and Burn to Replanting: Green Revolutions in the Indonesian Uplands*, edited by F. Ruf and F. Lançon, 1–32. Washington, DC: World Bank.

Ruf, François, and Yoddang. 2001. "Cocoa Migrants from Boom to Bust." In *Agriculture in Crisis: People, Commodities and Natural Resources in Indonesia, 1996–2000*, edited by F. Ruf and F. Gérard, 97–156. Richmond, UK: Curzon.

Sachs, Jeffrey D., Kaitlin Y. Cordes, James Rising, Perrine Toledano, and Nicolas Maennling. 2019. *Ensuring Economic Viability and Sustainability of Coffee Production*. New York: Columbia Center on Sustainable Investment. https://papers.ssrn.com/sol3/papers.cfm?abstract_id=3660936.

Salmudin. 2012. *Hukum Waris Adat: Pengurusan Sawah Tunggu Tubang dalam Dinamika Pranata dan Kelembagaan Hokum Waris Adat Daerah Semende Kabupaten Mura Enim*. Yogyakarta: Idea.

Samper, Luis F., Daniele Giovannucci, and Luciana Marques Vieira. 2017. "The Powerful Role of Intangibles in the Coffee Value Chain." Economic Research Working Paper 39, World Intellectual Property Organization (WIPO), Geneva, Switzerland.

Sayer, Jeffrey, Chris Margules, Agni Klintuni Boedhihartono, Allan Dale, Terry Sunderland, Jatna Supriatna, and Ria Saryanthi. 2015. "Landscape Approaches: What Are the Pre-conditions for Success?" *Sustainability Science* 10 (2): 345–355.

SCA (Specialty Coffee Association). 2021. "About SCA." https://sca.coffee/about.

Schrieke, B. (1928) 1966. "The Causes and Effects of Communism on the West Coast of Sumatra." In *Indonesian Sociological Studies: Selected Writings of B. Schrieke*, 83–166. The Hague: W. van Hoeve.

Schroth, Götz, Peter Läderach, Diana Sofia Blackburn Cuero, Jeffrey Neilson, and Christian Bunn. 2015. "Winner or Loser of Climate Change? A Modeling Study of Current and Future Climatic Suitability of Arabica Coffee in Indonesia." *Regional Environmental Change* 15 (7): 1473–1482.

Scoones, Ian. 1998. "Sustainable Rural Livelihoods: A Framework for Analysis." IDS Working Paper 72, Sussex University, Institute of Development Studies, Brighton, UK.

Scoones, Ian. 2009. "Livelihoods Perspectives and Rural Development." *Journal of Peasant Studies* 36 (1): 171–196.

Scoones, Ian. 2015. *Sustainable Livelihoods and Rural Development*. Rugby, UK: Practical Action.

Scott, James C. 1972. "Patron-Client Politics and Political Change in Southeast Asia." *American Political Science Review* 66 (1): 91–113.

Scott, James C. 1976. *The Moral Economy of the Peasant: Rebellion and Subsistence in Southeast Asia*. New Haven, CT: Yale University Press.

Scott, James C. 2009. *The Art of Not Being Governed: An Anarchist History of Upland Southeast Asia*. New Haven, CT: Yale University Press.

Sen, Amartya. 1984. *Resources, Values and Development*. Cambridge, MA: Harvard University Press.

Shoup, Mary Ellen. 2018. "Staking Claim to Online Coffee Sales: Coffee Brands Lead E-commerce Grocery Sales." *Food Navigator*, December 20. https://www.food navigator-usa.com/Article/2018/12/19/Staking-claim-to-online-coffee-sales-Coffee-brands-lead-e-commerce-grocery-sales.

Sitorus, Henry, and John F. McCarthy. 2023. "Affluence, Generational Poverty and Food Security in the Oil Palm Landscapes of North Sumatra." In *The Paradox of Agrarian Change: Food Security and the Politics of Social Protection in Indonesia*, edited by John F. McCarthy, Andrew McWilliam, and Gerben Nooteboom, 167–196. Singapore: NUS Press.

Slaats, Herman, Erman Rajagukguk, Nurul Elmiyah, and Akhmad Safik. 2009. "Land Law in Indonesia." In *Legalising Land Rights: Local Practices, State Responses and Tenure Security in Africa, Asia and Latin America*, edited by Janine M. Ubink, André J. Hoekema, and Willem J. Assies, 493–526. Leiden: Leiden University Press.

Smith, Glenn. 1999. "Migrants in South Sumatra's Forests: Development Pioneers or Destructive Interlopers?" In *L'homme et la forêt tropicale*, edited by Serge Bahuchet, Daniel Bley, Hélène Pagezy, and Nicole Vernazza-Licht, 417–428. Châteauneuf de Grasse: Éditions du Bergier.

Starbucks. 2021. "Our Heritage: Starbucks in Indonesia." https://www.starbucks.co.id/about-us/our-heritage/starbucks-in-indonesia.

Studwell, Joe. 2013. *How Asia Works: Success and Failure in the World's Most Dynamic Region*. London: Profile Books.

Sukarno. (1957) 1960. "Marhaen and Proletarian." Speech before the Indonesian Nationalist Party at the party's thirtieth anniversary, at Bandung, July 3, 1957, translated by Clare Holt, Modern Indonesia Project, Cornell University, Ithaca, NY. http://collections.library.cornell.edu/cmip/browse.html.

Sutherland, Heather. 1983. "Power and Politics in South Sulawesi: 1860–1880." *Review of Indonesian and Malaysian Affairs* 17:161–207.

Sutherland, Heather. 2015. "On the Edge of Asia: Maritime Trade in East Indonesia, Early Seventeenth to Mid-twentieth Century." In *Commodities, Ports and Asian Maritime Trade since 1750*, edited by U. Bosma and A. Webster, 59–78. London: Palgrave Macmillan.

Suyanto, S., Rizki Pandu Permana, Noviana Khususiyah, and Laxman Joshi. 2005. "Land Tenure, Agroforestry Adoption, and Reduction of Fire Hazard in a Forest Zone: A Case Study from Lampung, Sumatra, Indonesia." *Agroforestry Systems* 65 (1): 1–11.

Talbot, John M. 2004. *Grounds for Agreement: The Political Economy of the Coffee Commodity Chain*. Lanham, MD: Rowman & Littlefield.

Tanner, Thomas, David Lewis, David Wrathall, Robin Bronen, Nick Cradock-Henry, Saleemul Huq, Chris Lawless, et al. 2015. "Livelihood Resilience in the Face of Climate Change." *Nature Climate Change* 5 (1): 23–26.

Tchibo. 2015. *Sustainability Report 2015 Update*. https://www.tchibo.com/servlet/cb/909748/data/-/SustainabilityReport2015.pdf.

TechnoServe. 2014. "Indonesia: A Business Case for Sustainable Coffee Production." An industry study by TechnoServe by the Sustainable Coffee Program (SCP), powered by IDH.

Timmer, Charles Peter. 1993. "Rural Bias in the East and South-East Asian Rice Economy: Indonesia in Comparative Perspective." *Journal of Development Studies* 29 (4): 149–176.

Timmer, Charles Peter. 2004. "The Road to Pro-poor Growth: The Indonesian Experience in Regional Perspective." *Bulletin of Indonesian Economic Studies* 40 (2): 177–207.

Timmer, Charles Peter. 2018. "Pro-poor Growth in Indonesia: Challenging the Pessimism of Myrdal's Asian Drama." WIDER Working Paper No. 2018/103, UNU-WIDER, Helsinki. https://www.wider.unu.edu/publication/pro-poor-growth-indonesia.

Touwen, Lourens Jeroen. 2001. *Extremes in the Archipelago: Trade and Economic Development in the Outer Islands of Indonesia, 1900–1942.* Leiden: KITLV.

Tsubouchi, Yoshihiro. 1980. "History of Settlement Formation along the Komering-Ogan-Lower Musi Rivers." In *South Sumatra, Man and Agriculture*, edited by Yoshihiro Tsubouchi, N. Iljas, Y. Takaya, and A. R. Hanafiah. Center for Southeast Asian Studies, Kyoto University.

Ukers, William H. 1922. *All about Coffee.* New York: Tea and Coffee Trade Journal.

UNICEF, UNDP, Prospera, and SMERU. 2021. *Analysis of the Social and Economic Impacts of COVID-19 on Households and Strategic Policy Recommendations for Indonesia.* Jakarta: UNICEF. https://www.unicef.org/indonesia/coronavirus/reports/socio-economic-impact-covid-19-households-indonesia.

United Nations. 2019. *World Population Prosects 2019. UN Department of Economic and Social Affairs, Population Division.* New York: United Nations. https://population.un.org/.

United Nations Comtrade. 2021. "UN Comtrade Database." https://comtrade.un.org/.

United Nations Comtrade. 2024. "UN Comtrade Database." https://comtradeplus.un.org/.

USDA. 2019. "Indonesia Coffee Annual Report 2016, GAIN Report Number ID1616." www.fas.usda.gov.

Utomo, Kampto. 1967. "Villages of Unplanned Resettlers in the Subdistrict Kaliredjo, Central Lampung." In *Villages in Indonesia*, edited by Koentjaraningrat, 281–298. Ithaca, NY: Cornell University Press.

van der Eng, Pierre. 2016. "After 200 Years, Why Is Indonesia's Cadastral System Still Incomplete?" In *Land and Development in Indonesia: Searching for the People's Sovereignty*, edited by J. F. McCarthy and K. Robinson, 227–244. Singapore: ISEAS.

van der Muur, Willem, Jacqueline Vel, Micah R. Fisher, and Kathryn Robinson. 2019. "Changing Indigeneity Politics in Indonesia: From Revival to Projects." *Asia Pacific Journal of Anthropology* 20 (5): 379–396.

van der Ploeg, Jan Douwe. 2008. *The New Peasantries: Struggles for Autonomy and Sustainability in an Era of Empire and Globalization.* London: Earthscan.

van der Ploeg, Jan Douwe. 2013. *Peasants and the Art of Farming: A Chayanovian Manifesto.* Halifax, NS: Fernwood.

van der Veen, H. 1965. *The Merok Feast of the Sa'dan Toradja.* The Hague: Martinus Nijhoff / Brill.

van Klinken, Gerry. 2009. "Patronage Democracy in Provincial Indonesia." In *Rethinking Popular Representation*, edited by Olle Törnquist, Neil Webster, and Kristian Stokke, 141–159. New York: Palgrave Macmillan.

van Lijf, J. M. 1948. "Kentrekken en problemen van de geschiedenis der Sa'dan-Toraja-Landen." *Indonesie*, no. 1: 518–538.

van Noordwijk, Meine, Beria Leimona, and Sacha Amaruzaman. 2019. "Sumber Jaya from Conflict to Source of Wealth in Indonesia: Reconciling Coffee Agroforestry and Watershed Functions." In *Sustainable Development through Trees on Farms:*

Agroforestry in Its Fifth Decade, edited by M. van Noordwijk, 177–192. Bogor: World Agroforestry Centre (ICRAF) Indonesia.

van Noordwijk, Meine, Olk Mulyoutami, Niken Sakuntaladewi, and Fahmuddin Agus. 2008. "Swiddens in Transition: Shifted Perceptions on Shifting Cultivators in Indonesia." World Agroforestry Centre (ICRAF) Occasional Paper 09, World Agroforestry Centre Southeast Asia Regional Program, Bogor, Indonesia.

van Rijn, A. P. 1902. "Tocht naar de boven' sadang (Midden celebes)." *Tijdschrift van het Koninklijk Nederlandsch Aardrijksskundig Genootschap* 29: 328–372.

Verbist, Bruno, Andree Eka Dinata Putra, and Suseno Budidarsono. 2005. "Factors Driving Land Use Change: Effects on Watershed Functions in a Coffee Agroforestry System in Lampung, Sumatra." *Agricultural Systems* 85 (3): 254–270.

Vicol, Mark. 2019. "Potatoes, Petty Commodity Producers and Livelihoods: Contract Farming and Agrarian Change in Maharashtra, India." *Journal of Agrarian Change* 19 (1): 135–161.

Vicol, Mark, Niels Fold, Bill Pritchard, and Jeffrey Neilson. 2019. "Global Production Networks, Regional Development Trajectories and Smallholder Livelihoods in the Global South." *Journal of Economic Geography* 19 (4): 973–993.

Vicol, Mark, Jeffrey Neilson, Diany Faila Sophia Hartatri, and Peter Cooper. 2018. "Upgrading for Whom? Relationship Coffee, Value Chain Interventions and Rural Development in Indonesia." *World Development* 110:26–37.

von Benda-Beckmann, Keebet. 2019. "Anachronism, Agency, and the Contextualisation of Adat: Van Vollenhoven's Analyses in Light of Struggles over Resources." *Asia Pacific Journal of Anthropology* 20 (5): 397–415.

von Essen, Marius, and Eric F. Lambin. 2021. "Jurisdictional Approaches to Sustainable Resource Use." *Frontiers in Ecology and the Environment* 19 (3): 159–167.

Wade, Robert H. 2018. "The Developmental State: Dead or Alive?" *Development and Change* 49 (2): 518–546.

Wallace, Alfred Russel. 1869. *The Malay Archipelago: The Land of the Orang-utan and the Bird of Paradise; A Narrative of Travel with Studies of Man and Nature*. London: Macmillan.

Ward, Neil. 1993. "The Agricultural Treadmill and the Rural Environment in the Postproductivist era." *Sociologia Ruralis* 33 (3–4): 348–364.

Waterson, Roxana. 2009. *Paths and Rivers; Sa'dan Toraja Society in Transformation*. Singapore: NUS Press.

Watts, Michael. 1994. "Life under Contract: Contract Farming, Agrarian Restructuring, and Flexible Accumulation." In *Living under Contract: Contract Farming and Agrarian Transformation in Sub-Saharan Africa*, edited by P. Little and M. Watts, 21–77. Madison: University of Wisconsin Press.

White, Benjamin. 1983. "'Agricultural Involution' and Its Critics: Twenty Years After." *Bulletin of Concerned Asian Scholars* 15 (2): 18–31.

White, Benjamin. 1989. "Problems in the Empirical Analysis of Agrarian Differentiation." In *Agrarian Transformations: Local Processes and the State in Southeast Asia*, edited by G. Hart, A. Turton, and B. White, 15–30. Berkeley: University of California Press.

White, Benjamin. 2018. "Marx and Chayanov at the Margins: Understanding Agrarian Change in Java." *Journal of Peasant Studies* 45 (5–6): 1108–1126. https://doi.org/1 0.1080/03066150.2017.1419191.

White, Ben, Colum Graham, and Laksmi Savitri. 2023. "Agrarian Movements and Rural Populism in Indonesia." *Journal of Agrarian Change* 23 (1): 68–84.

White, Benjamin, and Gunawan Wiradi. 1989. "Agrarian and Nonagrarian Bases for Inequality in Nine Javanese Villages." In *Agrarian Transformations: Local*

Processes and the State in Southeast Asia, edited by G. Hart, A. Turton, and B. White, 266–302. Berkeley: University of California Press.

Wijaya, Atika, Pieter Glasbergen, and Surip Mawardi. 2017. "The Mediated Partnership Model for Sustainable Coffee Production: Experiences from Indonesia." *International Food and Agribusiness Management Review* 20 (5): 689–708.

Williams, Maxine. 2020. "The Pandemic, Patronage and Politics: Exploring the Impacts of COVID-19 on Rural Livelihoods and Local Patronage Networks in the Toraja Region of Indonesia." Honors thesis, University of Sydney.

Wilson, Geoff A., and Rob J. F. Burton. 2015. "'Neo-productivist' Agriculture: Spatio-temporal versus Structuralist Perspectives." *Journal of Rural Studies* 38:52–64.

World Bank. 1993. *The East Asian Miracle: Economic Growth and Public Policy.* New York: Oxford University Press.

World Bank. 2007. *World Development Report 2008: Agriculture for Development.* Washington, DC: World Bank. https://openknowledge.worldbank.org/handle/10986/5990.

World Bank. 2010. *Indonesia Jobs Report: Towards Better Jobs and Security for All.* Washington, DC: World Bank. https://openknowledge.worldbank.org/handle/10986/27901.

World Bank. 2024. "World Development Indicators." https://data.worldbank.org/indicator.

Yeung, Henry Wai-chung. 2016. *Strategic Coupling: East Asian Industrial Transformation in the New Global Economy.* Ithaca, NY: Cornell University Press.

Yulisman, Linda. 2020. "Indonesians Fight Coronavirus with Gotong-royong." *Straits Times*, April 19. https://www.straitstimes.com/asia/se-asia/indonesians-fight-coronavirus-with-gotong-royong.

Zhan, Shaohua. 2019. "Accumulation by and without Dispossession: Rural Land Use, Land Expropriation, and Livelihood Implications in China." *Journal of Agrarian Change* 19 (3): 447–464.

Zhan, Shaohua, and Ben Scully. 2018. "From South Africa to China: Land, Migrant Labor and the Semi-proletarian Thesis Revisited." *Journal of Peasant Studies* 45 (5–6): 1018–1038.

Index

Figures and tables are indicated by "f" and "t" following page numbers.

www.ingramcontent.com/pod-product-compliance
Lightning Source LLC
Chambersburg PA
CBHW031408270326
41929CB00010BA/1370